CISSP®

FOR

DUMMIES®

4TH EDITION

CISSP® FOR DUMMIES® 4TH EDITION

by Lawrence Miller and Peter H. Gregory

WILEY

John Wiley & Sons, Inc.

CISSP® For Dummies®, 4th Edition

Published by
John Wiley & Sons, Inc.
111 River Street
Hoboken, NJ 07030-5774

www.wiley.com

For general information on our other products and services, please contact our Customer Care Department within the U.S. at 877-762-2974, outside the U.S. at 317-572-3993, or fax 317-572-4002.

For technical support, please visit www.wiley.com/techsupport.

Wiley also publishes its books in a variety of electronic formats and by print-on-demand. Not all content that is available in standard print versions of this book may appear or be packaged in all book formats. If you have purchased a version of this book that did not include media that is referenced by or accompanies a standard print version, you may request this media by visiting http://booksupport. wiley.com. For more information about Wiley products, visit us www.wiley.com.

Library of Congress Control Number: 2012942107

ISBN 978-1-118-36239-6 (pbk); ISBN 978-1-118-41710-2 (ebk); ISBN 978-1-118-42037-9 (ebk); ISBN 978-1-118-46755-8 (ebk)

Manufactured in the United States of America

10 9 8 7 6 5 4 3 2 1

WILEY

About the Authors

Lawrence Miller, CISSP, has worked in information security and technology management for more than 15 years. He received his MBA from Indiana University and has earned numerous technical certifications throughout his career. He is currently working as the Director of Information Technology for an e-commerce and event merchandising company. He has previously worked as the Operations Manager for a Top 100 U.S. law firm, as an internetworking security engineer and a security consultant for service providers and clients in the retail, financial, and manufacturing sectors in the U.S. and Japan; he was a Chief Petty Officer in the U.S. Navy, serving in various roles, including information systems security manager and "weather guesser." He is the author of *Home Networking Do-It-Yourself For Dummies* (John Wiley & Sons, Inc.) and has also written more than 25 *For Dummies* Custom Edition books on numerous topics, including information security, unified communications, virtualization, and archiving.

Peter H. Gregory, C I CISO, CISA, CISSP, CRISC, DRCE, CCSK, is the author of more than thirty books on security and technology, including *Solaris Security* (Prentice Hall), *Biometrics For Dummies* (John Wiley & Sons, Inc.), *IT Disaster Recovery Planning For Dummies* (John Wiley & Sons, Inc.), and *CISA Certified Information Systems Auditor All-In-One Study Guide* (McGraw-Hill/ Osborne Media Group).

Peter is a career technologist and the global manager of information security and risk management at Concur (www.concur.com), a Redmond, WA–based leading provider of integrated travel and expense management solutions. Prior to this, he held tactical and strategic security positions in large wireless telecommunications organizations. He has also held development and operations positions in casino management systems, banking, government, nonprofit organizations, and academia since the late 1970s. Peter is the lead instructor and advisory board member for the University of Washington certificate program in information systems security and a graduate of the FBI Citizens' Academy. He is a certified RiderCoach for the Motorcycle Safety Foundation and teaches people how to ride motorcycles in the Seattle area.

Peter can be found at www.peterhgregory.com.

Dedication

From Lawrence Miller:
To Michelle.

From Peter H. Gregory:
To Rebekah.

Authors' Acknowledgments

Lawrence Miller would like to thank all the wonderful folks I have worked with on so many projects over the years. You all make writing so enjoyable and fulfilling: Amy, Barry, Chris, Dan, . . . E, F, G, . . . Heidi, I, Jen, Katie, Laura, Mike, N, O, Paul, . . . Q, Rev, Susan, . . . T, U, V, . . . W, X, Y, and Zoë! Finally, thank you Peter for working with me on yet another great book, and Kevin for helping to keep us (technically) honest and on our toes!

Peter H. Gregory would like to thank Katie Feltman, Senior Acquisitions Editor at Wiley, for her perseverance and patience. Thank you to Christopher Morris, Senior Project Editor at Wiley, for your help throughout this project, and to Barry Childs-Helton, for your really helpful copy editing. Thank you, Larry, for agreeing once again to coauthor this book. It's great as always to work with you on security books.

There are many more people at Wiley and other organizations without whom this book could not be published and reach readers. I don't know who you are, but I know you are out there, and I am grateful for your dedication and hard work.

My contribution to this book would not have been possible without support from my wife, business manager and best friend, Rebekah Gregory. Thanks also to Carole Jelen, my literary agent, for guidance on this and other projects over the past five years.

Publisher's Acknowledgments

We're proud of this book; please send us your comments at http://dummies.custhelp.com. For other comments, please contact our Customer Care Department within the U.S. at 877-762-2974, outside the U.S. at 317-572-3993, or fax 317-572-4002.

Some of the people who helped bring this book to market include the following:

Acquisitions, Editorial, and Vertical Websites

Senior Project Editor: Christopher Morris

Senior Acquisitions Editor: Katie Feltman

Senior Copy Editor: Barry Childs-Helton

Technical Editor: Kevin Beaver

Editorial Manager: Kevin Kirschner

Vertical Websites Project Manager:
Laura Moss-Hollister

Vertical Websites Assistant Project Manager:
Jenny Swisher

Vertical Websites Associate Producers:
Josh Frank, Marilyn Hummel, Douglas Kuhn, Shawn Patrick

Editorial Assistant: Leslie Saxman

Sr. Editorial Assistant: Cherie Case

Cover Photos:
© Victor Habbick/iStockphoto.com

Cartoons: Rich Tennant
(www.the5thwave.com)

Composition Services

Project Coordinator: Patrick Redmond

Layout and Graphics: Jennifer Creasey, Joyce Haughey, Corrie Niehaus

Proofreaders:
BIM Indexing & Proofreading Services

Indexer: BIM Indexing & Proofreading Services

Publishing and Editorial for Technology Dummies

Richard Swadley, Vice President and Executive Group Publisher

Andy Cummings, Vice President and Publisher

Mary Bednarek, Executive Acquisitions Director

Mary C. Corder, Editorial Director

Publishing for Consumer Dummies

Kathleen Nebenhaus, Vice President and Executive Publisher

Composition Services

Debbie Stailey, Director of Composition Services

Contents at a Glance

Table of Contents

Introduction

· ·

For more than 15 years now, security practitioners around the world have been pursuing a well-known and highly regarded professional credential: the Certified Information Systems Security Professional (CISSP) certification.

And security-minded companies have been actively seeking individuals who have earned the coveted CISSP certification. It has surpassed the demand for many vendor-sponsored technical certifications and is widely held as *the* professional standard in the information security field.

With more than 75,000 CISSPs worldwide, some have argued that, because more people have earned it, the CISSP certification is becoming less relevant. However, the CISSP certification isn't less relevant because more people are attaining it — more people are attaining it because it's now more relevant than ever. Information security is far more important than at any time in the past because more organizations are using information systems in increasingly complex ways to support increasingly critical business processes — and the threats to information security have become increasingly sophisticated.

Most organizations today understand that information security needs to be a part of their overall business strategy. They also realize that security at the detail level is much more difficult, as businesses have adopted increasingly complex application environments. The CISSP certification covers both ends of this broad spectrum, and everything in between.

Protecting information-related assets has always been important, but for many organizations information security was optional. These days, organizations and businesses of all sizes — in all industries — are legally required to protect their information assets. Organizations are now past the point of deciding whether or not information protection is needed; now they need to understand *how* to protect their information assets. Experienced security professionals with the CISSP certification understand this complex task.

About This Book

Our goal in this book is simple: to help you prepare for and pass the CISSP examination so that you can join the ranks of respected certified security professionals who dutifully serve organizations and industries around the world. Although we've stuffed it chock-full of good information, we don't expect that this book will be a weighty desktop reference on the shelf of every security professional — although we certainly wouldn't object.

And we don't intend for this book to be an all-purpose, be-all-and-end-all, one-stop shop that has all the answers to life's great mysteries. Given the broad base of knowledge required for the CISSP certification, we strongly recommend that you use multiple resources to prepare for the exam. This book can provide you with a road map to the CISSP certification and sufficient information to help you pass the exam. But it won't make you an instant security expert!

As a security professional, you may find that earning the CISSP certification is only a beginning. Business and technology, which have associated risks and vulnerabilities, require that each of us — as security professionals — constantly press forward, consuming vast volumes of knowledge and information in a constant tug-of-war against the bad guys. Thus, when you prepare for your CISSP certification, study as much relevant information as your time and resources allow. *CISSP For Dummies,* 4th Edition, provides the framework and the blueprint for your study effort and gives you some great experience in practicing for the test, to boot.

How This Book Is Organized

This book is organized in four parts. We cover the International Information Systems Security Certifications Consortium (ISC)[2] and examination basics in Part I, the Common Body of Knowledge (CBK) domains in Part II, the Part of Tens in Part III, and several useful tools in the appendixes in Part IV.

Part I: Certification Basics

In Part I, we introduce the International Information Systems Security Certifications Consortium (ISC)[2], how you earn the CISSP certification, and an overview of the Common Body of Knowledge (CBK). Then we provide some helpful guidance for your study efforts. Chapter 3 is a guide for actions and activities that you may consider pursuing to maintain your CISSP certification and your good standing as a security professional.

Part II: Domains

Part II contains the domains of the CBK and covers the core concepts and key information that you need to understand in order to pass the CISSP exam. A CISSP candidate must have practical work experience with many, but not necessarily all, of the concepts and technologies that we cover in this part.

Part III: The Part of Tens

The much-loved and revered Part of Tens contains five chapters that are more than mere lists. We include information to help you prepare for the CISSP exam and to also help you in your career as a security professional.

Part IV: Appendixes

You'll be glad that we didn't perform an appendectomy on this book — and you definitely don't want to skip this part!

Appendix A contains 250 practice exam questions that you can use to simulate the actual testing environment. Building up your stamina and figuring out how to pace yourself can be well worth the effort when it comes time to take your actual CISSP exam.

Finally, Appendix B contains a helpful glossary, but it's not just any ordinary glossary: The CISSP exam requires you to select the *best* answer for a given question. You definitely need to know and understand very concise terms and definitions in order to recognize any obviously wrong answers on the exam.

How the Chapters Are Organized

CISSP For Dummies (now in its fourth edition) is unique in the *For Dummies* series. Because the CISSP examination covers such a broad base of information, we don't recommend skipping any of the material in this book. You may find some of the information that we present in some of the chapters familiar or easy to understand, but we still recommend at least a quick, cursory read of those chapters. For this reason, we don't include a quick assessment test at the beginning of each chapter, like other *For Dummies* certification books do. Instead, we packed this book with as much useful information as possible to help you succeed in your quest for the CISSP certification.

Chapter introductions

The first page of each domain chapter begins with a brief introduction to the domain covered in that chapter. You can also find a list of chapter objectives that closely correlates to the CISSP knowledge objectives for that domain.

Study subjects

At the heart of each CISSP domain chapter, we extensively cover the knowledge objectives listed in the CISSP Common Body of Knowledge (CBK), and we include relevant information for the CISSP exam and enough detail to put the information into proper context.

Tables and illustrations

To help you study, we provide tables and illustrations of important information or concepts whenever we can. However, because CISSP is a vendor-neutral certification, don't expect to find screen captures or simulation-type graphics. More room for good, old-fashioned information!

Prep Tests

Finally, we conclude each CISSP domain chapter with a quick, ten-question multiple-choice Prep Test. *Note:* The Prep Tests at the end of each of these chapters do *not* contain the types of questions that you find on the actual CISSP examination. Instead, the Prep Tests are meant to help you recall important information that we present in the chapter so that you can use that information to answer questions on the actual exam.

Icons Used in This Book

Throughout this book, you occasionally see icons in the left margin that call attention to important information that's particularly worth noting. No smiley faces winking at you or any other cute little emoticons, but you'll definitely want to take note! Here's what to look for and what to expect:

Instant Answer icons highlight important information to help you answer questions on the actual exam. To help you succeed on the CISSP exam, look for these icons to highlight critical points that you're likely to see again.

This icon identifies general information and core concepts that are well worth committing to your non-volatile memory, your gray matter, or your noggin — along with anniversaries, birthdays, and other important stuff! You should certainly understand and review this information before taking your CISSP exam.

Thank you for reading; we hope you enjoy the book; please take care of your writers! (Now, where's that jar . . . ?) Seriously, this icon includes helpful suggestions and tidbits of useful information that may save you some time and headaches.

Proceed at your own risk . . . well, okay — it's actually nothing *that* hazardous. These helpful alerts point out easily confused or difficult-to-understand terms and concepts.

Cross Reference icons point you toward other places in this book that have additional information on particular subjects — kind of a low-tech Fast-Forward and Reverse button!

You won't find a map of the human genome or the secret to cold fusion in this book (or maybe you will, hmm), but if you're an insufferable insomniac or hoping to be the life of a World of Warcraft party, take note. The Technical Stuff icon points out explanations of the jargon beneath the jargon, breaks down complicated topics into common terms, and is the stuff legends — well, at least nerds — are made of. So, if you're seeking to attain the seventh level of NERD-vana, keep an eye out for these icons!

Where to Go from Here

With our apologies to Lewis Carroll, Alice, and the Cheshire Cat:

"Would you tell me, please, which way I ought to go from here?"

"That depends a good deal on where you want to get to," said the Cat — err, the Dummies Man.

"I don't much care where..." said Alice.

"Then it doesn't matter which way you go!"

That's certainly true of *CISSP For Dummies,* which, like *Alice in Wonderland,* is also destined to become a timeless classic!

If you don't know where you're going, any chapter will get you there — but Chapter 1 may be a good place to start! However, if you see a particular topic that piques your interest, feel free to jump ahead to that chapter. Each chapter is individually wrapped (but not packaged for individual sale) and written to stand on its own, so feel free to start reading anywhere and skip around! Read this book in any order that suits you (though we don't recommend upside down or backwards). We promise you won't get lost falling down the rabbit hole!

Once you feel comfortable with the material, head to www.dummies.com/go/cisspfd4e to take an online practice test.

Part I
Certification
Basics

The 5th Wave   By Rich Tennant

©RICHTENNANT

"You know, this was a situation question on my CISSP exam, but I always thought it was just hypothetical."

In this part . . .

CBK? (ISC)²? CISSP? No, it's not the latest text-messaging lingo for your cell phone! The chapters in this part describe the *who, what, when, where, how,* and *why* of the CISSP certification and the subject areas tested, as well as the *now what?* after you earn your certification.

Chapter 1

(ISC)² and the CISSP Certification

Some say that the Certified Information Systems Security Professional (CISSP) candidate requires a breadth of knowledge 50 miles across and 2 inches deep. To embellish on this statement, we believe that the CISSP candidate is more like the Great Wall of China, with a knowledge base extending over 3,500 miles — maybe a few holes here and there, stronger in some areas than others, but nonetheless one of the Seven Wonders of the Modern World.

The problem with many currently available CISSP preparation materials is in defining how high the Great Wall actually is: Some material overwhelms and intimidates CISSP candidates, leading them to believe that the wall is as high as it is long. Other study materials are perilously brief and shallow, giving the unsuspecting candidate a false sense of confidence while he or she merely attempts to step over the Great Wall, careful not to stub a toe. To help you avoid either misstep, *CISSP For Dummies* answers the question, "What level of knowledge must a CISSP candidate possess to succeed on the CISSP exam?"

About (ISC)² and the CISSP Certification

The International Information Systems Security Certification Consortium (ISC)² (www.isc2.org) was established in 1989 as a nonprofit, tax-exempt corporation chartered for the explicit purpose of developing a standardized security curriculum and administering an information security certification process for security professionals worldwide. In 1994, the Certified Information Systems Security Professional (CISSP) credential was launched.

The CISSP was the first information security credential to be accredited by the American National Standards Institute (ANSI) to the ISO/IEC 17024:2003 standard. This international standard helps to ensure that personnel certification processes define specific competencies and identify required knowledge, skills, and personal attributes. It also requires examinations to be independently administered and designed to properly test a candidate's competence for the certification. This process helps a certification gain industry acceptance and credibility as more than just a marketing tool for certain vendor-specific certifications (a widespread criticism that has caused many vendor certifications to lose relevance over the years).

The ISO (International Organization for Standardization) and IEC (International Electrotechnical Commission) are two organizations that work together to prepare and publish international standards for businesses, governments, and societies worldwide.

The CISSP certification is based on a Common Body of Knowledge (CBK) identified by the (ISC)² and defined through ten distinct domains:

- ✔ Access Control
- ✔ Telecommunications and Network Security
- ✔ Information Security Governance and Risk Management
- ✔ Software Development Security
- ✔ Cryptography
- ✔ Security Architecture and Design
- ✔ Security Operations
- ✔ Business Continuity and Disaster Recovery Planning
- ✔ Legal, Regulations, Investigations and Compliance
- ✔ Physical (Environmental) Security

You Must Be This Tall to Ride (and Other Requirements)

The CISSP candidate must have a minimum of five cumulative years of professional, full-time, direct work experience in two or more of the domains listed in the preceding section. The work experience requirement is a hands-on one — you can't satisfy the requirement by just having "information security" listed as one of your job responsibilities. You need to have specific knowledge of information security — and perform work that requires you to apply that knowledge regularly.

However, you can get a waiver for a maximum of one year of the five-year professional experience requirement if you have one of the following:

- A four-year college degree

- An advanced degree in information security from a U.S. National Center of Academic Excellence in Information Assurance Education (CAEIAE) or a regional equivalent

- A credential that appears on the (ISC)²–approved list, which includes more than 30 technical and professional certifications, such as various SANS GIAC certifications, Microsoft certifications, and CompTIA Security+ (For the complete list, go to www.isc2.org/credential_waiver/default.aspx.)

In the U.S., CAEIAE programs are jointly sponsored by the National Security Agency and the Department of Homeland Security. For more information, go to www.nsa.gov/ia/academic_outreach/nat_cae/index.shtml.

Registering for the Exam

As of June 1, 2012, the CISSP exam is now being administered via computer-based testing (CBT) at local Pearson VUE testing centers worldwide. To register for the exam, go to the (ISC)² website (www.isc2.org), click the Certifications tab, click Computer Based Testing (CBT), and then click the Register Now – Pearson VUE button; alternatively, go directly to the Pearson VUE website (http://pearsonvue.com/isc2/).

On the Pearson VUE website, you have to create a web account first; then you can register for the CISSP exam, schedule your test, and pay your testing fee. You can also locate a nearby test center, take a Pearson VUE testing tutorial, practice taking the exam (which definitely you should do if you've never taken a CBT), and then download the (ISC)² non-disclosure agreement (NDA).

Download and read the (ISC)² NDA when you register for the exam. You're given five minutes to read and accept the agreement at the start of your exam. If you don't accept the NDA in the allotted five minutes, your exam will end and you forfeit your exam fees!

When you register, you're required to quantify your work experience in information security, answer a few questions regarding criminal history and related background, and agree to abide by the (ISC)² Code of Ethics.

The current exam fee in the U.S. is $599. You can cancel or re-schedule your exam by contacting VUE by telephone at least 24 hours in advance of your scheduled exam or online at least 48 hours in advance. The fee to re-schedule is $20.

If you fail to show up for your exam, you'll forfeit your entire exam fee!

Great news! If you're a U.S. military veteran and are eligible for Montgomery GI Bill benefits, the Veteran's Administration (VA) will reimburse you for the full cost of the exam, regardless of whether you pass or fail.

Preparing for the Exam

Many resources are available to help the CISSP candidate prepare for the exam. Self-study is a major part of any study plan. Work experience is also critical to success, and you can incorporate it into your study plan. For those who learn best in a classroom or training environment, (ISC)² offers CISSP review seminars.

We recommend that you commit to an intense 60-day study plan leading up to the CISSP exam. How intense? That depends on your own personal experience and learning ability, but plan on a minimum of two hours a day for 60 days. If you're a slow learner or reader, or perhaps find yourself weak in many areas, plan on four to six hours a day — and more on the weekends. But stick to the 60-day plan. If you feel you need 360 hours of study, you may be tempted to spread this study out over a six-month period for 2 hours a day. Consider, however, that committing to six months of intense study is much harder (on you, as well as your family and friends) than two months. In the end, you'll find yourself studying only as much as you would have in a 60-day period anyway.

Studying on your own

Self-study can include books and study references, a study group, and practice exams.

Begin by downloading the free official *CISSP Candidate Information Bulletin (CIB)* from the (ISC)² website. This booklet provides a good outline of the subjects on which you'll be tested.

Next, read this book, take the practice exam, and review the materials on the Dummies website (www.dummies.com). *CISSP For Dummies* is written to provide the CISSP candidate an excellent overview of all the broad topics covered on the CISSP exam.

You can also find several study guides at www.cissp.com, www.cccure.org, and www.cramsession.com.

Joining or creating your own study group can help you stay focused and also provide a wealth of information from the broad perspectives and experiences of other security professionals.

No practice exams exactly duplicate the CISSP exam (and forget about brain dumps — using or contributing to brain dumps is unethical and is a violation of your NDA which could result in losing your CISSP certification permanently). However, many resources are available for practice questions. Some practice questions are too hard, others are too easy, and some are just plain irrelevant. Don't despair! The repetition of practice questions helps reinforce important information that you need to know in order to successfully answer questions on the CISSP exam. For this reason, we recommend taking as many practice exams as possible. Use the Practice Exam on the Dummies website (www.dummies.com), and try the practice questions at Clément Dupuis and Nathalie Lambert's CCCure website (www.cccure.org).

Getting hands-on experience

Getting hands-on experience may be easier said than done, but keep your eyes and ears open for learning opportunities while you prepare for the CISSP exam.

For example, if you're weak in networking or applications development, talk to the networking group or programmers in your company. They may be able to show you a few things that can help make sense of the volumes of information that you're trying to digest.

Your company or organization should have a security policy that's readily available to its employees. Get a copy and review its contents. Are critical elements missing? Do any supporting guidelines, standards, and procedures exist? If your company doesn't have a security policy, perhaps now is a good time for you to educate management about issues of due care, due diligence, and other concepts from the Legal, Regulations, Investigations, and Compliance security domain.

Review your company's plans for business continuity and disaster recovery. They don't exist? Perhaps you can lead this initiative to help both you and your company.

Attending an (ISC)² CISSP CBK Review or Live OnLine Seminar

The (ISC)² also administers five-day CISSP CBK Review Seminars and Live OnLine seminars to help the CISSP candidate prepare. You can find schedules and registration forms for the CBK Review Seminar and Live OnLine on the (ISC)² website at www.isc2.org.

The early rate for the CISSP CBK Review or Live OnLine seminar in the U.S. is $2,495 if you register 16 days or more in advance (the standard rate is $2,695).

If you generally learn better in a classroom environment or find that you have knowledge or actual experience in only two or three of the domains, you might seriously consider attending a review seminar.

If it's not convenient or practical for you to travel to a seminar, Live Online provides the benefit of learning from an (ISC)² Authorized Instructor on your computer. Live OnLine provides all the features of classroom based seminars, real-time delivery, access to archived modules, and all official courseware.

Attending other training courses or study groups

Other reputable organizations, such as SANS (www.sans.org), offer high-quality training in both classroom and self-study formats. Before signing up and spending your money, we suggest that you talk to someone who has completed the course and can tell you about its quality. Usually, the quality of a classroom course depends on the instructor; for this reason, try to find out from others whether the proposed instructor is as helpful as he or she is reported to be.

Many cities have self-study groups, usually run by CISSP volunteers. You may find a study group where you live; or, if you know some CISSPs in your area, you might ask them to help you organize a self-study group.

Always confirm the quality of a study course or training seminar before committing your money and time.

See Chapter 3 for more information on starting a CISSP study group.

Take the testing tutorial and practice exam

If you are not familiar with the operations of computer-based testing, you may want to take a practice exam. Go to the Pearson VUE website and look for the Pearson VUE Tutorial and Practice Exam (at www.pearsonvue.com/athena).

The tutorial and practice exam are available for Windows computers only. To use them, you must have at least 512 MB of RAM, 60 MB of available disk space, Windows 2000 or newer (XP, Vista, 7, or 8), and Microsoft Internet Explorer 5 or a newer browser.

Are you ready for the exam?

Are you ready for the big day? We can't answer this question for you. You must decide, on the basis of your individual learning factors, study habits, and professional experience, when you're ready for the exam. We don't know of any magic formula for determining your chances of success or failure on the CISSP examination. If you find one, please write to us so we can include it in the next edition of this book!

In general, we recommend a minimum of two months of focused study. Read this book and continue taking the practice exams — in this book and on the Dummies website — until you can consistently score 80 percent or better in all areas. *CISSP For Dummies* covers *all* the information you need to know if you want to pass the CISSP examination. Read this book (and reread it) until you're comfortable with the information presented and can successfully recall and apply it in each of the ten domains.

Continue by reviewing other materials (particularly in your weak areas) and actively participating in an online or local study group. Take as many practice exams from as many different sources as possible. You can't find any brain dumps for the CISSP examination, and no practice test can exactly duplicate the actual exam (some practice tests are simply too easy, and others are too difficult), but repetition can help you retain the important knowledge required to succeed on the CISSP exam.

About the CISSP Examination

The CISSP examination itself is a grueling six-hour, 250-question marathon. To put that into perspective, in six hours, you could walk about 20 miles, watch a Kevin Costner movie 1½ times, or sing "My Way" 540 times on a karaoke machine. Each of these feats, respectively, closely approximates the physical, mental (not intellectual), and emotional toll of the CISSP examination.

As described by the (ISC)^2, you need a scaled score of 700 or better to pass the examination. Not all the questions are weighted equally, so we can't absolutely state the number of correct questions required for a passing score.

You won't find any multiple-answer, fill-in-the-blank, scenario-based, or simulation questions on the CISSP exam. However, all 250 multiple-choice questions require you to select the *best* answer from four possible choices. So the correct answer isn't always a straightforward, clear choice. In fact, you can count on many questions to appear initially as if they have more than one correct answer. (ISC)^2 goes to great pains to ensure that you really, *really* know the material. For instance, a sample question might resemble the following:

> Which of the following is the FTP control channel?
>
> **A** TCP port 21
>
> **B** UDP port 21
>
> **C** TCP port 25
>
> **D** IP port 21

Many readers almost instinctively know that FTP's control channel is port 21, but is it TCP, UDP, or IP?

Increasingly, CISSP exam questions are based more on *situations* than on simple knowledge of facts. For instance, here's a question you might get:

> A system administrator has found that a former employee has successfully logged in to the system. The system administrator should:
>
> **A** Shut down the system.
>
> **B** Confirm the breach in the security logs.
>
> **C** Lock or remove the user account.
>
> **D** Contact law enforcement.

You won't find the answer to this in a book (well, probably not). But every exam question still has a *best* answer — perhaps not an ideal answer, but definitely a *best* answer.

A common and effective test-taking strategy for multiple-choice questions is to carefully read each question and then eliminate any obviously wrong choices. The CISSP examination is no exception.

Wrong choices aren't necessarily obvious on the CISSP examination. You may find a few obviously wrong choices, but they only stand out to someone who has studied thoroughly for the examination and has a good grasp of all ten of the security domains.

Only 225 questions are actually counted toward your final score. The other 25 are trial questions for future versions of the CISSP examination. However, the exam doesn't identify these questions for the test-taker, so you have to answer all 250 questions as if every one of them is the real thing.

The CISSP examination is currently available in English, Brazilian Portuguese, Chinese, French, German, Japanese, Korean, and Spanish. You're permitted to bring a foreign language dictionary (non-electronic) for the exam, if needed. You need to indicate your language preference when you register for the exam.

Chapter 15 contains suggestions for preparation on the day of the exam.

After the Examination

After passing the CISSP examination, you must submit a qualified third-party endorsement (from another CISSP, your employer, or any licensed, certified, or commissioned professional — such as a banker, attorney, or certified public accountant) to validate your work experience. This endorsement must be submitted within 90 days of your exam; otherwise your application and exam results are voided. (ISC)² randomly audits a percentage of submitted applications, requiring additional documentation (normally a résumé and confirmation from employers of work history) and review by (ISC)². Within one business day (seven business days, if audited) after it receives the endorsement, (ISC)² normally sends final notification of certification via e-mail.

After you earn your CISSP certification, you must remain an (ISC)² member in good standing and renew your certification every three years. You can renew the CISSP certification by accumulating 120 Continuing Professional

Education (CPE) credits or by retaking the CISSP examination. You must earn a minimum of 20 CPE credits during each year of your three-year recertification cycle. You earn CPE credits for various activities, including taking educational courses or attending seminars and security conferences, belonging to association chapters and attending meetings, viewing vendor presentations, completing university or college courses, providing security training, publishing security articles or books, serving on relevant industry boards, taking part in self-study, and doing related volunteer work. You must document your annual CPE activities on the secure (ISC)^2 website to receive proper credit. You also have to pay an $85 annual maintenance fee, payable to (ISC)^2. Maintenance fees are billed in arrears for the preceding year, and you can pay them online, also in the secure area of the (ISC)^2 website.

See Chapter 3 for more information on earning CPE credits and maintaining your CISSP certification.

Chapter 2

The Common Body of Knowledge (CBK)

In This Chapter

▶ Getting up close and personal with the CBK

▶ Reviewing the ten domains of information security

▶ Understanding knowledge objectives and study topics

*T*he *Common Body of Knowledge* (CBK) defines a basic and common knowledge base for all security professionals, collectively referred to as the *ten domains of information security*. The CBK also provides minimum knowledge requirements for the Certified Information Systems Security Professional (CISSP) exam. Although these knowledge requirements are similar to test objectives, they have some distinct differences. For one thing, test objectives require a candidate to perform specific tasks or demonstrate skill with a specific technology, but the CBK is relatively abstract and changes little over time.

The CBK is periodically updated by the CBK Committee, which the International Information Systems Security Certification Consortium [(ISC)^2] Board of Directors appoints.

In this chapter, we describe the ten domains of information security, as defined in the CBK, introducing each with its official (ISC)^2 definition in italics. You can also find descriptions of each domain online at www.isc2.org.

Access Control

The Access Control domain covers the mechanisms by which a system grants or revokes the right to access data or perform an action on an information system.

Access Control systems include

- ✔ *File permissions, such as "create," "read," "edit," or "delete" on a file server.*

- ✔ *Program permissions, such as the right to execute a program on an application server.*

- ✔ *Data rights, such as the right to retrieve or update information in a database.*

CISSP candidates should fully understand access control concepts, methodologies, and their implementation within centralized and decentralized environments across an organization's computing environment.

Chapter 4 covers this domain in detail. Major Access Control topics include

- ✔ Reviewing concepts, methodologies, and techniques of access control

- ✔ Knowing the risks, vulnerabilities, and attacks that target access control

- ✔ Assessing the effectiveness of access controls

- ✔ Provisioning identity and access throughout the information life cycle

Telecommunications and Network Security

The Telecommunications and Network Security domain encompasses the structures, techniques, transport protocols, and security measures used to provide integrity, availability, confidentiality and authentication for transmissions over private and public communication networks.

The candidate is expected to demonstrate an understanding of communications and network security as it relates to data communications in local area and wide area networks, remote access, and internet/intranet/extranet configurations. Candidates should be knowledgeable with network equipment such as switches, bridges and routers, as well as networking protocols (such as TCP/IP and IPsec), and VPNs.

Such is the definition that (ISC)² gives you as a starting point. We give you the detailed lowdown on this domain in Chapter 5. Its major topics include

- ✔ Reviewing network architecture and design

- ✔ Defining network components

- ✔ Securing communication channels

- ✔ Guarding against (and responding to) network attacks

Information Security Governance and Risk Management

The Information Security Governance and Risk Management domain entails the identification of an organization's information assets and the development, documentation, implementation and updating of policies, standards, procedures and guidelines that ensure confidentiality, integrity and availability. Management tools such as data classification, risk assessment, and risk analysis are used to identify threats, classify assets, and to rate their vulnerabilities so that effective security measures and controls can be implemented.

The candidate is expected to understand the planning, organization, roles and responsibilities of individuals in identifying and securing organization's information assets; the development and use of policies stating management's views and position on particular topics and the use of guidelines, standards, and procedures to support the policies; security training to make employees aware of the importance of information security, its significance, and the specific security-related requirements relative to their position; the importance of confidentiality, proprietary and private information; third-party management and service-level agreements related to information security; employment agreements, employee hiring and termination practices, and risk management practices and tools to identify, rate, and reduce the risk to specific resources.

Chapter 6 covers this domain, which deals with these major topics:

- Understanding and aligning security functions with organizational goals, missions, and objectives
- Understanding and applying security governance, including concepts, processes, and compliance
- Meeting demands for confidentiality, integrity, and availability
- Developing and implementing security policies, procedures, standards, guidelines, and documentation
- Managing the information life cycle
- Managing third-party governance
- Defining concepts and principles of risk management
- Establishing policies, practices, and controls for personnel security
- Maintaining security education, training, and awareness
- Managing security functions, including budgets, metrics, and resources

Software Development Security

The *Software Development Security* domain refers to the controls that are included within systems and application software and the steps used in their development (for example, the Software Development Life Cycle, or SDLC).

Software refers to system software (operating systems) and application programs such as agents, applets, software, databases, data warehouses, and knowledge-based systems. These applications may be used in distributed or centralized environments.

The candidate should fully understand the security and controls of the systems development process, system life cycle, application controls, change controls, data warehousing, data mining, knowledge-based systems, program interfaces, and concepts used to ensure data and application integrity, security, and availability.

We talk about this domain in Chapter 7. Here are the major topics:

✔ Maintaining security throughout the life cycle of software development

✔ Setting up appropriate security controls for your environment

✔ Assessing the effectiveness of software security

Cryptography

The *Cryptography* domain addresses the principles, means, and methods of applying mathematical algorithms and data transformations to information to ensure its integrity, confidentiality, and authenticity.

The candidate is expected to know basic concepts within cryptography; public and private key algorithms in terms of their applications and uses; algorithm construction, key distribution and management, and methods of attack; the applications, construction and use of digital signatures to provide authenticity of electronic transactions, and non-repudiation of the parties involved; and the organization and management of the Public Key Infrastructures (PKIs) and digital certificates distribution and management.

We discuss this domain in Chapter 8. Its major topics include

✔ Applying and using cryptography to achieve security goals

✔ Reviewing the cryptographic life cycle

✔ Comparing encryption concepts

- ✔ Managing public and private keys
- ✔ Using digital signatures for authentication
- ✔ Setting up non-repudiation
- ✔ Examining cryptanalytic attack methods
- ✔ Putting cryptography in the context of network security
- ✔ Using cryptography to secure applications
- ✔ Defining Public Key Infrastructure (PKI)
- ✔ Reviewing certificate-related issues
- ✔ Deciding when to hide information (and what to hide)

Security Architecture and Design

The Security Architecture and Design domain contains the concepts, principles, structures, and standards used to design, implement, monitor, and secure operating systems, equipment, networks, applications, and those controls used to enforce various levels of confidentiality, integrity, and availability.

Information security architecture and design covers the practice of applying a comprehensive and rigorous method for describing a current and/or future structure and behavior for an organization's security processes, information security systems, personnel and organizational sub-units, so that these practices and processes align with the organization's core goals and strategic direction.

The candidate is expected to understand security models in terms of confidentiality, integrity, data flow diagrams; Common Criteria (CC) protection profiles; technical platforms in terms of hardware, firmware, and software; and system security techniques in terms of preventative, detective, and corrective controls.

Chapter 9 delves into this domain, which has the following major topics:

- ✔ Reviewing security models and concepts
- ✔ Evaluating information systems security using various models
- ✔ Outlining security capabilities of information systems
- ✔ Spotting vulnerabilities of system architectures
- ✔ Reviewing vulnerabilities and threats to software and systems
- ✔ Applying countermeasure principles

Security Operations

The Security Operations domain identifies critical information and the execution of selected measures that eliminate or reduce adversary exploitation of critical information. It includes the definition of the controls over hardware, media, and the operators with access privileges to any of these resources. Auditing and monitoring are the mechanisms, tools and facilities that permit the identification of security events and subsequent actions to identify the key elements and report the pertinent information to the appropriate individual, group, or process.

The candidate is expected to know the resources that must be protected, the privileges that must be restricted, the control mechanisms available, the potential for abuse of access, the appropriate controls, and the principles of good practice.

You can get the scoop on this domain in Chapter 10. This domain's major topics include

- ✔ Reviewing concepts of operations security
- ✔ Protecting resources
- ✔ Responding to incidents
- ✔ Preventing and responding to attacks
- ✔ Managing patches and vulnerabilities
- ✔ Managing change and configuration
- ✔ Defining system resilience and fault tolerance

Business Continuity and Disaster Recovery Planning

The Business Continuity and Disaster Recovery Planning domain addresses the identification of an organization's exposure to internal and external threats, and preservation of the business in the face of major disruptions to normal business operations. Business Continuity and Disaster Recovery Planning involve the preparation, testing and updating of specific actions to protect critical business processes from the effect of major system and network failures.

Business Continuity Planning (BCP) helps to identify the organization's exposure to internal and external threats; synthesize hard and soft assets to provide effective prevention and recovery for the organization, and maintains competitive advantage and value system integrity. BCP counteracts interruptions to business activities and should be available to protect critical business processes from the effects of major failures or disasters. It deals with the natural and man-made events and the consequences, if not dealt with promptly and effectively.

Business Impact Analysis (BIA) determines the proportion of impact an individual business unit would sustain subsequent to a significant interruption of computing or telecommunication services. These impacts may be financial, in terms of monetary loss, or operational, in terms of inability to deliver.

Disaster Recovery Plans (DRP) contain procedures for emergency response, extended backup operation and post-disaster recovery, should a computer installation experience a partial or total loss of computer resources and physical facilities. The primary objective of the disaster recovery plan is to provide the capability to process mission-essential application, in a degraded mode, and return to normal mode of operation within a reasonable amount of time.

The candidate is expected to know the difference between business continuity planning and disaster recovery; business continuity planning in terms of project scope and planning, business impact analysis, recovery strategies, recovery plan development, and implementation. Moreover, the candidate should understand disaster recovery in terms of recovery plan development, implementation and restoration.

You can read about this domain in Chapter 11. This domain has the following major topics:

✔ Setting requirements for business continuity

✔ Analyzing business impact

✔ Outlining backup and recovery strategies

✔ Reviewing processes of disaster recovery

✔ Testing plans for business continuity and disaster recovery

Legal, Regulations, Investigations, and Compliance

The Legal, Regulations, Investigations and Compliance domain addresses ethical behavior and compliance with regulatory frameworks. It includes the investigative measures and techniques that can be used to determine if a crime has been committed, and methods used to gather evidence. This domain also includes understanding the computer incident forensic response capability to identify the Advanced Persistent Threat (APT) that many organizations face today.

We go over this domain in Chapter 12. Major topics include

- ✔ Identifying legal issues and complying with international laws
- ✔ Defining professional ethics
- ✔ Conducting investigations and gathering evidence
- ✔ Applying forensic procedures
- ✔ Developing procedures for regulatory compliance
- ✔ Reviewing contractual agreements and procurement processes

Physical (Environmental) Security

The Physical (Environmental) Security domain addresses the threats, vulnerabilities and countermeasures that can be utilized to physically protect an enterprise's resources and sensitive information. These resources include people, the facility in which they work, and the data, equipment, support systems, media, and supplies they utilize.

Physical security describes measures that are designed to deny access to unauthorized personnel (including attackers) from physically accessing a building, facility, resource, or stored information; and guidance on how to design structures to resist potentially hostile acts.

The candidate is expected to know the elements involved in choosing a secure site, its design and configuration, and the methods for securing the facility against unauthorized access, theft of equipment and information, and the environmental and safety measures needed to protect people, the facility, and its resources.

We talk about this domain in Chapter 13. The major topics for this domain include

- ✔ Taking the site and facility design into consideration
- ✔ Establishing perimeter security
- ✔ Reviewing internal security
- ✔ Establishing facilities security
- ✔ Setting up equipment security
- ✔ Providing for personnel privacy and safety

Chapter 3

Putting Your Certification to Good Use

*Y*ou may divide your life into two halves: life before you earned your CISSP certification and life afterwards. Much of this book is devoted to helping you get from the "before" half to the "after" half. This chapter is entirely devoted to "after."

So what do you do after you earn your CISSP? Plenty of things. Some activities are mandatory, such as living the Code of Ethics (provided that you want to *keep* your hard-won certification — we presume that you do), getting security training, and paying your annual maintenance fee. Other activities, such as earning more certifications and volunteering your time, are optional but highly recommended. (We think obtaining additional certifications is a very good idea to enrich your professional life and the professional lives of others.) Table 3-1 lists required and optional post-CISSP activities.

Table 3-1	Post-CISSP Activities	
Activity	**Required**	**Optional**
Live the Code of Ethics	✓	
Maintain your certification	✓	
Be an active (ISC)² member		✓
Volunteer for (ISC)²		✓
Get active in local security chapters		✓
Start or aid a study group		✓
Be a public speaker		✓
Help others learn more about security		✓
Promote the CISSP certification		✓
Be an agent of change		✓
Earn other certifications		✓

Following the (ISC)² Code of Ethics

The (ISC)² Code of Ethics contains a preamble, four canons, and objectives for guidance. The Code of Ethics is

Preamble:

Safety of the commonwealth, duty to our principals (employers, contractors, people we work for) and to each other requires that we adhere, and be seen to adhere, to the highest ethical standards of behavior.

Therefore, strict adherence to this Code is a condition of certification.

Canons:

- ✔ Protect society, the commonwealth, and the infrastructure.
- ✔ Act honorably, honestly, justly, responsibly, and legally.
- ✔ Provide diligent and competent service to principals.
- ✔ Advance and protect the profession.

Objectives for Guidance:

The committee is mindful of its responsibility to:

✔ Give guidance for resolving good versus good, and bad versus bad, dilemmas.

✔ To encourage right behavior such as

- Research

- Teaching

- Identifying, mentoring, and sponsoring candidates for the profession

- Valuing the certificate

✔ To discourage such behavior as

- Raising unnecessary uncertainty

- Giving unwarranted comfort or reassurance

- Consenting to bad practice

- Attaching weak systems to the public network

- Professional association with non-professionals, amateurs, or criminals

When you earn the CISSP certification, you're obligated to do these things. In fact, you're *required* to take on a new responsibility as a protector of the organizations with which you're directly or indirectly involved.

 The best approach to complying with the (ISC)² Code of Ethics is to never partake in any activity that provides even the *appearance* of an ethics violation. Making questionable moves puts your certification at risk, and it may also convey to others that such activity is acceptable. Remember to lead by example!

Keeping Your Certification Current

They say that if you don't use it, you lose it. So it goes with your CISSP certification, anyway. After you earn your CISSP certification, you must do a few things in order to maintain your hard-won CISSP certification:

✔ **Keep your contact information current.** As soon as you receive your certification, register on the (ISC)² website and provide your contact information. (ISC)² reminds you about your annual maintenance fee, Board of Directors elections, annual meetings, and events, but *only* if you maintain your contact info, particularly your e-mail address.

✔ **Pay your annual maintenance fee (AMF).** You're required to pay the annual maintenance fee (AMF — currently US $85) each year in order to continue to hold your CISSP certification. You can easily pay the AMF online at the (ISC)² website (`www.isc2.org`).

✔ **Attending training and conferences to earn CPEs.** CPEs are *Continuing Professional Education* credits. You're required to continue to earn CPEs through security- and professional-related education opportunities in order to maintain your CISSP certification. During each three-year certification cycle, you have to earn a minimum of 120 CPEs; you must earn at least 20 CPEs each year. (You can't wait until the last minute in a three-year cycle to earn all of your CPEs.) More information about earning and recording your CPEs is available at `www.isc2.org` in the document entitled *Continuing Professional Education (CPE) Policies and Guidelines*.

To submit your CPEs, log in to the (ISC)²website and register your training and other qualified events, one at a time.

You can earn a lot of CPEs by attending conferences and training courses, but you can find many more ways to earn CPEs, such as by providing training, attending chapter meetings, or publishing articles or books.

You must maintain complete records for your CPEs. (ISC)² randomly audits its members to verify that they've actually participated in educational events and really earned those CPEs. You don't want to be caught with your bytes down.

Remaining an Active (ISC)² Member

Besides volunteering (see the following section), you can participate in several other activities, including voting in annual elections and attending the annual meeting and other events:

✔ **Vote in (ISC)² elections.** Every year, the election for the (ISC)² Board of Directors takes place. Board members serve three-year terms, and every year, one-third of the members are re-elected. In any democracy, eligible voters need to participate in the election process; this concept is just as true for the (ISC)² board. If you maintain your contact information with (ISC)², you receive notifications of upcoming elections.

✔ **Attend the (ISC)² annual meeting.** Each year, the (ISC)² annual meeting takes place. In the annual meeting, Board of Directors election results are announced, along with any voted changes in bylaws, a reading of the treasurer's report, and other items of business. (ISC)² bestows awards and honors on worthy recipients.

✔ **Attend (ISC)² events.** (ISC)² conducts several events each year, from networking receptions to conferences and educational events. Check back regularly on the (ISC)² website to find out more about events in your area.

✔ **Join an (ISC)² chapter.** (ISC)² is forming chapters around the world, much as other organizations like ISSA have been doing for years. You can find out more at www.isc2.org/chapters/. In a chapter environment you will find many opportunities to get involved, including chapter leadership, participation in chapter activities, and participation in community outreach projects.

Considering (ISC)² Volunteer Opportunities

Volunteers perform much of the work done by the (ISC)². When you take your CISSP certification exam, most or all of the officials in the room are volunteers. Volunteers write the questions in the CISSP exam itself. Most or all of the speakers at (ISC)² events are volunteers.

(ISC)² is much more than a certification or an organization: It's a *cause*. It's security professionals' *raison d'être,* the reason we exist — professionally, anyway. As one of us, consider throwing your weight into the cause.

Volunteers have made (ISC)² what it is today and contributed toward your certification. You can't stand on the sidelines and watch others do the work. Use your talents to help those who'll come after you. You can help in many ways. For information about volunteering, see the (ISC)² website (www.isc2.org).

Most sanctioned (ISC)² volunteer activities earn CPE credits. Check with (ISC)² for details.

Writing certification exam questions

The state of technology, laws, and practices within the (ISC)² Common Body of Knowledge (CBK) is continually changing and advancing. In order to be effective and relevant, CISSP exams need to have exam questions that reflect how security is done today. Therefore people working in the industry — such as you — need to write new questions. If you're interested in being a question writer, visit the (ISC)² website and apply.

Speaking at events

(ISC)² now holds more security-related events around the world than it has at any other time in its history. More often than not, (ISC)² speakers are local volunteers, experts in their professions who want to share with others what they know and have figured out. If you have an area of expertise or a unique perspective on CISSP-related issues, consider educating others with a speaking engagement. For more information, visit the (ISC)² website.

Joining the InterSeC Community

The InterSeC Community is a vetted "community within a community." InterSeC provides means for members to communicate with one another through a LinkedIn-style social networking site. Perhaps the most compelling reason for joining InterSeC is the opportunity to volunteer in the *(ISC)² Safe and Secure Online* program. Through this program members can volunteer their time through public speaking at public and private schools on the subject of safe Internet usage. All materials are provided, and *Safe and Secure Online* supports its volunteers through marketing activities. One of us is a member; in our opinion, this is a great way to network with other CISSPs and contribute to the community.

Supervising examinations

Volunteers who have already earned their CISSP certifications supervise local certification exams. Exam volunteers check in candidates, proctor exams, and observe test-takers to ensure that no one cheats on the certification exam.

If you proctor CISSP examinations, you're ineligible for many other activities — in particular, performing any instructional activities, such as teaching a CISSP class or study group. If you're interested in proctoring CISSP exams (a noble activity, in our opinion), make sure that your other activities aren't in conflict with (ISC)²'s terms and conditions for proctoring. Don't hesitate to contact (ISC)² if you're not sure which other outside teaching activities you may participate in if you're considering being a proctor.

Read and contribute to (ISC)² publications

The *InfoSecurity Professional* digital magazine benefits from articles submitted by (ISC)² members. The entire security community benefits by reading about what others have discovered. Find the magazine at https://www.isc2.org/infosecurity_professional/.

(ISC)² publishes a quarterly online magazine called Insights that is associated with InfoSecurity Professional. You can find out more at https://www.isc2.org/infosecurity_professional_insights/.

The *(ISC)² Blog* is a free online publication for all (ISC)² members. Find the blog, as well as information about writing articles, at `http://blog.isc2.org/isc2_blog/`.

The *(ISC)² Journal* is a fee-based publication that's published bimonthly. Find information about subscribing and writing articles on the journal's home page (`https://www.isc2.org/isc2-journal.aspx`). The annual subscription is currently US$45.

Contribute to the (ISC)² Cyber Exchange

The *(ISC)² Cyber Exchange* is a great online repository of security awareness information in several different formats, including posters, slides, flyers, and brochures. In organizations, the realization of a successful security strategy relies heavily on the good judgment and best practices of all computer users.

If you're responsible for a security awareness program in your organization, you can upload any awareness materials that you create. Others can vote on your materials, and — who knows? — maybe your materials will get high votes, a lot of people will download them, and those people will help to improve security awareness in many other organizations.

The *(ISC)² Cyber Exchange* provides a link to the *Safe and Secure Online* program discussed earlier in this chapter.

You can find the Cyber Exchange at `http://cyberexchange.isc2.org`.

Participating in (ISC)² focus groups

(ISC)² has developed focus groups and quality assurance (QA) testing opportunities. (ISC)² is developing new services, and it needs to receive early feedback during the requirements and design phases of its projects. By participating in these groups and tests, you can influence future (ISC)² services that will aid current and future certification holders.

Getting involved with a CISSP study group

Many communities have CISSP study groups that consist of volunteer mentors and instructors who help those who want to earn the certification.

If your community doesn't have a CISSP study group, consider starting one. Many communities have them already, and the organizers there can give you advice on how to start your own.

Helping others learn more about data security

In no way are we being vain or arrogant when we say that we (the writers of this book, and you the readers) know more about data security and safe Internet usage than perhaps 97% of the general population. There are two main reasons for this:

- ✔ Security is our profession
- ✔ Security is not always easy to do

A legion of volunteer opportunities is available out there to help others keep their computers (and mobile computing devices) secure and to use the Internet safely. Here is a very short list of places where you can help:

- ✔ Service clubs
- ✔ Senior centers
- ✔ Schools (and be sure to read about Safe and Secure Online earlier in this chapter)
- ✔ Your place of employment

In using a little imagination, certainly you can come up with additional opportunities. The world is hungry for the information you possess!

Why volunteer?

Why should you consider volunteering for (ISC)² — or for any other professional organization? Here are two main reasons:

- ✔ Volunteerism of any kind is about giving back to a larger community. Consider the volunteers who helped you to earn your CISSP certification.

- ✔ Volunteering looks good on your résumé . Personally, we consider this a byproduct of volunteering, and not the primary reason for doing it.

Volunteering for (ISC)², or any other cause, should be a reflection of your character, and not simply an activity to embellish your résumé.

While your intention through volunteering may be to help others, volunteering will also change you — for the better.

Consider it a good idea to check in periodically on the (ISC)² website to see other ways you can help.

Becoming an Active Member of Your Local Security Chapter

Relatively recently, (ISC)² started a chapter program, and chapters are springing up all over. Find a local chapter here: http://www.isc2.org/chapters/.

Many other security organizations around the world also have local chapters, perhaps in or near your community. Here's a short list of some organizations that you may be interested in:

- **International Systems Security Association (ISSA):** www.issa.org
- **Information Systems Audit and Control Association (ISACA):** www.isaca.org
- **Society for Information Management (SIM):** www.simnet.org
- **InfraGard:** www.infragard.net
- **Electronic Crimes Task Force:** www.secretservice.gov/ectf.shtml
- **Open Web Application Security Project (OWASP):** www.owasp.org
- **ASIS International:** www.asisonline.org
- **High Technology Crime Investigation Association (HTCIA):** www.htcia.org
- **Risk and Insurance Management Society (RIMS):** www.rims.org
- **Institute of Internal Auditors (IIA):** www.theiia.org
- **Disaster Recovery Institute International (DRII):** www.drii.org
- **Computer Technology Investigators Network (CTIN):** www.ctin.org

Local security groups provide excellent opportunities to find peers in other organizations and to discover more about your trade. Many people find that the contacts they make as part of their involvement with local security organizations can be especially valuable when looking for new career opportunities.

You certainly can find many, many more security organizations that have local chapters, beyond the ones we include in the preceding list. Ask your colleagues and others about security organizations and clubs in your community. If you can't find one, start one!

Spreading the Good Word about CISSP Certification

As popular as the CISSP certification is, many people still don't know about it. And many who may have heard of it don't understand what it's all about. Tell people about your CISSP certification and explain the certification process to your peers. Here are some facts that you can share with anyone and everyone you meet:

- CISSP is the top-tier information security professional certification.
- Over 75,000 security professionals around the world have the CISSP certification.
- The CISSP certification started in 1989.
- CISSP was the first credential to be accredited by the ANSI (American National Standards Institute) to ISO (International Organization for Standardization) Standard 17024:2003.
- The organization that manages the CISSP certification has other certifications for professionals who specialize in various fields of information security. The organization also promotes information security awareness through education programs and events.

Promote the fact that you're certified. How can you promote it? After you earn your CISSP, you can simply put the letters CISSP after your name on your business cards, stationery, e-mail signature, resume, blog, and website. While you're at it, put the CISSP or (ISC)² logo on there, too (just be sure to abide by any established terms of use).

Promoting other certifications

Some of your peers may not be ready to pursue the CISSP certification. They may not have the career experience or knowledge required to go for the CISSP now. These certifications may be suitable for your friends:

- **Associate of (ISC)²:** If you can pass the CISSP or SSCP certification exams but don't yet possess the required professional experience, you can become an Associate of (ISC)². Read about this option on the (ISC)²website.
- **SSCP (Systems Security Certified Practitioner):** This midlevel certification is for hands-on security techs and analysts.

Your colleagues can use these two certs as steppingstones, and eventually, they may be ready for the big one.

Wearing the colors proudly

The (ISC)² online store has a lot of neat stuff, from jackets to shirts to mugs to caps. You can find something for everybody there. The organization introduces new items now and again, and it runs closeout specials on the stuff no one wanted in the first place.

Consider adding a few nice khaki shirts that sport the (ISC)² and CISSP logos to your wardrobe. Or a bright yellow CISSP grip for your computer bag. Or really splurge and consider buying an (ISC)² or CISSP bag!

Lead by example

Like it or not, security professionals, particularly those with the CISSP and other "top drawer" certifications, are role models for those around them. From a security perspective, whatever we do — and how we do it — is seen as the standard for correct behavior.

Being mindful of this, we need to conduct ourselves as though someone were looking — even if no one is — in everything we do.

Using Your CISSP Certification to Be an Agent of Change

As a certified security professional, you're an *agent of change* in your organization: The state of threats and regulations is ever-changing, and you must respond by ensuring that your employer's environment and policies continue to defend your employer's assets against harm. Here are some of the important principles regarding successful agents of change:

- ✔ Identify and promote only essential changes.
- ✔ Promote only those changes that have a chance to succeed.
- ✔ Anticipate sources of resistance.
- ✔ Distinguish resistance from well-founded criticism.
- ✔ Involve all affected parties the right way.
- ✔ Don't promise what you can't deliver.
- ✔ Use sponsors, partners, and collaborators as co-agents of change.

    ✔ Change metrics and rewards to support the changed world.

    ✔ Provide training.

    ✔ Celebrate all successes.

Your job as a security professional doesn't involve preaching; instead, you need to recognize opportunities for improvement and lower risks to the business. Work within your organization's structure to bring about change in the right way. That's the best way to reduce security risks.

Earning Other Certifications

In business and technology, no one's career stays in one place. You're continuously growing and changing, and ever-changing technology also influences organizations and your role within them.

You shouldn't consider your quest for certifications finished when you earn your CISSP — even if it *is* the highest-level information security certification out there! Security is a journey, and your CISSP certification isn't the end goal, but a milestone along the way.

Other (ISC)² certifications

(ISC)² has several other certifications, including some that you may aspire to earn after (or instead of) receiving your CISSP. These certifications are

    ✔ **CSSLP (Certified Secure Software Lifecycle Professional):** A certification that was introduced in 2009. Designed for software development professionals, the CSSLP recognizes software development in which security is a part of the software requirements, design, and testing — so that the finished product has security designed in and built in, rather than added on afterwards.

    ✔ **JGISP (Japanese Government Information Security Professional):** A country-specific certification that validates a professional's knowledge, skills, and experience related to Japanese government regulations and standards.

    ✔ **CAP (Certification and Accreditation Professional):** Jointly developed by the U.S. Department of State's Office of Information Assurance and (ISC)², the CAP credential reflects the skills required to assess risk and establish security requirements for complex systems and environments.

CISSP concentrations

(ISC)² has developed follow-on certifications (think *accessories*) that accompany your CISSP. (ISC)² calls these certifications *concentrations* because they represent the three areas you may choose to specialize in:

- ✔ **ISSAP (Information Systems Security Architecture Professional):** Suited for technical systems security architects

- ✔ **ISSEP (Information Systems Security Engineering Professional):** Demonstrates competence for security engineers

- ✔ **ISSMP (Information Systems Security Management Professional):** About security management (of course!)

All the concentrations require that you first be a CISSP in good standing, and each has its own exam. Read about these concentrations and their exams on the (ISC)² website.

Non- (ISC)² certifications

Organizations other than (ISC)² have security-related certifications, one or more of which may be right for you. None of these certifications directly compete with CISSP, but some of them do overlap with CISSP somewhat.

Non-technical/non-vendor certifications

There are many other certifications available that are not tied to specific hardware or software vendors. Some of the better ones include

- ✔ **CISA (Certified Information Systems Auditor):** Consider this certification if you work as an internal auditor or your organization is subject to one or more security regulations, such as Sarbanes-Oxley, HIPAA, GLBA, PCI, and so on. The Information Systems Audit and Control Association and Foundation (ISACA) manages this certification. Find out more about CISA at www.isaca.org/cisa.

- ✔ **CISM (Certified Information Security Manager):** Similar to (ISC)²'s Information Systems Security Management Professional (ISSMP) certification (which we talk about in the section "CISSP concentrations," earlier in this chapter), you may want the CISM certification if you're in security management. Like CISA, ISACA manages this certification. Read more about it at www.isaca.org/cism.

- ✔ **CRISC (Certified in Risk and Information Systems Control):** This is a relatively new certification that concentrates on organization risk management. Learn more at www.isaca.org/crisc.

- ✔ **CGEIT (Certified in the Governance of Enterprise IT):** Look into this certification if you want to demonstrate your skills and knowledge in the areas of IT management and governance. Effective security in an IT organization definitely depends on *governance,* which involves the management and control of resources to meet long-term objectives. You can find out more about CGEIT at www.isaca.org/cgeit.

- ✔ **CPP (Certified Protection Professional):** Primarily a security management certification, CPP is managed by ASIS International, at www.asisonline.org/certification. The CPP certification designates individuals who have demonstrated competency in all areas constituting security management.

- ✔ **PSP (Physical Security Professional):** ASIS International also offers this certification, which caters to those professionals whose primary responsibility focuses on threat surveys and the design of integrated security systems. Read more at www.asisonline.org/certification.

- ✔ **CIPP (Certified Information Privacy Professional):** The International Association of Privacy Professionals has this and other country-specific privacy certifications for security professionals with knowledge and experience in personal data protection. Find out more at www.privacy association.org.

- ✔ **C|CISO (Certified Chief Information Security Officer):** This certification demonstrates the skills and knowledge required for the typical CISO position. Learn more at www.eccouncil.org.

- ✔ **CBCP (Certified Business Continuity Planner):** A business continuity planning certification offered by the Disaster Recovery Institute. You can find out more at www.drii.org.

- ✔ **DRCE (Disaster Recovery Certified Expert):** This certification is a recognition of knowledge and experience in disaster recovery planning. For more information visit www.bcm-institute.org/bcmi10/drce.

- ✔ **PMP (Project Management Professional):** A good project manager — someone you can trust with organizing resources and schedules — is a wonderful thing, especially on large projects. The Project Management Institute, at www.pmi.org, offers this certification.

- ✔ **GIAC (Global Information Assurance Certification):** The GIAC family of certifications includes categories in Audit, Management, Operations, and Security Administration. One of the GIAC non-vendor-specific certifications that complement CISSP is the GIAC Certified Forensics Analyst (GCFA) and GIAC Certified Incident Handler (GCIH). Find more information at www.giac.org/certifications. There are also several vendor-related GIAC certifications mentioned in the next section.

Technical/vendor certifications

We won't even pretend to list all the technical and vendor certifications here. But these are some of the well-known vendor-related security certifications:

- ✔ **CCSP (Cisco Certified Security Professional) and CCIE (Cisco Certified InternetworkingExpert) Security:** Cisco also offers several product-related certifications for specific products, including PIX firewalls and intrusion prevention systems. Find out more at www.cisco.com/certifications.

- ✔ **Check Point Security Administration certifications:** You can earn certifications related to Check Point's firewall and other security products. Visit www.checkpoint.com/certification.

- ✔ **MCSA (Microsoft Certified Solutions Associate): Security and MCSE (Microsoft Certified Solutions Expert): Security:** These are two specializations for the Microsoft Certified Systems Administrator and Microsoft Certified Systems Engineer certifications from Microsoft. Read more at www.microsoft.com/certification.

- ✔ **C|EH (Certified Ethical Hacker):** We know, we know. A contradiction in terms to some, real business value for others. Read carefully before signing. Offered by the International Council of E-Commerce Consultants (EC-Council). You can find out more at www.eccouncil.org .

- ✔ **E|NSA (Network Security Administrator).** Also from EC Council, this is the certification that recognizes the defensive view — as opposed to the offensive view of C|EH. You can learn more at https://cert.eccouncil.org/certification/certificate-categories/ensa-2.

- ✔ **L|PT (Licensed Penetration Tester).** Another certification from the EC Council, this takes penetration testing to a higher level than C|EH. Learn more at https://cert.eccouncil.org/certification/certificate-categories/licensed-penetration-tester-lpt.

- ✔ **C|HFI (Certified Hacking Forensics Investigator).** Also from EC Council, this certification recognizes the skills and knowledge of a forensic expert who can detect computer crime and gather forensic evidence. Find out more here: https://cert.eccouncil.org/certification/certificate-categories/computer-hacking-forensic-investigator-chfi.

- ✔ **CSFA (CyberSecurity Forensic Analyst):** This certification demonstrates the knowledge and skills for conducting computer forensic examinations. Part of the certification exam is an actual forensics assignment in the lab. Check out www.cybersecurityforensicanalyst.com for more.

- ✔ **RHCSS (Red Hat Certified Security Specialist):** This certification demonstrates advanced skills and knowledge for securing the Red Hat distribution of the Linux operating system. You can find out more at www.redhat.com/certification/rhcss.

✔ **Security+:** A security competency certification for PC techs and the like. We consider this an entry-level certification that may not be for you, but you may well advise your aspiring colleagues who want to get into information security that this certification is a good place to start. You can find out more at `certification.comptia.org`.

✔ **Security|5:** Like Security+, this is an entry-level security competency certification for anyone interested in learning computer networking and security basics. Find out more at `www.eccouncil.org`. Go to Courses ➪ Entry Level Certifications.

You can find many other security certifications out there. Use your favorite search engine and search for phrases such as "security certification" to find information.

Choosing the right certifications

Regularly, technology and security professionals ask us which certifications they should earn next. Our answer is almost always the same: Your decision depends on where you are now and where you want your career to go. You can't find a single "right" certification for everyone — determining which certification you should seek is a very individual thing.

When considering other certifications, ask yourself the following questions:

✔ **Where am I in my career right now?** Are you more focused on technology, policy, operations, development, or management?

✔ **Where do I want my career to go in the future?** If (for example) you're stuck in operations but you want to be focusing on policy, let that goal be your guide.

✔ **What qualifications for certifications do I possess right now?** Some people tackle certifications based on the skills they already possess, and they use those newly earned certifications to climb the career ladder.

✔ **What do I need to do in my career to earn more qualifications?** You need to consider not only what certifications you may be qualified to earn right now, but also what experience you must develop in order to earn future certifications.

If you're honest with yourself, answering these questions should help you discern what certifications are right for you. We recommend that you take time every few years to do some long-term career planning; most people will find that the answers to the questions we've listed here will change.

You might even find that one or more of the certifications you have no longer reflect your career direction. If so, give yourself permission to let those certifications lapse. No sense hanging on to old certifications that no longer exhibit (or help you attain) your career objectives. Each of us has done this at least once, and we may again someday.

Most nontechnical certifications require you to prove that you *already* possess the required job experience in order to earn them. People make this common mistake: They want to earn a certification in order to land a particular kind of job. But that's not the purpose of a certification. Instead, a certification is evidence that you *already* possess both knowledge *and experience.*

Pursue Security Excellence

We think that the best way to succeed in a security career is to pursue excellence every day, regardless of whether you're already in your dream security job or just starting out.

The pursuit of excellence may sound like a lofty or vague term, but you can make a difference every day by doing the following:

- ✔ **Do your best job daily.** No matter what you do for a living, be the very best at it.

- ✔ **Maintain a positive outlook.** Happiness and job satisfaction are due in large part to your attitude. Having a good attitude helps make each day better and helps you to do a better job. Because optimism is contagious, your positive outlook will encourage your co-workers, and pretty soon everyone will be whistling, humming, or whatever they do when they like their jobs.

- ✔ **Improve yourself.** Take the time to read about security practices, advances, developments, and changes in the industry. Try to figure out how innovation in the industry can help you and your organization reduce risk even more, with less effort.

- ✔ **Understand your value.** Take the time to understand how your work adds value to the organization and try to come up with more ways to add value and reduce risk.

- ✔ **Understand the security big picture in your organization.** Whether or not you're responsible for some aspect of security, take the time to understand the principles that your organization uses to increase security and reduce risk. Use the security and risk management principles in Chapter 6, and see how those principles can help improve security even more. Think about the role you can play in advancing the cause of asset and information protection in your organization.

If you make the pursuit of excellence a habit, you can slowly change for the better over time. You end up with an improved security career, and your organization gets better security and reduced risk.

Part II
Domains

The 5th Wave   By Rich Tennant

"We take network security here very seriously."

In this part . . .

The ten chapters of this part cover all the domains of the CISSP exam. We're not talking about `.biz`, `.com`, `.edu`, `.gov`, `.net`, `.org`, and all their dot-dot-dot friends. Instead, we cover the subject areas of the exam: access control, cryptography, physical security, and much more.

Chapter 4

Access Control

*A*ccess control is at the heart of information security. For that matter, access control is at the heart of *all* security. During medieval times, castles were built to provide safety and security. The castle was normally built in a strategic location with towering walls surrounded by a moat. Battlements were positioned along the top of the wall with bastions at the corners. A heavily fortified and guarded entrance was secured by a drawbridge to control entry to (and departure from) the castle. (See Chapter 13 for more information about building a secure castle, uhh, *facility*.) These measures created a security perimeter, preventing hostile forces from freely roaming through the castle grounds and attacking its inhabitants. Breaching the perimeter and gaining entry to the castle was the key to victory for an attacking force. The castle's inner defenses were relatively simple; after getting in, the attackers were free to burn and pillage. Hard and crunchy on the outside, chewy in the middle!

Similarly, computer security requires a strong perimeter and elaborate defenses. Unfortunately, a drawbridge doesn't suffice for access control in computer security. Threats to computer security are much more sophisticated and prevalent than marauding bandits and the occasional fire-breathing dragon. Access control is still critical to securing a perimeter, but it's not limited to a single point of entry. Instead, security professionals must protect their systems from a plethora of threats, including Internet-based attacks, viruses and Trojan horses, insider attacks, covert channels, software bugs, and honest mistakes. And the perimeter now extends well beyond a corporate firewall and has become more of a virtual boundary that typically includes laptops, tablets, mobile devices, and other endpoints that people can use — and that you must secure — from virtually anywhere, including home offices, airport terminals, hotel rooms, and coffee shops!

Finally, you need to ensure that the drawbridge operator (the firewall administrator) is properly trained on how and when to raise or lower the drawbridge (following policies and procedures), and you must be sure that he or she isn't sleeping on the job (that he or she is actually monitoring your logs).

The Certified Information Systems Security Professional (CISSP) candidate must fully understand access control concepts (including control types and authentication, authorization, and accounting), *system access controls* (including identification and authentication techniques, methodologies and implementation, and methods of attack), and *data access controls* (including access control techniques and models) within centralized and decentralized computing environments.

Basic Concepts of Access Control

Access control, in the context of information security, permits an organization's management to define and control which systems or resources a user has access to, and what that user can do on that system or resource. More formally, access control is the ability to permit or deny the use of an *object* (a passive entity, such as a system or file) by a *subject* (an active entity, such as an individual or process). Such use is normally defined through sets of rules or permissions (such as Read, Write, Execute, List, Change, and Delete) and combinations of various security mechanisms (such as administrative, technical, and physical controls).

A subject is always the active entity that attempts to perform an action on (in this case, access) an object, which is always the passive entity being acted upon. You can't always identify an object or subject in absolute terms. For example, a process isn't always an object. An individual user (subject) may be attempting to access a database (object) or run a batch process (object). However, for example, a batch process may actually be the subject attempting to access a database (object) or write run results to a disk (object). In another example, an individual user runs an application to access a specific file. In this example, the user is always a subject, but the application is both an object and a subject. It's an object being run by the user, but it's a subject accessing a file on a file server (which are both objects). See Figure 4-1.

A *subject* is an active entity (such as an individual or process) that accesses or acts on an object. An *object* is a passive entity (such as a system or process) that a subject acts upon or accesses.

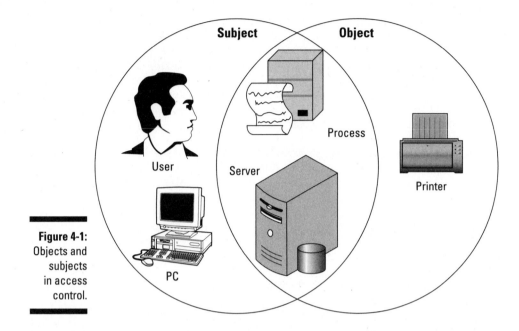

Figure 4-1:
Objects and
subjects
in access
control.

Control Types and Purposes

You achieve access control through an entire set of controls which, identified by purpose, include

- ✔ Preventive controls, for reducing risk
- ✔ Detective controls, for identifying violations and incidents
- ✔ Corrective controls, for remedying violations and incidents and improving existing preventive and detective controls
- ✔ Deterrent controls, for discouraging violations
- ✔ Recovery controls, for restoring systems and information
- ✔ Compensating controls, for providing alternative ways of achieving a task

You implement most access control mechanisms with the primary goal of reducing risk (that is, they're preventive in nature). Detective, corrective, deterrent, recovery, and compensating controls work in a complementary manner with preventive controls to help create an organization's overall security posture.

For example, detective controls help to determine when preventive controls have failed, been bypassed, or are otherwise ineffective or non-existent. Corrective controls help an organization appropriately address access violations or other security incidents. Deterrent controls dissuade malicious or unauthorized activity. Recovery controls return systems and information to their original capabilities when damage has occurred, and compensating controls provide substitute control options for management when other more effective controls aren't possible or feasible.

Many access control mechanisms aren't mutually exclusive in purpose or function. For example, a security guard serves primarily a preventive and detective function, but can also be a strong deterrent and, with proper equipment and training, can assist in correcting and recovering from a security incident.

To keep all these concepts nicely organized, the various controls mentioned in the preceding list are often divided up into three distinct control categories: administrative, technical, and physical.

Access controls can be administrative, technical, or physical.

Administrative controls

Administrative controls include the policies and procedures that an organization implements as part of its overall information security strategy. Administrative controls ensure that technical and physical controls are understood and properly implemented in accordance with the organization's security policy. The purpose of administrative controls is most often preventive and detective, although you can also implement them as deterrent and compensating controls. Administrative controls may include

- Policies, standards, guidelines, and procedures
- Security awareness training
- Asset classification and control
- Employment policies and personnel practices (background checks, job rotations, and separation of duties and responsibilities)
- Account administration
- Account, log, and journal monitoring
- Review of audit trails

We discuss administrative controls in greater detail in Chapters 6 and 10.

Technical controls

Technical (or *logical*) *controls* use hardware and software technology to implement access control.

Technical controls (or logical controls) are the hardware and software mechanisms used to implement access controls. The CISSP exam uses both terms interchangeably, and they refer to the same thing.

Preventive technical controls include

- **Encryption:** Data Encryption Standard (DES), Advanced Encryption Standard (AES), and Merkle-Hellman Knapsack
- **Access control mechanisms:** Biometrics, smart cards, and tokens
- **Access control lists:** Permission lists that define what a subject can or cannot do to an object
- **Remote access authentication protocols:** Password Authentication Protocol (PAP), Challenge Handshake Authentication Protocol (CHAP), Remote Authentication Dial-In User Service (RADIUS), and Lightweight Directory Access Protocol (LDAP)

Detective technical controls include

- Violation reports
- Audit trails
- Network monitoring and intrusion detection

Although technical controls are primarily preventive and detective, you may also use them for corrective, deterrent, and recovery purposes.

Technical controls are the focus of this chapter; we also discuss them in Chapters 5 through 8.

Physical controls

Physical controls ensure the safety and security of the physical environment. These are primarily preventive or detective in nature.

Preventive physical controls include

- Security perimeters, such as fences, locked doors, and restricted areas
- Guards and dogs

Detective physical controls include

- ✔ Motion detectors
- ✔ Video cameras

Often, physical controls are also deterrent in nature. For example, fences, locked doors, security guards and dogs, motion detectors, and video cameras, in addition to being preventive and detective controls, also function as effective deterrent controls, in many cases.

We discuss physical controls in Chapter 13.

Access Control Services

Access control systems provide three essential services:

- ✔ Authentication
- ✔ Authorization
- ✔ Accountability

We devote a subsection to each of these services.

Authentication

Authentication (who can log in) is actually a two-step process consisting of identification and authentication (I&A). *Identification* is the means by which a user (subject) presents a specific identity (such as a username) to a system (object). *Authentication* is the process of verifying that identity. For example, a username/password combination is one common technique (albeit a weak one) that demonstrates the concepts of identification (username) and authentication (password).

Authentication determines whether a subject can log in.

Authorization

Authorization (also referred to as *establishment*) defines the rights and permissions granted to a user account or process (what you can do). After a system authenticates a user, authorization determines what that user can do with a system or resource.

Authorization (or establishment) determines what a subject can do (as defined by assigned rights and permissions).

Accountability

Accountability is the capability to associate users and processes with their actions (what they did). Audit trails and system logs are components of accountability.

An important security concept that's closely related to accountability is non-repudiation. *Non-repudiation* means that a user (username Madame X) can't deny an action because her identity is positively associated with her actions. Non-repudiation is an important legal concept. If a system permits users to log in using a generic user account, or a user account that has a widely known password, or no user account at all, then you can't absolutely associate any user with a given (malicious) action or (unauthorized) access on that system, which makes it extremely difficult to prosecute or otherwise discipline that user.

Accountability determines what a subject did.

Non-repudiation means that a user can't deny an action because you can irrefutably associate him or her with that action.

Categories of Access Control

The two categories of access controls are

- ✔ **System access controls:** Controls in this category protect the entire system and provide a first line of defense for the data contained on the system.
- ✔ **Data access controls:** Controls in this category are specifically implemented to protect the data contained on the system.

System access controls

System access controls are the hard and crunchy outside of a system, providing the first line of defense in information security. They protect systems and information by restricting access to the system.

Although system access controls can provide complete authentication, authorization, and accountability (AAA), they're renowned for authentication.

You can base authentication on any of three factors:

- ✔ **Something you know, such as a password or a personal identification number (PIN):** This concept is based on the assumption that only the owner of the account knows the secret password or PIN needed to access the account. Username and password combinations are the simplest, least expensive, and therefore most common authentication mechanism implemented today. Of course, passwords are often shared, stolen, guessed, or otherwise compromised — thus they're also one of the weakest authentication mechanisms.

- ✔ **Something you have, such as a smart card or token:** This concept is based on the assumption that only the owner of the account has the necessary key to unlock the account. Smart cards, USB tokens, and key fobs are becoming more common, particularly in relatively secure organizations, such as government or financial institutions. Although smart cards and tokens are somewhat more expensive and complex than other, less-secure authentication mechanisms, they're not (usually) prohibitively expensive or overly complicated to implement, administer, and use, and they provide a *significant* boost to authentication security. Of course, keys are often lost, stolen, or damaged.

- ✔ **Something you are, such as fingerprint, voice, retina, or iris characteristics:** This concept is based on the assumption that the finger or eyeball attached to your body is actually yours and uniquely identifies you. (Of course, fingers and eyes can be lost or . . . .) Actually, the major drawback with this authentication mechanism is acceptance — people are sometimes uneasy about using these systems. Biometric systems are also among the most expensive authentication mechanisms to deploy.

Authentication is based on something you know, something you have, or something you are.

Two-factor authentication requires two of these three authentication factors for authentication. *Three-factor authentication* requires all three factors for authentication.

Strong authentication requires at least two of the factors in the preceding list (something you know, something you have, and/or something you are).

A commonly cited example of an access control system that uses two-factor authentication is an automatic teller machine (ATM) card and a PIN. Purists might argue that the ATM card is actually a form of identification that you present to the ATM machine to establish your identity and that the PIN is the only authentication factor involved; thus an ATM doesn't provide two-factor authentication. Save this debate for engaging conversation at a wild party. For the CISSP exam, this scenario is considered two-factor authentication.

Identification and authentication

The various identification and authentication (I&A) techniques that we discuss in the following sections include passwords/passphrases and PINs (knowledge-based); biometrics and behavior (characteristic-based); and one-time passwords, tokens, and single sign-on (SSO).

The identification component is normally a relatively simple mechanism based on a username or, in the case of a system or process, based on a computer name, Media Access Control (MAC) address, Internet Protocol (IP) address, or Process ID (PID). Identification requirements include only that it must uniquely identify the user (or system/process) and shouldn't identify that user's role or relative importance in the organization (the identification shouldn't include labels such as *accounting* or *CEO*). Common or shared accounts, such as *root, admin,* or *system* should not be permitted. Such accounts provide no account-ability and are prime targets for malicious beings.

Identification is the act of claiming a specific identity. Authentication is the act of verifying that identity.

Passwords and passphrases

"A password should be like a toothbrush. Use it every day; change it regularly; and DON'T share it with friends." –USENET

Passwords are easily the most common — and weakest — authentication mechanism in use today. Although there are more advanced and secure authentication technologies available, including tokens and biometrics, organizations typically use those technologies as supplements to or in combination with — rather than as replacements for — traditional usernames and passwords.

A *passphrase* is a variation on a password; it uses a sequence of characters or words, rather than a single password. Generally, attackers have more difficulty breaking passphrases than breaking regular passwords because longer passphrases are generally more difficult to break than complex passwords. Passphrases also have the following advantages:

- ✔ Users frequently use the same passwords to access numerous accounts; their corporate networks, their home PCs, their Hotmail or Yahoo! e-mail accounts, their eBay accounts, and their Amazon.com accounts, for example. So an attacker who targets a specific user may be able to gain access to his or her work account by going after a less secure system, such as his or her home PC, or by compromising an Internet account (because the user has passwords conveniently stored in that bastion of security — Internet Explorer!). Internet sites and home PCs typically don't use passphrases, so you improve the chances that your users have to use different passwords/passphrases to access their work accounts.

✔ Users can actually remember and type passphrases more easily than they can remember and type a much shorter, cryptic password that requires contorted finger acrobatics to type on a keyboard.

✔ A passphrase (or a password for that matter) that is 15 characters or longer **cannot** be stored in Active Directory or in the local Security Account Manager (SAM) accounts database using the LanManager hash, which effectively eliminates the well-known vulnerabilities associated with this hash function.

However, passphrases also have a downside:

✔ Users can find passphrases inconvenient, so you may find passphrases difficult to implement. ("You mean I need to have a 20-character password now?!")

✔ Not all systems support passphrases. Such systems ignore anything longer than the system limit (for example, eight characters).

✔ Many command-line interfaces and tools don't support the space character that separates words in a passphrase.

✔ Ultimately, a passphrase is still just a password (albeit, a much longer and better one) and thus shares some of the same problems associated with passwords.

You, as a CISSP candidate, should understand the general problems associated with passwords, as well as common password controls and management features.

Password/passphrase problems include that they're

✔ **Insecure:** Passwords are generally insecure for several reasons, including

• **Human nature:** In the case of user-generated passwords, users often choose passwords that they can easily remember and consequently attackers can easily guess (such as a spouse's or pet's name, birthday, anniversary, or hobby). Users may also be inclined to write down passwords (particularly complex, system-generated passwords) or share their passwords with others.

• **Transmission and storage:** Many applications and protocols (such as file transfer protocol [FTP] and password authentication protocol [PAP]) transmit passwords in clear text. These applications and protocols may also store passwords in plaintext files, or in a security database that uses a weak hashing algorithm.

✔ **Easily broken:** Passwords are susceptible to brute-force and dictionary attacks (which we discuss in the section "Methods of attack," later in this chapter) by readily available programs such as John the Ripper and L0phtCrack (pronounced *loft-crack*).

✔ **Inconvenient:** Easily agitated users can find entering passwords tiresome. In an attempt to bypass these controls, users may select an easily typed, weak password; they may automate log-ons (for instance, selecting the Remember My Password check box in a browser); and they can neglect to lock their workstations or log out when they leave their desks.

✔ **Refutable:** Transactions authenticated with only a password don't necessarily provide absolute proof of a user's identity. Authentication mechanisms must guarantee non-repudiation, which is a critical component of accountability. (For more on non-repudiation, see the section "Accountability," earlier in this chapter.)

Passwords have the following login controls and management features that you should configure in accordance with an organization's security policy and security best practices:

✔ **Length:** Generally, the longer the better. A password is, in effect, an encryption key. Just as larger encryption keys (such as 1024-bit or 2048-bit) are more difficult to crack, so too are longer passwords. You should configure systems to require a minimum password length of six to eight characters. Of course, users can easily forget long passwords or simply find them too inconvenient, leading to some of the human-nature problems discussed earlier in this section.

✔ **Complexity:** Strong passwords contain a mix of upper- and lowercase letters, numbers, and special characters such as # and $. Be aware that some systems may not accept certain special characters, or those characters may perform special functions (for example, in terminal emulation software).

✔ **Aging:** You should set maximum password aging to require password changes at regular intervals: 30-, 60-, or 90-day periods are common. You should also set minimum password aging — one day is usually recommended — to prevent users from easily circumventing password history controls (for example, by changing their password five times within a few minutes, then setting it back to the original password).

✔ **History:** Password history settings (five is usually recommended) allow a system to remember previously used passwords for a specific account. This security setting prevents users from circumventing maximum password aging by alternating between two or three familiar passwords when they're required to change their passwords.

✔ **Limited attempts:** This control limits the number of unsuccessful log-on attempts and consists of two components: counter threshold (for example, three or five) and counter reset (for example, 5 or 30 minutes). The *counter threshold* is the maximum number of consecutive unsuccessful attempts permitted before some action occurs (such as automatically disabling the account). The *counter reset* is the amount of time between unsuccessful attempts. For example, three unsuccessful log-on attempts within a 30-minute period may result in an account lockout for a set period (for example, 24 hours); but two unsuccessful attempts in 25 minutes, and then a third unsuccessful attempt 10 minutes later, wouldn't result in an account lockout. A successful log-on attempt also resets the counter.

✔ **Lockout duration (or intruder lockout):** When a user exceeds the counter threshold that we describe in the preceding bullet, the account is locked out. Organizations commonly set the lockout duration to 30 minutes, but you can set it for any duration. If you set the duration to forever, an administrator must unlock the account. Some systems don't notify the user when it locks out an account, instead quietly alerting the system administrator to a possible break-in attempt. Of course, an attacker can use the lockout duration as a simple means to perform a *Denial of Service attack* (intentionally making repeated bad log-on attempts to keep the user's account locked).

✔ **Limited time periods:** This control restricts the time of day that a user can log in. For example, you can effectively reduce the period of time that attackers can compromise your systems by limiting users' access to business hours only. However, this type of control is becoming less common in the modern age of the workaholic and the global economy, both of which require users to legitimately perform work at all hours of the day.

✔ **System messages:** System messages include the following:

- **Login banner:** Welcome messages literally invite criminals to access your systems. Disable any welcome message and replace it with a legal warning that requires the user to click OK to acknowledge the warning and accept the legal terms of use.

- **Last username:** Many popular operating systems display the username of the last successful account log-on. Users (who only need to type in their password) find this feature convenient — and so do attackers (who only need to crack the password without worrying about matching it to a valid user account). Disable this feature.

- **Last successful log-on:** After successfully logging on to the system, this message tells the user the last time that he or she logged on. If the system shows that the last successful log-on for a user was Saturday morning at 2:00 a.m. and the user knows that he couldn't possibly have logged in at that time because he has a life, he knows that someone has compromised his account, and he can report the incident accordingly.

We're sure that you know many of the following widely available and well-known guidelines for creating more secure passwords, but just in case, here's a recap:

✔ Use a mix upper- and lowercase letters, numbers, and special characters (for example, !@#$%).

✔ Do not include your name or other personal information (such as spouse, street address, school, birthdays, and anniversaries).

✔ Replace some letters with numbers (for example, replace *e* with *3*).

✔ Use nonsense phrases, misspellings, substitutions, or before-and-after words and phrases (combining two unrelated words or phrases, such as "Wheel of Fortune Cookies").

✔ Combine two words by using a special character (for example, sALT&pEPPER or BaCoN+EgGs).

✔ Use a combination of all the other tips in this list (for example, "Snow White and the Seven Habits of Highly Effective People" becomes SW&t7HoH3P!).

✔ Do not use repeating patterns between changes (for example, password1, password2, password3).

✔ Do not use the same passwords for work and personal accounts.

✔ Do not use passwords that are too difficult to remember.

✔ Do not use any passwords you see in a published book, including this one. (But you knew that.)

The problem with these guidelines is that they're *widely available and well known!* In fact, attackers use some of these same guidelines to create their aliases or handles: *super-geek* becomes *5up3rg33k.* Also, a password such as *Qwerty12* technically satisfies these guidelines, but it's not really a good password because it's a relatively simple and obvious pattern (the first row on your keyboard). Many dictionary attacks include not only word lists, but also patterns such as this one.

You can use a software tool that helps users evaluate the quality of their passwords when they create them. These tools are commonly known as *password/ passphrase generators* or *password appraisers.*

Personal Identification Numbers (PINs)

A PIN in itself is a relatively weak authentication mechanism because you have only 10,000 possible combinations for a four-digit numeric PIN. Therefore, organizations usually use some other safeguard in combination with a PIN. For example, most ATMs confiscate your ATM card after three incorrect PIN attempts. A PIN used with a one-time token password and an account lockout policy is also very effective, allowing a user to attempt only one PIN/password combination per minute and then locking the account after three or five failed attempts as determined by the security policy.

Biometrics and behavior

The only absolute method for positively identifying an individual is to base authentication on some unique physiological or behavioral characteristic of that individual. Biometric identification uses physiological characteristics, including fingerprints, hand geometry, and facial features such as retina and iris patterns. Behavioral biometrics are based on measurements and data derived from an action, and they indirectly measure characteristics of the human body. Behavioral characteristics include voice, signature, and keystroke patterns.

Biometrics are based on the third factor of authentication — something you are. Biometric access control systems apply the concept of identification and authentication (I&A) slightly differently, depending on their use:

- **Physical access controls:** The individual presents the required biometric characteristic and the system attempts to *identify* the individual by matching the input characteristic to its database of authorized personnel. This type of control is also known as a *one-to-many* search.

- **Logical access controls:** The user enters a username or PIN (or inserts a smart card), and then presents the required biometric characteristic for verification. The system attempts to *authenticate* the user by matching the claimed identity and the stored biometric image file for that account. This type of control is also known as a *one-to-one* search.

Biometric authentication, in and of itself, doesn't provide *strong* authentication because it's based on only one of the three authentication requirements — something you *are*. To be considered a truly strong authentication mechanism, biometric authentication must include either something you *know* or something you *have*. (Although you might argue that your hand or eye is both something you have *and* something you are, for the purposes of the CISSP exam you'd be wrong!)

The necessary factors for an effective biometrics access control system include

- **Accuracy:** The most important characteristic of any biometric system. The *uniqueness* of the body organ or characteristic that the system measures to guarantee positive identification is an important element of accuracy. In common biometric systems today, the only organs that satisfy this requirement are the fingers/hands and the eyes.

  Another important element of accuracy is the system's ability to detect and reject forged or counterfeit input data. The accuracy of a biometric system is normally stated as a percentage, in the following terms:

  - **False Reject Rate (FRR) or Type I error:** Authorized users to whom the system incorrectly denies access, stated as a percentage. Reducing a system's sensitivity reduces the FRR but increases the False Accept Rate (FAR).

The False Reject Rate (or Type I error) is the percentage of authorized users to whom the system incorrectly denies access.

- **False Accept Rate (FAR) or Type II error:** Unauthorized users to whom the system incorrectly grants access, stated as a percentage. Increasing a system's sensitivity reduces the FAR but increases the FRR.

The False Accept Rate (or Type II error) is the percentage of unauthorized users to whom the system incorrectly grants access.

- **Crossover Error Rate (CER):** The point at which the FRR equals the FAR, stated as a percentage. (See Figure 4-2.) Because you can adjust the FAR and FRR by changing a system's sensitivity, the CER is considered the most important measure of biometric system accuracy.

The Crossover Error Rate is the point at which the FRR equals the FAR, stated as a percentage.

✔ **Speed and throughput:** The length of time required to complete the entire authentication procedure. This time measurement includes stepping up to the system, inputting a card or PIN (if required), entering biometric data (such as inserting a finger or hand in a reader, pressing a sensor, aligning an eye with a camera or scanner, speaking a phrase, or signing a name), processing the input data, and opening and closing an access door (in the case of a physical access control system). Another important measure is the initial enrollment time required to create a biometric file for a user account. Generally accepted standards are a speed of less than five seconds, a throughput rate of six to ten per minute, and enrollment time of less than two minutes.

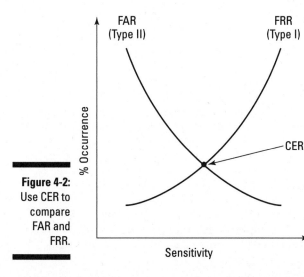

Figure 4-2: Use CER to compare FAR and FRR.

✔ **Data storage requirements:** Though less significant these days, data storage requirements are still an interesting issue because costs have decreased for data storage media. The size of a biometric system's input files can be as small as 9 bytes or as large as 10,000 bytes, averaging 256 to 1,000 bytes.

✔ **Reliability:** Reliability is an important factor in any system. The system must operate continuously and accurately without frequent maintenance outages.

✔ **Acceptability:** Getting users to accept a biometric system is the biggest hurdle to widespread implementation. Certain privacy and ethics issues arise with the prospect of organizations using these systems to collect medical or other physiological data about employees. Other factors that might potentially alarm users include intrusiveness of the data collection procedure and undesirable physical contact with common system components, such as pressing an eye against a plastic cup or placing lips close to a microphone for voice recognition.

Gaining user acceptance is the most common difficulty with biometric systems.

Table 4-1 summarizes the generally accepted standards for the factors described in the preceding list.

Table 4-1 Generally Accepted Standards for Biometric Systems

Characteristic	Standard
Accuracy	CER < 10%
Speed	5 seconds
Throughput	6–10 per minute
Enrollment time	< 2 minutes

Common types of physiological biometric access control systems include

✔ **Fingerprint recognition and finger scan systems:** The most common biometric systems in use today. They analyze the ridges, whorls, and minutiae (bifurcations and ridge endings, dots, islands, ponds and lakes, spurs, bridges, and crossovers) of a fingerprint to create a digitized image that uniquely identifies the owner of the fingerprint. A *fingerprint recognition* system stores the entire fingerprint as a digitized image. A disadvantage of this type of system is that it can require a lot of storage space and resources. More commonly, organizations use a *finger scan system,* whichstores only sample points or unique features of a fingerprint and therefore requires less storage and processing resources.

Also, users may more readily accept the technology because no one can re-create an entire fingerprint from the data in a finger scan system. See Table 4-2 for general characteristics of finger scan systems.

Finger scan systems, unlike fingerprint recognition systems, don't store an image of the entire fingerprint — only a digitized file describing its unique characteristics. This fact should allay the privacy concerns of most users.

✔ **Hand geometry systems:** Like finger scan systems, *hand geometry systems* are also nonintrusive and therefore generally more easily accepted than other biometric systems. These systems generally can more accurately uniquely identify an individual than finger scan systems, and they have some of the smallest file sizes compared with other biometric system types. A digital camera simultaneously captures a vertical and a horizontal image of the subject's hand, acquiring the three-dimensional hand geometry data. The digitized image records the length, width, height, and other unique characteristics of the hand and fingers. See Table 4-2 for general characteristics of hand geometry systems.

Table 4-2 **General Characteristics of Finger Scan and Hand Geometry Systems**

Characteristic	Finger Scan	Hand Geometry
Accuracy	< 1%–5% (CER)	< 1%–2% (CER)
Speed	1–7 seconds	3–5 seconds
File size	~250–1500 bytes	~10 bytes
Advantages	Nonintrusive, inexpensive	Small file size
Disadvantages	Sensor wear and tear; accuracy may be affected by swelling, injury, or wearing rings	Sensor wear and tear; accuracy may be affected by swelling, injury, or wearing rings

✔ **Retina pattern:** These systems record unique elements in the vascular pattern of the retina. Major concerns with this type of system are fears of eye damage from a laser (which is actually only a camera with a focused low-intensity light) directed at the eye and, more feasibly, privacy concerns. Certain health conditions, such as diabetes and heart disease, can cause changes in the retinal pattern, which these types of systems may detect. See Table 4-3 for general characteristics of retina pattern systems.

✔ **Iris pattern:** By far the most accurate of any type of biometric system. The *iris* is the colored portion of the eye surrounding the pupil. The complex patterns of the iris include unique features such as coronas, filaments, freckles, pits, radial furrows, rifts, and striations. The characteristics of the iris, formed shortly before birth, remain stable throughout life. The iris is so unique that even the two eyes of a single individual have different patterns. A camera directed at an aperture mirror scans the iris pattern. The subject must glance at the mirror from a distance of approximately 3 to 10 inches. It's technically feasible — but perhaps prohibitively expensive — to perform an iris scan from a distance of several feet. See Table 4-3 for general characteristics of iris pattern systems.

Table 4-3	General Characteristics of Retina and Iris Pattern Systems	
Characteristic	*Retina Pattern*	*Iris Pattern*
Accuracy	1.5% (CER)	< 0.5% (CER)
Speed	4–7 seconds	2.5–4 seconds
File size	~96 bytes	~256–512 bytes
Advantages	Overall accuracy	Best overall accuracy
Disadvantages	Perceived intrusiveness; sanitation and privacy concerns	Subject must remain absolutely still; subject can't wear colored contact lenses or glasses (clear contacts are generally okay)

Common types of behavioral biometric systems include

- **Voice recognition:** These systems capture unique characteristics of a subject's voice and may also analyze phonetic or linguistic patterns. Most voice recognition systems are text-dependent, requiring the subject to repeat a specific phrase. This functional requirement of voice recognition systems also helps improve their security by providing two-factor authentication: something you know (a phrase) and something you are (your voice). More advanced voice recognition systems may present a random phrase or group of words, which prevents an attacker from recording a voice authentication session and later replaying the recording to gain unauthorized access. See Table 4-4 for general characteristics of voice recognition systems.

- **Signature dynamics:** These systems typically require the subject to sign his or her name on a signature tablet. The enrollment process for a signature dynamics system captures numerous characteristics, including the signature pattern itself, the pressure applied to the signature pad, and the speed of the signature. Of course, signatures commonly exhibit some slight changes because of different factors, and they can be forged. See Table 4-4 for general characteristics of signature dynamics systems.

✔ **Keystroke or typing dynamics:** These systems typically require the subject to type a password or phrase. The keystroke dynamic identification is based on unique characteristics such as how long a user holds down a key on the keyboard (dwell time) and how long it takes a user to get to and press a key (seek or flight time). These characteristics are measured by the system to form a series of mathematical data representing a user's unique typing pattern or signature, which is then used to authenticate the user.

Digital signatures (discussed in detail in Chapter 8) and *electronic signatures* — which are electronic copies of people's signatures — are not the same as the signatures used in biometric systems. These terms are *not* related and are *not* interchangeable.

Table 4-4	General Characteristics of Voice Recognition and Signature Dynamics Systems	
Characteristic	*Voice Recognition*	*Signature Dynamics*
Accuracy	< 10% (CER)	1% (CER)
Speed	10–14 seconds	5–10 seconds
File size	~1,000–10,000 bytes	~1,000–1,500 bytes
Advantages	Inexpensive; nonintrusive	Nonintrusive
Disadvantages	Accuracy, speed, file size; affected by background noise, voice changes; can be fooled by voice imitation	Signature tablet wear and tear; speed; can be fooled by a forged signature

In general, the CISSP candidate doesn't need to know the specific characteristics and specifications of the different biometric systems, but you should know how they compare with each other. For example, know that iris pattern systems are more accurate than retina pattern systems.

One-time passwords

A *one-time password* is a password that's valid for one log-on session only. After a single log-on session, the password is no longer valid. Thus, if an attacker obtains a one-time password that someone has already used, that password has no value. A one-time password is a *dynamic password,* meaning it changes at some regular interval or event. Conversely, a *static password* is a password that remains the same for each log-on. Similar to the concept of a one-time pad in cryptography (which we discuss in Chapter 8), a one-time password provides maximum security for access control.

Two examples of one-time password implementations are tokens (which we discuss in the following section) and the S/Key protocol. The *S/Key protocol*, developed by Bell Communications Research and defined in Internet Engineering Task Force (IETF) Request For Comment (RFC) 1760, is client/server based and uses MD4 and MD5 to generate one-time passwords. (*MD4* and *MD5* are algorithms used to verify data integrity by creating a 128-bit message digest from data input. We discuss both in Chapter 8.)

Tokens

Tokens are access control devices such as key fobs, dongles, smart cards, magnetic cards, software (known as *soft tokens* and installed on a tablet, mobile device, smartphone, laptop, or PC), and keypad or calculator-type cards that store static passwords (or digital certificates) or that generate dynamic passwords. The three general types of tokens are

- ✔ **Static password tokens:** Store a static password or digital certificate.

- ✔ **Synchronous dynamic password tokens:** Continuously generate a new password or passcode at a fixed time interval (for example, 60 seconds) or in response to an event (such as each time you press a button). Typically, the passcode is valid only during a fixed time window (say, one minute) and only for a single log-on (so, if you want to log on to more than one system, you must wait for the next passcode).

- ✔ **Asynchronous (or *challenge-response*) dynamic password tokens:** Generate a new password or passcode asynchronously by calculating the correct response to a system-generated random challenge string (known as a *nonce*) that the owner manually enters into the token.

Tokens provide two-factor authentication (something you have and something you know) by either requiring the owner to authenticate to the token first or by requiring that the owner enters a secret PIN along with the generated password. Both RADIUS and Terminal Access Controller Access Control System (TACACS+; which we discuss in the section "Centralized access controls," later in this chapter) support various token products.

A soft token that's installed on a laptop or PC doesn't provide strong (two-factor) authentication because the "something you have" is the computer you're trying to log on to!

You can use tokens to generate one-time passwords and provide two-factor authentication.

Single sign-on (SSO)

The concept of single sign-on (SSO) addresses a common problem for users and security administrators alike. Multiple accounts mean multiple vulnerabilities. Every account that exists in a system, network, or application is a potential point of unauthorized access. Multiple accounts belonging to a single user represent an even greater vulnerability:

✔ Users who require access to multiple systems or applications must often maintain numerous different passwords, which inevitably leads to short-cuts in creating and recalling passwords. Users create weak passwords that have only slight variations, and they likely write down those passwords.

✔ Multiple accounts also affect user productivity (and sanity!) because the user must stop to log in to different systems. Someone also has to create and maintain accounts, which involves supporting, removing, resetting, and disabling passwords, as well as unlocking accounts.

At first glance (alas), SSO seems the "perfect" solution that users and security administrators alike thirst for and seek. SSO allows a user to present a single set of log-on credentials, typically to an authentication server, which then transparently logs the user in to *all* other enterprise systems and applications for which that user is authorized. Of course, SSO does have some disadvantages, which include

✔ **Woo-hoo!:** After you're authenticated, you have the keys to the kingdom. Read that as *unrestricted access to all authorized resources!* The security professional's nightmare.

✔ **Complexity:** Implementing SSO can be difficult and time-consuming. You have to address interoperability issues between different systems and applications. But, hey — that's why you get paid (or should get paid) the big bucks!

SSO is commonly implemented by third-party ticket-based solutions, including

✔ **Kerberos:** *Kerberos,* commonly used in the Sun Network File System (NFS) and Windows 2000, 2003, and 2008, is perhaps the most popular ticket-based symmetric key authentication protocol in use today. Kerberos is named for the fierce, three-headed dog that guards the gates of Hades in Greek mythology. (Not to be confused with Ker-beer-os, the fuzzy, six-headed dog sitting at the bar that keeps looking better and better!) Researchers at the Massachusetts Institute of Technology (MIT, also known as *Millionaires in Training*) developed this open-systems protocol in the mid-1980s. The CISSP exam requires a general understanding of Kerberos operation. Unfortunately, Kerberos is a complex protocol that has many different implementations and no simple explanation. The following step-by-step discussion is a basic description of Kerberos operation:

  1. The client prompts the subject (such as a user) for identification and authentication (for example, username and password). Using the authentication information (password), the client temporarily generates and stores a secret key for the subject by using a one-way hash function and then sends only the subject's identification (username) to the Key Distribution Center's (KDC) Authentication Server (AS). The password/secret key *isn't* sent to the KDC. See Figure 4-3.

See Chapter 8 for a discussion of hash functions.

2. The AS on the KDC verifies that the subject (known as a *principal*) exists in the KDC database. The KDC Ticket Granting Service (TGS) then generates a Client/TGS Session Key encrypted with the subject's secret key, which only the TGS and the client know. The TGS also generates a Ticket Granting Ticket (TGT), consisting of the subject's identification, the client network address, the valid period of the ticket, and the Client/TGS Session Key. The TGS encrypts the TGT by using its secret key, which only the TGS knows, then sends the Client/TGS Session Key and TGT back to the client. See Figure 4-4.

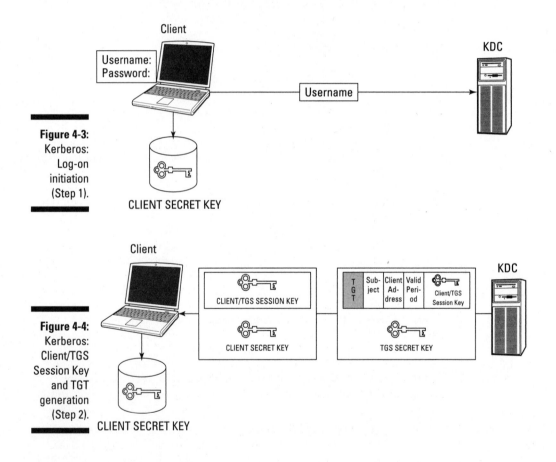

Figure 4-3: Kerberos: Log-on initiation (Step 1).

Figure 4-4: Kerberos: Client/TGS Session Key and TGT generation (Step 2).

3. The client decrypts the Client/TGS Session Key — using the stored secret key that it generated by using the subject's password — authenticates the subject (user), and then erases the stored secret key to avoid possible compromise. The client can't decrypt the TGT, which the TGS encrypted by using the TGS secret key. See Figure 4-5.

4. When the subject requests access to a specific object (such as a server, also known as a *principal*), it sends the TGT, the object identifier (such as a server name), and an authenticator to the TGS on the KDC. (The *authenticator* is a separate message that contains the client ID and a timestamp, and uses the Client/TGS Session Key to encrypt itself.) See Figure 4-6.

5. The TGS on the KDC generates both a Client/Server Session Key (which it encrypts by using the Client/TGS Session Key) and a Service Ticket (which consists of the subject's identification, the client network address, the valid period of the ticket, and the Client/Server Session Key). The TGS encrypts the Service Ticket by using the secret key of the requested object (server), which only the TGS and the object know. The TGS then sends the Client/Server Session Key and Service Ticket back to the client. See Figure 4-7.

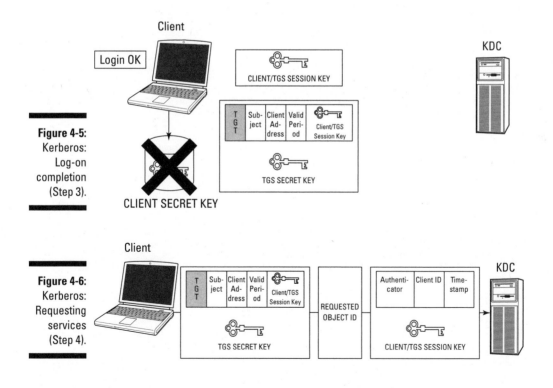

Figure 4-5: Kerberos: Log-on completion (Step 3).

Figure 4-6: Kerberos: Requesting services (Step 4).

6. The client decrypts the Client/Server Session Key by using the Client/TGS Session Key. The client can't decrypt the Service Ticket, which the TGS encrypted by using the secret key of the requested object. See Figure 4-8.

7. The client can then communicate directly with the requested object (server). The client sends the Service Ticket and an authenticator to the requested object (server). The client encrypts the authenticator (comprising the subject's identification and a timestamp) by using the Client/Server Session Key that the TGS generated. The object (server) decrypts the Service Ticket by using its secret key. The Service Ticket contains the Client/Server Session Key, which allows the object (server) to then decrypt the authenticator. If the subject identification and timestamp are valid (according to the subject identification, client network address, and valid period specified in the Service Ticket), then communication between the client and server is established. The Client/Server Session Key is then used for secure communications between the subject and object. See Figure 4-9.

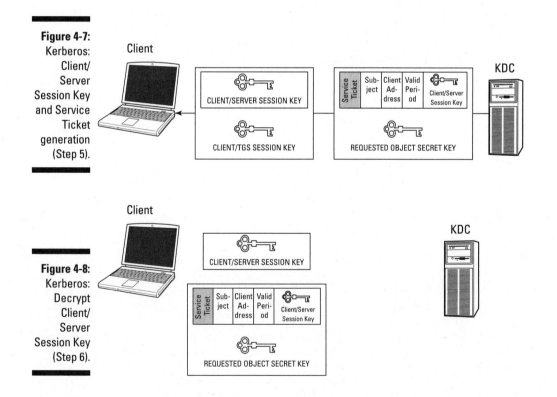

Figure 4-7:
Kerberos:
Client/
Server
Session Key
and Service
Ticket
generation
(Step 5).

Figure 4-8:
Kerberos:
Decrypt
Client/
Server
Session Key
(Step 6).

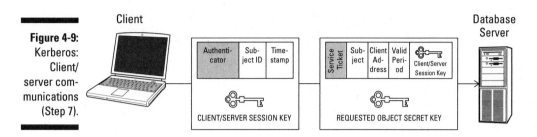

See Chapter 8 for more on symmetric key cryptography.

In Kerberos, a *session key* is a dynamic key that is generated when needed, shared between two principals, then destroyed when it is no longer needed. A *secret* key is a static key that is used to encrypt a session key.

✓ **SESAME:** The *Secure European System and Applications in a Multi-vendor Environment* (SESAME) project, developed by the European Computer Manufacturer's Association (ECMA), is a ticket-based system, like Kerberos, with some additional functionality. It uses both symmetric and asymmetric cryptography to distribute secret keys and securely transmit data. By using public key cryptography, SESAME can securely communicate between different organizations or security domains. It incorporates a trusted authentication server at each host (known as a *Privileged Attribute Server,* or PAS), employs MD5 and CRC-32 one-way hash functions, and uses two separate certificates (known as a *Privileged Attribute Certificates,* or PACs) to provide authentication and define access privileges. However, SESAME also has some serious security flaws in its basic implementation, including these:

It uses an XOR function for encryption.

It performs authentication based on a small segment of the message rather than on the entire message.

Its key generation is not really very random.

It's vulnerable to password-guessing attacks. (Want to bet that somebody thought "open" was a pretty clever password?)

See Chapter 8 for more information on one-way hash functions, XOR functions, and key generation.

✓ **KryptoKnight:** Developed by IBM, *KryptoKnight* is another example of a ticket-based SSO authentication and key distribution system that establishes peer-to-peer relationships between the Key Distribution Center (KDC) and its principals. In addition to user authentication with SSO, KryptoKnight provides two-party authentication, key distribution, and data integrity services. KryptoKnight is an extremely compact and flexible protocol that can be easily exported to other systems and applications, and it can function at any layer of the OSI model. Unlike Kerberos, KryptoKnight doesn't require clock synchronization (it uses nonces instead).

A *nonce* is literally a *number used once.* Similar in concept to an initialization vector (see Chapter 8), a nonce is a randomly generated value (usually based on a timestamp) that can be used only once to authenticate a session.

See Chapter 5 for a complete discussion of the OSI model.

Kerberos, SESAME, and KryptoKnight are three examples of ticket-based authentication technologies that provide SSO services.

Methodologies and implementation

Access control methodologies are generally classified as either centralized or decentralized. Each of these classifications contains numerous protocols and models for implementation. For the CISSP exam, you should be able to identify the various protocols and models used in centralized and decentralized access control systems.

Centralized access controls

Centralized access control systems maintain user account information in a central location. Centralized access control systems allow organizations to implement a more consistent, comprehensive security policy, but they may not be practical in extremely large enterprises. For example, an enterprise that has several thousand employees working at major locations throughout the world may find it burdensome and bureaucratic to contact a main office in another region of the world for account provisioning or to change an individual's access rights. In such cases, a decentralized access control system (described in the following section) may be more appropriate.

Examples of centralized access control systems and protocols commonly used for authentication of remote users include

- ✔ **LDAP:** *Lightweight Directory Access Protocol* (LDAP) is both an IP protocol and a data model. LDAP (pronounced *EL-dap*) is used to support authentication and directory functions for both people and resources. Several vendors have implemented LDAP, including

  - Microsoft Active Directory

  - CA eTrust Directory

  - Apache Directory Server

  - Novell eDirectory

  - IBM SecureWay and Tivoli Directory Server

  - Sun Directory Server

  You can also find several open-source versions of LDAP available, including OpenLDAP and tinyldap.

✔ **RAS:** *Remote Access Service* (RAS) servers utilize the Point-to-Point Protocol (PPP) to encapsulate IP packets and establish dial-in connections over serial and ISDN links. PPP incorporates the following three authentication protocols:

- **PAP:** The *Password Authentication Protocol* (PAP) uses a two-way handshake to authenticate a peer to a server when a link is initially established. PAP transmits passwords in clear text and provides no protection from replay attacks (in which part of a session is captured or recorded, then played back to the system) or brute force attacks.

  A *two-way handshake* refers to a communications session in which the communicating devices, for example a remote PC and a remote access server, establish a connection by sending an initial TCP SYN (Synchronize) packet to each other, each device receiving the other's SYN packet before receiving an ACK (Acknowledgment) packet to indicate that its own SYN packet has reached the other device and been accepted.

- **CHAP:** The *Challenge Handshake Authentication Protocol* (CHAP) uses a three-way handshake to authenticate both a peer and server when a link is initially established and, optionally, at regular intervals throughout the session. CHAP requires both the peer and server to be preconfigured with a shared secret that must be stored in plain text. The peer uses the secret to calculate the response to a server challenge by using an MD5 one-way hash function. *MS-CHAP,* a Microsoft enhancement to CHAP, allows the shared secret to be stored in an encrypted form.

- **EAP:** The *Extensible Authentication Protocol* (EAP) adds flexibility to PPP authentication by implementing various authentication mechanisms, including MD5-challenge, S/Key, generic token card, digital certificates, and so on. Many wireless networks implement EAP.

✔ **RADIUS:** The *Remote Authentication Dial-In User Service* (RADIUS) protocol is an open-source, client-server networking protocol — defined in more than 25 current IETF (Internet Engineering Task Force) RFCs (Request For Comments) — that provides authentication, authorization, and accountability (AAA) services. RADIUS is an Application Layer protocol that utilizes User Datagram Protocol (UDP) packets for transport. UDP is a connection-less protocol, which means it's fast but not as reliable as other transport protocols.

See Chapter 5 for a complete discussion of UDP.

RADIUS is commonly implemented in Internet service provider (ISP) networks, as well as corporate remote access service (RAS) and virtual private networks (VPNs). RADIUS is also becoming increasingly popular in corporate wireless networks. A user provides username/password information to a RADIUS client by using PAP or CHAP. The RADIUS client encrypts the password and sends the username and encrypted password to the RADIUS server for authentication.

Note: Passwords exchanged between the RADIUS client and RADIUS server are encrypted, but passwords exchanged between the PC client and the RADIUS client are not necessarily encrypted — if using PAP authentication, for example. If the PC client happens to also be the RADIUS client, however, all password exchanges are encrypted, regardless of the authentication protocol used.

✔ **Diameter:** This next-generation RADIUS protocol was developed to overcome some of RADIUS's deficiencies, but it has yet to overcome RADIUS's popularity, so it's not yet widely implemented.

Like RADIUS, Diameter provides AAA services and is an open protocol standard defined in 11 current RFCs.

Unlike RADIUS, Diameter utilizes Transmission Control Protocol (TCP) and Stream Control Transmission Protocol (SCTP) packets to provide a more reliable, connection-oriented transport mechanism. Also, Diameter uses Internet Protocol Security (IPSec) or Transport Layer Security (TLS) to provide network security or transport layer security (respectively) — rather than PAP or CHAP (used in RADIUS) — to provide a more secure connection.

See Chapter 5 for a complete discussion of TCP and SCTP, IPSec and TLS, and the OSI model.

Diameter isn't fully backward-compatible with RADIUS, but it does provide an upgrade path for RADIUS-based environments. Diameter isn't an acronym, but a pun on the term RADIUS. (In geometry, the diameter of a circle is twice its radius.)

✔ **TACACS:** The *Terminal Access Controller Access Control System* (TACACS) is a remote authentication control protocol, originally developed for the MILNET (U.S. Military Network), which provides AAA services. The original TACACS protocol has been significantly enhanced, as XTACACS (no longer used) and TACACS+ (which is the most common implementation of TACACS). However, TACACS+ is a completely new protocol and therefore isn't backward-compatible with either TACACS or XTACACS. TACACS+ is TCP based on (port 49) and supports practically any authentication mechanism (PAP, CHAP, MS-CHAP, EAP, token cards, Kerberos, and so on). The major advantages of TACACS+ are its wide support of various authentication mechanisms and granular control of authorization parameters. TACACS+ can also use dynamic passwords; TACACS uses static passwords only.

LDAP, RAS (PAP and CHAP), RADIUS, Diameter, and TACACS are examples of centralized access control for remote access.

Decentralized access controls

Decentralized access control systems keep user account information in separate locations, maintained by different administrators, throughout an organization or enterprise. This type of system makes sense in extremely large organizations or in situations where very granular control of complex user access rights and relationships is necessary. In such a system, administrators typically have a more thorough understanding of their users' needs and can apply the appropriate permissions — say, in a research and development lab or a manufacturing facility. However, decentralized access control systems also have various potential disadvantages. For example, organizations may apply security policies inconsistently across various systems, resulting in the wrong level of access (too much or not enough) for particular users; and if you need to disable numerous accounts for an individual user, the process becomes much more labor-intensive and error-prone.

Examples of decentralized access control systems include

- ✔ **Multiple domains and trusts:** A *domain* is a collection of users, computers, and resources (such as printers) that have a common security policy and single administration. Smaller organizations may have a single domain defined, which is considered a *centralized access control*. Larger organizations or enterprises may establish multiple domains (or a *Forest* in Microsoft-speak) along organizational or geographical boundaries — such as separate Marketing, Accounting, Sales, and Research domains, or separate Chicago, Seattle, Paris, and Tokyo domains. One-way *trust relationships* or *trust models* facilitate communications between multiple domains. For example, if the Marketing domain explicitly trusts the Research domain, then all users in the Research domain can access resources in the Marketing domain. Unless the Research domain establishes a trust relationship in the reverse direction (Research trusts Marketing), users in the Marketing domain *can't* access resources in the Research domain.

- ✔ **Databases:** A *database management system* (DBMS) controls access to databases. A DBMS restricts access by different subjects (users) to various objects (such as data and operations) in a database. A *view* is a logical operation that can be used to restrict access to specific information in a database, hide attributes, and restrict the queries available to a user. Views are a type of constrained user interface that can restrict access to specific functions by not allowing a user to request those functions.

We cover additional database security methods in Chapter 7.

A database view is a type of constrained user interface.

Data access controls

Data access controls are, well, the hard and crunchy middle. Probably not your favorite candy (freeze-dried Cadbury's Creme Egg, anyone?), but effective information security requires defense in depth.

Data access controls protect systems and information by restricting access to system files and user data based on object identity. Data access controls also provide authorization and accountability, relying on system access controls to provide identification and authentication.

Access control techniques

Data access control techniques are generally categorized as either discretionary or mandatory. You, as a CISSP candidate, must fully understand the concept of discretionary and mandatory access controls and be able to describe specific access control methods that fall under each category.

Discretionary access control

A *discretionary access control* (DAC) is an access policy determined by the owner of a file (or other resource). The owner decides who's allowed access to the file and what privileges they have.

In DAC, the owner determines the access policy.

Two important concepts in DAC are

- ✔ **File and data ownership:** Because the owner of the resource (including files, directories, data, system resources, and devices) determines the access policy, every object in a system must have an owner. Theoretically, an object without an owner is left unprotected. Normally, the *owner* of a resource is the person who created the resource (such as a file or directory), but in certain cases, you may need to explicitly identify the owner.

- ✔ **Access rights and permissions:** The controls that an owner can assign to individual users or groups for specific resources. Various systems (Windows-based, UNIX-based, and Novell-based) define different sets of permissions that are essentially variations or extensions of three basic types of access:

    - **Read (R):** The subject can read contents of a file or list contents of a directory.

    - **Write (W):** The subject can change the contents of a file or directory (including add, rename, create, and delete).

    - **Execute (X):** If the file is a program, the subject can run the program.

Access control lists (ACLs) provide a flexible method for applying discretionary access controls. An ACL lists the specific rights and permissions that are assigned to a subject for a given object.

Various operating systems implement ACLs differently. Although the CISSP exam doesn't directly test your knowledge of specific operating systems or products, you should be aware of this fact. Also, understand that ACLs in this context are different from ACLs used on routers (see Chapter 5), which have nothing to do with DAC.

Role-based access control is another method for implementing discretionary access controls. Role-based access control assigns group membership based on organizational or functional roles. Individuals may belong to one or many groups (acquiring cumulative permissions or limited to the most restrictive set of permissions for all assigned groups), and a group may contain only a single individual (corresponding to a specific organizational role assigned to one person). Access rights and permissions for objects are assigned to groups, rather than (or in addition to) individuals. This strategy greatly simplifies the management of access rights and permissions, particularly in organizations that have large functional groups or departments, and organizations that routinely rotate personnel through various positions or otherwise experience high turnover.

Major disadvantages of discretionary access control techniques such as ACLs or role-based access control include

- ✔ Lack of centralized administration
- ✔ Dependence on security-conscious resource owners
- ✔ Many popular operating systems defaulting to full access for everyone if the owner doesn't explicitly set permissions
- ✔ Difficult, if not impossible, auditing because of the large volume of log entries that can be generated

Mandatory access control

A *mandatory access control* (MAC) is an access policy determined by the system, rather than by the owner. Organizations use MAC in multilevel systems that process highly sensitive data, such as classified government and military information. A *multilevel system* is a single computer system that handles multiple classification levels between subjects and objects. Two important concepts in MAC are

- ✔ **Sensitivity labels:** In a MAC-based system, all subjects and objects must have assigned labels. A subject's sensitivity label specifies its level of trust. An object's sensitivity label specifies the level of trust required for access. In order to access a given object, the subject must have a sensitivity level equal to or higher than the requested object. For example, a user (subject) with a Top Secret clearance (sensitivity label) is permitted to access a file (object) that has a Secret classification level (sensitivity label) because his or her clearance level exceeds the minimum required for access.

We discuss classification systems in Chapter 6.

> ✔ **Data import and export:** Controlling the import of information from other systems and the export to other systems (including printers) is a critical function of MAC-based systems, which must ensure that the system properly maintains and implements sensitivity labels so that sensitive information is appropriately protected at all times.

In MAC, the system determines the access policy.

Rule-based access control is one method of applying mandatory access control. Actually, all MAC-based systems implement a simple form of rule-based access control by matching an object's sensitivity label and a subject's sensitivity label to determine whether the system should grant or deny access. You can apply additional rules by using rule-based access control to further define specific conditions for access to a requested object.

Lattice-based access controls are another method of implementing mandatory access controls. A *lattice model* is a mathematical structure that defines greatest lower-bound and least upper-bound values for a pair of elements, such as a subject and an object. Organizations can use this model for complex access control decisions involving multiple objects and/or subjects. For example, given a set of files that have multiple classification levels, the lattice model determines the minimum clearance level that a user requires to access all the files.

Major disadvantages of mandatory access control techniques include

> ✔ Lack of flexibility
>
> ✔ Difficulty in implementing and programming
>
> ✔ User frustration

Access control models

Applications use models to express access control requirements in a theoretical or mathematical framework that precisely describes or quantifies the application's function. Common access control models include Bell-La Padula, Biba, Clark-Wilson, noninterference, access matrix, and information flow.

We introduce these models in the following sections and also cover them more in Chapter 9.

Bell-La Padula (Basic security theorem)

Published in 1973 and designed for the U.S. military to address storage and protection of classified information, the Bell-La Padula model was the first formal confidentiality model of a mandatory access control system. *Bell-La Padula* is a state machine model that addresses only the confidentiality of information. A *state machine model* defines and maintains a secure state during transitions between states. The basic premise of Bell-La Padula is that information can't flow downward. Bell-La Padula defines the following two properties:

- ✓ **simple security property (ss property):** A subject can't read information from an object that has a higher sensitivity label (no read up, or NRU).

- ✓ ***-property (star property):** A subject can't write information to an object that has a lower sensitivity label (no write down, or NWD).

Bell-La Padula addresses confidentiality.

Biba

Published in 1977, the *Biba integrity model* (sometimes referred to as *Bell-La Padula upside down*) was the first formal integrity model. Biba is a lattice-based model that addresses the first goal of integrity — ensuring that unauthorized users or processes don't make modifications to data. For more on lattice-based models, read the section "Mandatory access control," earlier in this chapter. See Chapter 6 for a complete discussion of the three goals of integrity. Biba defines the following two properties:

- ✓ **simple integrity property:** A subject can't read information from an object that has a lower integrity level (no read down).

- ✓ ***-integrity property (star integrity property):** A subject can't write information to an object that has a higher integrity level (no write up).

Clark-Wilson

Published in 1987, the *Clark-Wilson integrity model* establishes a security framework for use in commercial activities, such as the banking industry. Using the Clark-Wilson model, data cannot be directly accessed by a user. Instead, it must be accessed through an application which controls the access. Clark-Wilson addresses all three goals of integrity (read more about these goals in Chapter 6) and identifies special requirements for inputting data based on the following items and procedures:

- ✓ **Unconstrained data item (UDI):** Data outside the control area, such as input data

- ✓ **Constrained data item (CDI):** Data inside the control area (integrity must be preserved)

- ✓ **Integrity verification procedures (IVP):** Checks validity of CDIs

- ✓ **Transformation procedures (TP):** Maintains integrity of CDIs

Biba and Clark-Wilson both address integrity.

Noninterference model

A *noninterference model* ensures that objects and subjects don't see the actions of different objects and subjects on the same system — and that those actions don't interfere with them. For example, if a user with a higher level of access made a change to a file, a user with a lower level of access would not see those changes and would not be able to deduce any information from those changes.

Access matrix model

An *access matrix model* provides object access rights (read/write/execute, or R/W/X) to subjects in a DAC system. An access matrix consists of access control lists (ACLs) and capability lists. For more on DAC and ACLs, peruse the section "Discretionary access control," earlier in this chapter.

Information flow model

An *information flow model* is a lattice-based model in which the system assigns objects a security class and value, and a security policy controls their direction of flow.

Access Control Attacks

Gaining access (getting through that hard and crunchy outside) to a system or network is an attacker's first objective. Attackers commonly use several methods of attack against access control systems, including

- ✔ **Brute-force or dictionary attack:** The attacker attempts every possible combination of letters, numbers, and characters to crack a password, passphrase, or PIN. A *dictionary attack* is essentially a more focused type of brute force attack in which the attacker uses a predefined word list. You can find such word lists or dictionaries, including foreign language and special-interest dictionaries, widely available on the Internet for use in password-cracking utilities such as L0phtCrack and John the Ripper. Attackers typically run these password-cracking utilities against a copy of the target system's (or network's) security accounts database or password file. The utility creates hashes of passwords contained in its dictionary or word list, and then compares the resulting hash to the password file. These types of programs work very quickly and effectively (see the sidebar "How much brute force does it take to crack your passwords?" in this chapter), even when organizations use complex passwords, so the key to defending against a brute-force or dictionary attack is to protect your security accounts databases and password files.

✔ **Buffer or stack overflow:** *Buffer or stack overflows* constitute the most common and successful type of computer attacks today. Although often used in Denial of Service attacks, buffer overflows in certain systems or applications may enable an attacker to gain unauthorized access to a system or directory. An overflow occurs when an application or protocol attempts to store more information than the allotted resources will allow. This causes previously entered data to become corrupted, the protocol or application to crash, or other unexpected or erratic behavior to occur. A *teardrop attack* is a type of stack overflow attack that exploits vulnerabilities in the IP protocol. The best defense against buffer or stack overflow attacks is to identify and patch vulnerabilities in the system, network, and applications as quickly as possible after each vulnerability is identified (and ideally before the affected code or application is used in a production environment).

✔ **Man-in-the-Middle attacks:** Here an attacker intercepts messages between two parties and forwards a modified version of the original message to the intended recipient. For example, an attacker may substitute his or her own public key during a public-key exchange between two parties. The two parties believe that they're still communicating only with each other and unknowingly encrypt messages by using the attacker's public key, rather than the intended recipient's public key. The attacker can then decrypt secret messages between the two parties, modify their contents as desired, and send them on to the unwary recipient.

✔ **Packet (or password) sniffing:** An attacker uses an application or device, known as a *sniffer*, to capture network packets and analyze their contents, such as usernames and passwords, and shared keys.

✔ **Session hijacking:** Similar to a Man-in-the-Middle attack, except that the attacker impersonates the intended recipient, instead of modifying messages in transit.

✔ **Social engineering:** This low-tech method is one of the most effective and easily perpetrated forms of attack. Common techniques involve phishing (see the sidebar "Gone phishin'," in this chapter), dumpster diving, shoulder surfing, raiding cubicles (looking for passwords on monitors, under keyboards, and under mouse pads), and plain ol' asking. This latter brazen technique can simply involve the attacker calling a user, pretending to be a system administrator and asking for the user's password, or calling a help desk pretending to be a user and asking to have the password changed.

How much brute force does it take to crack your passwords?

Passwords remain the most ubiquitous form of access control used on systems and networks today. But password security is something of a misnomer. Assuming that an attacker has gained access to your system's password file or security accounts database, how long would it take for him or her to crack your user's passwords? One week? One day? One hour? Try 14 seconds! That's the approximate average time it takes to crack a Windows password. Most attackers can crack a password in less than a minute by using commonly available tools such as John the Ripper or L0phtCrack.

So, why even bother with passwords? But wait — don't be so quick to scuttle your passwords! You can still use passwords as an effective means of securing your systems and networks. Consider the following:

✔ The time and effort it takes for an attacker to crack a password is relatively inconsequential compared to the time and effort it takes to gain access to your password file or security accounts database. After all, if an attacker has already gained access to your systems, you may already have bigger problems than compromised passwords!

✔ Although attackers can usually crack most passwords in less than a minute, a security policy that requires a password of eight characters — using a mix of upper- and lowercase letters and numbers — yields more than 218 trillion possible passwords, which theoretically would take a maximum of 253 days for an attacker to crack.

✔ You can achieve password security not only through the passwords themselves, but also through the combination of password policies and enforcement mechanisms.

Consider your bank card's PIN — which is nothing more than a four-digit password. A four-digit password yields only 10,000 possible combinations, and an attacker can crack it easily in less than one second! Yet PINs are reasonably effective for many reasons. First, the bank keeps the security accounts database very secure, which means an attacker would have to mount a brute-force attack on the database in the old-fashioned way — manually entering PIN combinations into an ATM. After three bad attempts, the ATM literally eats the bank card. This card confiscation demonstrates effective use of an account lockout and lockout duration policy (three bad attempts and forever, respectively), as well as two-factor authentication — something you have becomes something you had, and you get no more guesses!

✔ When an organization implements passwords with an effective (and enforced) security policy, passwords can provide adequate internal security by preventing authorized users from logging in as other authorized users and establishing non-repudiation. Most users don't attempt to run a password-cracking utility against their organization's systems, but they might be tempted to log in with someone else's credentials if that other person has his or her password taped to a computer monitor or hidden under a mouse pad, or he or she carelessly shared it with others.

✔ A password policy that requires users to change their passwords frequently (such as every 30 days) can limit the damage — or, at least, the length of time that an attacker can do damage with a compromised account.

Gone phishin'

Phishing has become one of the most common (and successful) social engineering techniques in use today, tricking users into disclosing personal account information and passwords. Phishing attacks, which typically use e-mail or instant messaging, can be very sophisticated and use various techniques to convince a user that a solicitation for his or her account information is legitimate. Such techniques include using images and logos from a trusted institution's official website (such as a bank, online auction, or social networking site), using actual links to an official website, and using cleverly manipulated website links that look authentic.

Organizations should employ various tactics and processes to counter access control attacks, including

- ✔ **Threat modeling.** Ensures that security is a key design consideration early in the application development lifecycle. A security specification is created and tested during the design phase to identify likely threats, vulnerabilities and countermeasures for a specific application and its uses.

- ✔ **Asset valuation.** The process of assigning a financial value to an organization's information assets, thereby enabling an objective measure of the systems and data that require various levels of protection.

- ✔ **Vulnerability analysis.** The process of identifying defining, identifying and prioritizing a system's vulnerabilities.

- ✔ **Access aggregation.** Combines all of a user's access rights, privileges, and permissions in a single or multiple systems (for example, using single sign-on or SSO).

Evaluating and Testing Access Controls

Organizations need to both build an access control environment and test it to see how it performs and behaves. In many cases, access control is the only barrier between outsiders and sensitive information. A great example is online banking: The only thing protecting your bank account information is your user ID and password. Don't you want to be sure that the bank's access control mechanism is working properly to protect your precious information from outsiders?

Computer systems contain information, which, in many cases, must be accessible to only authorized persons. However, weaknesses or vulnerabilities in access control software may permit users without the necessary credentials to also access this information. Additionally, poorly defined or inadequate access control policies can result in users having unauthorized access to sensitive data. *User entitlement* refers to the data access privileges that are granted to an individual user. Organizations must routinely — if not continually — review user entitlement to ensure overall data access privileges are appropriately administered in the organization. The audit and review process should be automated to increase efficiency, reduce errors, ensure completeness, and improve overall effectiveness.

Why test?

Organizations should perform penetration and vulnerability testing on these systems to ensure that they don't possess any vulnerabilities or weaknesses that could permit unauthorized persons to view or alter information. You can carry out penetration testing (*pen testing*) manually, but more often than not, organizations use automated tools for faster identification of weaknesses in a system or its software applications.

Some terms used in pen testing that you need to know include

- **Port scanning:** The process of probing a system to determine which TCP/IP service ports are running on the system.

- **Application scanning:** The process of assessing whether an online application has any specific weaknesses that could permit exploitation. Some types of application scanning examine the source code itself in order to more easily identify vulnerabilities.

- **Black box testing:** The tester has no prior knowledge of the system he or she tests.

- **White box testing:** The person doing the testing has complete knowledge about the system that he or she tests. This testing provides maximum assurance that organizations can identify existing vulnerabilities — even if the organization gives the people doing the testing hints in advance.

- **Gray box testing:** You guessed it — the people doing the testing have some (but not all) knowledge about the system they test.

- **Host scanning:** The process of scanning a network in order to discover any host computers on the network.

- **Operating System (OS) detection:** Determining the host OS, or the version of the host.

You can find numerous open-source and commercial scanning tools available, each designed to identify vulnerabilities in software applications, database management systems, operating systems, and network devices.

When and how to test

Most experts agree that you must test systems for vulnerabilities *before* placing those systems into production use. This principle is especially true for systems that users will access through the Internet. If you don't test an Internet-facing system, attackers could exploit and "own" it faster than you can say "vulnerability testing."

You should also test software that users access over the Internet or company networks for vulnerabilities as part of the functional testing performed prior to the release of new versions of the software. This additional testing can help to prevent any serious weaknesses from ever seeing the light of day (or the dark side of the Internet).

Organizations should adopt a *software development life cycle* (SDLC) process to govern any activities in software development or integration. Testing the software for vulnerabilities should be a formal part of the SDLC.

Read more about the software development life cycle in Chapter 7.

Identity and Access Provisioning Lifecycle

Organizations must adopt formal policies and procedures to address account provisioning, review, and revocation.

When new or temporary employees, contractors, partners, auditors, and other third parties require access to an organization's systems and networks, the organization must have a formal methodology for assessing risk and assigning appropriate access rights. New accounts must be provisioned correctly and in a timely manner to ensure access is ready and available when the user needs it, but not too soon (so as to ensure that new accounts not yet in active use are not compromised by an attacker).

User and system accounts, along with their assigned privileges, should be reviewed on a regular basis to ensure that they are still appropriate. For example, an employee may no longer require the same privilege levels due to rotation of duties (see Chapter 6) or a transfer or promotion.

Finally, when access is no longer required, accounts must be promptly disabled.

Prep Test

1 General-purpose control types include all the following except

A ○ Detective
B ○ Mandatory
C ○ Preventive
D ○ Compensating

2 Violation reports and audit trails are examples of what type of control?

A ○ Detective technical
B ○ Preventive technical
C ○ Detective administrative
D ○ Preventive administrative

3 "A user cannot deny an action" describes the concept of

A ○ Authentication
B ○ Accountability
C ○ Non-repudiation
D ○ Plausible deniability

4 Authentication can be based on any combination of the following factors except

A ○ Something you know
B ○ Something you have
C ○ Something you need
D ○ Something you are

5 Unauthorized users that are incorrectly granted access in biometric systems are described as the

A ○ False Reject Rate (Type II error)
B ○ False Accept Rate (Type II error)
C ○ False Reject Rate (Type I error)
D ○ False Accept Rate (Type I error)

6 All the following devices and protocols can be used to implement one-time passwords except

A ○ Tokens
B ○ S/Key
C ○ Diameter
D ○ Kerberos

7 Which of the following PPP authentication protocols transmits passwords in clear text?

A ○ PAP

B ○ CHAP

C ○ MS-CHAP

D ○ FTP

8 Which of the following is not considered a method of attack against access control systems?

A ○ Brute force

B ○ Dictionary

C ○ Denial of Service

D ○ Buffer overflow

9 Sensitivity labels are a fundamental component in which type of access control systems?

A ○ Mandatory access control

B ○ Discretionary access control

C ○ Access control lists

D ○ Role-based access control

10 Which of the following access control models addresses availability issues?

A ○ Bell-La Padula

B ○ Biba

C ○ Clark-Wilson

D ○ None of the above

Answers

1 **B.** Mandatory. Control types identified by purpose include preventive, detective, corrective, deterrent, recovery, and compensating controls. *Review "Control types."*

2 **A.** Detective technical. Preventive technical controls include access control mechanisms and protocols. Review of audit trails is a detective administrative control, but the actual generating of audit trails is a technical function (control). *Review "Technical controls."*

3 **C.** Non-repudiation. Authentication and accountability are related to but aren't the same as non-repudiation. Plausible deniability is a bogus answer. *Review "Accountability."*

4 **C.** Something you need. The three factors of authentication are something you know, something you have, and something you are. *Review "System access controls."*

5 **B.** False Accept Rate (Type II error). You should know the biometric error types by both the name (False Accept Rate) and the classification (Type II). The False Reject Rate is a Type I error and describes the percentage of authorized users that are incorrectly denied access. *Review "Biometrics and behavior."*

6 **D.** Kerberos. Kerberos is a ticket-based authentication protocol. Although the tickets that are generated are unique for every log-on, Kerberos relies on shared secrets that are static. Therefore, Kerberos isn't considered a one-time password protocol. *Review these three sections: "One-time passwords," "Tokens," and "Single sign-on (SSO)."*

7 **A.** PAP. The Password Authentication Protocol (PAP) transmits passwords in clear text. CHAP and MS-CHAP authenticate by using challenges and responses that are calculated, using a one-way hash function. FTP transmits passwords in clear text but isn't a PPP authentication protocol. *Review "Centralized access controls."*

8 **C.** Denial of Service. The purpose of an attack against access controls is to gain access to a system. Brute-force and dictionary attacks are both password-cracking methods. Although commonly used in Denial of Service attacks, a buffer overflow attack can exploit vulnerabilities or flaws in certain applications and protocols that will allow unauthorized access. *Review "Methods of attack."*

9 **A.** Mandatory access control. The fundamental components in discretionary access controls are file (and data) ownership and access rights and permissions. Access control lists and role-based access control are types of discretionary access control systems. *Review "Access control techniques."*

10 **D.** None of the above. Bell-La Padula addresses confidentiality issues. Biba and Clark-Wilson address integrity issues. *Review "Access control models."*

Chapter 5

Telecommunications and Network Security

. . . .

In This Chapter

▶ Getting a handle on the OSI Reference Model and TCP/IP Model

▶ Keeping both wired and wireless networks secure

▶ Securing e-mail, Internet, facsimile, and telephone lines

▶ Understanding network attacks and countermeasures

. . . .

*T*he Telecommunications and Network Security domain is easily the most extensive domain in the Common Body of Knowledge (CBK) for the Certified Information Systems Security Professional (CISSP) examination. The CISSP candidate must thoroughly understand the various networking models, protocols, standards, services, technologies, and vulnerabilities. A networking background can definitely help you pass the exam. We highly recommend that you go out and get yourself a networking certification, such as the CompTIA Network+ or the Cisco Certified Network Associate (CCNA). Such certifications are extremely helpful in preparing for this portion of the CISSP exam.

Data Network Types

Data networks are most commonly classified as *local area networks* (LANs) and *wide area networks* (WANs). You should understand the fundamental distinctions between these two network classifications.

Local area network (LAN)

A *local area network* (LAN) is a data network that operates across a relatively small geographic area, such as a single building or floor. A LAN connects workstations, servers, printers, and other devices so that network resources, such as files and e-mail, can be shared. Key characteristics of LANs include the following:

  ✔ Can connect networked resources over a small geographic area, such as a floor, a building, or a group of buildings.

  ✔ Are relatively inexpensive to set up and maintain, typically consisting of readily available equipment such as servers, client workstations or PCs, printers, switches, hubs, bridges, repeaters, wireless access points (WAPs or simply, APs), and various security devices.

  ✔ Can be wired, wireless, or a combination of both wired and wireless.

  ✔ Perform at relatively high speeds — typically 10 megabits per second (Mbps), 100 Mbps, or 1000 Mbps (also referred to as 1 gigabit per second [1 Gbps]) for wired networks, and 11or 54 Mbps for wireless networks. In high-performance datacenters and storage area networks (SANs), 10 Gbps speeds are also becoming more common. We cover LAN speeds in the section "Physical Layer (Layer 1)," later in this chapter.

Be careful when referring to data speeds (and their abbreviations) and data storage. 100 Mbps is "100 megabits per second," and 100 MB is "100 megabytes." The distinction is subtle (a little b versus a big B, bits rather than bytes), but the difference is significant: A byte is equal to 8 bits. Data speeds are typically referred to in bits per second; data storage is typically referred to in bytes.

A local area network (LAN) is a data network that operates across a relatively small geographic area.

See the section "The OSI Reference Model," later in this chapter, for a discussion of the LAN function at the Physical and Data Link layers of the OSI Reference Model.

Wide area network (WAN)

A *wide area network* (WAN) connects multiple LANs and other WANs by using telecommunications devices and facilities to form an internetwork. Key characteristics of WANs include the following:

✔ Connect multiple LANs over large geographic areas, such as a small city (for example, a metropolitan area network [or MAN]), a region or country, a global corporate network, the entire planet (for example, the Internet), or beyond (for example, the International Space Station via satellite).

✔ Can be relatively expensive to set up and maintain, typically consisting of equipment such as routers, Channel Service Unit/Data Service Unit (CSU/DSU) devices, firewalls, Virtual Private Network (VPN) concentrators, and various other security devices.

✔ Perform at relatively low speeds by using various technologies, such as dial-up (56 kilobits per second [Kbps]); digital subscriber line, or DSL (for example, 128 Kbps to 3 Mbps); T-1 (1.544 Mbps); DS-3 (45 Mbps); OC-12 (622 Mbps); and OC-255 (13 Gbps). We cover WAN speeds in the section "Data Link Layer (Layer 2)," later in this chapter.

Examples of WANs include

✔ **Internet:** The mother of all WANs, the *Internet* is the global network of public networks originally developed by the U.S. Department of Defense (DoD) Advanced Research Projects Agency (ARPA). Users and systems connect to the Internet via *Internet service providers* (ISPs).

✔ **Intranet:** An *intranet* can be thought of as a private Internet. An *intranet* typically uses web-based technologies to disseminate company information that's available only to authorized users on the company network.

✔ **Extranet:** An *extranet* extends the basic concept of an intranet to include partners, vendors, or other related parties. For example, an automobile manufacturer may operate an extranet that connects networks belonging to parts manufacturers, distributors, and dealerships. Extranets are commonly operated across the Internet by using a Virtual Private Network (VPN) — discussed in the section "Virtual Private Networks (VPNs)," later in this chapter — or other secure connection.

See the following section for a discussion of the WAN function at the Physical, Data Link, and Network layers of the OSI Reference Model.

A wide area network (WAN) is a data network that operates across a relatively large geographic area.

The OSI Reference Model

In 1984, the International Organization for Standardization (ISO) adopted the Open Systems Interconnection (OSI) Reference Model (or simply, the *OSI model*) to facilitate interoperability between network devices independent of the manufacturer. The OSI model defines standard protocols for communication and interoperability by using a layered approach. This approach divides complex networking issues into simpler functional components that help the understanding, design, and development of networking solutions and provides the following specific advantages:

- ✔ Clarifies the general functions of a communications process, instead of focusing on specific issues
- ✔ Reduces complex networking processes into simpler sub-layers and components
- ✔ Promotes interoperability by defining standard interfaces
- ✔ Aids development by allowing vendors to change individual features at a single layer, instead of rebuilding the entire protocol stack
- ✔ Facilitates easier (and more logical) troubleshooting

The OSI model consists of seven distinct layers that describe how data is communicated between systems and applications on a computer network, as shown in Figure 5-1. These layers include

- ✔ Application (Layer 7)
- ✔ Presentation (Layer 6)
- ✔ Session (Layer 5)
- ✔ Transport (Layer 4)
- ✔ Network (Layer 3)
- ✔ Data Link (Layer 2)
- ✔ Physical (Layer 1)

Try creating a mnemonic to recall the layers of the OSI model, such as: *Adult People Should Try New Dairy Products.*

In the OSI model, data is passed from the highest layer (Application; Layer 7) downward through each layer to the lowest layer (Physical; Layer 1), and is then transmitted across the network medium to the destination node, where it's passed upward from the lowest layer to the highest layer. Each layer communicates only with the layer immediately above and below it *(adjacent layers)*. This communication is achieved through a process known as data encapsulation. *Data encapsulation* wraps protocol information from the layer immediately above in the data section of the layer immediately below. Figure 5-2 illustrates this process.

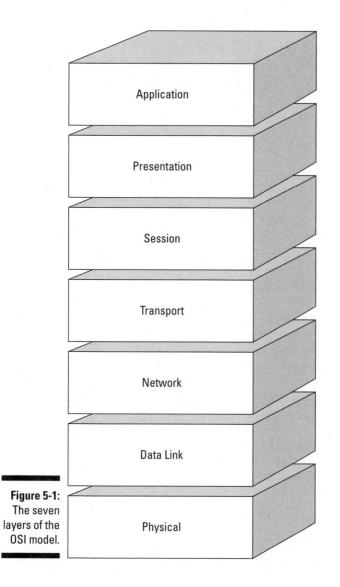

Figure 5-1:
The seven layers of the OSI model.

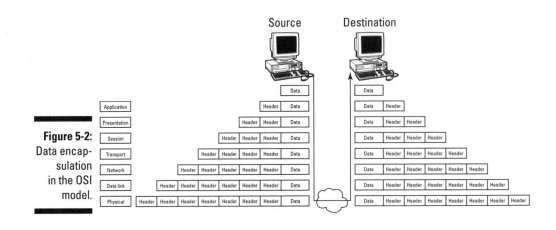

Figure 5-2:
Data encapsulation in the OSI model.

Fill-in-the-blank area networks (__AN)

Although networks are generally classified as LANs or WANs, you should familiarize yourself with a number of variations (and acronyms) — if for no other reason than to put together a winning combination in a friendly game of Scrabble:

✔ **Personal area network (PAN):** Connects an individual's electronic devices to each other or to a larger network, such as the Internet. Examples of devices that might be connected via a PAN include laptop computers, cellular phones, PDAs (personal digital assistants), and other mobile devices (such as BlackBerries and iPods). These devices can be connected via wired technologies such as USB and FireWire, or wireless technologies such as Wi-Fi, Bluetooth, and IrDA (Infrared Data Association). A wireless PAN is also sometimes referred to as a WPAN (that's worth nine points in Scrabble!).

✔ **Storage area network (SAN):** Connects servers to a separate physical storage device (typically a disk array). The server operating system sees the storage as if it were directly attached to the server. SANs typically comprise several terabytes or more of disk storage and incorporate highly sophisticated design architectures for fault tolerance and redundancy. Communications protocols used in SANs typically include SCSI (Small Computer System Interface, or "Scuzzy"), iSCSI (IP-based SCSI), Fibre Channel Protocol (FCP, SCSI over Fibre Channel), and FCoE (Fibre Channel over Ethernet). SANs are highly scalable, enable technologies such as virtualization and snapshots, provide flexibility in server deployment options, facilitate disaster recovery (for example, with real-time replication), and tend to reduce the overall cost of data storage.

✔ **Virtual local area network (VLAN):** Implemented on network switches in a LAN as a way of logically grouping users and resources together. Often, such VLANs correlate to department functions (such as Accounting, Sales, and Research & Development) and/or IP subnets. VLANs provide scalability, segmentation, and (some) security at Layer 2 (see the section "The OSI Reference Model," in this chapter) and can also work to limit the size of your Ethernet broadcast domains. VLANs are implemented by using IEEE 802.1q tagging to tag Ethernet frames with VLAN information.

✔ **Wireless local area network (WLAN):** Also known as a *WiFi network.* A wireless LAN that uses wireless access points (WAPs, or simply APs) to connect wireless-enabled devices to a wired LAN. We cover WLANs in more detail in the section "Wireless Network (WLAN) Security," later in this chapter.

✔ **Campus area network (CAN):** Connects multiple buildings across a high-performance backbone.

✔ **Metropolitan area network (MAN):** Extends across a large area, such as a small city.

✔ **Value-added network (VAN):** A type of extranet that allows businesses within an industry to share information or integrate shared processes. For example, Electronic Data Interchange (EDI) allows organizations to exchange structured documents — such as order forms, purchase orders, bills of lading, and invoices — over a secure network.

Physical Layer (Layer 1)

The Physical Layer sends and receives bits across the network cabling from one device to another.

It specifies the electrical, mechanical, and functional requirements of the network, including network topology, cabling and connectors, and interface types, as well as the process for converting bits to electrical (or light) signals that can be transmitted across the physical medium. Various network topologies, made from copper or fiber-optic wires and cables, hubs, and other physical materials, comprise the Physical Layer.

Network topologies

The four basic network topologies in common use at the Physical Layer today are star, mesh, ring, and bus. Although many variations of the basic types (Fiber Distributed Data Interface [FDDI], star-bus, star-ring) exist, we stick to the basics in the following sections.

Star

In a *star* topology, each individual node on the network is directly connected to a switch, hub, or concentrator. (See Figure 5-3.) All data communications must pass through the switch (or hub), which can become a bottleneck or single point of failure. A star topology is ideal for practically any size environment and is the most common basic topology in use today. A star topology is also easy to install and maintain, and network faults are easily isolated without affecting the rest of the network.

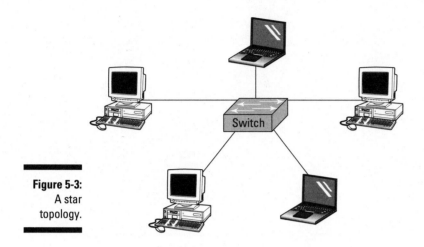

Figure 5-3:
A star
topology.

Mesh

In a *mesh* topology, all systems are interconnected to provide multiple paths to all other resources. See Figure 5-4 for a logical illustration of a mesh topology. In Figure 5-4, if Link 1 between Routers 1 and 2 is down, those routers and the attached systems and networks can still communicate via Router 3 over Links 5 and 6.

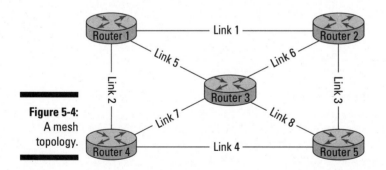

Figure 5-4:
A mesh
topology.

In most networks, a partial mesh is implemented for only the most critical network components, such as routers, switches, and servers (by using multiple network interface cards [NICs] or server clustering) to eliminate single points of failure.

See Chapter 6 for more on eliminating single points of failure.

Ring

A *ring* topology is a closed loop that connects end devices in a continuous ring (see Figure 5-5). Functionally, this is achieved by connecting individual devices to a Multistation Access Unit (MSAU or MAU). Physically, this setup gives the ring topology the appearance of a star topology. (See Figure 5-6.)

Ring topologies are common in token-ring and FDDI networks. In a ring topology, all communication travels in a single direction around the ring.

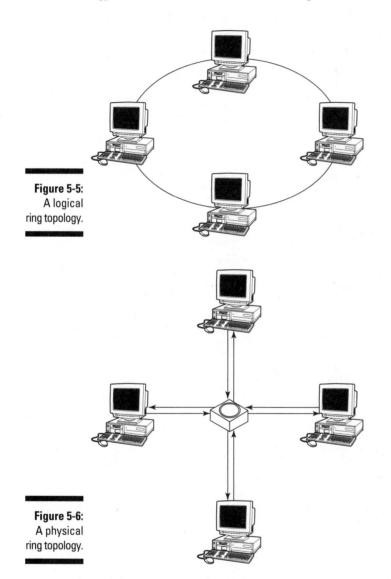

Figure 5-5:
A logical
ring topology.

Figure 5-6:
A physical
ring topology.

Bus

In a *bus* (or *linear bus*) topology, all devices are connected to a single cable (the *backbone*) that's terminated on both ends. (See Figure 5-7.) Bus networks were commonly used for very small networks because they're inexpensive and easy to install. However, in large environments, they're impractical because the media has physical limitations, the backbone is a single point of failure (a break anywhere on the network affects the entire network), and tracing a fault in a large network can be extremely difficult. Bus networks are extremely rare today and are no longer the least-expensive or easiest-to-install network option.

Figure 5-7:
A bus
topology.

Cable and connector types

Cables carry the electrical or light signals that represent data between devices on a network. Data signaling is described by several characteristics, including type (see the sidebar "Analog and digital signaling," in this chapter), control mechanism (see the sidebar "Asynchronous and synchronous communications," in this chapter), and classification (either baseband or broadband). *Baseband* signaling uses a single channel for transmission of digital signals and is common in LANs that use twisted-pair cabling. *Broadband* signaling uses many channels over a range of frequencies for transmission of analog signals, including voice, video, and data. The four basic cable types used in networks are coaxial, twinaxial, twisted-pair, and fiber-optic.

Coaxial cable

Coaxial (abbreviated as coax and pronounced *KOH-axe*) cable was very common in the early days of LANs and is rebounding (sort of) with the emergence of broadband networks. *Coax* cable consists of a single, solid-copper-wire core, surrounded by a plastic or Teflon insulator, braided-metal shielding, and (sometimes) a metal foil wrap, all covered with a plastic sheath. This construction makes the cable very durable and resistant to Electromagnetic Interference (EMI) and Radio Frequency Interference (RFI) signals. Coax cable is commonly used to connect cable or satellite television receivers (the cable that goes from the black box to the wall).

Coax cable comes in two flavors, thick and thin:

- **Thick:** Also known as *RG8* or *RG11* or *thicknet.* Thicknet cable uses a screw-type connector, known as an *Attachment Unit Interface (AUI).*

- **Thin:** Also known as *RG58* or *thinnet.* Thinnet cable is typically connected to network devices by using a bayonet-type connector, known as a *BNC (Bayonet Neill-Concelman) connector.*

Analog and digital signaling

Analog signaling conveys information through a continuous signal by using variations of wave amplitude, frequency, and phase.

Digital signaling conveys information in pulses through the presence or absence (on-off) of electrical signals.

Twinaxial cable

Twinaxial (also known as twinax) cable is very similar to coax cable, but it consists of *two* solid copper-wire cores, rather than a single core. Twinax is used to achieve high data transmission speeds (for example, 10 Gb Ethernet [abbreviated as GE, GbE or GigE]) over very short distances (for example, 10 meters) at a relatively low cost. Typical applications for twinax cabling include SANs and top-of-rack network switches that connect critical servers to a high-speed core. Other advantages of twinax cabling include lower transceiver latency (delay in transmitter/receiver devices) and power consumption (compared to 10 GbE twisted-pair cables), and low bit error ratios (BERs).

Bit error ratio (BER) is the ratio of incorrectly received bits to total received bits over a specified period of time.

Twisted-pair cable

Twisted-pair cable is the most popular LAN cable in use today. It's lightweight, flexible, inexpensive, and easy to install. One easily recognized example of twisted-pair cable is common telephone wire. Twisted-pair cable consists of four copper-wire pairs that are twisted together to improve the transmission quality of the cable by reducing crosstalk and attenuation. The tighter the twisted pairs, the better the transmission speed and quality. *Crosstalk* occurs when a signal transmitted over one channel or circuit negatively affects the signal transmitted over another channel or circuit. An (ancient) example of crosstalk occurred over analog phone lines when you could hear parts of other conversations over the phone. *Attenuation* is the gradual loss of intensity of a wave (for example, electrical or light) while it travels over (or through) a medium.

Currently, ten categories of twisted-pair cabling exist, although only four (Cat 3, Cat 5e, Cat 6, and Cat 6a) are currently defined as standards by the TIA/EIA (Telecommunications Industry Association/Electronics Industries Alliance). Cat 5, Cat 5e, and Cat 6 cable are typically used for networking today. (See Table 5-1.)

The International Organization of Standardization (ISO) also defines cabling standards corresponding to the TIA/EIA standards and including some of the other cabling categories. These standards include Class D (Cat 5e), Class E (Cat 6), Class E_A (Cat 6a), Class F (Cat 7), and Class F_A (Cat 7a).

Twisted-pair cable can be either unshielded (UTP) or shielded (STP). UTP cabling is more common because it's easier to work with and less expensive than STP. STP is used when noise is a problem or when security is a major concern. Noise is produced by external sources and can distort or otherwise impair the quality of a signal. Examples of noise include RFI and EMI from sources such as electrical motors, radio signals, fluorescent lights, microwave ovens, and electronic equipment. Shielded cabling also reduces electromagnetic emissions that may be intercepted by an attacker.

TEMPEST is a (previously classified) U.S. military term that refers to the study of electromagnetic emissions from computers and related equipment.

Cat 7 and Cat 7a cable is available as STP only. In addition to the entire Cat 7 or Cat 7a cable, the individual wire pairs are also shielded.

Twisted-pair cable is terminated with an RJ-type terminator. The three common types of RJ-type connectors are RJ-11, RJ-45, and RJ-49. Although these connectors are all similar in appearance (particularly RJ-45 and RJ-49), only RJ-45 connectors are used for LANs. RJ-11 connectors are used for analog phone lines, and RJ-49 connectors are commonly used for Integrated Services Digital Network (ISDN) lines and WAN interfaces.

Table 5-1	Twisted-Pair Cable Categories	
Category	**Use and Speed**	**Example**
1 (not a TIA/EIA standard)	Voice only	Telephone
2 (not a TIA/EIA standard)	Data (up to 4 Mbps)	Token-ring at 4 Mbps
3	Data (up to 10 Mbps) and voice	Ethernet and telephone
4 (not a TIA/EIA standard)	Data (up to 20 Mbps)	Token-ring at 16 Mbps
5 (not a TIA/EIA standard)	Data (up to 100 Mbps)	Fast Ethernet
5e	Data (up to 1000 Mbps at 100 MHz)	Gigabit Ethernet
6	Data (up to 1000 Mbps at 250 MHz)	Gigabit Ethernet
6a	Data (up to 10 Gbps at 500 MHz)	10 Gigabit Ethernet
7 (not a TIA/EIA standard)	Data (up to 10 Gbps at 600 MHz up to 100 meters)	10 Gigabit Ethernet
7a (not a TIA/EIA standard)	Data (up to 100 Gbps at 1000 MHz up to 15 meters)	40 Gigabit Ethernet

Cat 7 and 7a cabling is terminated by using various non-RJ-type connectors.

Fiber-optic cable

Fiber-optic cable, the most expensive type of network cabling — but also the most reliable — is typically used in backbone networks and high-availability networks (such as FDDI). Fiber-optic cable carries data as light signals, rather than as electrical signals. Fiber-optic cable consists of a glass core or bundle, a glass insulator (commonly known as *cladding*), Kevlar fiber strands (for strength), and a polyvinyl chloride (PVC) or Teflon outer sheath. Advantages of fiber-optic cable include high speeds, long distances, and resistance to interception and interference. Fiber-optic cable is terminated with an SC-type, ST-type, or LC-type connector.

See Table 5-2 for a comparison of the various cable types and their characteristics.

Ethernet designations, such as 10Base-T or 100Base-TX, refer to the speed of the cable and the signaling type (baseband). The last part of the designation is less strictly defined. It may refer to the approximate maximum length (as in 10Base-2 and 10Base-5), the type of connector (as in 10Base-T, 100Base-TX, and 100Base-F), or the type and speed of the connector (as in 1000Base-T/GbE).

Table 5-2	Cable Types and Characteristics		
Cable Type	**Ethernet Designation**	**Maximum Length**	**EMI/RFI Resistance**
RG58 (thinnet)	10Base-2	185 m	Good
RG8/11 (thick-net)	10Base-5	500 m	Better
UTP	10Base-T 100Base-TX 1000Base-T 10GbE	100 m	Poor
STP	10Base-T 100Base-TX 1000Base-T 10GbE	100 m	Fair to good
Fiber-optic	100Base-F	2,000 m	Best (EFI and RFI have no effect on fiber-optic cable)

Interface types

The interface between the Data Terminal Equipment (DTE) and Data Communications Equipment (DCE), which we discuss in the following section, is specified at the Physical Layer.

Network topologies, cable and connector types, and interfaces are defined at the Physical Layer of the OSI model.

Common interface standards include

- **EIA/TIA-232:** This standard supports circuits at signal speeds of up to 115,200 bits per second (formerly known as *RS-232*).

- **EIA/TIA-449:** A faster version of EIA/TIA-232, this standard supports longer cable runs and speeds of up to 2 Mbps.

- **V.24. CCITT:** Formerly ITU-T. This standard is essentially the same as the EIA/TIA-232 standard.

- **V.35. CCITT:** Formerly ITU-T. This standard describes a synchronous communications protocol between network access devices and a packet network that supports speeds of up to 48 Kbps.

- **X.21bis. CCITT:** Formerly ITU-T. This standard defines the communications protocol between DCE and DTE in an X.25 network. It's essentially the same as the EIA/TIA-232 standard.

- **High-Speed Serial Interface (HSSI):** This network standard was developed to address the need for high-speed (up to 52 Mbps) serial connections over WAN links.

Networking equipment

Networking devices that operate at the Physical Layer include network interface cards (NICs), network media (cabling, connectors, and interfaces, all of which we discuss in the section "Cable and connector types," earlier in this chapter), repeaters, and hubs.

Network interface cards (NICs) are used to connect a computer to the network. NICs may be integrated on a computer motherboard or installed as an adapter card, such as an ISA, PCI, or PC card. Similar to a NIC, a WIC (WAN interface card) contains a built-in CSU/DSU and is used to connect a router to a digital circuit. Variations of WICs include HWICs (high-speed WAN interface cards) and VWICs (voice WAN interface cards).

A *repeater* is a non-intelligent device that simply amplifies a signal to compensate for *attenuation* (signal loss) so that one can extend the length of the cable segment.

A *hub* (or *concentrator*) is used to connect multiple LAN devices together, such as servers and workstations. The two basic types of hubs are

- **Passive:** Data enters one port and exits all other ports without any signal amplification or regeneration.

- **Active:** Combines the features of a passive hub and repeater. Also known as a *multi-port repeater.*

A *switch* is used to connect multiple LAN devices together. Unlike a hub, a switch doesn't send outgoing packets to all devices on the network, but instead sends packets only to actual destination devices. A switch typically operates at the Data Link Layer (discussed in the following section), but the physical interfaces (the RJ-45 input connections) are defined at the Physical Layer.

Data Link Layer (Layer 2)

The Data Link Layer ensures that messages are delivered to the proper device across a physical network link. This layer also defines the networking protocol (for example, Ethernet and token-ring) used to send and receive data between individual devices. The Data Link Layer formats messages from layers above into frames for transmission, handles point-to-point synchronization and error control, and can perform link encryption.

We go into detail about link encryption in Chapter 8.

The Data Link Layer consists of two sub-layers: the Logical Link Control (LLC) and Media Access Control (MAC) sub-layers. (See Figure 5-8.)

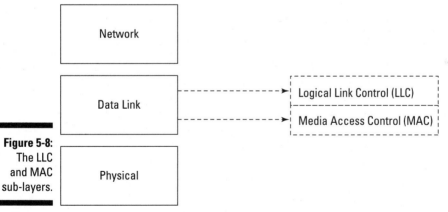

Figure 5-8:
The LLC
and MAC
sub-layers.

The Data Link Layer is responsible for ensuring that messages are delivered to the proper device across a physical network link.

The LLC sub-layer operates between the Network Layer above and the MAC sub-layer below. The LLC sub-layer performs the following three functions:

- ✔ Provides an interface for the MAC sub-layer by using Source Service Access Points (SSAPs) and Destination Service Access Points (DSAPs).
- ✔ Manages the control, sequencing, and acknowledgement of frames being passed up to the Network Layer or down to the Physical Layer.

✔ Bears responsibility for timing and flow control. *Flow control* monitors the flow of data between devices to ensure that a receiving device, which may not necessarily be operating at the same speed as the transmitting device, isn't overwhelmed.

The Logical Link Control (LLC) and Media Access Control (MAC) are sub-layers of the Data Link Layer.

The MAC sub-layer operates between the LLC sub-layer above and the Physical Layer below. It's primarily responsible for framing and has the following three functions:

✔ **Performs error control:** Error control uses a cyclic redundancy check (CRC). A *CRC* is a simple mathematical calculation or checksum used to create a message profile (analogous to a simple message digest, which we discuss in Chapter 8). The CRC is recalculated by the receiving device. If the calculated CRC doesn't match the received CRC, the packet is dropped and a request to re-send is transmitted back to the device that sent it.

✔ **Identifies hardware device (or MAC) addresses:** A *MAC address* (also known as a *hardware address* or *physical address*) is a 48-bit address that's encoded on each device by its manufacturer. The first 24 bits identify the manufacturer or vendor. The second 24 bits uniquely identify the device.

✔ **Controls media access:** The three basic types of media access are

• **Contention:** In contention-based networks, individual devices must vie for control of the physical network medium. This type of network is ideally suited for networks characterized by small bursts of traffic. Ethernet networks use a contention-based method, known as *Carrier-Sense Multiple Access Collision Detect* (CSMA/CD), in which all stations listen for traffic on the physical network medium. If the line is clear, any station can transmit data. However, if another station attempts to transmit data at the same time, a collision occurs, the traffic is dropped, and both stations must wait a random period of time before attempting to re-transmit. Another slight variation of the CSMA/CD method, used in Apple LocalTalk networks, is known as *Carrier-Sense Multiple Access Collision Avoidance* (CSMA/CA).

• **Token-passing:** In token-passing networks, individual devices must wait for a special frame, known as a *token,* before they transmit data across the physical network medium. This type of network is considered *deterministic* (transmission delay can be reliably calculated, and collisions don't occur) and is ideally suited for networks that have large, bandwidth-consuming applications that are delay-sensitive. Token-ring, FDDI, and ARCnet networks all use various token-passing methods for media access control.

• **Polling:** In polling networks, individual devices (secondary hosts) are polled by a primary host to see whether they have data to be transmitted. Secondary hosts can't transmit until permission is granted by the primary host. Polling is typically used in mainframe environments.

LAN protocols and transmission methods

Common LAN protocols are defined at the Data Link (and Physical) Layer. They include the following:

- ✔ **ARCnet:** The ARCnet protocol is one of the earliest LAN technologies developed. It transports data to the physical LAN medium by using the token-passing media access method that we discuss in the preceding section. It's implemented in a star topology by using coaxial cable. ARCnet provides slow-but-predictable network performance.

- ✔ **Ethernet:** The Ethernet protocol transports data to the physical LAN medium by using CSMA/CD (which we discuss in the preceding section) and is designed for networks characterized by sporadic, sometimes heavy traffic requirements. Ethernet is by far the most common LAN protocol used today — most often implemented with twisted-pair cabling (which we discuss in the section "Twisted-pair cable," earlier in the chapter). Ethernet operates at speeds up to 10 Mbps, Fast Ethernet operates at speeds up to 100 Mbps (over Cat 5 twisted-pair or fiber-optic cabling), and Gigabit Ethernet operates at speeds up to 1000 Mbps (over Cat 5e or Cat 6 twisted-pair or fiber-optic cabling).

- ✔ **Token-Ring:** The Token-Ring protocol transports data to the physical LAN medium by using the token-passing media access method that we discuss in the preceding section. In a token-ring network, all nodes are attached to a Multistation Access Unit (MSAU) in a logical ring (physical star) topology. One node on the token-ring network is designated as the *active monitor* and ensures that no more than one token is on the network at any given time. (Variations permit more than one token on the network.) If the token is lost, the active monitor is responsible for ensuring that a replacement token is generated. Token-ring networks operate at speeds of 4 and 16 Mbps.

- ✔ **Fiber Distributed Data Interface (FDDI):** The FDDI protocol transports data to the physical LAN medium by using the token-passing media access method that we discuss in the preceding section. It's implemented as a dual counter-rotating ring over fiber-optic cabling at speeds up to 100 Mbps. All stations on a FDDI network are connected to both rings. During normal operation, only one ring is active. In the event of a network break or fault, the ring wraps back through the nearest node onto the second ring.

- ✔ **Address Resolution Protocol (ARP):** ARP maps Network Layer IP addresses to MAC addresses. ARP discovers physical addresses of attached devices by broadcasting ARP query messages on the network segment. IP-address-to-MAC-address translations are then maintained in a dynamic table that's cached on the system.

- ✔ **Reverse Address Resolution Protocol (RARP):** RARP maps MAC addresses to IP addresses. This process is necessary when a system, such as a diskless machine, needs to discover its IP address. The system broadcasts a RARP message that provides the system's MAC address and requests to be informed of its IP address. A RARP server replies with the requested information.

Both ARP and RARP are Layer 2 protocols. ARP maps an IP address to a MAC address and is used to identify a device's hardware address when only the IP address is known. RARP maps a MAC address to an IP address and is used to identify a device's IP address when only the MAC address is known.

LAN data transmissions are classified as

- ✔ **Unicast:** Packets are sent from the source to a single destination device by using a specific destination IP address.

- ✔ **Multicast:** Packets are copied and sent from the source to multiple destination devices by using a special multicast IP address that the destination stations have been specifically configured to use.

- ✔ **Broadcast:** Packets are copied and sent from the source to every device on a destination network by using a broadcast IP address.

LAN data transmissions are classified as unicast, multicast, or broadcast.

WLAN technologies and protocols

WLAN (wireless LAN) technologies function at the lower layers of the OSI Reference Model. WLAN protocols define how frames are transmitted over the air. See Table 5-3 for a description of the most common IEEE 802.11 WLAN standards.

The IEEE (Institute of Electrical and Electronics Engineers) is an international organization that defines many standards, including numerous 802 networking standards.

Table 5-3		Wireless LAN Standards
Type	*Speed*	*Description*
802.11a	54 Mbps	Operates at 5 GHz (less interference than at 2.4 GHz)
802.11b	11 Mbps	Operates at 2.4 GHz (first widely used protocol)
802.11g	54 Mbps	Operates at 2.4 GHz (backward-compatible with 802.11b)
802.11n	600 Mbps	Operates at 5 GHz or 2.4 GHz

WLAN networks were first encrypted with the WEP (Wired Equivalent Privacy) protocol, which was soon proven to be insufficient. New standards of encryption include WPA (WiFi protected access) and WPA2. WPA using TKIP (Temporal Key Integrity Protocol) is also considered insufficient. We discuss wireless network security in greater detail in the section "Network Security," later in this chapter.

WAN technologies and protocols

WAN technologies function at the lower three layers of the OSI Reference Model (the Physical, Data Link, and Network Layers), primarily at the Data Link Layer. WAN protocols define how frames are carried across a single data link between two devices. These protocols include

- ✔ **Point-to-point links:** These links provide a single, pre-established WAN communications path from the customer's network, across a carrier network (such as a Public Switched Telephone Network [PSTN]), to a remote network. These point-to-point links include

  - **Layer 2 Forwarding Protocol (L2F):** A tunneling (data encapsulation) protocol developed by Cisco and used to implement VPNs, specifically Point-to-Point Protocol (PPP, discussed later in this section) traffic. L2F doesn't provide encryption or confidentiality.

  - **Layer 2 Tunneling Protocol (L2TP):** A tunneling protocol used to implement VPNs. L2TP is derived from L2F (described above) and PPTP (described below) and uses UDP port 1701 (see the section "Network Layer (Layer 3)" later in this chapter) to create a tunneling session. L2TP is commonly implemented along with an encryption protocol, such as IPSec, because it doesn't encrypt traffic or provide confidentiality by itself. We discuss L2TP and IPSec in more detail in the section "Virtual Private Networks (VPNs)," later in this chapter.

  - **Point-to-Point Protocol (PPP):** The successor to SLIP (see the discussion later in this section), PPP provides router-to-router and host-to-network connections over synchronous and asynchronous circuits. It's a more robust protocol than SLIP and provides additional built-in security mechanisms. PPP is far more common than SLIP in modern networking environments.

  - **Point-to-Point Tunneling Protocol (PPTP):** A tunneling protocol developed by Microsoft and commonly used to implement VPNs, specifically PPP traffic. PPTP doesn't provide encryption or confidentiality, instead relying on other protocols, such as PAP, CHAP, and EAP, for security. We discuss PPTP, PAP, CHAP, and EAP in more detail in the sections "Virtual Private Networks (VPNs)" and "Remote access," both later in this chapter.

  - **Serial Line IP (SLIP):** The predecessor of Point-to-Point Protocol (PPP), SLIP was originally developed to support TCP/IP networking over low-speed asynchronous serial lines (such as dial-up modems) for Berkeley UNIX computers.

- ✔ **Circuit-switched networks:** In a circuit-switched network, a dedicated physical circuit path is established, maintained, and terminated between the sender and receiver across a carrier network for each communications session (the *call*). This network type is used extensively in telephone company networks and functions similarly to a regular telephone call. Examples include

- **Digital Subscriber Line (xDSL):** xDSL uses existing analog phone lines to deliver high-bandwidth connectivity to remote customers. Table 5-4 describes several types of xDSL lines that are currently available.

- **Data Over Cable Services Interface Specification (DOCSIS):** DOCSIS is a communications protocol for transmitting high speed data over an existing cable TV system.

- **Integrated Services Digital Network (ISDN):** ISDN is a communications protocol that operates over analog phone lines that have been converted to use digital signaling. ISDN lines are capable of transmitting both voice and data traffic. ISDN defines a B-channel for data, voice, and other services, and a D-channel for control and signaling information. Table 5-5 describes the two levels of ISDN service that are currently available.

With the introduction and widespread adoption of DSL, ISDN has largely fallen out of favor in the United States and is no longer available in many areas.

Circuit-switched networks are ideally suited for *always-on* connections that experience constant traffic.

Table 5-4	xDSL Examples	
Type	*Characteristics*	*Description*
ADSL and ADSL2	Downstream rate: 1.5 to 12 Mbps Upstream rate: 0.5 to 3.5 Mbps Operating range: Up to 14,400 ft	Asymmetric Digital Subscriber Line; designed to deliver higher bandwidth downstream (as from a central office to a customer site) than upstream
SDSL	Downstream rate: 1.544 Mbps Upstream rate: 1.544 Mbps Operating range: Up to 10,000 ft	Single-line Digital Subscriber Line; designed to deliver high bandwidth both upstream and downstream over a single copper twisted pair
HDSL	Downstream rate: 1.544 Mbps Upstream rate: 1.544 Mbps Operating range: Up to 12,000 ft	High-rate Digital Subscriber Line; designed to deliver high bandwidth both upstream and downstream over two copper twisted pairs; commonly used to provide local access to T1 services

Type	Characteristics	Description
VDSL	Downstream rate: 13 to 52 Mbps Upstream rate: 1.5 to 2.3 Mbps Operating range: 1,000 to 4,500 ft	Very high Data-rate Digital Subscriber Line; designed to deliver extremely high bandwidth over a single copper twisted pair; VDSL2 provides simultaneous upstream and downstream data rates in excess of 100 Mbps

Table 5-5	ISDN Service Levels
Level	**Description**
Basic Rate Interface (BRI)	One 16-Kbps D-channel and two 64-Kbps B-channels (maximum data rate of 128 Kbps)
Primary Rate Interface (PRI)	One 64-Kbps D-channel and either 23 64-Kbps B-channels (U.S.) or 30 64-Kbps B-channels (EU), with a maximum data rate of 1.544 Mbps (U.S.) or 2.048 Mbps (EU)

✔ **Packet-switched networks:** In a packet-switched network, devices share bandwidth (by using statistical multiplexing) on communications links to transport packets between a sender and receiver across a carrier network. This type of network is more resilient to error and congestion than circuit-switched networks. We compare packet-switched and circuit-switched networks in Table 5-6. Examples of packet-switched networks include

- **Asynchronous Transfer Mode (ATM):** A very high-speed, low-delay technology that uses switching and multiplexing techniques to rapidly relay fixed-length (53-byte) cells that contain voice, video, or data. Cell processing occurs in hardware that reduces transit delays. ATM is ideally suited for fiber-optic networks that carry bursty (uneven) traffic.

- **Frame Relay:** A packet-switched, standard protocol that handles multiple virtual circuits by using High-level Data Link Control (HDLC) encapsulation (which we discuss later in this section) between connected devices. Frame Relay utilizes a simplified framing approach that has no error correction and Data Link Connection Identifiers (DLCIs) to achieve high speeds across the WAN. Frame Relay can be used on *Switched Virtual Circuits* (SVCs) or *Permanent Virtual Circuits* (PVCs). An *SVC* is a temporary connection that's dynamically created (in the circuit establishment phase) to transmit data (which happens during the data transfer phase) and then disconnected (in the circuit termination phase).

PVCs are permanently established connections. Because the connection is permanent, a PVC doesn't require the bandwidth overhead associated with circuit establishment and termination. However, PVCs are generally a more expensive option than SVCs.

- **Multi-Protocol Label Switching (MPLS):** A packet-switched, high-speed, highly scalable and highly versatile technology used to create fully meshed Virtual Private Networks (VPNs). It can carry IP packets, as well as ATM, SONET (Synchronous Optical Networking), or Ethernet frames. MPLS is specified at both Layer 2 and Layer 3. Label Edge Routers (LERs) in an MPLS network push or encapsulate a packet (or frame) with an MPLS label. The label information is used to switch the payload through the MPLS cloud at very high speeds. Label Switch Routers (LSRs) within the MPLS cloud make routing decisions based solely on the label information, without actually examining the payload. At the egress point, an LER *pops* (decapsulates) the packet, removing the MPLS label when the packet exits the MPLS network. One disadvantage of an MPLS network is that a customer loses visibility into the Cloud. Or, if you're a glass-is-half-full type, one advantage of an MPLS network is that an attacker loses visibility into the Cloud.

- **Synchronous Optical Network (SONET) and Synchronous Digital Hierarchy (SDH):** A high-availability, high-speed, multiplexed, low-latency technology used on fiber-optic networks. SONET was originally designed for the public telephone network and is widely used throughout the U.S. and Canada, particularly within the energy industry. SDH was developed after SONET and is used throughout the rest of the world. Data rates for SONET and SDH are defined at OC (optical carrier) levels (see Table 5-7).

- **Switched Multimegabit Data Service (SMDS):** A high-speed, packet-switched, connectionless-oriented, datagram-based technology available over public switched networks. Typically, companies that exchange large amounts of data bursts with other remote networks use SMDS.

A *datagram* is a self-contained unit of data that is capable of being routed between a source and a destination. Similar to a packet, which is used in the Internet Protocol (IP), datagrams are commonly used in UDP and other protocols such as AppleTalk.

- **X.25:** The first packet-switching network, X.25 is a CCITT (formerly ITU-T) standard that defines how point-to-point connections between a DTE and a DCE (which we discuss in the following section) are established and maintained. X.25 specifies the Link Access Procedure, Balanced (LAPB) protocol at the Data Link Layer and the Packet Level Protocol (PLP; also known as X.25 Level 3) at the Network Layer. X.25 is more common outside the United States but is being superseded by Frame Relay.

Table 5-6	Circuit Switching versus Packet Switching
Circuit Switching	*Packet Switching*
Ideal for always-on connections, constant traffic, and voice communications	Ideal for bursty traffic and data communications
Connection-oriented	Connectionless-oriented
Fixed delays	Variable delays

Packet-switched networks are ideally suited for on-demand connections that have bursty traffic.

✔ **Other WAN protocols:** Two other important WAN protocols defined at the Data Link Layer include

- **High-level Data Link Control (HDLC):** A bit-oriented, synchronous protocol that was created by the ISO to support point-to-point and multipoint configurations. Derived from SDLC, it specifies a data encapsulation method for synchronous serial links and is the default for serial links on Cisco routers. Unfortunately, various vendor implementations of the HDLC protocol are incompatible.

- **Synchronous Data Link Control (SDLC):** A bit-oriented, full-duplex serial protocol that was developed by IBM to facilitate communications between mainframes and remote offices. It defines and implements a polling method of media access, in which the *primary* (front end) polls the *secondaries* (remote stations) to determine whether communication is required.

Asynchronous and synchronous communications

Asynchronous communication transmits data in a serial stream that has control data (start and stop bits) embedded in the stream to indicate the beginning and end of characters. Asynchronous devices must communicate at the same speed, which is controlled by the slower of the two communicating devices. Because no internal clocking signal is used, parity bits are used to reduce transmission errors.

Synchronous communications utilize an internal clocking signal to transmit large blocks of data, known as *frames*. Synchronous communication is characterized by very high-speed transmission rates.

WAN protocols and technologies are implemented over telecommunications circuits. See Table 5-7 for a description of common telecommunications circuits and speeds.

Table 5-7		Common Telecommunications Circuits
Type	*Speed*	*Description*
DS0	64 Kbps	Digital Signal Level 0. Framing specification used in transmitting digital signals over a single channel at 64 Kbps on a T1 facility.
DS1	1.544 Mbps or 2.048 Mbps	Digital Signal Level 1. Framing specification used in transmitting digital signals at 1.544 Mbps on a T1 facility (U.S.) or at 2.048 Mbps on an E1 facility (EU).
DS3	44.736 Mbps	Digital Signal Level 3. Framing specification used in transmitting digital signals at 44.736 Mbps on a T3 facility.
T1	1.544 Mbps	Digital WAN carrier facility. Transmits DS1-formatted data at 1.544 Mbps (24 DS0 user channels at 64 Kbps each).
T3	44.736 Mbps	Digital WAN carrier facility. Transmits DS3-formatted data at 44.736 Mbps (672 DS0 user channels at 64 Kbps each).
E1	2.048 Mbps	Wide-area digital transmission scheme used primarily in Europe that carries data at a rate of 2.048 Mbps.
E3	34.368 Mbps	Wide-area digital transmission scheme used primarily in Europe that carries data at a rate of 34.368 Mbps (16 E1 signals).
OC-1	51.84 Mbps	SONET (Synchronous Optical Networking) Optical Carrier WAN specification
OC-3	155.52 Mbps	SONET
OC-12	622.08 Mbps	SONET
OC-48	2.488 Gbps	SONET
OC-192	9.9 Gbps	SONET

Networking equipment at the Data Link Layer

Networking devices that operate at the Data Link Layer include bridges, switches, DTEs, and DCEs.

✔ A *bridge* is a semi-intelligent repeater used to connect two or more (similar or dissimilar) network segments. A bridge maintains an Address Resolution Protocol (ARP) cache that contains the MAC addresses of individual devices on connected network segments. When a bridge receives a data signal, it checks its ARP cache to determine whether the destination MAC address is on the local network segment. If the data signal turns out to be local, it isn't forwarded; if the MAC address isn't local, however, the bridge forwards (and amplifies) the data signal to all other connected network segments. A serious networking problem associated with bridges is a *broadcast storm,* in which broadcast traffic is automatically forwarded by a bridge, effectively flooding a network.

✔ A *switch* is essentially an intelligent hub that uses MAC addresses to route traffic. Unlike a hub, a switch transmits data only to the port connected to the destination MAC address. This transmission method creates separate collision domains (called *network segments*) and effectively increases the data transmission rates available on the individual network segments. Additionally, a switch can be used to implement virtual LANs (VLANs), which logically segregate a network and limit broadcast domains. Switches are traditionally considered to be Layer 2 (or Data Link Layer) devices, although newer technologies allow switches to function at the upper layers, including Layer 3 (the Network Layer) and Layer 7 (the Application Layer).

✔ *Data Terminal Equipment* (DTE) is a general term used to classify devices at the user end of a user-to-network interface (such as computer workstations). A DTE connects to *Data Communications Equipment* (DCE; also know as Data Circuit-Terminating Equipment), which consists of devices at the network end of a user-to-network interface. The DCE provides the physical connection to the network, forwards network traffic, and provides a clocking signal to synchronize transmissions between the DCE and the DTE. Examples of DCEs include NICs (Network Interface Cards), modems, and CSUs/DSUs (Channel Service Units/Data Service Units).

Network Layer (Layer 3)

The Network Layer (Layer 3) provides routing and related functions that enable data to be transported between systems on the same network or on interconnected networks (or *internetworks*). *Routing* protocols, such as the Routing Information Protocol (RIP), Open Shortest Path First (OSPF), and Border Gateway Protocol (BGP), are defined at this layer. Logical addressing of devices on the network is accomplished at this layer by using *routed* protocols, including the Internet Protocol (IP) and Internetwork Packet Exchange (IPX).

The Network Layer is primarily responsible for routing.

Routing protocols move *routed* protocol messages across a network. Routing protocols include RIP, OSPF, and BGP. Routed protocols include IP and IPX.

Routing protocols

Routing protocols are defined at the Network Layer and specify how routers communicate with one another on a WAN. Routing protocols are classified as static or dynamic.

A *static* routing protocol requires an administrator to create and update routes manually on the router. If the route is down, the network is down. The router can't reroute traffic dynamically to an alternate destination (unless a different route is specified manually). Also, if a given route is congested, but an alternate route is available and relatively fast, the router with static routes can't route data dynamically over the faster route. Static routing is practical only in very small networks or for very limited, special-case routing scenarios (for example, a destination that's reachable only via a single router). Despite the limitations of static routing, it has a few advantages, such as low bandwidth requirements (routing information isn't broadcast across the network) and some built-in security (users can only get to destinations that are specified in the routing table).

A *dynamic* routing protocol can discover routes and determine the best route to a given destination at any given time. The routing table is periodically updated with current routing information. Dynamic routing protocols are further classified as link-state and distance-vector (for intra-domain routing) and path-vector (for inter-domain routing) protocols.

A *distance-vector* protocol makes routing decisions based on two factors: the distance (hop count or other metric) and vector (the egress router interface). It periodically informs its peers and/or neighbors of topology changes. *Convergence,* the time it takes for all routers in a network to update their routing table with the most current information (such as link status changes), can be a significant problem for distance-vector protocols. Without convergence, some routers in a network may be unaware of topology changes, causing the router to send traffic to an invalid destination. During convergence, routing information is exchanged between routers, and the network slows down considerably. Routing Information Protocol (RIP), discussed in the following section, is an example of a distance-vector routing protocol.

Hop count generally refers to the number of router nodes that a packet must pass through to reach its destination.

A *link-state* protocol requires every router to calculate and maintain a complete map, or *routing table,* of the entire network. Routers that use a link-state protocol periodically transmit updates that contain information about adjacent connections (these are called *link states*) to all other routers in the network. Link-state protocols are computation-intensive but can calculate the most efficient route to a destination, taking into account numerous factors such as link speed, delay, load, reliability, and cost (an arbitrarily assigned weight or metric). Convergence occurs very rapidly (within seconds) with link-state protocols; distance-vector protocols usually take longer (several minutes, or even hours in very large networks). Open Shortest Path First (OSPF) — discussed in the section "Open Shortest Path First (OSPF)," later in this chapter — is an example of a link-state routing protocol.

A *path-vector* protocol is similar in concept to a distance-vector protocol, but without the scalability issues associated with limited hop counts. Border Gateway Protocol (BGP), which we talk about in the section "Border Gateway Protocol (BGP)," later in this chapter, is an example of a path-vector protocol.

Routing Information Protocol (RIP)

Routing Information Protocol (RIP) is a distance-vector routing protocol that uses hop count as its routing metric. In order to prevent *routing loops,* in which packets effectively get stuck bouncing between various router nodes, RIP implements a hop limit of 15, which significantly limits the size of networks that RIP can support. After a data packet crosses 15 router nodes (hops) between a source and a destination, the destination is considered unreachable. In addition to hop limits, RIP employs three other mechanisms to prevent routing loops:

- ✔ **Split horizon:** Prevents a router from advertising a route back out through the same interface from which the route was learned.

- ✔ **Route poisoning:** Sets the hop count on a bad route to 16, effectively advertising the route as unreachable if it takes more than 15 hops to reach.

- ✔ **Holddown timers:** Cause a router to start a timer when the router first receives information that a destination is unreachable. Subsequent updates about that destination will not be accepted until the timer expires. This also helps avoid problems associated with *flapping.* Flapping occurs when a route (or interface) repeatedly changes state (up, down, up, down) over a short period of time.

RIP uses UDP port 520 as its transport protocol and thus is a connectionless-oriented protocol. Other disadvantages of RIP include slow convergence and insufficient security (RIPv1 has no authentication, and RIPv2 transmits passwords in cleartext). RIP is a legacy protocol, but it's still in widespread use on networks today, despite its limitations, because of its simplicity.

Open Shortest Path First (OSPF)

OSPF is a link-state routing protocol widely used in large enterprise networks. It's considered an Interior Gateway Protocol (IGP) because it performs routing within a single autonomous system (AS). OSPF is encapsulated directly into IP datagrams, as opposed to using a Transport Layer protocol such as TCP or UDP. OSPF networks are divided into areas identified by 32-bit area identifiers. *Area identifiers* can (but don't have to) correspond to network IP addresses and can duplicate IP addresses without conflicts. Special OSPF areas include the *backbone area* (also known as *area 0*), *stub area,* and *not-so-stubby area* (NSSA).

An *autonomous system (AS)* is a group of contiguous IP address ranges under the control of a single Internet entity. Individual autonomous systems are assigned a 16-bit or 32-bit AS Number (ASN) that uniquely identifies the network on the Internet. ASNs are assigned by the Internet Assigned Numbers Authority (IANA).

Intermediate System to Intermediate System (IS-IS)

IS-IS is a link-state routing protocol used to route datagrams through a packet-switched network. It is an interior gateway protocol used for routing within an autonomous system, used extensively in large service-provider backbone networks.

Border Gateway Protocol (BGP)

BGP is a path-vector routing protocol used between separate autonomous systems (ASs). It's considered an Exterior Gateway Protocol (EGP) because it performs routing between separate autonomous systems. It's the core protocol used by Internet service providers (ISPs) and on very large private IP networks. When BGP runs between autonomous systems (such as between ISPs), it's called external BGP (eBGP). When BGP runs within an AS (such as on a private IP network), it's called internal BGP (iBGP).

Routed protocols

Routed protocols are Network Layer protocols, such as Internet Protocol (IP) and Internetwork Packet Exchange (IPX), that address packets with routing information, which allows those packets to be transported across networks by using routing protocols (discussed in the section "Routing protocols," earlier in this chapter).

Internet Protocol (IP)

Internet Protocol (IP) contains addressing information that enables packets to be routed. IP is part of the TCP/IP (Transmission Control Protocol/Internet Protocol) suite, which is the language of the Internet. IP has two primary responsibilities:

✔ Connectionless, best-effort (no guarantee of) delivery of datagrams

✔ Fragmentation and reassembly of datagrams

IP Version 4 (IPv4), which is currently the most commonly used version, uses a 32-bit logical IP address that's divided into four 8-bit sections *(octets)* and consists of two main parts: the network number and the host number.

IP addressing supports five different address classes, indicated by the high-order (leftmost) bits in the IP address, as listed in Table 5-8.

Table 5-8		IP Address Classes		
Class	*Purpose*	*High-Order Bits*	*Address Range*	*Maximum Number of Hosts*
A	Large networks	0	1 to 126	16,777,214 (224-2)
B	Medium networks	10	128 to 191	65,534 (216-2)
C	Small networks	110	192 to 223	254 (28-2)
D	Multicast	1110	224 to 239	N/A
E	Experimental	1111	240 to 254	N/A

The address range 127.0.0.1 to 127.255.255.255 is a loopback network used for testing and troubleshooting. Packets sent to a 127 address are immediately routed back to the source device. The most commonly used loopback address for devices is 127.0.0.1, although any address in the 127 network range can be used for this purpose.

Several IP address ranges are also reserved for use in private networks, including

✔ 10.0.0.0 – 10.255.255.255 (Class A)

✔ 172.16.0.0 – 172.31.0.0 (Class B)

✔ 192.168.0.0 – 192.168.255.255 (Class C)

These addresses aren't routable on the Internet and are thus often implemented on firewalls and gateways by using Network Address Translation (NAT) to conserve IP addresses, mask the network architecture, and enhance security. NAT translates private, non-routable addresses on internal network devices to registered IP addresses when communication across the Internet is required.

IP Version 6 (IPv6) uses a 128-bit logical IP address (versus 32 bits for IPv4) and incorporates additional functionality to provide security, multimedia support, plug-and-play compatibility, and backward compatibility with IPv4. The main reason for developing IPv6 was to provide more network addresses than are available with IPv4 addresses. However, the widespread use of NAT has somewhat delayed the inevitable depletion of IPv4 addresses. As a result, IPv6 hasn't yet been widely implemented on the Internet (although it is being actively implemented and experimented with in Asia).

Internetwork Packet Exchange (IPX)

Internetwork Packet Exchange (IPX) is a connectionless protocol used primarily in older Novell NetWare networks for routing packets across the network. It's part of the IPX/SPX (Internetwork Packet Exchange/Sequenced Packet Exchange) protocol suite, which is analogous to the TCP/IP suite.

Other Network Layer protocols

Other protocols defined at the Network Layer include the Internet Control Message Protocol (ICMP) and Simple Key Management for Internet Protocols (SKIP).

Internet Control Message Protocol (ICMP)

The Internet Control Message Protocol (ICMP) reports errors and other information back to the source regarding the processing of transmitted IP packets.

Common ICMP messages include Destination Unreachable, Echo Request and Reply, Redirect, and Time Exceeded. The Packet Internet Groper (PING) is a popular utility that uses ICMP messages to test the reachability of a network device.

Simple Key Management for Internet Protocols (SKIP)

SKIP is a Network Layer key management protocol used to share encryption keys. An advantage of SKIP is that it doesn't require a prior communication session to be established before it sends encrypted keys or packets. However, SKIP is bandwidth-intensive because of the size of additional header information in encrypted packets.

Networking equipment at the Network Layer

The primary networking equipment defined at Layer 3 are *routers* and *gateways.*

Routers

Routers are intelligent devices that link dissimilar networks and use logical or physical addresses to forward data packets only to the destination network (or along the network path). Routers consist of both hardware and software components, and they employ various routing algorithms (for example, RIP, OSPF, and BGP) to determine the best path to a destination, based on different variables that include bandwidth, cost, delay, and distance.

Gateways

Gateways are created with software running on a computer (workstation or server) or router. Gateways link dissimilar programs and protocols by examining the entire data packet so as to translate incompatibilities. For example, a gateway can be used to link an IP network to an IPX network or a Microsoft Exchange mail server to a Lotus Notes server (a mail gateway).

Transport Layer (Layer 4)

The Transport Layer (Layer 4) provides transparent, reliable data transport and end-to-end transmission control. The Transport Layer hides the details of the lower layer functions from the upper layers.

Specific Transport Layer functions include

- ✔ **Flow control:** Manages data transmission between devices, ensuring that the transmitting device doesn't send more data than the receiving device can process.

- ✔ **Multiplexing:** Enables data from multiple applications to be transmitted over a single physical link.

- ✔ **Virtual circuit management:** Establishes, maintains, and terminates virtual circuits.

- ✔ **Error checking and recovery:** Implements various mechanisms for detecting transmission errors and taking action to resolve any errors that occur, such as requesting that data be retransmitted.

The Transport Layer is responsible for providing transparent, reliable data transport and end-to-end transmission control.

Several important protocols defined at the Transport Layer include

- ✔ **Transmission Control Protocol (TCP):** A *full-duplex* (capable of simultaneous transmission and reception), connection-oriented protocol that provides reliable delivery of packets across a network. A *connection-oriented* protocol requires a direct connection between two communicating devices before any data transfer occurs. In TCP, this connection is accomplished via a three-way handshake. The receiving device acknowledges packets, and packets are retransmitted if an error occurs. The following characteristics and features are associated with TCP:

- **Connection-oriented:** Establishes and manages a direct virtual connection to the remote device.

- **Reliable:** Guarantees delivery by acknowledging received packets and requesting retransmission of missing or corrupted packets.

- **Slow:** Because of the additional overhead associated with initial handshaking, acknowledging packets, and error correction, TCP is generally slower than other connectionless protocols, such as User Datagram Protocol (UDP).

TCP is a connection-oriented protocol.

A three-way handshake is the method used to establish a TCP connection. A PC attempting to establish a connection with a server initiates the connection by sending a TCP SYN (Synchronize) packet. This is the first part of the handshake. In the second part of the handshake, the server replies to the PC with a SYN ACK packet (Synchronize Acknowledgement). Finally, the PC completes the handshake by sending an ACK or SYN-ACK-ACK packet, acknowledging the server's acknowledgement, and the data communications commence.

- **User Datagram Protocol (UDP):** A connectionless protocol that provides fast best-effort delivery of datagrams across a network. A connectionless protocol doesn't guarantee delivery of transmitted packets (datagrams) and is thus considered unreliable. It doesn't

  - Attempt to establish a connection with the destination network prior to transmitting data.

  - Acknowledge received datagrams.

  - Perform re-sequencing.

  - Perform error checking or recovery.

UDP is ideally suited for data that requires fast delivery, as long as that data isn't sensitive to packet loss and doesn't need to be fragmented. Examples of applications that use UDP include Domain Name System (DNS), Simple Network Management Protocol (SNMP), and streaming audio or video. The following characteristics and features are associated with UDP:

- **Connectionless:** Doesn't pre-establish a communication circuit with the destination network.

- **Best effort:** Doesn't guarantee delivery and is thus considered unreliable.

- **Fast:** Has no overhead associated with circuit establishment, acknowledgement, sequencing, or error-checking and recovery.

UDP is a connectionless protocol.

✓ **Sequenced Packet Exchange (SPX):** The protocol used to guarantee data delivery in older Novell NetWare IPX/SPX networks. SPX sequences transmitted packets, reassembles received packets, confirms all packets are received, and requests retransmission of packets that aren't received. SPX is to IPX as TCP is to IP, though it might be confusing because the order is stated as IPX/SPX, rather than SPX/IPX (as in TCP/IP): SPX and TCP are Layer 4 protocols, and IPX and IP are Layer 3 protocols. Just think of it as yang and yin, rather than yin and yang!

Several examples of connection-oriented and connectionless-oriented protocols are identified in Table 5-9.

Table 5-9	Connection-oriented and Connectionless-oriented Protocols	
Protocol	*Layer*	*Type*
TCP (Transmission Control Protocol)	4 (Transport)	Connection-oriented
UDP (User Datagram Protocol)	4 (Transport)	Connectionless-oriented
IP (Internet Protocol)	3 (Network)	Connectionless-oriented
IPX (Internetwork Packet Exchange)	3 (Network)	Connectionless-oriented
SPX (Sequenced Packet Exchange)	4 (Transport)	Connection-oriented

✓ **Secure Sockets Layer/Transport Layer Security (SSL/TLS):** The SSL/TLS protocol provides session-based encryption and authentication for secure communication between clients and servers on the Internet. SSL/TLS provides server authentication with optional client authentication, which we discuss further in Chapter 8.

Session Layer (Layer 5)

The Session Layer (Layer 5) establishes, coordinates, and terminates communication sessions (service requests and service responses) between networked systems.

The Session Layer is responsible for establishing, coordinating, and terminating communication sessions.

A communication session is divided into three distinct phases:

✔ **Connection establishment:** Initial contact between communicating systems is made, and the end devices agree on communications parameters and protocols to be used, including the mode of operation:

- **Simplex mode:** In simplex mode, a one-way communications path is established with a transmitter at one end of the connection and a receiver at the other end. An analogy is AM radio, where a radio station broadcasts music and the radio receiver can only receive the broadcast.

- **Half-duplex mode:** In half-duplex mode, both communicating devices are capable of transmitting and receiving messages, but they can't do it at the same time. An analogy is a two-way radio in which a button must be pressed to transmit and then released to receive a signal.

- **Full-duplex mode:** In full-duplex mode, both communicating devices are capable of transmitting and receiving simultaneously. An analogy is a telephone with which you can transmit and receive signals (but not necessarily communicate) at the same time.

✔ **Data transfer:** Information is exchanged between end devices.

✔ **Connection release:** After data transfer is completed, end devices systematically end the session.

Some examples of Session Layer protocols include

✔ **NetBIOS:** Network Basic Input/Output System (NetBIOS) is a Microsoft protocol that allows applications to communicate over a LAN. When NetBIOS is combined with other protocols such as TCP/IP, known as NetBIOS over TCP/IP (or NBT), applications can communicate over large networks.

✔ **Network File System (NFS):** Developed by Sun Microsystems to facilitate transparent user access to remote resources on a UNIX-based TCP/IP network.

✔ **Remote Procedure Call (RPC):** A client-server network redirection tool. Procedures are created on clients and performed on servers.

✔ **Secure Shell (SSH and SSH-2):** SSH provides a secure alternative to Telnet (discussed in the section "Application Layer (Layer 7)" later in this chapter) for remote access. SSH establishes an encrypted tunnel between the client and the server, and can also authenticate the client to the server. (For more on SSH and other encryption-related topics, read Chapter 8.)

✔ **Session Initiation Protocol (SIP):** An open signaling protocol standard for establishing, managing and terminating real-time communications — such as voice, video, and text — over large IP-based networks.

Presentation Layer (Layer 6)

The Presentation Layer (Layer 6) provides coding and conversion functions that are applied to data being presented to the Application Layer (Layer 7). These functions ensure that data sent from the Application Layer of one system are compatible with the Application Layer of the receiving system.

The Presentation Layer is responsible for coding and conversion functions.

Tasks associated with this layer include

- **Data representation:** Use of common data representation formats (standard image, sound, and video formats) enable application data to be exchanged between different types of computer systems.

- **Character conversion:** Information is exchanged between different systems by using common character conversion schemes.

- **Data compression:** Common data compression schemes enable compressed data to be properly decompressed at the destination.

- **Data encryption:** Common data encryption schemes enable encrypted data to be properly decrypted at the destination.

Some examples of Presentation Layer protocols include

- **American Standard Code for Information Interchange (ASCII):** A character-encoding scheme based on the English alphabet, consisting of 128 characters.

- **Extended Binary-Coded Decimal Interchange Code (EBCDIC):** An 8-bit character-encoding scheme largely used on mainframe and mid-range computers.

- **Graphics Interchange Format (GIF):** A widely used bitmap image format that allows up to 256 colors and is suitable for images or logos (but not photographs).

- **Joint Photographic Experts Group (JPEG):** A photographic compression method widely used to store and transmit photographs.

- **Motion Picture Experts Group (MPEG):** An audio and video compression method widely used to store and transmit audio and video files.

Application Layer (Layer 7)

The Application Layer (Layer 7) is the highest layer of the OSI model. It supports the components that deal with the communication aspects of an application that requires network access, and it provides an interface to the user. So, both the Application Layer and the end-user interact directly with the application.

The Application Layer is responsible for the following:

- ✔ Identifying and establishing availability of communication partners
- ✔ Determining resource availability
- ✔ Synchronizing communication

The Application Layer is responsible for identifying and establishing availability of communication partners, determining resource availability, and synchronizing communication.

Don't confuse the Application Layer with software applications such as Microsoft Word or Excel. Applications that function at the Application Layer include

- ✔ **File transfer protocol (FTP):** A program used to copy files from one system to another over a network.

- ✔ **HyperText Transfer Protocol (HTTP):** The language of the World Wide Web (WWW). Attacks typically exploit vulnerabilities in web browsers or programming languages such as CGI, Java, and ActiveX. HTTP operates on TCP port 80.

- ✔ **HyperText Transfer Protocol Secure (HTTPS):** The language of commercial transactions on the World Wide Web (WWW). HTTPS is actually the HTTP protocol used in combination with SSL/TLS (discussed earlier in the section "Transport Layer (Layer 4)").

- ✔ **Internet Message Access Protocol (IMAP):** A store-and-forward electronic mail protocol that allows an e-mail client to access, manage, and synchronize e-mail on a remote mail server. IMAP provides more functionality than POP3, such as requiring users to explicitly delete e-mails from the server. The most current version is IMAPv4 (or IMAP4), which operates on TCP port 143. E-mail clients that use IMAP can be secured by using TLS or SSL encryption.

- ✔ **Post Office Protocol Version 3 (POP3):** An e-mail retrieval protocol that allows an e-mail client to access e-mail on a remote mail server by using TCP port 110. Inherently insecure, POP3 allows users to authenticate over the Internet by using plaintext passwords. E-mail clients that use POP3 can be secured by using TLS or SSL encryption.

- ✔ **Privacy Enhanced Mail (PEM):** *PEM* is a proposed IETF (Internet Engineering Task Force) standard for providing e-mail confidentiality and authentication. Read more about this in Chapter 8.

- ✔ **Secure Electronic Transaction (SET):** The *SET* specification was developed by MasterCard and Visa to provide secure e-commerce transactions by implementing authentication mechanisms while protecting the confidentiality and integrity of cardholder data. Find more information on this in Chapter 8.

✔ **Secure HyperText Transfer Protocol (S-HTTP):** *S-HTTP* is an Internet protocol that provides a method for secure communications with a web server. S-HTTP is a connectionless-oriented protocol that encapsulates data after security properties for the session have been successfully negotiated. We discuss this further in Chapter 8.

Do not confuse HTTPS and S-HTTP. They are two distinctly different protocols with several differences. For example, HTTPS encrypts an entire communications session and is commonly used in VPNs, whereas S-HTTP encrypts individual messages between a client and server pair.

✔ **Secure Multipurpose Internet Mail Extensions (S/MIME):** *S/MIME* is a secure method of sending e-mail incorporated into several popular browsers and e-mail applications. We discuss this further in Chapter 8.

✔ **Secure Remote Procedure Call (S-RPC):** *S-RPC* is a secure client-server protocol that's defined at the upper layers of the OSI model, including the Application Layer. RPC is used to request services from another computer on the network. S-RPC provides public and private keys to clients and servers by using Diffie-Hellman. (Read more about this in Chapter 8.) After S-RPC operations initially authenticate, they're transparent to the end-user.

✔ **Simple Mail Transfer Protocol (SMTP):** Used to send and receive e-mail across the Internet. This protocol has several well-known vulnerabilities that make it inherently insecure. SMTP operates on TCP/UDP port 25.

✔ **Simple Network Management Protocol (SNMP):** Used to collect network information by polling stations and sending *traps* (or alerts) to a management station. SNMP has many well-known vulnerabilities, including default cleartext community strings (passwords). SNMP operates on TCP/UDP port 161.

✔ **Telnet:** Provides terminal emulation for remote access to system resources. Passwords are sent in cleartext and are therefore inherently insecure. Telnet operates on TCP/UDP port 23.

✔ **Trivial File Transfer Protocol (TFTP):** A lean, mean version of FTP without directory-browsing capabilities or user authentication. Generally considered less secure than FTP, TFTP operates on UDP port 69.

The TCP/IP Model

The Transmission Control Protocol/Internet Protocol (TCP/IP) Model is similar to the OSI Reference Model. It was originally developed by the U.S. Department of Defense and actually preceded the OSI model. However, the TCP/IP model is not as widely used as the OSI model today. The most notable difference between the TCP/IP model and the OSI model is that the TCP/IP model consists of only four layers, rather than seven (see Figure 5-9):

- ✔ **Application Layer:** Consists of network applications and processes, and loosely corresponds to the upper layers of the OSI model (Application, Presentation, and Session layers)
- ✔ **Transport Layer:** Provides end-to-end delivery and corresponds to the OSI Transport Layer
- ✔ **Internet Layer:** Defines the IP datagram and routing, and corresponds to the OSI Network Layer
- ✔ **Network Access (or Link) Layer:** Contains routines for accessing physical networks and corresponds to the OSI Data Link and Physical layers

The OSI Model		The TCP/IP Model
Application	→	Application
Presentation	→	
Session	→	
Transport	→	Transport
Network	→	Internet
Data Link	→	Network Access
Physical	→	

Figure 5-9: Comparing the OSI model and the TCP/IP Model.

Network Security

Network security is implemented with various technologies, including firewalls, intrusion detection systems (IDSs) and intrusion prevention systems (IPSs), remote access authentication mechanisms, and Virtual Private Networks (VPNs).

Intrusion detection systems (IDS) and intrusion prevention systems (IPS) are sometimes referred to as intrusion detection and prevention systems (IDPS).

Firewalls

A *firewall* controls traffic flow between a trusted network (such as a corporate LAN) and an untrusted or public network (such as the Internet). A firewall can comprise hardware, software, or a combination of both hardware and software. The CISSP candidate must understand the various types of firewalls and common firewall architectures.

Firewall types

Three basic classifications of firewalls have been established: packet-filtering, circuit-level gateway, and application-level gateway.

Three basic types of firewalls are packet-filtering, circuit-level gateway, and application-level gateway.

Packet-filtering

A packet-filtering firewall (or *screening router*), one of the most basic (and inexpensive) types of firewalls, is ideally suited for a low-risk environment. A *packet-filtering firewall* permits or denies traffic based solely on the TCP, UDP, ICMP, and IP headers of the individual packets. It examines the traffic direction (inbound or outbound), the source and destination IP addresses, and the source and destination TCP or UDP port numbers. This information is compared with predefined rules that have been configured in an access control list (ACL) to determine whether a packet should be permitted or denied. A packet-filtering firewall typically operates at the Network Layer or Transport Layer of the OSI model. Some advantages of a packet-filtering firewall are that

✔ It's inexpensive. (It can be implemented as a router ACL, which is free — the ACL, not the router!)

✔ It's fast and flexible.

✔ It's transparent to users.

Disadvantages of packet-filtering firewalls are that

✔ Access decisions are based only on address and port information, rather than more sophisticated information such as context or application.

✔ It has no protection from IP or DNS address spoofing (forged addresses).

✔ It doesn't support strong user authentication.

✔ Configuring and maintaining ACLs can be difficult.

✔ Logging information may be limited.

A more advanced variation of the packet-filtering firewall is the *dynamic packet-filtering firewall.* This type of firewall supports dynamic modification of the firewall rule base by using context-based access control (CBAC) or reflexive ACLs — both of which create dynamic access list rules for individual sessions as they are established. For example, an ACL might be automatically created to allow a user working from the corporate network (inside the firewall) to connect to an FTP server outside the firewall in order to upload and download files between her PC and the FTP server. When the file transfer is completed, the ACL is automatically deleted from the firewall.

Circuit-level gateway

A circuit-level gateway controls access by maintaining state information about established connections. When a permitted connection is established between two hosts, a *tunnel* (or virtual circuit) is created for the session, allowing packets to flow freely between the two hosts without the need for further inspection of individual packets. This type of firewall operates at the Session Layer (Layer 5) of the OSI model.

Advantages of this type of firewall include

- ✔ Speed (After a connection is established, individual packets aren't analyzed.)
- ✔ Support for many protocols
- ✔ Easy maintenance

Disadvantages of this type of firewall include

- ✔ Dependence on the trustworthiness of the communicating users or hosts. (After a connection is established, individual packets aren't analyzed.)
- ✔ Limited logging information about individual data packets is available after the initial connection is established.

A *stateful inspection firewall* is a type of circuit-level gateway that captures data packets at the Network Layer and then queues and *analyzes* (examines the state and context of) these packets at the upper layers of the OSI model.

Application-level gateway

An application-level (or Application Layer) gateway operates at the Application Layer of the OSI model, processing data packets for specific IP applications. This type of firewall is generally considered the most secure and is commonly implemented as a proxy server. In a *proxy server,* no direct communication between two hosts is permitted. Instead, data packets are intercepted by the proxy server, which analyzes the packet's contents and — if permitted by the firewall rules — sends a copy of the original packet to the intended host.

Advantages of this type of firewall include

> ✔ Data packets aren't transmitted directly to communicating hosts, a tactic that masks the internal network's design and prevents direct access to services on internal hosts.

> ✔ It can be used to implement strong user authentication in applications.

Disadvantages of this type of firewall include

> ✔ It reduces network performance because every packet must be passed up to the Application Layer of the OSI model to be analyzed.

> ✔ It must be tailored to specific applications. (Such customization can be difficult to maintain or update for new or changing protocols.)

Firewall architectures

The basic firewall *types* that we discuss in the preceding sections may be implemented by using one of the firewall *architectures* described in the following sections. The four basic types of firewall architectures are screening router, dual-homed gateway, screened-host gateway, and screened-subnet.

Screening router

A *screening router* is the most basic type of firewall architecture employed. An external router is placed between the untrusted and trusted networks, and a security policy is implemented by using ACLs. Although a router functions as a choke point between a trusted network and an untrusted network, an attacker — after gaining access to a host on the trusted network — may potentially be able to compromise the entire network.

Advantages of a screening router architecture include these:

> ✔ It's completely transparent.
> ✔ It's relatively simple to use and inexpensive.

Disadvantages of the screening router architecture include these:

> ✔ It may have difficulty handling certain traffic.
> ✔ It has limited or no logging available.
> ✔ It doesn't employ user authentication.
> ✔ It makes masking the internal network structure difficult.
> ✔ It has a single point of failure.
> ✔ It doesn't truly implement a firewall choke-point strategy because it isn't truly a firewall or a choke-point — it's a router that passes traffic between two networks (the "private" and "public" network).

Still, using a screening router architecture is better than using nothing.

Dual-homed gateways

Another common firewall architecture is the dual-homed gateway. A *dual-homed gateway* (or bastion host) is a system that has two network interfaces (NICs) and sits between an untrusted network and a trusted network. A *bastion host* is a general term often used to refer to proxies, gateways, firewalls, or any server that provides applications or services directly to an untrusted network. Because it's often the target of attackers, a bastion host is sometimes referred to as a *sacrificial lamb*.

However, this term is misleading because a bastion host is typically a hardened system that employs robust security mechanisms. A dual-homed gateway is often connected to the untrusted network via an external screening router. The dual-homed gateway functions as a proxy server for the trusted network and may be configured to require user authentication. A dual-homed gateway offers a more fail-safe operation than a screening router does because, by default, data isn't normally forwarded across the two interfaces. Advantages of the dual-homed gateway architecture include

✔ It operates in a *fail-safe mode* — if it fails, it allows no access, rather than allowing full access for everyone.

✔ Internal network structure is masked.

Disadvantages of the dual-homed gateway architecture include

✔ Its use may inconvenience users by requiring them to authenticate to a proxy server or by introducing latency in the network.

✔ Proxies may not be available for some services.

✔ Its use may cause slower network performance.

Screened-host gateways

A *screened-host gateway* architecture employs an external screening router and an internal bastion host. The screening router is configured so that the bastion host is the only host accessible from the untrusted network (such as the Internet). The bastion host provides any required web services to the untrusted network, such as HTTP and FTP, as permitted by the security policy. Connections to the Internet from the trusted network are routed via an application proxy on the bastion host or directly through the screening router.

Here are some of the advantages of the screened-host gateway:

✔ It provides distributed security between two devices, rather than relying on a single device to perform all security functions.

✔ It has transparent outbound access.

✔ It has restricted inbound access.

Here are some disadvantages of the screened-host gateway:

✔ It's considered less secure because the screening router can bypass the bastion host for certain trusted services.

✔ Masking the internal network structure is difficult.

✔ It can have multiple single points of failure (on the router or bastion host).

Screened-subnet

The screened-subnet is perhaps the most secure of the currently designed firewall architectures. The screened-subnet employs an external screening router, a dual-homed (or multi-homed) host, and a second internal screening router. This implements the concept of a network DMZ (or *demilitarized zone*). Publicly available services are placed on bastion hosts in the DMZ.

Advantages of the screened-subnet architecture include these:

✔ It's transparent to end-users.

✔ It's flexible.

✔ Internal network structure can be masked.

✔ It provides *defense in depth* instead of relying on a single device to provide security for the entire network.

Disadvantages of a screened-subnet architecture, compared to other firewall architectures, include these:

✔ It's more expensive.

✔ It's more difficult to configure and maintain.

✔ It can be more difficult to troubleshoot.

Intrusion detection and prevention systems (IDSs, IPSs, and IDPSs)

Intrusion detection is defined as real-time monitoring and analysis of network activity and data for potential vulnerabilities and attacks in progress. One major limitation of current intrusion-detection-system (IDS) technologies is the requirement to filter false alarms to prevent the operator (the system or security administrator) from being overwhelmed with data. IDSs are classified in many different ways, including active and passive, network-based and host-based, and knowledge-based and behavior-based.

Active and passive IDS

Commonly known as an *intrusion prevention system* (IPS) or as an *intrusion detection and prevention system* (IDPS), an *active IDS* is a system that's configured to automatically block suspected attacks in progress without requiring any intervention by an operator. IPS has the advantage of providing real-time corrective action in response to an attack, but it has many disadvantages as well. An IPS must be placed inline along a network boundary; thus the IPS itself is susceptible to attack. Also, if false alarms and legitimate traffic haven't been properly identified and filtered, authorized users and applications may be improperly denied access. Finally, the IPS itself may be used to effect a *Denial of Service* (DoS) attack, which involves intentionally flooding the system with alarms that cause it to block connections until no connection or bandwidth is available.

A *passive* IDS is a system that's configured to monitor and analyze network traffic activity and alert an operator to potential vulnerabilities and attacks. It can't perform any protective or corrective functions on its own. The major advantages of passive IDS are that these systems can be easily and rapidly deployed and aren't normally susceptible to attack themselves.

Network-based and host-based IDS

A *network-based* IDS usually consists of a network appliance (or sensor) that includes a Network Interface Card (NIC) operating in *Promiscuous* mode (meaning it listens to, or "sniffs," all traffic on the network, not just traffic addressed to a specific host) and a separate management interface. The IDS is placed along a network segment or boundary, and it monitors all traffic on that segment.

A *host-based* IDS requires small programs (or *agents*) to be installed on the individual systems that are to be monitored. The agents monitor the operating system and write data to log files and/or trigger alarms. A host-based IDS can monitor only the individual host systems on which the agents are installed; it doesn't monitor the entire network.

Knowledge-based and behavior-based IDS

A *knowledge-based* (or *signature-based*) IDS references a database of previous attack profiles and known system vulnerabilities to identify active intrusion attempts. Knowledge-based IDSs are currently more common than behavior-based IDSs. Advantages of knowledge-based systems include

✔ They have lower false-alarm rates than behavior-based IDSs.

✔ Alarms are more standardized and more easily understood than behavior-based IDS alarms.

Disadvantages of knowledge-based systems include

✔ The signature database must be continually updated and maintained.

✔ New, unique, or original attacks may not be detected or may be improperly classified.

A *behavior-based* (or *statistical anomaly-based*) IDS references a baseline or learned pattern of normal system activity to identify active intrusion attempts. Deviations from this baseline or pattern cause an alarm to be triggered. Advantages of behavior-based systems include that they

✔ Dynamically adapt to new, unique, or original attacks.

✔ Are less dependent on identifying specific operating system vulnerabilities than knowledge-based IDSs are.

Disadvantages of behavior-based systems include

✔ Higher false alarm rates than knowledge-based IDSs.

✔ An inability to adapt to legitimate usage patterns that may change often and therefore aren't static enough to implement an effective behavior-based IDS.

Remote access

Remote access is provided through various technologies (such as cable modems and wireless devices) and protocols (such as asynchronous dial-up, ISDN, and xDSL), which we discuss in the section "WAN technologies and protocols," earlier in this chapter.

Remote access security is provided through various methods and technologies, which we describe in the following sections.

Remote access security methods

Remote access security methods include restricted allowed addresses, caller ID, and callback.

  ✔ **Restricted address:** The restricted address method restricts access to
    the network based on allowed IP addresses, essentially performing rudi-
    mentary *node* authentication, but not *user* authentication.

  ✔ **Caller ID:** The caller ID method restricts access to the network based on
    allowed phone numbers, thus performing a slightly more secure form of
    node authentication because phone numbers are more difficult to spoof
    than IP addresses. However, this method can be difficult to administer
    for road warriors that routinely travel to different cities.

  ✔ **Callback:** The callback method restricts access to the network by
    requiring a remote user to first authenticate to the remote access service
    (RAS) server. The RAS server then disconnects and calls the user back
    at a preconfigured phone number. As with caller ID, this method can be
    difficult to administer for road warriors.

  One limitation of callback is that it can be easily defeated by using call
  forwarding.

Remote access security technologies

Remote access security technologies include RAS servers that utilize various
authentication protocols associated with PPP, RADIUS, and TACACS.

  ✔ **RAS:** Remote access service (RAS) servers utilize the Point-to-Point
    Protocol (PPP) to encapsulate IP packets and establish dial-in connec-
    tions over serial and ISDN links. PPP incorporates the following three
    authentication protocols:

    • *PAP:* The Password Authentication Protocol (PAP) uses a two-way
      handshake to authenticate a peer to a server when a link is initially
      established. PAP transmits passwords in cleartext, and provides
      no protection from replay or brute force attacks.

    • *CHAP:* The Challenge Handshake Protocol (CHAP) uses a three-way
      handshake to authenticate both a peer and a server when a link is
      initially established and, optionally, at regular intervals through-
      out the session. CHAP requires both the peer and the server to be
      preconfigured with a shared secret that must be stored in cleartext.
      The peer uses the secret to calculate the response to a server
      challenge by using an MD5 one-way hash function. MS-CHAP, a
      Microsoft enhancement to CHAP, allows the shared secret to be
      stored in an encrypted form.

    • *EAP:* The Extensible Authentication Protocol (EAP) adds flexibility
      to PPP authentication by implementing various authentication
      mechanisms, including MD5-challenge, S/Key, generic token card,
      digital certificates, and so on. EAP is implemented in many wireless
      networks.

See Chapters 4 and 8 for more on tokens and digital certificates.

✓ **RADIUS:** The Remote Authentication Dial-In User Service (RADIUS) protocol is an open-source, UDP-based, client-server protocol, which provides authentication and accountability. A user provides username/password information to a RADIUS client by using PAP or CHAP.

The RADIUS client encrypts the password and sends the username and encrypted password to the RADIUS server for authentication.

Note: Passwords exchanged between the RADIUS client and the RADIUS server are encrypted, but passwords exchanged between the PC client and the RADIUS client aren't necessarily encrypted — if using PAP authentication, for example. However, if the PC client happens to also be the RADIUS client, all password exchanges are encrypted, regardless of the authentication protocol being used.

See Chapter 4 for more information about RADIUS.

✓ **Diameter:** The Diameter protocol is the next-generation RADIUS protocol. Diameter overcomes several RADIUS shortcomings. For instance, it uses TCP rather than UDP, supports IPSec or TLS, and has a larger address space than RADIUS.

See Chapter 4 for more on Diameter.

✓ **TACACS:** The Terminal Access Controller Access Control System (TACACS) is a UDP-based access control protocol (originally developed for the MILNET), which provides authentication, authorization, and accountability (AAA). The original TACACS protocol has been significantly enhanced, primarily by Cisco, as XTACACS (no longer used) and TACACS+ (the most common implementation of TACACS). TACACS+ is TCP-based (port 49) and supports practically any authentication mechanism (PAP, CHAP, MS-CHAP, EAP, token cards, Kerberos, and so on). The basic operation of TACACS+ is similar to RADIUS, including the caveat about encrypted passwords between client and server. The major advantages of TACACS+ are its wide support of various authentication mechanisms and granular control of authorization parameters.

See Chapter 4 for a more complete discussion of TACACS.

Virtual Private Networks (VPNs)

A *Virtual Private Network* (VPN) creates a secure tunnel over a public network, such as the Internet. Either encrypting or encapsulating the data as it's transmitted across the VPN creates a secure tunnel. The two ends of a VPN are commonly implemented by using one of the following methods:

> ✔ Client-to-VPN-Concentrator (or Device)
>
> ✔ Client-to-Firewall
>
> ✔ Firewall-to-Firewall
>
> ✔ Router-to-Router

Common VPN protocol standards include Point-to-Point Tunneling Protocol (PPTP), Layer 2 Forwarding Protocol (L2F), Layer 2 Tunneling Protocol (L2TP), Internet Protocol Security (IPSec), and Secure Sockets Layer (SSL).

Point-to-Point Tunneling Protocol (PPTP)

The Point-to-Point Tunneling Protocol (PPTP) was developed by Microsoft to enable the Point-to-Point Protocol (PPP) to be tunneled through a public network. PPTP uses native PPP authentication and encryption services (such as PAP, CHAP, and EAP), which we discuss in the section "RAS," earlier in this chapter. PPTP is commonly used for secure dial-up connections, using Microsoft Win9x or NT/2000 clients. PPTP operates at the Data Link Layer (Layer 2) of the OSI model and is designed for individual client-server connections.

Layer 2 Forwarding Protocol (L2F)

The Layer 2 Forwarding Protocol (L2F) was developed by Cisco and provides similar functionality to PPTP. Like its name implies, L2F operates at the Data Link Layer of the OSI model and permits tunneling of Layer 2 WAN protocols such as HDLC and SLIP.

Layer 2 Tunneling Protocol (L2TP)

The Layer 2 Tunneling Protocol (L2TP) is an IETF standard that combines Microsoft (and others') PPTP and Cisco L2F protocols. Like PPTP and L2F, L2TP operates at the Data Link Layer of the OSI model to create secure VPN connections for individual client-server connections. The L2TP addresses the following end-user requirements:

> ✔ **Transparency:** Requires no additional software.
>
> ✔ **Robust authentication:** Supports PPP authentication protocols, Remote Authentication Dial-In User Service (RADIUS), Terminal Access Controller Access Control System (TACACS), smart cards, and one-time passwords.
>
> ✔ **Local addressing:** The VPN entities, rather than the ISP, assign IP addresses.
>
> ✔ **Authorization:** Authorization is managed by the VPN server-side, similar to direct dial-up connections.
>
> ✔ **Accounting:** Both the ISP and the user perform AAA accounting.

IPSec

Internet Protocol Security (IPSec) is an IETF open standard for VPNs that operates at the Network Layer (Layer 3) of the OSI model. It's the most popular and robust VPN protocol in use today. IPSec ensures confidentiality, integrity, and authenticity by using Layer 3 encryption and authentication to provide an end-to-end solution. IPSec operates in two modes:

- ✔ **Transport mode:** Only the data is encrypted.
- ✔ **Tunnel mode:** The entire packet is encrypted.

The two main protocols used in IPSec are

- ✔ **Authentication Header (AH):** Provides integrity, authentication, and non-repudiation
- ✔ **Encapsulating Security Payload (ESP):** Provides confidentiality (encryption) and limited authentication

Each pair of hosts communicating in an IPSec session must establish a security association.

A *security association* (SA) is a one-way connection between two communicating parties; thus, two SAs are required for each pair of communicating hosts. Additionally, each SA supports only a single protocol (AH or ESP). Therefore, using both an AH and an ESP between two communicating hosts will require a total of four SAs. An SA has three parameters that uniquely identify it in an IPSec session:

- ✔ **Security Parameter Index (SPI):** The SPI is a 32-bit string used by the receiving station to differentiate between SAs terminating on that station. The SPI is located within the AH or ESP header.
- ✔ **Destination IP address:** The destination address could be the end station or an intermediate gateway or firewall, but it must be a unicast address.
- ✔ **Security Protocol ID:** The Security Protocol ID must be either an AH or ESP association.

Key management is provided in IPSec by using the Internet Key Exchange (IKE). *IKE* is actually a combination of three complementary protocols: the Internet Security Association and Key Management Protocol (ISAKMP), the Secure Key Exchange Mechanism (SKEME), and the Oakley Key Exchange Protocol.

SSL

The Secure Sockets Layer (SSL) protocol (discussed in greater detail in Chapter 8) operates at the Transport Layer (Layer 4) of the OSI model. SSL

VPNs have rapidly gained widespread popularity and acceptance in recent years because of their ease of use and low cost. An SSL VPN requires no special client hardware or software (other than a web browser), and little or no client configuration. SSL VPNs provide secure access to web-enabled applications and thus are somewhat more granular in control — a user is granted access to a specific application, rather than to the entire private network. This granularity can also be considered a limitation of SSL VPNs; not all applications will work over an SSL VPN, and many convenient network functions (file and print sharing) may not be available over an SSL VPN.

Wireless Network (WLAN) Security

Both residential and business wireless local area networks (WLANs) have proliferated around the world and are often an inviting target for attackers, whether those attackers want to compromise your data or resources, or simply get free access to the Internet.

The CISSP candidate should understand the basic WLAN components and architectures, and various WLAN security protocols and their vulnerabilities.

WLAN components and architectures

The basic components of a WLAN (also known as a *WiFi network*) include client devices, wireless network cards, and wireless access points (APs).

Client devices and wireless cards

Client devices in a WLAN include desktop and laptop PCs, PDAs, and other mobile devices (such as smartphones, iPhones, medical devices, and barcode scanners). Wireless network interface cards (WNICs), or wireless cards, come in a variety of form factors such as PCI adapters, PC cards, and USB adapters, or they are built into wireless-enabled devices, such as laptop PCs, PDAs, and smartphones.

Access points (APs)

Wireless access points (APs) are transceivers that connect wireless clients to the wired network. Access points are base stations for the wireless network. They're essentially hubs (or routers) operating in Half-Duplex mode — they can only receive or transmit at a given time; they can't do both at the same time. Wireless access points also need antennas so that they can transmit and receive data. The four basic types of wireless antennas include

✔ **Omni-directional:** The most common type of wireless antenna, *omni-directional antennas* are essentially short poles that transmit and receive wireless signals with equal strength in all directions around a horizontal axis.

✔ **Parabolic:** Also known as dish antennas, *parabolic antennas* are directional dish antennas made of meshed wire grid or solid metal. Parabolic antennas are used to extend wireless ranges over great distances.

✔ **Sectorized:** Similar in shape to omni-directional antennas, *sectorized antennas* have reflectors that direct transmitted signals in a specific direction (usually a 60- to 120-degree pattern) to provide additional range and decrease interference in a specific direction.

✔ **Yagi:** Similar in appearance to a small aerial TV antenna, *yagi antennas* are used for long distances in point-to-point or point-to-multipoint wireless applications.

Access points and the wireless cards that connect to them must use the same WLAN 802.11 standard or be backward-compatible. See the section "WLAN technologies and protocols," earlier in this chapter, for a list of the 802.11 specifications.

Access points (APs) can operate in one of three modes:

✔ **Root mode:** The default configuration for most APs. The AP is directly connected to the wired network, and wireless clients access the wired network via the wireless access point. Also known as *infrastructure* mode.

✔ **Repeater mode:** The AP doesn't connect directly to the wired network, but instead provides an upstream link to another AP, effectively extending the range of the WLAN. Also known as *stand-alone* mode.

✔ **Bridge mode:** A rare configuration that isn't supported in most APs. Bridge mode is used to connect two separate wired network segments via a wireless access point.

Ad hoc is a type of WLAN architecture that doesn't have any APs. The wireless devices communicate directly with each other in a peer-to-peer network.

WLAN security techniques and protocols

Security on wireless networks, as with all security, is best implemented by using a defense-in-depth approach. Security techniques and protocols include SSIDs, WEP, and WPA.

Service Set Identifier (SSID)

An SSID is a name (up to 32 characters) that uniquely identifies a wireless network. A wireless client must know the SSID to connect to the WLAN. However, most APs broadcast their SSID (or the SSID can be easily sniffed), so the security provided by an SSID is largely inconsequential.

Wired Equivalent Privacy (WEP)

As its name implies, WEP was originally conceived as a security protocol to provide the same level of confidentiality that wired networks have. However, significant weaknesses were quickly uncovered in the WEP protocol.

WEP uses an RC4 stream cipher for confidentiality and a CRC-32 checksum for integrity. WEP uses either a 40-bit or 104-bit key with a 24-bit initialization vector (IV) to form a 64-bit or 128-bit key. (See Chapter 8 for more on stream ciphers, checksums, and initialization vectors.) Because of the relatively short initialization vector used (and other flaws), WEP keys can be easily cracked by readily available software in a matter of minutes.

WEP supports two methods of authentication:

- **Open System authentication:** Doesn't require a wireless client to present credentials during authentication. After the client associates with the access point, WEP encrypts the data that's transmitted over the wireless network.

- **Shared Key authentication:** Uses a four-way handshake to authenticate and associate the wireless client with the access point, then encrypts the data.

Despite its many security flaws, WEP is still widely used in both residential and business networks as the default security protocol. WEP security can be enhanced by using tunneling protocols such as IPSec and SSH (see Chapter 8), but other security protocols are available to enhance WLAN security, as discussed in the following section.

WiFi Protected Access (WPA and WPA2)

WPA and WPA2 provide significant security enhancements over WEP and were introduced as a quick fix to address the flaws in WEP while the 802.11i wireless security standard was being developed.

WPA uses the Temporal Key Integrity Protocol (TKIP) to address some of the encryption problems in WEP. TKIP combines a secret root key with the initialization vector by using a key-mixing function. WPA also implements a sequence counter to prevent replay attacks and a 64-bit message integrity check. Despite these improvements, WPA that uses TKIP is now considered insufficient because of some well-known attacks.

WPA and WPA2 also support various EAP extensions (see the section "Remote access," earlier in this chapter) to further enhance WLAN security. These extensions include EAP-TLS (Transport Layer Security), EAP-TTLS (Tunneled Transport Layer Security), and Protected EAP (PEAPv0 and v1).

Further security enhancements were introduced in WPA2. WPA2 uses the AES-based algorithm Counter Mode with Cipher Block Chaining Message Authentication Code Protocol (CCMP), which replaces TKIP and WEP to produce a fully secure WLAN protocol.

E-mail, Web, Facsimile, and Telephone Security

The CISSP candidate should understand common issues associated with e-mail, web, facsimile, and telephone security.

E-mail security

E-mail has emerged as one of the most important communication mediums in our global economy, with over 50 billion e-mail messages sent worldwide every day. Unfortunately, spam accounts for as much as 85 percent of that e-mail volume. Spam is more than a minor nuisance — it's a serious security threat to all organizations worldwide.

The Simple Mail Transfer Protocol (SMTP) is used to send and receive e-mail across the Internet. It operates on TCP/UDP port 25 and contains many well-known vulnerabilities. Most SMTP mail servers are configured by default to forward (or *relay*) all mail, regardless of whether the sender's or recipient's address is valid.

Failing to secure your organization's mail servers may allow spammers to misuse your servers and bandwidth as an open relay to propagate their spam. The bad news is that you'll eventually (it usually doesn't take more than a few days) get blacklisted by a large number of organizations that maintain real-time blackhole lists (RBLs) against open relays, effectively preventing most (if not all) e-mail communications from your organization reaching their intended recipients. It usually takes several months to get removed from those RBLs after you've been blacklisted, and it does significant damage to your organization's communications infrastructure and credibility.

Using RBLs is only one method to combat spam, and it's generally not even the most effective or reliable method, at that. The organizations that maintain these massive lists aren't perfect and do make mistakes. If a mistake is made with your domain or IP addresses, you'll curse their existence — it's a case in which the cure is sometimes worse than the disease.

Failure to make a reasonable effort towards spam prevention in your organization is a failure of due diligence. An organization that fails to implement appropriate countermeasures may find itself a defendant in a sexual harassment lawsuit from an employee inundated with pornographic e-mails sent by a spammer to his or her corporate e-mail address.

Other risks associated with spam e-mail include

- ✔ **Missing or deleting important e-mails:** Your boss might inadvertently delete that e-mail authorizing your promotion and pay raise because her inbox is flooded with spam and she gets trigger-happy with the Delete button — at least it's a convenient excuse!

- ✔ **Viruses and other mail-icious code:** Although you seem to hear less about viruses in recent years, they're still prevalent, and e-mail remains the favored medium for propagating them.

- ✔ **Phishing and pharming scams:** *Phishing* and *pharming* attacks, in which victims are lured to an apparently legitimate website (typically online banking or auctions) ostensibly to validate their personal account information, are usually perpetrated through mass mailings. It's a complex scam increasingly perpetrated by organized criminals. Ultimately, phishing and pharming scams cost the victim his or her moolah — and possibly his or her identity.

Countering these threats requires an arsenal of technical solutions and user-awareness efforts and is — at least, for now — a never-ending battle. Begin by securing your servers and client PCs. Mail servers should always be placed in a DMZ, and unnecessary or unused services should be disabled — and change that default relay setting! Most other servers, and almost all client PCs, should have port 25 disabled. Implement a spam filter or other secure mail gateway. Also, consider the following user-awareness tips:

- ✔ **Never unsubscribe or reply to spam e-mail.** Unsubscribe links in spam e-mails are often used to confirm the legitimacy of your e-mail address, which can then be added to mass-mailing lists that are sold to other spammers. And, as tempting as it is to tell a spammer what you really think of his or her irresistible offer to enhance your social life or improve your financial portfolio, most spammers don't actually read your replies and (unfortunately) aren't likely to follow your suggestion that they jump off a cliff.

Although legitimate offers from well-known retailers or newsletters from professional organizations may be thought of as spam by many people, it's likely that, at some point, a recipient of such a mass mailing actually signed up for that stuff — so it's technically not spam. Everyone seems to want your e-mail address whenever you fill out an application for something, and providing your e-mail address often translates to an open invitation for them to tell you about every sale from here to eternity. In such cases, senders are required by law to provide an Unsubscribe hyperlink in their mass mailings, and clicking it does remove the recipient from future mailings.

✔ **Don't send auto-reply messages to Internet e-mail addresses (if possible).** Mail servers can be configured not to send auto-reply messages (such as out-of-office messages) to Internet e-mail addresses. However, this setting may not be (and probably isn't) practical in your organization. Be aware of the implications — auto-reply rules don't discriminate against spammers, so the spammers know when you're on vacation, too!

✔ **Get a firewall for your home computer** *before* **you connect it to the Internet.** This admonishment is particularly true if you're using a high-speed cable or DSL modem. Typically, a home computer that has high-speed access will be scanned within minutes of being connected to the Internet. And if it isn't protected by a firewall, this computer will almost certainly be compromised and become an unsuspecting zombie in some spammer's bot-net army (over 250,000 new zombies are added to the Internet every day!). Then, you'll become part of the problem because your home computer and Internet bandwidth are used to send spam and phishing e-mails to thousands of other victims around the world, and you'll be left wondering why your brand-new state-of-the-art home computer is suddenly so slow and your blazing new high-speed Internet connection isn't so high-speed just two weeks after you got it.

Your end-users don't have to be CISSP-certified to secure their home computers. A simple firewall software package that has a basic configuration is usually enough to deter the majority of today's hackers — most are using automated tools to scan the Internet and don't bother to slow down for a computer that presents even the slightest challenge. Size matters in these bot-net armies, and far too many unprotected computers are out there to waste time (even a few minutes) defeating your firewall.

Spam is only the tip of the iceberg. Get ready for emerging threats such as *SPIM* (spam over instant messaging) and *SPIT* (spam over Internet telephony) that will up the ante in the battle for messaging security.

Several protocols exist for secure e-mail, including S/MIME, PEM, and PGP. We discuss several of these protocols in the section "Application Layer (Layer 7)," earlier in this chapter, and also in Chapter 8.

Other e-mail security considerations include malicious code contained in attachments, lack of privacy, and lack of authentication. These considerations can be countered by implementing antivirus scanning software, encryption, and digital signatures, respectively.

Web security

The two principal protocols that make up the World Wide Web are the HyperText Transport Protocol (HTTP) and the HyperText Markup Language (HTML). HTTP is the command-and-response language used by browsers to communicate with web servers, and HTML is the display language that defines the appearance of web pages.

HTTP and HTML are the means used to facilitate all sorts of high-value activities, such as online banking and business applications. It should be of no surprise, then, to know that these protocols are under constant attack by hackers. Some of the types of attacks are

- ✔ **Script injection:** Hackers attempt to inject scripting language commands into form fields on web pages in an attempt to fool the web server into sending the contents of back-end databases to the hacker.

- ✔ **Buffer overflow:** Hackers try to send machine language instructions as parts of queries to web servers in an attempt to run those instructions. If successful, the hacker can execute commands of his or her own choosing on the server, with potentially disastrous results.

- ✔ **Denial of Service (DoS):** Hackers can send specially crafted queries to a web server in order to cause it to malfunction and stop working. Another form of Denial of Service involves merely sending huge volumes of queries to the web server in an attempt to clog its inputs and make it unavailable for legitimate use.

These and other types of attacks have made web security testing a necessity. Many organizations that have web applications, especially ones that facilitate high-value activities (such as banking, travel, and information management), employ tools and other methods to make sure that no vulnerabilities exist which could permit malicious attacks to expose sensitive information or cause the application to malfunction.

Facsimile security

Facsimile transmissions are often taken for granted, but they definitely present major security issues. A fax transmission, like any other electronic transmission, can be easily intercepted or re-created. General administrative and technical controls for fax security include

- ✔ Using cover pages (that include appropriate routing and classification markings)
- ✔ Placing fax machines in secure areas
- ✔ Using secure phone lines
- ✔ Encrypting fax data

Many faxes are lost in situations in which the recipient doesn't know a fax is coming, and someone else in the office takes too many pages from the fax machine, including the fax destined for the unaware recipient! If you're sending a fax that contains sensitive information, inform the recipient in advance so that he or she can be sure to grab it from the fax machine!

PBX, POTS, and VoIP fraud and abuse

PBX (Private Branch Exchange) switches, POTS (Plain Old Telephone Systems), and VoIP (Voice over IP) switches are some of the most overlooked and costly aspects of a corporate telecommunications infrastructure. Many employees don't think twice about using a company telephone system for extended personal use, including long-distance calls. Personal use of company-supplied mobile phones and pagers is another area of widespread abuse. Perhaps the simplest and most effective countermeasure against internal abuses is to publish and enforce a corporate telephone-use policy. Regular auditing of telephone records is also effective for deterring and detecting telephone abuses.

PBX, POTS, and VoIP are information systems, too. Unless security measures are taken, such as strong passwords and security patches, attacks on telephone switches and systems are more likely to succeed, resulting in toll fraud and other headaches.

Caller ID fraud and abuse

A new and growing problem is that of forged caller IDs. Several methods are available for hiding a caller ID — in some cases, in a way that can be deliberately misleading or used to perpetrate fraud. These methods include

- ✔ **Using a calling card:** Using a long-distance calling card often masks the true origin of a call.
- ✔ **Using caller ID services:** A number of commercial services are available that will generate any desired caller ID.

✔ **Blocking caller ID:** Many wireline and wireless telephone services have means that can block caller ID, either on a per-call basis or universally.

✔ **Reconfigure your telephone switch:** Often, a telephone switch that is connected via a trunk to a telephone network can send Caller ID data that is configured into the telephone switch.

✔ **VoIP:** Simple IP smartphone or PC software can often be used to generate false caller ID data from VoIP phones.

The use of caller ID spoofing as part of a scheme to commit fraud is in its infancy and may grow over time.

Network Attacks and Countermeasures

Most attacks against networks are Denial of Service (DoS) or Distributed Denial of Service (DDoS) attacks in which the objective is to consume a network's bandwidth so that network services become unavailable. But several other types of attacks exist, some of which are discussed in the following sections.

Bluejacking and bluesnarfing

With Bluetooth technology becoming wildly popular, several new attack methods have evolved, including *bluejacking* (sending anonymous, unsolicited messages to Bluetooth-enabled devices) and *bluesnarfing* (stealing personal data, such as contacts, pictures, and calendar information from a Bluetooth-enabled phone). Even worse, in a bluesnarfing attack, information about your cellular phone (such as its serial number) can be downloaded, then used to clone your phone.

Fraggle

A *Fraggle* attack is a variant of a Smurf attack (see the section "Smurf," later in this chapter) that uses UDP Echo packets (UDP port 7) rather than ICMP packets. Cisco routers can be configured to disable the TCP and UDP services (known as *TCP and UDP small servers*) that are most commonly used in Fraggle attacks.

ICMP flood

In an *ICMP flood* attack, large numbers of ICMP packets (usually Echo Request) are sent to the target network to consume available bandwidth and/or system resources. Because ICMP isn't required for normal network operations, the easiest defense is to drop ICMP packets at the router or filter them at the firewall.

Session hijacking (spoofing)

IP *spoofing* involves altering a TCP packet so that it appears to be coming from a known, trusted source, thus giving the attacker access to the network.

Smurf

A *Smurf* attack is a variation of the ICMP flood attack. (Check out the section "ICMP flood," earlier in this section.) In a Smurf attack, ICMP Echo Request packets are sent to the broadcast address of a target network by using a spoofed IP address on the target network. The target, or *bounce site,* then transmits the ICMP Echo Request to all hosts on the network. Each host then responds with an Echo Reply packet, overwhelming the available bandwidth and/or system resources. Countermeasures against Smurf attacks include dropping ICMP packets at the router.

SYN flood

In a *SYN flood* attack, TCP packets with a spoofed source address request a connection (SYN bit set) to the target network. The target responds with a SYN-ACK packet, but the spoofed source never replies. *Half-open connections* are incomplete communication sessions awaiting completion of the TCP three-way handshake. These connections can quickly overwhelm a system's resources while the system waits for the half-open connections to time out, which causes the system to crash or otherwise become unusable.

SYN floods are countered on Cisco routers by using two features: *TCP Intercept,* which effectively proxies for the half-open connections; and *Committed Access Rate* (CAR), which limits the bandwidth available to certain types of traffic. Checkpoint's FW-1 firewall has a feature known as *SYN Defender* that functions in way similar to the Cisco TCP Intercept feature. Other defenses include changing the default maximum number of TCP half-open connections and reducing the timeout period on networked systems.

Teardrop

In a *Teardrop* attack, the Length and Fragmentation offset fields of sequential IP packets are modified, causing the target system to become confused and crash.

UDP flood

In a *UDP flood* attack, large numbers of UDP packets are sent to the target network to consume available bandwidth and/or system resources. UDP floods can generally be countered by dropping unnecessary UDP packets at the router. However, if the attack uses a required UDP port (such as DNS port 53), other countermeasures need to be employed.

Prep Test

1 A data network that operates across a relatively large geographic area defines what type of network?

A ○ LAN

B ○ MAN

C ○ CAN

D ○ WAN

2 The process of wrapping protocol information from one layer in the data section of another layer describes

A ○ Data encryption

B ○ Data encapsulation

C ○ Data hiding

D ○ TCP wrappers

3 The LLC and MAC are sub-layers of what OSI model layer?

A ○ Data Link

B ○ Network

C ○ Transport

D ○ Session

4 The Ethernet protocol is defined at what layer of the OSI model and in which IEEE standard?

A ○ Data Link Layer, 802.3

B ○ Network Layer, 802.3

C ○ Data Link Layer, 802.5

D ○ Network Layer, 802.5

5 All the following are examples of packet-switched WAN protocols, except

A ○ X.25

B ○ Frame Relay

C ○ ISDN

D ○ SMDS

6 Which of the following is an example of a Class C IP address?

A ○ 17.5.5.1

B ○ 127.0.0.1

C ○ 192.167.4.1

D ○ 224.0.0.1

7 **The TCP/IP Protocol Model consists of the following four layers:**

A ○ Application, Presentation, Session, Transport

B ○ Application, Session, Network, Physical

C ○ Application, Session, Transport, Internet

D ○ Application, Transport, Internet, Link

8 **Which of the following firewall architectures employs external and internal routers, as well as a bastion host?**

A ○ Screening router

B ○ Screened-subnet

C ○ Screened-host gateway

D ○ Dual-homed gateway

9 **Which of the following is not a common VPN protocol standard?**

A ○ IPSec

B ○ PPTP

C ○ TFTP

D ○ L2TP

10 **A type of network attack in which TCP packets are sent from a spoofed source address with the SYN bit set describes**

A ○ Smurf

B ○ Fraggle

C ○ Teardrop

D ○ SYN flood

Answers

1 **D.** WAN. A LAN operates across a relatively small geographic area. MANs and CANs are LAN variations. *Review "Wide area network (WAN)."*

2 **B.** Data encapsulation. Data encapsulation wraps protocol information from one layer in the data section of another layer. The other choices are incorrect. Review *"The OSI Reference Model."*

3 **A.** Data Link. The Data Link Layer is the only layer of the OSI model that defines sub-layers (the Logical Link Control and Media Access Control sub-layers). *Review "Data Link Layer (Layer 2)."*

4 **A.** Data Link Layer, 802.3. LAN protocols are defined at the Data Link Layer. IEEE 802.5 defines the Token-Ring standard. *Review "Data Link Layer (Layer 2)."*

5 **C.** ISDN. ISDN is circuit-switched. Packet-switched network technologies include X.25, Frame Relay, SMDS, ATM, and VoIP. *Review "WAN technologies and protocols."*

6 **C.** 192.167.4.1. 17.5.5.1 is a Class A address, 127.0.0.1 is an interface loopback address, and 224.0.0.1 is a multicast address (Class D). *Review "Internet Protocol (IP)."*

7 **D.** Application, Transport, Internet, Link (or Network). *Review "The TCP/IP Model."*

8 **B.** Screened-subnet. The screened-subnet employs an external screening router, a dual-homed (or multi-homed) host, and a second internal screening router. *Review "Firewall architectures."*

9 **C.** TFTP. TFTP is the Trivial File Transfer Protocol, a basic variation of the FTP protocol that provides limited file transfer capabilities. It has absolutely nothing to do with VPNs. *Review "Virtual Private Networks (VPNs)."*

10 **D.** SYN flood. Smurf attacks exploit vulnerabilities in the ICMP protocol. Fraggle attacks exploit vulnerabilities in the UDP protocol. A Teardrop attack exploits vulnerabilities in the TCP protocol by using the length and fragmentation offset fields. *See "Network Attacks and Countermeasures."*

Chapter 6

Information Security Governance and Risk Management

• •

In This Chapter

▶ Understanding security governance, data classification, and risk management concepts

▶ Knowing your missions, goals, and objectives

▶ Practicing security policies, standards, guidelines, and procedures

▶ Taking stock of information security management practices

▶ Identifying security education, training, and awareness needs and opportunities

• •

*T*he Information Security Governance and Risk Management domain introduces many important concepts and overlaps with several other domains. Fortunately, it's not an extremely technical domain, and the concepts that we discuss in this chapter are fairly straightforward and easy to understand.

Information Security Governance Concepts and Principles

As a CISSP candidate, you must fully understand the three fundamental information security concepts that comprise the *C-I-A* triad and form the basis of information security (see Figure 6-1):

▸ Confidentiality

▸ Integrity

▸ Availability

As with any triangular shape, all three sides depend on each other (think of a three-sided pyramid or a three-legged stool) to form a stable structure. If one piece falls apart, the whole thing falls apart. All other domains within the CISSP Common Body of Knowledge (CBK) are based on these three important concepts.

Where security is concerned, you also need to understand the defense-in-depth concept, how to avoid single points of failure, and how to incorporate these concepts into security planning.

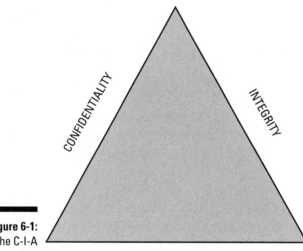

Figure 6-1:
The C-I-A
triad.

Confidentiality

Confidentiality prevents the unauthorized use or disclosure of information, ensuring that only those who are authorized to access information can do so. *Privacy* is a closely related concept that's most often associated with personal data. Various U.S. and international laws exist to protect the privacy (confidentiality) of personal data.

Personal data most commonly refers to *personally identifiable information* (PII), which includes names, addresses, Social Security numbers, contact information, and financial or medical data. Personal data, in more comprehensive legal definitions (particularly in Europe), may also include race, marital status, sexual orientation or lifestyle, religious preference, political affiliations, and any number of other unique personal characteristics that may be collected or stored about an individual.

Read more about U.S. and international privacy laws in Chapter 12.

Privacy ensures the confidentiality of personal data.

Integrity

Integrity safeguards the accuracy and completeness of information and processing methods. It ensures that

- Unauthorized users or processes don't make modifications to data.
- Authorized users or processes don't make unauthorized modifications to data.
- Data is internally and externally consistent, meaning a given input produces an expected output.

Availability

Availability ensures that authorized users have reliable and timely access to information, and associated systems and assets, when needed. Availability is easily one of the most overlooked aspects of information security. In addition to Denial of Service attacks, other threats to availability include single points of failure, inadequate capacity (such as storage, bandwidth, and processing) planning, equipment malfunctions, fail-safe control mechanisms, and business interruptions or disasters.

The opposite of C-I-A is *D-A-D:* disclosure, alteration, and destruction.

Defense in depth

Defense in depth is an information security strategy based on multiple layers of defense. It's often the (desired) result of a holistic approach to information security. Here's a rundown of the integral parts of a defense-in-depth strategy:

- **Security management principles:** Include data classification, personnel security policies and practices, and information security awareness programs
- **Security technologies:** Include firewalls, antivirus software, and intrusion detection systems

✔ **Vendor solutions:** These include software solutions that are implemented in your technology infrastructure.

For example, to achieve defense in depth, an organization might deploy antivirus software from one vendor on servers and a completely different vendor's antivirus software on user workstations.

Although using multiple solutions increases the management burden for these systems (different support issues and requirements, incompatible logs, and so on), it does produce a blended, dense, diverse defense — and typically helps to eliminate single points of failure. In short, a security posture that doesn't rely on any single vendor or solution is more likely to be a successful one.

See Chapter 7 for more on defense in depth.

Data Classification

You must understand the purpose of a data classification scheme, and be familiar with commercial data classification criteria and the government data classification scheme.

Information and data, in all their various forms, are valuable business assets. As with other, more tangible assets, the information's value determines the level of protection required by the organization. Applying a single protection standard uniformly across all an organization's assets is neither practical nor desirable.

A data classification scheme helps an organization assign a value to its information assets based on its sensitivity to loss or disclosure, as well as determine the appropriate level of protection. Additionally, data classification schemes may be required for regulatory or other legal compliance.

An organization's employees also need to understand the classification schema being used, how to classify information assets, handling and safeguarding requirements, and proper destruction or disposal procedures.

Commercial data classification

Commercial data classification schemes are typically implemented to protect information that has a monetary value, to comply with applicable laws and protect privacy, and to limit liability. Criteria by which commercial data is classified include

✔ **Value:** The most common classification criterion in commercial organizations. It's based on monetary value or some other intrinsic value.

✔ **Age/useful life:** Information that loses value over time, becomes obsolete or irrelevant, or becomes common/public knowledge is classified this way.

✔ **Regulatory requirements:** Private information, such as medical records subject to HIPAA (Health Insurance Portability and Accountability Act of 1996) and HITECH (Health Information Technology for Economic and Clinical Health Act) regulations and educational records subject to the Privacy Act (see Chapter 12), may have legal requirements for protection. Classification of such information may be based not only on compliance but also on liability limits.

Descriptive labels are often applied to company information, such as *Confidential and Proprietary* and *Internal Use Only*. However, the organizational requirements for protecting information labeled as such are often not formally defined or are unknown. Organizations should formally identify standard classification levels as well as specific requirements for labeling, handling, storage, and destruction/disposal.

Government data classification

Government data classification schemes are generally implemented to

✔ Protect national interests or security.

✔ Comply with applicable laws.

✔ Protect privacy.

One of the more common systems, used within the U.S. Department of Defense (DoD), consists of five broad categories for information classification: Unclassified, Sensitive but Unclassified (SBU), Confidential, Secret, and Top Secret. (We discuss all these categories in the following sections.)

Within each classification level, certain safeguards are required in the use, handling, reproduction, transport, and destruction of Defense Department information. In addition to having an appropriate clearance level at or above the level of information being processed, individuals must have a need to know before they can access the information. Those who need to know are those who require the information so as to perform an assigned job function.

Unclassified

The lowest government data classification level is unclassified. *Unclassified* information isn't sensitive, and unauthorized disclosure won't cause any harm to national security. Unclassified information may include information that was once classified at a higher level but has since been declassified by an appropriate authority. Unclassified information isn't automatically releasable to the public and may include additional modifiers such as *For Official Use Only* or *For Internal Use Only*.

Sensitive but Unclassified (SBU)

Sensitive but Unclassified information is a common modifier of unclassified information. It generally includes information of a private or personal nature. Examples include test questions, disciplinary proceedings, and medical records.

Confidential

Confidential information is information that, if compromised, could cause damage to national security. Confidential information is the lowest level of classified government information.

Secret

Secret information is information that, if compromised, could cause *serious* damage to national security. Secret information must normally be accounted for throughout its life cycle, all the way to its destruction.

Top Secret

Top Secret information is information that, if compromised, could cause grave damage to national security. Top Secret information may require additional safeguards, such as special designations and handling restrictions.

Mission Statements, Goals, and Objectives

As a CISSP candidate, you must understand the differences and relationships between an organization's mission statement, goals, and objectives. You should also know how these elements can affect the organization's information security policies and program.

Mission (not-so-impossible)

Corny heading, yes, but there's a good chance you're humming the *Mission Impossible* theme song now — mission accomplished!

An organization's *mission statement* expresses its reason for existence. A good mission statement is an easily understood, general-purpose statement that says what the organization is, what it does, and why it exists, doing what it does in the way that it has chosen. The mission statement is sometimes referred to as a *company philosophy* or a *vision statement.*

Goals and objectives

A *goal* is something (or many somethings) that an organization hopes to accomplish. A goal should be consistent with the organization's mission statement or philosophy, and it should help define a vision for the organization. It should also whip people into a wild frenzy, running around their offices, waving their arms in the air, and yelling "GOOOAAALLL!" (Well, maybe only if they're World Cup fans.)

An *objective* is a milestone or a specific result that is expected and, as such, helps an organization attain its goals and achieve its mission.

Organizations often use the terms *goals* and *objectives* interchangeably without distinction. Worse yet, some organizations refer to goals as long-term objectives, and objectives as short-term goals! For our purposes, an *objective* (short-term) supports a *goal* (intermediate-term), which supports a *mission* (long-term).

Policies, Standards, Guidelines, and Procedures

Policies, standards, guidelines, and procedures are all subtly different from each other, but they also interact with each other in a variety of ways. It's your job as a CISSP candidate to study these differences and relationships, and also to recognize the different types of policies and their applications. To successfully develop and implement information security policies, standards, guidelines, and procedures, you must ensure that your efforts are consistent with the organization's mission, goals, and objectives (see the preceding sections).

Policies, standards, guidelines, and procedures all work together as the blueprints for a successful information security program. They

- ✔ Establish governance.
- ✔ Provide valuable guidance and decision support.
- ✔ Help establish legal authority.

Too often, technical security solutions are implemented without these important blueprints. The results are often expensive and ineffective controls that aren't uniformly applied and don't support an overall security strategy.

Governance is a term that collectively represents the system of policies, standards, guidelines, and procedures that help steer an organization's day-to-day operations and decisions.

Policies

A *security policy* forms the basis of an organization's information security program. RFC 2196, *The Site Security Handbook,* defines a security policy as "a formal statement of rules by which people who are given access to an organization's technology and information assets must abide."

The four main types of policies are

- ✔ **Senior Management:** A high-level management statement of an organization's security objectives, organizational and individual responsibilities, ethics and beliefs, and general requirements and controls.
- ✔ **Regulatory:** Highly detailed and concise policies usually mandated by federal, state, industry, or other legal requirements.
- ✔ **Advisory:** Not mandatory, but highly recommended, often with specific penalties or consequences for failure to comply. Most policies fall into this category.
- ✔ **Informative:** Only informs, with no explicit requirements for compliance.

Standards, guidelines, and procedures are supporting elements of a policy and provide specific implementation details of the policy.

ISO/IEC 27002 (formerly ISO 17799), *Information Technology — Security Techniques — Code of Practice for Information Security Management,* is an international standard for information security policy originally based on BS (British Standard) 7799. ISO/IEC is the International Organization for Standardization and International Electrotechnical Commission. ISO/IEC 27002 consists of 12 sections that largely (but not completely) overlap the ten (ISC)[2] security domains.

Standards (and baselines)

Standards are specific, mandatory requirements that further define and support higher-level policies. For example, a standard may require the use of a specific technology, such as a minimum requirement for encryption of sensitive data using 3DES. A standard may go so far as to specify the exact brand, product, or protocol to be implemented.

Baselines are similar to and related to standards. A baseline can be useful for identifying a consistent basis for an organization's security architecture, taking into account system-specific parameters, such as different operating systems. After consistent baselines are established, appropriate standards can be defined across the organization.

Guidelines

Guidelines are similar to standards but they function as recommendations rather than as compulsory requirements. For example, a guideline may provide tips or recommendations for determining the sensitivity of a file and whether encryption is required.

Procedures

Procedures provide detailed instructions on how to implement specific policies and meet the criteria defined in standards. Procedures may include Standard Operating Procedures (SOPs), run books, and user guides. For example, a procedure may be a step-by-step guide for encrypting sensitive files by using a specific software encryption product.

Information Security Governance Practices

We introduce several common information security governance practices in the following sections and describe them in greater detail in other chapters (conveniently cross-referenced, of course!).

Third-party governance

Organizations commonly outsource many IT functions (particularly call-center or contact-center support and application development) today. Information security policies and procedures must address outsourcing security and the use of vendors or consultants, when appropriate. Access control, document exchange and review, maintenance hooks, on-site assessment, process and policy review, and service level agreements (SLAs) are good examples of outsourcing security considerations.

Service-level agreements (SLAs)

Service-level agreements (SLAs) establish minimum performance standards for a system, application, network, or service. An organization establishes internal SLAs to provide its end-users with a realistic expectation of the performance of its information systems and services. For example, a help desk SLA might prioritize incidents as 1, 2, 3, and 4, and establish SLA response times of ten minutes, 1 hour, 4 hours, and 24 hours, respectively. In third-party relationships, SLAs provide contractual performance requirements that an outsourcing partner or vendor must meet. For example, an SLA with an Internet service provider might establish a maximum acceptable downtime which, if exceeded within a given period, results in invoice credits or (if desired) cancellation of the service contract.

See Chapter 7 for more on Service Level Agreements.

Identity management

Identity management is accomplished through account provisioning and de-provisioning (creating and disabling user accounts), access control, and directory services. Its purpose is to identify a subject or object (see "Uncovering Concepts of Access Control" in Chapter 4) within an application, system, or network.

A Public Key Infrastructure (PKI) is an example of a component of an identity management system that facilitates authentication, non-repudiation, and access control, using digital certificates.

See Chapter 4 for more on identity management, and see Chapter 8 for a complete discussion of PKI.

Personnel Security Policies and Practices

CISSP candidates must have a basic understanding of various employment policies and practices, as well as how these policies achieve information security objectives. You should also know the various information security roles and responsibilities within an organization.

We also discuss various components of personnel security in Chapter 9.

Background checks and security clearances

Pre- and post-employment background checks can provide an employer with valuable information about an individual whom an organization is considering for a job or position within an organization. Such checks can give an immediate indication of an individual's integrity and can help screen out unqualified applicants.

Basic background checks should be conducted for all personnel with access to sensitive information or systems within an organization. A basic background check should include

- ✔ **Reference checks:** Personal, professional, and employment
- ✔ **Verification of data in employment applications and resumes:** Social Security numbers, education, professional/technical certifications, military records, and previous employment
- ✔ **Other records:** Court, local law enforcement, and motor vehicle records

Personnel who fill sensitive positions should undergo a more extensive pre-employment screening and background check, possibly including

- ✔ **Credit records**
- ✔ **Drug testing**
- ✔ **Special background investigation:** FBI and INTERPOL records, field interviews with former associates, or a personal interview with a private investigator

Periodic post-employment screenings (such as credit records and drug testing) may also be necessary, particularly for personnel with access to financial data, cash, or high-value assets, or for personnel being considered for promotions to more sensitive or responsible positions.

Employment agreements

Various employment agreements should be signed when an individual joins an organization or is promoted to a more sensitive position within an organization. Typical employment agreements include non-compete/non-disclosure agreements and acceptable use policies.

Hiring and termination practices

Hiring and termination practices should be formalized within an organization to ensure fair and uniform treatment and to protect the organization and its information assets.

Standard hiring practices should include background checks and employment agreements (as we discuss in the preceding sections), as well as a formal indoctrination and orientation process. This process may include formal introductions to key organizational personnel, creating user accounts and assigning IT resources (PCs and notebook computers, for example), assigning security badges and parking permits, and a general policy discussion with Human Resources personnel.

Formal termination procedures should be implemented to help protect the organization from potential lawsuits, property theft and destruction, unauthorized access, or workplace violence. Procedures should be developed for various scenarios including resignations, termination, layoffs, accident or death, immediate departures versus prior notification, and hostile situations. Termination procedures may include

- Having the former employee surrender keys, security badges, and parking permits
- Conducting an exit interview
- Making security escort the former employee to collect his or her personal belongings and/or to leave the premises
- Asking the former employee to return company materials (notebook computers, mobile phones and devices, PDAs, and so on)
- Changing door locks and system passwords
- Formally turning over duties and responsibilities
- Removing network and system access and disabling user accounts
- Enforcing policies regarding retention of e-mail, personal files, and employment records
- Notifying customers, partners, vendors, and contractors, as appropriate

Job descriptions

Concise job descriptions that clearly identify an individual's responsibility and authority, particularly on information security issues, can help

- Reduce confusion and ambiguity.
- Provide legal basis for an individual's authority or actions.

✔ Demonstrate any negligence or dereliction in carrying out assigned duties.

Security roles and responsibilities

The truism that information security is "everyone's responsibility" is too often put into practice as *Everyone is responsible, but no one is accountable.* To avoid this pitfall, specific roles and responsibilities for information security should be defined in an organization's security policy, individual job or position descriptions, and third-party contracts. These roles and responsibilities should apply to employees, consultants, contractors, interns, and vendors. And they should apply to every level of staff, from C-level executives to line employees. Several broad categories for information security roles and common responsibilities are discussed in the following sections.

Management

Senior-level management is often responsible for information security at several levels, including the role as an information owner, which we discuss in the following section. However, in this context, management has a responsibility to demonstrate a strong commitment to an organization's information security program through the following actions:

✔ **Creating a corporate information security policy:** This policy should include a statement of support from management and should also be signed by the CEO, COO, or CIO.

✔ **Leading by example:** A CEO who refuses to carry a mandatory identification badge or who bypasses system access controls sets a poor example.

✔ **Rewarding compliance:** Management should expect proper security behavior and acknowledge, recognize, and/or reward employees accordingly.

Management is always ultimately responsible for an organization's overall information security and for any information security decisions that are made (or not made). Our role as information security professionals is to report security issues and to make appropriate information security recommendations to management.

Owner

An information owner is normally assigned at an executive or senior-management level within an organization, such as director or vice-president. An information owner doesn't legally own the information assigned to him or her; the information owner is ultimately responsible for safeguarding assigned information assets and may have fiduciary responsibility or be held personally liable for negligence in protecting these assets under the concept of due care.

For more on due care, read Chapter 12.

Typical responsibilities of an information owner may include

- Determining information classification levels for assigned information assets
- Determining policy for access to the information
- Maintaining inventories and accounting for assigned information assets
- Periodically reviewing classification levels of assigned information assets for possible downgrading, destruction, or disposal
- Delegating day-to-day responsibility (but not accountability) and functions to a custodian

Custodian

An *information custodian* is the individual who has day-to-day responsibility for protecting information assets. IT systems administrators or network administrators often fill this role. Typical responsibilities may include

- Performing regular backups and restoring data, when necessary
- Ensuring that directory and file permissions are properly implemented and provide sufficient protection
- Assigning new users to appropriate permission groups and revoking user privileges, when required
- Maintaining classified documents or other materials in a vault or secure file room

The distinction between owners and custodians, particularly regarding their different responsibilities, is an important concept in information security management. The information owner has ultimate responsibility for the security of the information, whereas the information custodian is responsible for the day-to-day security administration.

Users

An *end-user* (or *user*) includes just about everyone within an organization. Users aren't specifically designated. They can be broadly defined as anyone who has authorized access to an organization's internal information or information systems. Typical user responsibilities include

✔ Complying with all security requirements defined in organizational policies, standards, and procedures; applicable legislative or regulatory requirements; and contractual requirements (such as non-disclosure agreements and Service Level Agreements).

✔ Exercising due care in safeguarding organizational information and information assets.

✔ Participating in information security training and awareness efforts.

✔ Reporting any suspicious activity, security violations, security problems, or security concerns to appropriate personnel.

Separation of duties and responsibilities

The concept of separation (or segregation) of duties and responsibilities ensures that no single individual has complete authority and control over a critical system or process. This practice promotes security in the following ways:

✔ Reduces opportunity for waste, fraud, or abuse.

✔ Provides two-man control (also called dual-control or two-person integrity).

✔ Reduces dependence on individuals (see the section "Avoiding single points of failure," earlier in this chapter).

Smaller organizations may find this practice difficult to implement because of limited personnel and resources.

Job rotation

Job rotation (or *rotation of duties*) provides another effective security control with many benefits to an organization. Similar to the concept of separation of duties and responsibilities (discussed in the preceding section), job rotations involve regularly transferring key personnel into different positions or departments within an organization. Job rotations benefit an organization in the following ways:

✔ Reduce opportunity for waste, fraud, or abuse.

✔ Reduce dependence, through cross-training opportunities, on individuals, as well as promote professional growth.

✔ Reduce monotony and/or fatigue for individuals.

As with the practice of separation of duties, job rotations can be difficult to implement in smaller organizations.

A side benefit of job rotations is that people are far less likely to commit fraudulent activities, for fear that they will be caught if they are unexpectedly rotated into another position.

Risk Management Concepts

Beyond basic security fundamentals, the concepts of risk management are perhaps the most important and complex part of the information security and risk management domain. The CISSP candidate must fully understand the risk management triple: Quantitative (compared with qualitative) risk assessment methodologies, risk calculations, and safeguard selection criteria and objectives.

The business of information security is all about risk management. A *risk* consists of a threat and a vulnerability of an asset:

- ✓ **Threat:** Any natural or man-made circumstance or event that could have an adverse or undesirable impact, minor or major, on an organizational asset.

- ✓ **Vulnerability:** The absence or weakness of a safeguard in an asset that makes a threat potentially more harmful or costly, more likely to occur, or likely to occur more frequently.

- ✓ **Asset:** A resource, process, product, or system that has some value to an organization and must therefore be protected. Assets may be tangible (computers, data, software, records, and so on) or intangible (privacy, access, public image, ethics, and so on), and those assets may likewise have a tangible value (purchase price) or intangible value (competitive advantage).

Threat × Vulnerability = Risk

The *risk management triple* consists of an asset, a threat, and vulnerability.

Risk can never be completely eliminated. Given sufficient time, resources, motivation, and money, any system or environment, no matter how secure, can eventually be compromised. Some threats or events, such as natural disasters, are entirely beyond our control and are largely unpredictable. Therefore the main goal of risk management is *risk mitigation:* reducing risk to a level that's acceptable to an organization. Risk management consists of three main elements (each treated in an upcoming section):

✔ Identification

✔ Analysis

✔ Risk treatment

Risk identification

A preliminary step in risk management *risk identification* — detecting and defining specific elements of the three components of risk: assets, threats, and vulnerabilities.

The process of risk identification occurs during a *risk assessment*.

Asset valuation

Identifying an organization's assets and determining their value is a critical step in determining the appropriate level of security. The value of an asset to an organization can be both *quantitative* (related to its cost) and *qualitative* (its relative importance). An inaccurate or hastily conducted asset valuation process can have the following consequences:

✔ Poorly chosen or improperly implemented controls

✔ Controls that aren't cost-effective

✔ Controls that protect the wrong asset

A properly conducted asset valuation process has several benefits to an organization:

✔ Supports quantitative and qualitative risk assessments, Business Impact Assessments (BIAs), and security auditing

✔ Facilitates cost-benefit analysis and supports management decisions regarding selection of appropriate safeguards

✔ Can be used to determine insurance requirements, budgeting, and replacement costs

✔ Helps demonstrate due care, thus (potentially) limiting personal liability

Three basic elements used to determine the value of an asset are

✔ **Initial and maintenance costs:** Most often, a tangible dollar value that may include purchasing, licensing, development, maintenance, and support costs.

✔ **Organizational (or internal) value:** Often a difficult and intangible value. It may include the cost of creating, acquiring, and re-creating information, and the business impact or loss if the information is lost or compromised. It can also include liability costs associated with privacy issues, personal injury, and death.

✔ **Public (or external) value:** Another difficult and often intangible cost, public value can include loss of proprietary information or processes, as well as loss of business reputation.

Threat analysis

To perform threat analysis, you follow these four basic steps:

1. **Define the actual threat.**

2. **Identify possible consequences to the organization if the threat event occurs.**

3. **Determine the probable frequency of a threat event.**

4. **Assess the probability that a threat will actually materialize.**

For example, a company that has a major distribution center located along the Gulf Coast of the United States may be concerned about hurricanes. Possible consequences include power outages, wind damage, and flooding. Using climatology, the company can determine that an annual average of three hurricanes pass within 50 miles of its location between June and September, and that a high probability exists of a hurricane actually affecting the company's operations during this period. During the remainder of the year, the threat of hurricanes has a low probability.

The number and types of threats that an organization must consider can be overwhelming, but you can generally categorize them as

✔ **Natural:** Earthquakes, floods, hurricanes, lightning, fire, and so on.

✔ **Man-made:** Unauthorized access, data-entry errors, strikes/labor disputes, theft, terrorism, social engineering, malicious code and viruses, and so on.

Not all threats can be easily or rigidly classified. For example, fires and utility losses can be both natural and man-made. See Chapter 11 for more on disaster recovery.

Vulnerability assessment

A *vulnerability assessment* provides a valuable baseline for determining appropriate and necessary safeguards. For example, an organization may have a Denial of Service (DoS) threat, based on a vulnerability found in Microsoft's implementation of Domain Name System (DNS). However, if an organization's DNS servers have been properly patched or the organization uses a UNIX-based BIND (Berkeley Internet Name Domain) server, the specific vulnerability may already have been adequately addressed, and no additional safeguards may be necessary for that threat.

Risk Analysis (RA)

The next element in risk management is *risk analysis* — a methodical examination that brings together all the elements of risk management (identification, analysis, and control) and is critical to an organization for developing an effective risk management strategy.

A risk analysis involves the following four steps:

1. **Identify the assets to be protected, including their relative value, sensitivity, or importance to the organization.**

   This component of risk identification is asset valuation.

2. **Define specific threats, including threat frequency and impact data.**

   This component of risk identification is threat analysis.

3. **Calculate Annualized Loss Expectancy (ALE).**

   The ALE calculation is a fundamental concept in risk analysis; we discuss this calculation later in this section.

4. **Select appropriate safeguards.**

   This process is a component of both risk identification (vulnerability assessment) and risk control (which we discuss in the section "Risk control," later in this chapter).

The *Annualized Loss Expectancy (ALE)* provides a standard, quantifiable measure of the impact that a realized threat has on an organization's assets. Because it's the estimated annual loss for a threat or event, expressed in dollars, ALE is particularly useful for determining the cost-benefit ratio of a safeguard or control. You determine ALE by using this formula:

$$SLE \times ARO = ALE$$

Here's an explanation of the elements in this formula:

- ✔ **Single Loss Expectancy (SLE):** A measure of the loss incurred from a single realized threat or event, expressed in dollars. You calculate the SLE by using the formula Asset value × Exposure Factor (EF).

  Exposure Factor (EF) is a measure of the negative effect or impact that a realized threat or event would have on a specific asset, expressed as a percentage.

- ✔ **Annualized Rate of Occurrence (ARO):** The estimated annual frequency of occurrence for a threat or event.

The two major types of risk analysis are qualitative and quantitative, which we discuss in the following sections.

Qualitative risk analysis

Qualitative risk analysis is more subjective than a quantitative risk analysis; unlike quantitative risk analysis, this approach to analyzing risk can be purely qualitative and avoid numbers altogether. The challenge of such an approach is developing real scenarios that describe actual threats and potential losses to organizational assets.

Qualitative risk analysis has some advantages when compared with quantitative risk analysis; these include

- ✔ No complex calculations are required.
- ✔ Time and work effort involved is relatively low.
- ✔ Volume of input data required is relatively low.

Disadvantages of qualitative risk analysis, compared with quantitative risk analysis, include

- ✔ No financial costs are defined; therefore cost-benefit analysis isn't possible.
- ✔ The qualitative approach relies more on assumptions and guesswork.
- ✔ Generally, qualitative risk analysis can't be automated.
- ✔ Qualitative analysis is less easily communicated. (Executives seem to understand *"This will cost us $3 million over 12 months"* or *"This could do long-term damage to our brand"* better than *"This will cause an unspecified loss at an undetermined future date."*)

A qualitative risk analysis is scenario-driven and doesn't attempt to assign numeric values to the components (the assets and threats) of the risk analysis.

Quantitative risk analysis

A fully quantitative risk analysis requires all elements of the process, including asset value, impact, threat frequency, safeguard effectiveness, safeguard costs, uncertainty, and probability, to be measured and assigned a numeric value. However, assigning a value to every component associated with a risk (safeguard effectiveness and uncertainty) isn't possible, so you must apply some qualitative measures.

A *quantitative risk analysis* attempts to assign an objective numeric value (cost) to the components (assets and threats) of the risk analysis.

Achieving a purely quantitative risk analysis is impossible.

Advantages of a quantitative risk analysis, compared with qualitative risk analysis, include the following:

- ✔ Financial costs are defined; therefore, cost-benefit analysis is possible.
- ✔ More concise, specific data supports analysis; thus fewer assumptions and less guesswork are required.
- ✔ Analysis and calculations can often be automated.
- ✔ Specific quantifiable results are easier to communicate to executives and senior-level management.

Disadvantages of a quantitative risk analysis, compared with qualitative risk analysis, include the following:

- ✔ Many complex calculations are usually required.
- ✔ Time and work effort involved is relatively high.
- ✔ Volume of input data required is relatively high.
- ✔ Some assumptions are required. Purely quantitative risk analysis is generally not possible or practical.

Risk treatment

A properly conducted risk analysis provides the basis for selecting appropriate safeguards and countermeasures. A *safeguard* is a control or countermeasure that reduces risk associated with a specific threat. The absence of a safeguard against a threat creates vulnerability and increases risk.

Safeguards counter risks through one of four general methods of risk treatment:

✔ **Risk reduction:** Mitigating risk by implementing the necessary security controls, policies, and procedures to protect an asset. This can be achieved by altering, reducing, or eliminating the threat and/or vulnerability associated with the risk.

This is the most common risk control remedy.

✔ **Risk assignment (or transference):** Transferring the potential loss associated with a risk to a third party, such as an insurance company.

✔ **Risk avoidance:** Eliminating the risk altogether through a cessation of the activity or condition that introduced the risk in the first place.

✔ **Risk acceptance:** Accepting the loss associated with a potential risk. This is sometimes done for convenience (not prudent) but more appropriately when the cost of other countermeasures is prohibitive and the potential risk probability is low.

Several criteria for selecting safeguards include cost-effectiveness, legal liability, operational impact, and technical factors.

Cost-effectiveness

The most common criterion for safeguard selection is cost-effectiveness, which is determined through cost-benefit analysis. Cost-benefit analysis for a given safeguard or collection of safeguards can be computed as follows:

ALE before safeguard – ALE after safeguard – Cost of safeguard = Value of safeguard to the organization

For example, if the ALE associated with a specific threat (data loss) is $1,000,000; the ALE after a safeguard (enterprise tape backup) has been implemented is $10,000 (recovery time); and the cost of the safeguard (purchase, installation, training, and maintenance) is $140,000; then the value of the safeguard to the organization is $850,000.

When calculating the cost of the safeguard, you should consider the *total cost of ownership* (TCO), including

✔ Purchase, development, and licensing

✔ Architecture and design

✔ Testing and installation

✔ Normal operating costs

✔ Resource allocation

✔ Maintenance and repair

✔ Production or service disruptions

The total cost of a safeguard is normally stated as an annualized amount.

Legal liability

An organization that fails to implement a safeguard against a threat is exposed to legal liability if the cost to implement a safeguard is less than the loss resulting from a realized threat. The legal liability we're talking about here could encompass statutory liability (as a result of failing to obey the law) or civil liability (as a result of failing to comply with a legal contract). A cost-benefit analysis is a useful tool for determining legal liability.

Operational impact

The operational impact of a safeguard must also be considered. If a safeguard is too difficult to implement and operate, or interferes excessively with normal operations or production, it will be circumvented or ignored and thus not be effective.

Technical factors

The safeguard itself shouldn't introduce new vulnerabilities. For example, improper placement, configuration, or operation of a safeguard can cause new vulnerabilities; lack of fail-safe capabilities, insufficient auditing and accounting features, or improper reset functions can cause asset damage or destruction; finally, covert channel access or other unsafe conditions are technical issues that can create new vulnerabilities.

Security Education, Training, and Awareness Programs

The CISSP candidate should be familiar with the tools and objectives of security awareness, training, and education programs.

Security awareness is an often-overlooked factor in an information security program. Although security is the focus of security practitioners in their day-to-day functions, it's often taken for granted that common users possess this same level of security awareness. As a result, users can unwittingly become the weakest link in an information security program. Several key factors are critical to the success of a security awareness program:

- ✔ **Senior-level management support:** Under ideal circumstances, senior management is seen attending and actively participating in training efforts.

- ✔ **Clear demonstration of how security supports the organization's business objectives:** Employees need to understand why security is important to the organization and how it benefits the organization as a whole.

✔ **Clear demonstration of how security affects all individuals and their job functions:** The awareness program needs to be relevant for everyone, so that everyone understands that "security is everyone's responsibility."

✔ **Taking into account the audience's current level of training and understanding of security principles:** Training that's too basic will be ignored; training that's too technical will not be understood.

✔ **Action and follow-up:** A glitzy presentation that's forgotten as soon as the audience leaves the room is useless. Find ways to incorporate the security information you present with day-to-day activities and follow-up plans.

The three main components of an effective security awareness program are a general awareness program, formal training, and education.

Awareness

A *general security awareness program* provides basic security information and ensures that everyone understands the importance of security. Awareness programs may include the following elements:

✔ **Indoctrination and orientation:** New employees and contractors should receive basic indoctrination and orientation. During the indoctrination, they may receive a copy of the corporate information security policy, be required to acknowledge and sign acceptable-use statements and non-disclosure agreements, and meet immediate supervisors and pertinent members of the security and IT staff.

✔ **Presentations:** Lectures, video presentations, and interactive computer-based training (CBTs) are excellent tools for disseminating security training and information. Employee bonuses and performance reviews are sometimes tied to participation in these types of security awareness programs.

✔ **Printed materials:** Security posters, corporate newsletters, and periodic bulletins are useful for disseminating basic information such as security tips and promoting awareness of security.

Training

Formal training programs provide more in-depth information than an awareness program and may focus on specific security-related skills or tasks. Such training programs may include

- ✔ **Classroom training:** Instructor-led or other formally facilitated training, possibly at corporate headquarters or a company training facility

- ✔ **On-the-job training:** May include one-on-one mentoring with a peer or immediate supervisor

- ✔ **Technical or vendor training:** Training on a specific product or technology provided by a third party

- ✔ **Apprenticeship or qualification programs:** Formal probationary status or qualification standards that must be satisfactorily completed within a specified time period

Education

An *education program* provides the deepest level of security training, focusing on underlying principles, methodologies, and concepts.

An education program may include

- ✔ **Continuing education requirements:** Continuing Education Units (CEUs) are becoming popular for maintaining high-level technical or professional certifications such as the CISSP or Cisco Certified Internetworking Expert (CCIE).

- ✔ **Certificate programs:** Many colleges and universities offer adult education programs that have classes about current and relevant subjects for working professionals.

- ✔ **Formal education or degree requirements:** Many companies offer tuition assistance or scholarships for employees enrolled in classes that are relevant to their profession.

Prep Test

1 **The three elements of the C-I-A triad include**

A ○ Confidentiality, integrity, authentication

B ○ Confidentiality, integrity, availability

C ○ Confidentiality, integrity, authorization

D ○ Confidentiality, integrity, accountability

2 **Which of the following government data classification levels describes information that, if compromised, could cause serious damage to national security?**

A ○ Top Secret

B ○ Secret

C ○ Confidential

D ○ Sensitive but Unclassified

3 **The practice of regularly transferring personnel into different positions or departments within an organization is known as**

A ○ Separation of duties

B ○ Reassignment

C ○ Lateral transfers

D ○ Job rotations

4 **The individual responsible for assigning information classification levels for assigned information assets is**

A ○ Management

B ○ Owner

C ○ Custodian

D ○ User

5 **Most security policies are categorized as**

A ○ Informative

B ○ Regulatory

C ○ Mandatory

D ○ Advisory

6 **A baseline is a type of**

A ◯ Policy

B ◯ Guideline

C ◯ Procedure

D ◯ Standard

7 **ALE is calculated by using the following formula:**

A ◯ SLE × ARO × EF = ALE

B ◯ SLE × ARO = ALE

C ◯ SLE + ARO = ALE

D ◯ SLE − ARO = ALE

8 **Which of the following is not considered a general remedy for risk management?**

A ◯ Risk reduction

B ◯ Risk acceptance

C ◯ Risk assignment

D ◯ Risk avoidance

9 **Failure to implement a safeguard may result in legal liability if**

A ◯ The cost to implement the safeguard is less than the cost of the associated loss.

B ◯ The cost to implement the safeguard is more than the cost of the associated loss.

C ◯ An alternate but equally effective and less expensive safeguard is implemented.

D ◯ An alternate but equally effective and more expensive safeguard is implemented.

10 **A cost-benefit analysis is useful in safeguard selection for determining**

A ◯ Safeguard effectiveness

B ◯ Technical feasibility

C ◯ Cost-effectiveness

D ◯ Operational impact

Answers

1 **B.** Confidentiality, integrity, availability. Confidentiality, integrity, and availability are the three elements of the C-I-A triad. Authentication, authorization, and accountability are access control concepts. *Review "Information Security Governance Concepts and Principles."*

2 **B.** Secret. Top Secret information leaks could cause *grave damage*. Confidential information breaches could cause *damage*. Sensitive but Unclassified information doesn't have a direct impact on national security. *Review "Government data classification."*

3 **D.** Job rotations. Separation of duties is related to job rotations, but is distinctly different. Reassignment and lateral transfers are functionally equivalent to job rotations but aren't necessarily done for the same reasons and aren't considered security employment practices. *Review "Job rotations."*

4 **B.** Owner. Although an information owner may be in a management position and also considered a user, the information owner role has the responsibility for assigning information classification levels. An information custodian is responsible for day-to-day security tasks. *Review "Security roles and responsibilities."*

5 **D.** Advisory. Although not mandatory, advisory policies are highly recommended and may provide penalties for failure to comply. *Review "Policies."*

6 **D.** Standard. A baseline takes into account system-specific parameters to help an organization identify appropriate standards. *Review "Standards (and baselines)."*

7 **B.** SLE × ARO = ALE. SLE × ARO = ALE is the correct formula for calculating ALE, where SLE is the Single Loss Expectancy, ARO is the Annualized Rate of Occurrence, and ALE is the Annualized Loss Expectancy (expressed in dollars). *Review "Risk analysis."*

8 **D.** Risk avoidance. Although risk avoidance is a valid concept, it's impossible to achieve and therefore not considered a general remedy for risk management. *Review "Risk control."*

9 **A.** The cost to implement the safeguard is less than the cost of the associated loss. This basic legal liability test determines whether the cost of the safeguard is less than the cost of the associated loss if a threat event occurs. *Review "Legal liability."*

10 **C.** Cost-effectiveness. A cost-benefit analysis can't help an organization determine the effectiveness of a safeguard, its technical feasibility, or its operational impact. *Review "Cost-effectiveness."*

Chapter 7

Software Development Security

The Software Security domain introduces many important concepts that overlap with other CBK domains.

You must fully understand the principles of software, software development, software vulnerabilities, and databases. Software and data are the foundation of information processing; software can't exist apart from software development. An understanding of the software development process is essential for the creation and maintenance of software that's appropriate, reliable, and secure. After all, if you don't understand how information systems work, how can you be expected to know how to protect them?

Additionally, the CISSP candidate must understand how malicious code works, how hackers attack systems, and how to stop malicious users. Security professionals should be familiar with these issues so they can guide software developers to create software that strengthens and defends systems and applications against attacks.

The scope of this domain applies to all types of software, including applications, operating systems, utilities, and even embedded systems.

Distributed Applications

Applications escaped the well-controlled computer-room environment in the early 1980s with the advent of personal computers and networks. Perhaps it was the computer operators' white lab coats, the pocket protectors, or the horn-rimmed glasses, but applications couldn't take it anymore. They needed a break and wanted a life. Can you blame them?

While application technology developed, we saw smart terminals that had field editing capabilities (cough . . . most of you readers weren't yet *born* when these terminals were prevalent) and, later on, two-tier and three-tier client-server applications in which some of the application logic ran on a server and some of it ran on a PC. Client-server technology looked really good on paper (and on those fancy new whiteboards), but it never measured up to its potential.

Then in 1990-1993, Eric Bina, Marc Andreesson, Tim Berners-Lee, and Robert Cailliau developed the hypertext transfer protocol (HTTP) and the first popular web browser called *Mosaic,* which sported such features as hyper-links and web pages that contained pictures *and* text. Thousands of people downloaded Mosaic, which was available for PC, Mac, and UNIX-based operating systems. *Distributed applications* (applications made up of distinct components on networked computers) were on the rise, and the Web was cool and really fast — until the general public found out about it and ruined it. Seriously, though, a lot of neat and relevant technologies were born out of the Web, many of which we discuss in this chapter.

In effect, the Web was the death-knell for client-server applications and other legacy application technologies.

A *distributed application* is an application that consists of components that reside on separate, networked systems.

Security in distributed systems

Securing distributed systems is anything but easy, and it boils down to three distinct issues:

✔ **Software integrity:** In a distributed system, the application may consist of software components located on various systems located in different physical locations, some of which may be owned or managed by other parties. Hundreds (or even thousands) of workstations may exist on the system, and all must have the right version of client software. Keeping track of the versions of all these separate components can be a night-mare, particularly if different parts of the organization (or even different companies!) support the various hardware platforms. Imagine the sce-nario if, a few days after a new release of an application is installed on all the systems, one of those systems suffers a catastrophic failure and must be rebuilt from backups — or if a new software release proves dif-ficult to install properly on many workstations. Not our idea of a fun day.

✔ **Data integrity:** The data in a distributed system may reside in many physical locations. And with advanced technologies such as data replication and cloud computing, the data often resides in *many* locations at the same time, introducing new problems. How, for instance, do you make sure that the data in these different locations remains accurate and in sync? Say you make a set of backup tapes before an application upgrade and you have a hardware platform that runs an older version of some part of the application. Perhaps the changes in the application upgrade were subtle, but they can be devastating. For example, now every customer's middle name has been changed to *Celine.* (Royalty checks not included.)

✔ **Access control:** All those distributed components need to talk with each other via the networks that connect them. Most easily, you can have the systems just talk with each other with full and complete trust. Well, Kevin Mitnick (cyber-criminal turned quasi-celebrity), Robert Morris (of the infamous 1988 Morris Worm), and scores of other infamous characters taught us that trusting everybody isn't such a great idea, so the best approach is to make the various components in a distributed environment prove their identity to one another. This means setting up some sort of authentication, access control, or maybe even a full-blown Kerberos environment so that the various parts of a distributed application know that the other parts they're talking to are the real deal and not hackers looking for credit card numbers to steal. It's enough for the over-55 set to wish for green-screens and mainframes again.

Distributed systems were a great idea at the time, but the tradeoff between offloading application logic from centralized servers and the additional complexity in the distributed environment didn't pan out very well. It was a stepping-stone on the path of progress; thankfully we didn't stay there very long.

But wait! Distributed systems have made a huge comeback in the form of mobile apps. Now, users will install and use applications in devices such as tablet computers and smartphones. These applications communicate with other systems: application servers, database servers, and even other devices.

The rise in popularity of mobile apps once again proves that, given enough time, almost anything once rejected will be back in style.

Working with agents in distributed systems

An *agent* is a software component in a distributed system that performs a particular service. An example of an agent might be a system that takes a credit card number (with expiration date, customer name, purchase amount, and so on) and builds a merchant transaction to send to the bank. The agent processes the transaction and gives a yea or nay response back to the main application, which then gives the customer placing the order on the Web the good or bad news.

Today, you most often see agents in systems management software rather than in business applications. Several examples of agents include

- **Patch management:** An agent determines what patches are installed on a server and facilitates the installation or removal of patches. A central management console controls the whole process.

- **Host-based intrusion detection systems (HIDSs):** Agents use various means to detect signs of attempted tampering and send alarm messages to a central console, which alerts personnel about potentially serious events.

- **Performance and capacity monitoring:** Agents periodically measure the utilization of computer resources such as CPU time, memory, and disk space.

An *agent* is a component in a distributed system that performs a particular function.

Adding applets to the mix

An *applet* is a component in a distributed environment that's downloaded and executed by a web browser. Web browsers, which are designed to display text and graphics, and also to accept data input from users on forms, can't process information locally on the client system very effectively, so applets were invented to solve this problem and enrich the user's web-surfing experience.

The neat thing about applets is that they run seamlessly right in a web browser, and you can't even tell whether an applet is running or you're just dealing with straight HTML. Ignorance is bliss.

The two most popular environments for applets are Java and ActiveX. Java code runs in a constrained environment called a *sandbox*, which means the Java code can communicate only with the host from which it was downloaded. Java can also display things on the screen and accept keyboard or mouse input. However, Java applets can't access a PC's hard drive, memory, or any other devices. Web browsers today get a lot of practice saying to Java applets, "Go play in your sandbox and leave my hard drive alone!" And rarely do Java applets escape from their sandboxes. Personally, we think they're surrounded by the digital equivalent of razor wire.

ActiveX, which is really just a cool name for *OLE over the Internet,* is Microsoft's "not invented here" response to Java. ActiveX uses a completely different security philosophy than Java, and it goes something like this: People running web browsers get to decide whether they trust *all* ActiveX applets that come from a particular server. Digital certificates prove whether the ActiveX applet is genuine.

A rogue developer can write some pretty nasty ActiveX code that (say) melts your hard drive and plays old Alice Cooper songs through your PC's speakers. ActiveX has no concept of a sandbox. If you trust the server that the ActiveX applet comes from, then you're basically saying that you give *all* control of your PC over to the ActiveX applet, and it can do *whatever it wants*. This setup is all fine and good in an ideal world (for a 3-mile radius around Redmond, Washington) where everyone is trustworthy. In the real world, though, programmers who have an attitude — or even honest and ethical programmers who make a mistake — can permit bad things to happen to your system. Always turn down your speaker volume before running ActiveX applets — unless you're in a closed room or you *really like* Alice Cooper.

Administrators can configure many proxy servers to filter out ActiveX applets (and most administrators put in extra hours to do this). You can also configure web browsers to not run Java or ActiveX applets, but the last time that we checked, users can just change this setting back so that they can see their stock tickers or the cool pictures at `www.time.gov`. Enterprises that are serious about protecting themselves — even at the expense of disabling some cool websites — really need to block ActiveX applets at the firewall or proxy server.

Applets are also known as *mobile code* because they're downloaded from a server and run on a client.

Web 2.0

The cumulative innovation of interactive information sharing, communities, mashups, web services, wikis, blogs, and other web features is collectively called Web 2.0. In Web 2.0, applications are far more collaborative and distributed, utilizing features on other websites to create truly creative user experiences.

Assessing the security of some Web 2.0 applications is, how shall we say, complicated. A lot of *really serious* business applications heavily utilize Web 2.0 features. CISSPs will have their work cut out for them as they pursue data protection, data sharing, and privacy in the new web world.

Closely related to the development and adoption of Web 2.0 applications is the trend known as *consumerization*, which Gartner (a well-known research firm found at `www.gartner.com`) predicts will be the most significant IT trend through 2015. Consumerization occurs as users increasingly find personal technology and applications that are more convenient, less expensive, quicker to install, and easier to use, than corporate IT solutions. Common examples include Google Docs, various mobile applications, and web-based e-mail. Web 2.0 applications often blur the traditional "black or white" distinctions between business and personal use, and as our work and personal lives become more commingled, users are practically demanding that these same tools be available to them in the workplace.

Another interesting use of applets is the *mashup,* which is a web page or application that combines functionality from external applications through their published application programming interfaces (APIs). Online maps that display locations which come from a different online application implement mashups. You can see an example of a mashup application — one that shows real estate listings superimposed on an interactive map — in Figure 7-1.

Figure 7-1: A mashup web application.

Object-Oriented Environments

Offering some much-needed competition to distributed systems, object-oriented applications have their foundation based in a completely different approach to information systems and processes — one based on *objects* and *reusability* (yes, it really is more environmentally friendly to recycle old computer code). Object orientation is an entire computing universe, comprising object-oriented analysis, design, programming, and even databases.

The object-oriented religion is based on a fundamental principle: Objects, after they're written, can be reused again and again, thereby making the enterprise's entire software development effort more and more efficient over time.

Object orientation is known as *OO,* pronounced *oh-oh* (not *uh-oh*).

An object is *encapsulated,* which means that the inner workings of an object are hidden and can remain so. Objects communicate with each other by using messages. When an object receives a message, it performs whatever function it was designed to do, which is its *method.*

An object that's running is an *instance.* The process of starting an instance is *instantiation.* But an *instance* can also refer to an object that's a member of a class of objects. For example, a chocolate cake recipe is a *method,* and a cake that has been baked using the recipe is an *instance* of the recipe.

As you can see, OO has quite a vocabulary, and you haven't seen half of it yet. But now you can be sure that when you hear a couple of guys talking about someone's objects *(ahem),* you have the secret decoder ring to know that they're computer-science types, probably even hip web developers.

If you're tiring of reading about OO terms buried in paragraphs, here they are in a little glossary:

- **Behavior:** The results of an object having received a message.

- **Class:** In his book *Business Engineering with Object Technology* (Wiley), author David Taylor describes a class as "a template that defines the methods and variables to be included in a particular type of object." The class itself contains the common methods and variables, and objects in the class contain only those characteristics that make them unique. OO also includes *subclasses* (parts of a class) and *superclasses* (collections of classes).

  An example of a class is the class `Cake`. From this class, an object called `Chocolate Cake` can be created. Also, objects such as `Bundt Cake`, `Carrot Cake`, `Layer Cake`, and `Cup Cake` are objects in the class `Cake`. The methods associated with these objects describe the unique details of each type of cake. The method associated with each type could be a recipe for making a cake or for eating a cake (we prefer the latter).

- **Class hierarchy:** The tree structure of a collection of objects and classes.

- **Delegation:** What happens when an object receives a message requesting a method that it doesn't have. The object delegates the message to the object that does contain the requested method.

- **Encapsulation:** The packaging of an object. Everything inside the object is hidden, or encapsulated.

- **Inheritance:** An object that gets some of its characteristics from a class. An object inherits characteristics from the class when it's instantiated. (It doesn't have to wait for the class to grow old and die.)

- **Instance:** A particular object that's a member of a class.

- **Message:** How objects communicate with one another. A message contains the name of an object to which it wants to communicate, the method it should perform, and usually one or more parameters. The object sending the message is the sender; the object receiving it is the receiver.

- **Method:** The procedure (code) contained in an object.

Objective trivia

Object orientation has its roots in two programming languages: Simula and Smalltalk. Simula was developed in the 1960s, and Smalltalk in the early 1970s. C++ was developed at AT&T Bell Laboratories in the early 1980s as an add-on to the popular C language, which was also developed at Bell Labs. You can find many newer OO languages, including C# (pronounced C-sharp; not D-flat), Java/JavaScript, Perl, PHP, Ruby, ColdFusion, Groovy, and Python.

✔ **Multiple inheritance:** When an object or class inherits characteristics from more than one class.

✔ **Object:** The basic unit in OO.

✔ **Polyinstantiation:** The process of developing one object from another object, but with different values in the new object.

✔ **Polymorphism:** Taylor describes this as "the ability to hide implementation details behind a common message interface." This permits new objects to be added to a system without having to rewrite existing procedures.

Databases

A *database* is a mechanism used to define, store, and manipulate data. It contains data used by one or more applications, as well as a programming and command interface used to create, manage, and administer data. In many modern software applications, database management systems exist on a server that is logically or physically separate from the server containing the application programs.

CROSS-REFERENCE

DBMSs (database management systems) generally contain an access-control mechanism used to protect data and permit only certain users, or classes of users, to view or modify data residing in certain portions of the database. We describe access control mechanisms in databases more fully in Chapter 4.

The three most common types of databases in use today are *relational databases, hierarchical databases,* and *object-oriented databases.*

Database security

The *granularity* of access control means how finely you can control who can see and manipulate data in which databases, tables, rows, and fields. An example of low granularity is Read or Read/Write access to all rows and fields in a table. High granularity restricts access to certain fields and even certain rows. High granularity means that either the database administrator (good if this isn't you) or the security administrator (bad if this is you) has to work a lot of extra hours managing all those permissions.

You can employ views to simplify security issues. A *view* is a virtual table that consists of the rows and fields from one or more tables in the database. Then, you give users access to these views, rather than to the actual tables. You can manage this setup really easily, meaning that the database administrator or security administrator can manage security with somewhat higher granularity and still have a life.

Aggregation is a matter of serious concern from a security and privacy perspective. *Aggregation* refers to the process of combining low-sensitivity data items together, resulting in high-sensitivity data. Consider this example: If you get Conan O'Brien's home address from one database, his Social Security Number from another, his driver's license number from another, and his date of birth from yet another, then you have some potentially damaging — or valuable — information. Add a diabolical, hungry mind, some motivation, and soon you're buying Brooks Brothers suits and driving shiny red Italian sports cars, all "courtesy of" Conan O'Brien. If you still don't get it, we're talking about *identity theft* here. By themselves, dates of birth or a home address don't mean a lot, but put them together, you've got something. That's the power — and risk — of aggregation.

The term *aggregation* refers to the process of combining separate low-sensitivity data items to produce a high-sensitivity data item.

We'd be remiss if we didn't mention *inference*. This concept refers to the ability of someone to deduce or infer something about sensitive information that's beyond normal reach because of its sensitivity level. For example, an application that cites the existence of highly sensitive information will make users (and potential intruders) think that there is a treasure trove of data waiting to be stolen.

Data dictionaries

A *data dictionary* is a database of databases. In a large application that has many tables (some applications have *hundreds* of tables), a data dictionary exists as a database that contains all the information about all the tables and fields in a given application. The DBMS, the application, and security tools (such as access control) use a data dictionary. You can use a data dictionary to create or re-create tables, to manage security access, and as a control point for managing the schema of the application's database.

Data warehouses

A *data warehouse* is a special-purpose database that's used for business research, decision support, and planning; comparatively, typical databases support daily business operations.

Why have a data warehouse? Ultimately it's for performance reasons. Every large company has a department full of people who play what-if games with the corporate data — and they get paid for it! For instance, a bank executive may want a list of customers who have more than $35,000 in their checking accounts who haven't made any deposits in the past month and live in the 98039 Zip code. (You know, the Redmond billionaires.) The people in Operations may get a little upset if the VP ties up computer resources combing through the database all day long doing queries on nonindexed fields. The tellers who have to wait 45 seconds for deposits to clear because of all this extra processing might get a little miffed, too.

The point is that the company's main production database isn't the place for the what-iffers to go play (okay, work). You can tune the database for *inserts and updates* (activities typical in regular production databases) or large *queries* (activities typical of data warehouses), but not both. These two activities require opposite tuning settings in the database. They don't get along. Here's an analogy: If you want to drive fast, pick the sports car; if you want to haul stuff, choose the pickup truck. Use the right tool for the right job. The same goes for business data processing versus research and forecasting.

The old-school term for the game that what-iffers play with scenarios is *decision support.* These folks try to figure out trends about their customers, their business activities, or what-have-you, in order to support strategic decisions. The new fancy-pants terms for decision support are *data mining* and *business intelligence.* Data mining should conjure up a vivid word-picture of a strip mine where frantic diggers comb through tons of ore for grams of gold, uranium, and kryptonite. Data mining is like that: Executives and business planners do comb through gigabytes of historical data in order to find hard-to-spot and potentially valuable trends that could help them to unlock future value.

Another common application of data mining is fraud detection. Banks and credit card companies sift through mountains of transactions looking for spending trends in individual accounts to sniff out whether someone may have stolen a credit card number from a poorly protected e-commerce company's data warehouse. (Talk about a cruel irony.)

Someone who needed to sell more databases came up with the idea that building a separate database optimized for humongous queries to sustain decision support would, in the end, be better than trying to accommodate production operations and decision support on the same system. History bears this out; data warehouses work pretty well when they're well designed and well managed.

The type of database used for decision support is called a *data warehouse*.

Types of databases

Because designers first developed them over 40 years ago, several types of databases have enjoyed commercial use. These different types of databases refer to various *data architectures*, or methods for organizing data. We describe the more common types in the following sections. Figure 7-2 depicts the types of databases discussed.

Hierarchical database

Data in a hierarchical database is arranged in a tree structure, with parent records at the top of the database, and a hierarchy of child records in successive layers.

One of the most well-known hierarchical databases is IBM's IMS (Information Management System) product, which was first used in the 1960s. IBM mainframes still use IMS widely today.

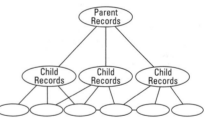

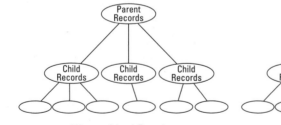

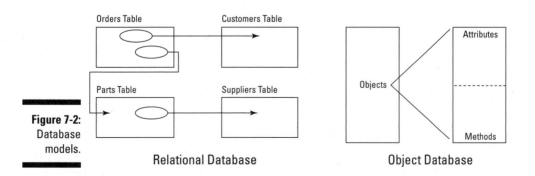

Figure 7-2: Database models.

Network database

Network databases represent an improvement in the design of hierarchical databases. In the hierarchical model, relationships between records are defined by the database's tree structure. In a network database, records can be networked to other records through paths that are different from the hierarchy itself.

Relational database

The designers of hierarchical and network databases were on to something good. Relational databases are the culmination of database design. A relational database has relationships between data sets with the freedom of a network database, but without the constraints of a hierarchical database. Instead, application developers or database administrators customize the relationships between data sets to meet the exact needs of the business.

The structure of a relational database is defined by its *schema*. Records are often called *rows,* and rows are stored in *tables.* A table can have a *primary key,* which is one of the fields in the table that contains a unique value. A primary key permits rapid table *lookups* (queries to find specific records) through binary searches and other data lookup algorithms. An *index* can also be built for any of the other fields in a table, to facilitate more rapid lookups.

One of the most powerful features of a relational database is the use of a *foreign key,* which is a field in a table that points to a primary key in a different table.

Stored procedures are subroutines that can be accessed by software applications. As their name suggests, stored procedures are actually stored in the relational database.

Prepared statements (sometimes called *parameterized* statements) are basically canned statements that can be called by the application.

Both stored procedures and prepared statements can help an application be more resistant to *SQL Injection* attacks.

Distributed database

A *distributed database* is a database whose components exist in multiple physical locations. A distributed database is so named because of its location, not because of its design. A distributed database can be hierarchical, network, relational, object, or any other design.

Object database

An *object database* model is a part of the overall object-oriented application design — the objects in an object database include data records, as well as their methods (application code). Like OO application programming languages, object databases can have classes (data types), instantiations (individual data records), inheritance, and encapsulation.

Object databases are a niche player in the market for database management systems, where relational databases dominate.

Database transactions

A *transaction* is an action that is performed on a database that results in the addition, alteration, or removal of data. An application program performs transactions through function calls, using the database management system's API. One of the advantages of using a database management system is that the software developer can leave the details of data management to the relational database and concentrate on the application's main functions.

The dominant computer language used to manipulate data in a database is Structured Query Language (SQL). Developed in the 1970s, SQL (pronounced SEE-kwul) is used to query a database, update data, define the structure of the database, and perform access management. An application program can dynamically construct SQL statements and pass them to the database management system in order to perform queries or update data.

The principal SQL commands are SELECT (which queries a database by requesting that it return specific records), UPDATE (which changes one or more fields or rows in a table), and INSERT (which adds new rows to a table).

SQL statements can also be grouped together in a transaction, to ensure that all of the statements are executed together, thus guaranteeing the integrity of the database. For example, a business transaction might consist of updates to several tables at the same time, and all the updates must occur — or none of them do — in an all-or-nothing arrangement.

Databases employ a mechanism known as *locking* in order to avoid collisions in which two or more programs may be trying to update the same table or row at the same time. A lock can be placed on a field, an entire row, or an entire table. The database management system manages these locks, and it follows certain rules if parts of a database are locked for a long time.

Knowledge-Based Systems

Also known as *artificial intelligence,* knowledge-based systems are so named because they accumulate knowledge and, with it, the ability to make decisions or predict the future based on knowledge of historical data.

Two well-known types of knowledge-based systems are *expert systems* and *neural networks.* We explain each in the following sections.

Expert systems

Expert systems build a database of past events in order to predict outcomes in future situations. An inference engine analyzes the past events to see whether it can find a match between a past event and the current problem. For instance, if a stock-picking program knows that IBM always goes up two points when the Mets are in town under a full moon, then it tells you to buy IBM when the Mets are in town and the moon is full.

Expert systems are designed to work with degrees of uncertainty, and they do so in one of two ways:

- ✔ **Fuzzy logic:** Breaks down the factors influencing a decision or outcome into its components, evaluates each individual component, and then recombines the individual evaluations in order to arrive at the yes/no or true/false conclusion for the big question or problem.

- ✔ **Certainty factors:** Operate on the numeric probability of yes/no, true/false, rain/snow, or whatever the expert system is working on. The individual probabilities are aggregated, and the final conclusion is reached. For example: Tomorrow it will snow in Buffalo.

Fuzzy logic is the component of an expert system that produces a quantitative result based on uncertainties.

Neural networks

Neural networks mimic the biological function of the brain. If the sum of a set of inputs exceeds a threshold, the neuron fires, or discharges. A neural network accumulates knowledge by observing events; it measures their inputs and outcome. Over time, the neural network becomes proficient at correctly predicting an outcome because it has observed several repetitions of the circumstances and is also told the outcome each time. Then, when confronted with a fresh set of inputs for a new situation, the neural network predicts outcomes with increasing reliability over time.

Neural networks learn that input components are *weighted*, which is to say that their specific degree of influence on the outcome is calculated.

Operating Systems

Operating system (OS) software is a set of programs that manage computer hardware resources and facilitate the use of application programs. Examples of modern operating systems are Linux, Mac OS X, Microsoft Windows, iOS, and Android.

The central component of an operating system is the *kernel*; this is the core software in an operating system that performs the functions listed below. Modern operating systems also have *device drivers*, as well as a selection of tools or *utility* programs that are used to manage and monitor the computer.

The activities carried out by the kernel typically include:

- **Process management.** A running computer operating system typically has several programs running at once. The kernel controls the initiation, execution, and termination of these programs, as well as the allocation of hardware components (such as CPUs, memory, and peripherals) between the running programs.

- **Memory management.** The kernel allocates memory to itself as well as to processes that are running. The kernel responds to processes that request more (or less) memory. Programs are permitted to use only the memory allocated to them; the kernel enforces this restriction.

- **Interrupts.** An *interrupt* is a signal sent to the kernel that directs the kernel to temporarily suspend processing in order to take care of something else. Typically an interrupt comes from one of the computer's hardware components when some event requires attention from the operating system.

- **Hardware resource management.** The kernel manages each process's access to the computer's hardware, including memory, hard disks, network adaptors, and bus adaptors (such as USB and FireWire).

Another important part of the OS is its *device drivers*. These are programs used to permit interaction between the kernel and specific hardware devices that are connected to the computer.

A vital part of the OS is the *user interface*. This is the part of the OS that we lowly humans use to communicate with the computer. The two primary types of user interfaces are

- **Command line.** The *command line* is simple interface controlled by a keyboard. The computer's user types in a command, and the computer responds. OSs that use a command-line interface include Microsoft DOS, and older version of UNIX.

- **Graphical.** This interface divides the screen into "windows"or "panes," typically controlled by a pointing device (such as a mouse or touchpad) and perhaps also a keyboard. OSs that use a graphical interface include Linux, Mac OS, Android, and Microsoft Windows.

Operating systems carry out many security functions on a computer, including

- **Authentication:** Before any local or remote user may access any programs or data, the OS needs to know who is performing the access request. The OS requires that the user identify him or herself, typically by entering a userid and password.

✔ **Access control:** Most OSs control which users are permitted to access resources on the system, such as a printer or scanner.

✔ **Process isolation:** The OS restricts processes by forbidding any process from accessing or modifying memory allocated to any other process. This prevents any process from tampering with other processes.

✔ **Network communication:** The OS includes basic network protocols to facilitate communication to other computers.

✔ **Filesystem access:** The OS restricts access to files and directories in file systems, basing access on permission labels affixed to each file and directory. Only authorized processes may access specific files. This is the mechanism used to restrict users' access to files on workstations and servers.

Operating systems use these controls not only to protect processes and resources, but also to protect themselves. A good OS is resistant to many kinds of attacks, which in turn helps to protect information stored in the system.

Systems Development Life Cycle

The *systems development life cycle* (SDLC, often called the *software development life cycle*) refers to all the steps required to develop a system from conception through implementation, support, and (ultimately) retirement. In other words, we mean the entire life of a system, from birth to death.

The life cycle is a development process designed to achieve two objectives: a system that performs its intended function correctly and securely, and a development project that's completed on time and on budget.

A typical *waterfall model* of system development contains all the steps required to take a project from conception to completion. See an illustration of the waterfall model in Figure 7-3. (We describe other models in the section "Other systems development life cycle models," later in this chapter.)

The waterfall model is so-called because its steps progress like a series of waterfalls. And in a software development project performed using the waterfall model, each of the stages is performed sequentially, one at a time.

In the following sections, we take a look at each of the steps of the waterfall model in detail to understand what happens in each.

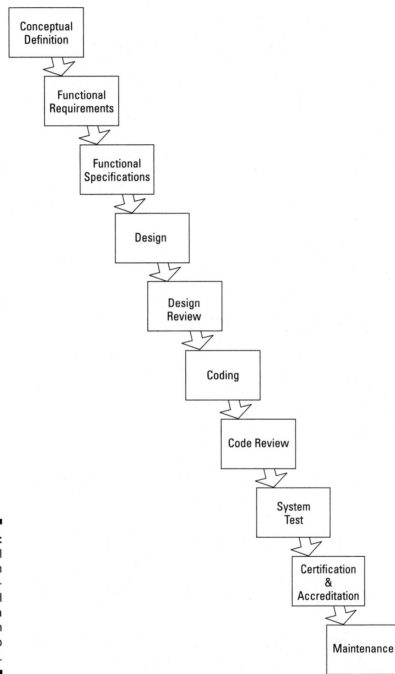

Figure 7-3:
A typical
system
develop-
ment model
takes a
project from
start to
finish.

Conceptual definition

Conceptual definition is a high-level description of a system. It generally contains no details — it's the sort of description that you want to give to the business and finance people (you know, those folks who fund your projects and keep you employed). You don't want to scare them with details.

A typical conceptual definition for the Apple iPad would read something like this: "Attractive, sleek tablet computer, touch-screen controls, crisp high-resolution display, long battery life, holds a wide variety of content that is all sold by Apple."

No detail here is too specific. Conceptual is just that — describing the concept.

Functional requirements

Functional requirements are basically a list of required characteristics of the system. Rather than a design, the functional requirements are a collection of things that the system must do. Continuing the iPad example, some functional requirements would include

- **Weight:** No more than 1 pound
- **Connectivity:** Connects to Internet via WiFi, Bluetooth, Wireless USB, WiMax, and 3G cellular
- **Battery life:** 200 hours
- **Capacity:** 200 GB of data
- **Quality:** DVD-quality audio and video

Although functional requirements don't give you design-level material, this description contains more details than the conceptual definition. The Marketing or Product Concept people come up with these sorts of ideas.

Functional requirements usually include a test plan, which is a detailed list of characteristics of the system that must be tested. The test plan describes how each test should be performed and also what the expected results should be. Generally you have at least one test in the test plan for each requirement in the functional requirements.

Functional requirements must contain expected security requirements for the system.

A proposed system's list of desired features is its *functional requirements*.

Functional specifications

You could call the *functional specifications* the Engineering department's version of functional requirements. Rather than a list of have-to-have and nice-to-have items, the functional specification is more of a what-it-is (we hope) or a what-we-think-we-can-build statement. Continuing our iPad example:

- ✔ **Weight:** 1.5 pounds
- ✔ **Connectivity:** WiFi, Bluetooth, GSM 3G cellular
- ✔ **Battery life:** 10 hours of video playback, 150 hours of audio playback
- ✔ **Capacity:** 8 GB to 64 GB of data
- ✔ **Quality:** DVD-quality video and audio

Functional specifications aren't quite a design, but rather a list of characteristics that Engineering thinks they can create in the real world. Note the compromises on weight and top speed from the preceding section's functional requirements: The people in Marketing didn't get what they wanted (64GB storage capacity and 500 hours of battery life), but then, those folks never do.

From a security perspective, the functional specifications for an operating system or application should contain all the details about authentication, authorization, access control, confidentiality, transaction auditing, integrity, and availability.

Design

Design is the process of developing highest-detail designs. In the application software world, design includes entity-relationship diagrams, data-flow diagrams, database schemas, over-the-wire protocols, and more.

For example, an iPad design review would consist of engineering drawings, bills of materials (a list of all the components required to build one Apple iPad), and building instructions.

Design review

The *design review* is the last step in the design process, in which a group of experts (some of whom are on the design team and some of whom aren't) examine the detailed designs. Those not on the design team give the design a set of fresh eyes and a chance to maybe catch a design flaw or two.

By the time a project is in the design review stage, the marketing people who came up with those wild and crazy specifications are getting a dose of reality; engineers who work on detailed designs sometimes have to "dial back" those initial wish-list specs to something that can actually be built.

Coding

Coding is the phase that the software developers yearn for. Most of them would prefer to skip all the preceding steps (described in the preceding sections) and start coding right away — even before the product people have a chance to develop formal requirements. It's scary to think about how much of the world's software was created with coding as the first activity. (Would you fly in an airplane that the machinists built before the designers could produce engineering drawings?)

Coding usually includes *unit testing,* which is the process of verifying all the modules that are built in this phase.

 Software developers need to follow secure coding practices! The Open Web Application Security Project (OWASP, at `www.owasp.org`) has a really great set of guidelines that members of the software industry generally accept. See the sidebar "The Open Web Applications Security Project," in this chapter, for more details.

Code review

As in the design phase (discussed in the section "Design review," earlier in this chapter), the coding phase ends with a code review in which a bunch of prima donna engineers examine each other's program code and get into religious arguments about levels of indenting and the correct use of curly braces. Seriously, though, during code review, engineers can discover any mistakes that would cost you a lot of money if you had to fix them later in the implementation process or in maintenance mode.

Several good tools exist that you can use to automatically identify security vulnerabilities and other errors in software code. Many organizations use these tools to ferret out programming errors that would otherwise remain and result in vulnerabilities that attackers might exploit.

Unit test

When portions of an application have been developed, it's often possible to test the pieces separately. This is called *unit testing.* Unit testing allows a developer or tester to verify the correct functioning of individual modules in an application.

Unit testing is usually done during coding, and doesn't always show up as a separate step in process diagrams.

System test

A system test occurs when all the components of the entire system have been assembled, and the entire system is tested from *end to end*. The test plan that was developed back in the functional requirements step (see the section "Functional requirements," earlier in this chapter) is carried out here.

Of course, the system test includes testing all the system's security functions because the program's designers included those functions in the test plan.

You can find some great tools available for rigorously testing for vulnerabilities in software applications. Many organizations consider use of such tools a necessary step in system tests so that they can ensure the system has no exploitable vulnerabilities.

The Open Web Application Security Project

The Open Web Application Security Project, or OWASP, has published a short list of security standards that organizations have adopted, most notably the Payment Card Industry Data Security Standard (PCI DSS). The top ten software risks cited by OWASP are

- Injection

- Cross-site scripting (XSS)

- Broken authentication and session management

- Insecure direct object reference

- Cross-site request forgery (CSRF)

- Security misconfiguration

- Insecure cryptographic storage

- Failure to restrict URL access

- Insufficient transport layer protection

- Invalidated redirects and forwards

Items in earlier versions of the OWASP top ten software vulnerabilities include malicious file execution, information leakage and improper error handling, and insecure communications. These are also important security considerations for any software development project.

Removal of these risks makes a software application more robust, reliable, and secure. You can find out more about OWASP — and even join or form a local chapter — by visiting the organization's website at www.owasp.org.

Certification & accreditation

Certification is the formal evaluation of the system. The system is declared fully functional. Every intended feature performs as planned.

Accreditation is a five-dollar word that means the people in the mahogany offices have said that it's okay to put the system into production. That could mean to offer it for sale, build it and ship it, or whatever *put into production* means in your organization.

(ISC)² now offers the Certification and Accreditation Professional (CAP) certification, which you might consider if you want to take accreditation to the next level in your career.

Maintenance

At this point, the system is in production, and now its customers start putting in change requests because of a bunch of boneheaded mistakes made while developing requirements and specifications. Here's where maintenance comes alive. The Change Management and Configuration Management processes (see the following sections) kick into play in order to maintain control of — and document all changes to — the system over its lifetime.

You need good documentation, in the form of those original specification and design documents, because the developers who wrote this system have probably moved on to some other cool project . . . and the new guys who don't know beans are left to maintain it.

Change Management

Change Management is the formal business process that ensures all changes made to a system receive formal review and approval from all stakeholders before implementation. Change Management gives everyone a chance to voice their opinions and concerns about any proposed change so that the change goes as smoothly as possible, with no surprises or interruptions in service.

A Change Review Board — which has members from departments such as Development, Operations, Customer Support, and Security as well as other stakeholders in the organization — usually performs Change Management.

The process of approving modifications to a production environment is called *Change Management.*

Configuration Management

Often confused with Change Management (and vice versa), Configuration Management has little to do with approvals but *everything* to do with recording all the facts about the change. Configuration Management captures actual changes to software code, end-user documentation, operations documentation, disaster recovery planning documentation, and anything else that's affected by the change. Configuration Management archives technical details for each change and release of the system, as well as for each instance of the system, if more than one instance exists.

Change Management and Configuration Management address two different aspects of change in a system's maintenance mode. Change Management is the what, and Configuration Management is the how.

The process of managing the changes being made to systems is called Change Management. The process of recording modifications to a production environment is called Configuration Management.

Notes about the life cycle

Larger organizations implement the system development life cycle by using a complex, formal process. Each step in the process contains its own steps, actions, deliverables, reviews, approvals, and recordkeeping. A formal process dictates knowing what step a project is in (product concept, functional requirements, functional specs, design, and so on), as well as whether a project is allowed to pass from one step to the next.

Large organizations implement such processes because they have such big projects. The seemingly expensive overhead of project management and all these reviews, approvals, and so on hopefully prevent the organization from making costly mistakes that might occur if they pushed a project along too fast and possibly skipped important steps.

Because of unexpected events, projects frequently must back up one step to make corrections. For instance, in the iPad example we use in the preceding sections, the Marketing people wanted the iPad to contain 200 GB of memory, but the Engineering folks could eke out only 64 GB and stay within budget. Such a discrepancy would trigger a return to the functional-requirements step to get the Marketing people back to Earth and get the functional requirements to align with realistic functional specifications. After the two groups settle their differences, they can move on to other projects with more experience through lessons learned.

Other models of the system development life cycle

We spend a lot of time describing the traditional waterfall life cycle in the preceding sections. The waterfall model is a comprehensive process that includes a lot of up-front planning and design to ensure that the actual development portion of it (the coding that developers always seem to want to start too soon) is done right. For all the integrity that the waterfall model provides, you can't say that it's a time-friendly approach to software development.

The waterfall model was developed back in the mainframe-computing era when a typical larger software development project could take two years. When breakthroughs in software development technology began in the 1980s, so too did the need to make the actual *process* of software development more efficient (timewise). So some other models — RAD (Rapid Application Development), Spiral, and Scrum, for example — have appeared that allow an organization to get software developed quickly.

Security principles in software development

No matter what development model is used, these principles are important in order to ensure that the resulting software is secure:

- ✓ **Security in the requirements:** Even before the developers design the software, the organization should determine what security features the software needs. This set of security requirements should range from thorough input field validation to authentication and access controls. If security is absent from requirements, it's likely to be absent in the design and implementation as well.

- ✓ **Security in the design:** The design of an application should include security features, ranging from vigorous input checking, strong authentication, audit logs, and privacy.

- ✓ **Security in testing:** An organization needs to test all the security requirements and design characteristics before declaring the software ready for production use. All test scripts and test results should be archived for later use, if needed. Automated tools should be used to test source code for security vulnerabilities and other types of defects.

- ✓ **Security in the implementation:** New applications need to be implemented on secure, hardened servers, and done in a way so that programmers do not have access to the production environment. If data was migrated from an older application, this migration must be done carefully so that security of any sensitive data is not compromised.

CSSLP Certification

There is a new kid on the block. In 2009, (ISC)² introduced a new certification, the Certified Secure Software Lifecycle Professional (CSSLP). This certification is recognition that the software professional is competent in incorporating security into every phase of the software lifecycle — not as an add-on as it has been for so many years.

The areas of concentration for the CSSLP certification are

✔ Secure Software Concepts

✔ Secure Software Requirements

✔ Secure Software Design

✔ Secure Software Implementation / Coding

✔ Secure Software Testing

✔ Software Acceptance

✔ Software Deployment, Operations, Maintenance, and Disposal

We hope you've noticed that these areas correspond to the phases of the software development life cycle.

You can find out more about the CSSLP certification at www.isc2.org/csslp.

✔ **Ongoing security testing:** After an application is implemented, security testing should be performed regularly, in order to make sure that no new security defects are introduced into the software. Also, because new security holes are discovered all the time, it is possible (and even likely) that a program that is secure at the beginning will be less secure in the future, because of these vulnerabilities that are discovered (and were always there).

When an organization makes security a part of a new application's design, that application is likely to experience far fewer security problems later on.

Application Security Controls

In the preceding sections in this chapter, our discussion centers on system architectures and development processes. You may wonder how you can make software secure in the first place. We discuss several techniques, characteristics, and mechanisms in the following sections.

Process isolation

With *process isolation,* running processes aren't allowed to view or modify memory and cache that's assigned to another process. For instance, if a user can see that a payroll program is running on the system, he (or any tool that he uses) won't be able to read the memory space used by the payroll program.

Process isolation is a service that's provided by the operating system. Mac OS X, Microsoft Windows, and Linux — and even much older OSs, such as RSTS/E, Kronos, and TOPS-10 — perform and provide this function. The system developer doesn't have to build a wall around his or her application because built-in process isolation prevents others from snooping on it.

Hardware segmentation

Hardware segmentation refers to the practice of isolating functions to separate hardware platforms as required to ensure the integrity and security of system functions. This concept can also refer to keeping developers' resource-intensive work off the production system. This is used to reinforce the concepts of *segregation of duties* and *least privilege* (these concepts are defined in Chapter 10) by preventing developers from accessing production systems.

Hardware segmentation is used to keep application developers off of production systems. It can also keep different applications or environments from interfering with each other.

Separation of privilege

Also known as *least privilege, separation of privilege* assures that no individuals or objects (such as programs that make requests of databases) have excessive functions on a system. For instance, in a finance application, you have at least three programs or functions involved in payments to others: those that request the payment, those that approve the payment, and those that perform the payment. Each of these individuals should have privileges that permit them to perform only their approved function, but no others.

Separation of privilege is quite similar to *segregation of duties*, which is the practice of dividing critical tasks among two or more persons, (discussed in more detail in Chapter 10).

Accountability

Accountability refers to an application's ability to record every auditable event by describing the event: who made the change, what the change was, and when the change was made. This feature makes it impossible (you hope) for an individual to make any change to data without the application (or database) capturing details about the change.

Accountability is only as strong as the underlying authentication and access control mechanisms. If employees habitually share passwords or use each other's accounts, then it's very difficult to associate any inappropriate data tampering with a specific individual.

Defense in depth

Also known as *layering, defense in depth* is a security architecture concept wherein multiple separate mechanisms form protective layers around assets that require protection. For example, a company may have a firewall, but additionally implement host-based access control and other mechanisms. Then, if any one of these protections fails, the others still presumably run and prevent or detect security problems in the environment.

The effective and not-so-tired cliché of defense in depth is the metaphor of a castle protected by its moat, drawbridge, layers of walls, and other defenses. All work together to protect the treasure hidden deep within.

The practice of protecting a system or network with several concurrent mechanisms is defense in depth.

Abstraction

Abstraction is a process of viewing an application from its highest-level functions, which makes all lower-level functions into abstractions. Lower-level functions are treated as black boxes — known to work, even if we don't know how.

Data hiding

Data hiding is an object-orientation term that refers to the practice of encapsulating an object within another in order to hide the first object's functioning details.

System high mode

System high mode refers to a system that operates at the highest level of information classification. Any user who wants to access such a system must have clearance at or above the information classification level.

Security kernel

The *security kernel* is composed of hardware, software, and firmware components that mediate access and functions between subjects and objects. The security kernel is a part of the protection rings model in which the operating system kernel occupies the innermost ring, and rings farther away from the innermost ring represent fewer access rights. The *security kernel* is the innermost ring and has full access to all system hardware and data. User programs occupy outer rings and have fewer access privileges.

Chapter 9 discusses security models in depth.

Reference monitor

The *reference monitor* is a component implemented by the security kernel that enforces access controls on data and devices on a system. In other words, when a user tries to access a file, the reference monitor ultimately performs the *Is This Person Allowed to Access This File?* function.

The system's reference monitor enforces access controls on a system.

Supervisor and User modes

Modern operating systems use the concept of privilege associated with user accounts. For instance, UNIX has the `root` account, and Windows Server has the Domain Administrator and Local Administrator roles. Only system or network administrators can use these accounts, with which they perform operating system and utility management functions.

Now and again, you may hear of administrators who grant `root` or administrator privileges to normal applications. Allowing a normal application these privileges is a serious mistake because applications that run in Supervisor mode bypass some or all security controls, which could lead to unexpected application behavior. For instance, any user of a payroll application could view or change anyone's data because the application running in Supervisor mode was never told *no* by the operating system.

You use Supervisor mode for system administration purposes only. Business applications should always run in User mode.

Hackers specifically target Supervisor and other privileged modes, because those modes have a great deal of power over systems. The use of Supervisor mode should be limited wherever possible, especially on end-user workstations.

Service-Level Agreements (SLAs)

In the real world, users of any business application need to know whether their application is going to function when they need it. Users need to know more than "Is it up?" or "Is it down *again?*" Their customers and superiors hold the users of an application accountable for getting a certain amount of work performed in a given period of time, so consequently, those users need to know whether they can depend on their application to help them deliver as promised.

The Service-Level Agreement (SLA) is a quasi-legal document (it's a real legal document when the application service provider is a different company than the organization that uses the application) that pledges the application performs to a set of minimum standards, such as

- ✓ **Hours of availability:** The wall-clock hours that the application will be available for users. This could be 24 x 7 (24 hours per day, 7 days per week) or something more limited, such as daily from 4:00 a.m. to 12:00 p.m. Availability specifications may also cite *maintenance windows* (for instance, Sundays from 2:00 a.m. to 4:00 a.m.) when users can expect the application to be down for testing, upgrades, and service.

- ✓ **Average and peak number of concurrent users:** The maximum number of users who can log on to the application at the same time.

- ✓ **Transaction throughput:** The number of transactions that the application can perform in a given time period. Usually, *throughput* is expressed as transactions per second, per minute, or per hour.

- ✓ **Data storage capacity:** The amount of data that the users can store in the application. Capacity may be expressed in raw terms (megabytes or gigabytes) or in numbers of transactions.

- ✓ **Application response times:** The maximum periods of time (in seconds) that key transactions take. All response times for long processes (nightly runs, and so on) should be in an application's SLA.

- ✓ **Service desk response times:** The amount of time (usually in hours) that a service desk (or help desk) will take to respond to requests for support.

- ✓ **Security incident response times:** The amount of time (usually in hours or days) between the realization of a security incident and any required notifications to data owners and other affected parties.

- ✓ **Escalation process during times of failure:** When things go wrong, how quickly the service provider will contact the customer, as well as what steps the provider will take to restore service.

Because the SLA is a quantified statement, the service provider and the user alike can take measurements to see how well the service provider is meeting the SLA's standards. This measurement, which is sometimes accompanied by analysis, is frequently called a *scorecard*.

How many nines?

Availability is often expressed in a percentage of uptime, usually in terms of "how many nines." In other words, an application, server, or site may be available 99 percent of the time, 99.9 percent of the time, or as much as 99.999 percent of the time. Approximate amounts of downtime per year are shown in the table below.

Percentage	Number of Nines	Downtime per year
99%	Two	88 hours
99.9%	Three	9 hours
99.99%	Four	53 minutes
99.999%	Five	5 minutes

System Attack Methods

Attackers develop new attack methods as fast as new products and technologies are introduced. It seems as though as soon as something new and cool comes out, only days — or even hours — later, you hear that someone has found a way to attack it.

Malicious code

As soon as data found a way to move easily from computer to computer, a creative individual with a bad attitude figured out that he could include some code that would play a not-so-practical joke, such as delete or alter files on someone else's computer. And more recently, criminal organizations have figured out that they can steal valuable information — such as bank account numbers and credit card numbers, or the login credentials to high-value sites such as online banking — from peoples' computers.

Unfortunately, several types of malicious code are out there; we define the most interesting ones here.

Viruses

The main purpose of a computer *virus*, a (usually) small program, is to replicate itself. Early computer viruses attached themselves to floppy disks' boot sectors or to executables (such as `.com` or `.exe` files). Boot-sector viruses spread if a user booted the PC with an infected diskette. Viruses attached to executable files would spread when a user ran those executable files. *Multipartite* viruses spread by using both the boot sector and executable files.

Today, viruses spread in many other ways, including macros found in documents, as well as in image files, JavaScript and ActiveX controls. We've also seen viruses spread through cross-site scripting vulnerabilities in websites and through instant messaging software. Virus writers — known as VXers — are always seeking new ways to propagate viruses and other malicious code.

Strictly speaking, a virus spreads by making (usually) identical copies of itself on files that are likely to be transported to other computers. Other types of malicious code, such as worms and Trojan horses, are often mistakenly called viruses.

If you find this topic fascinating (we sure do), you might consider picking up a copy of *Computer Viruses For Dummies* (John Wiley and Sons, Inc.; yes, one of us — Peter — wrote that book).

Worms

A *worm* is very similar to a virus: Both are designed to replicate quickly, but worms don't attach themselves to programs the way viruses do. Instead, worms propagate by attacking known weaknesses on computer systems. On those systems where the worm finds a weakness, it can successfully break in and enter. Whatever the weakness happens to be, the result is the same: The worm can assume enough control of the system (or just of the application whose weakness it exploited) to use it as a base to launch attacks against more systems. And in the meantime, the worm may also have some destructive characteristics as well: It could change or delete data on the system.

Some of the most successful malicious code events (Conficker, Storm, NIMDA, and Code Red) were worms.

The Morris Worm

In 1988, computer researcher Robert Tappan Morris developed and released what's now known as The Internet Worm. This worm was the first widely successful worm, in terms of the extent of its propagation and impact on the Internet. It exploited vulnerabilities in several UNIX utilities, as well as the transitive trust that existed between networks at that time. A report called "The Internet Worm Incident" gives a lucid description of the worm's composition and propagation techniques. You should be able to find this report by using your favorite search engine or online encyclopedia. The worm used techniques still in use today to exploit known vulnerabilities; understanding it can give you insight into present-day malicious code.

Rootkits

A *rootkit* is a malicious program that's designed to hide itself on the target system in order to evade detection. The purpose of a rootkit varies according to its maker. A rootkit may perform any of the actions that most other types of malware are capable of, including destroying, altering, or stealing data; intercepting or altering data transmissions; or changing the behavior of the target system.

What makes a rootkit different from other types of malware is the fact that it uses some means to hide itself. Types of rootkits include

- **Hardware:** Present in the computer's hardware. A hardware rootkit usually requires a compromise in the system manufacturer's supply chain that permits the substitution of an approved component in a computer with one that includes rootkit code. In 2008, such an attack was successful: A brand of credit card swipe readers in Europe was infiltrated with chips that captured credit card numbers and sent them to overseas crime syndicates.

- **Firmware:** Present in the target system's firmware. Most newer computers have firmware that firmware updates can overwrite. Malware can insert itself into a system's firmware, where it may then avoid detection: Most types of systems do nothing to check the integrity or contents of its firmware.

- **Hypervisor:** Operates as a virtual machine, running between the hardware and the operating system. The running operating system is a guest on the hypervisor's environment. Although you can find several "friendly" (we mean *commercial,* such as VMware) hypervisor software products, one that's malicious and even *transparent* (hidden from the user) may exist and be difficult to detect. A hypervisor-based rootkit can intercept all communications, as well as input-output with devices such as disk drives.

- **Kernel:** Utilizes malicious code that's been inserted into the operating system kernel. Done correctly, such code may be difficult or impossible to find.

- **Library:** Inserts rootkit code into an operating system's code library. Rather than alter the disk copy of a library file, a rootkit alters the memory image only, making its presence difficult to detect.

Antivirus programs have a difficult time detecting rootkits (once installed), because the rootkits exist in a location that the antivirus program is unable to access or is not designed to access. For example, antivirus programs do not typically examine a system's firmware (such as a ROM-BIOS) to see whether it's been altered, and an operating system can't detect whether it's a virtual machine guest of a hypervisor.

A *rootkit* is malware that uses one or more techniques to avoid detection.

Trojan horses

A *Trojan horse,* like its storybook namesake, is an object that claims to be one thing but turns out to be something far different (and not very nice).

Trojan horses generally don't spread by replicating themselves, but they can be very damaging nonetheless. Trojan horses became prevalent with the rise of the Internet and e-mail. A typical Trojan horse arrives in the payload of an e-mail message, usually an attached executable file or a file with macros. The text portion of the e-mail message may read something like `Viagra without a prescription, click here` or `See Britney Spears naked!!` or some other enticing message designed to lure people into executing the Trojan horse and aiding in its sword-wielding propagation through cyberspace.

Another type of Trojan horse is a pop-up window that appears on the screen with information that prompts the user to act by clicking it. The window may pretend to be a Microsoft Windows error message saying that the victim's computer has been infected by malware (in truth, it is *about to be!*) and that the user should "click here to install antivirus software." This class of Trojan is known as *scareware.*

Hoaxes

While the popularity of e-mail increased, viruses rode the rails and propagated themselves via e-mail. Conscientious people everywhere, hearing about real viruses, would write up warning messages and send them to their friends and colleagues. But chip-on-their-shoulder virus writers decided to attack on another front: creating phony virus-warning messages in order to instill panic and occasionally to get naive users to do harmful things unwittingly. Such false warnings, like their offline predecessors, are called *hoaxes.*

Typically, a virus hoax arrives via e-mail, making a plea such as `Please watch your inbox and DO NOT OPEN any message that has "Pictures for you" in the subject line. Whatever you do, do not open the message or your entire hard drive will be reformatted. I know — it happened to me two weeks ago, and I just got my computer back today.`

Even hoaxes serve a purpose: They can account for millions of productivity hours lost in companies around the world. Sometimes, hoax messages clog e-mail systems, which is often one of the intentions of the perpetrator of the hoax.

It's often a good idea to independently check out a rumor before spreading it to others. Snopes (at `www.snopes.com`) and Mythbusters (`www.mythbusters.com`) are good sites. Ask us how we know this (sheepish grin here).

Logic bombs

A *logic bomb* is a program designed to cause damage when some computer/ network event has occurred. For instance, a logic bomb could destroy files when a user invokes a certain program, such as a text editor. Logic bombs don't replicate themselves, but viruses or worms can leave them behind.

A common logic bomb is malicious code that activates on a certain date. Disgruntled programmers sometimes plant logic bombs that activate and destroy data long after those programmers leave their jobs. Nice parting gift, eh? This doozy alone justifies the use of code reviews and controls that prevent unauthorized changes from being inserted into software and systems.

Malicious applets

ActiveX and Java applets can carry malicious code and wreak havoc on users' computers. Strictly speaking, attackers can write destructive ActiveX applets more easily than Java applets because the applets have unfettered access to the entire computer. Destructive Java applets are far more difficult to write because they must exploit some weakness in the Java sandbox in order to break out of it and do whatever damaging deed it was designed to do. For more about applets, read the earlier section "Adding applets to the mix."

Trap doors

A *trap door* is a type of logic bomb that functions as part of a program. The trap door performs an undocumented function when certain conditions are met. Often these functions are designed to bypass security and other control mechanisms. One such trap door that we saw many years ago was planted in the /bin/login program on a UNIX system. When any ordinary user logged in to the system, the login program behaved normally. But when a special password was typed in (the publisher won't let us tell you what it is), the login program would log the person in as root; further, the login program, which usually logs the session to an audit file, would conveniently *forget* to log the trap-door session. The login program was hard to detect because its date, size, and checksum were the same as the software maker's original login program. It was a very effective — and terrible — trap door.

Hidden code

If an attacker can modify or replace programs on the target system, he or she may elect to install hidden code. *Hidden code* is a set of computer instructions hiding inside another program that carries out some usually-malicious act. An example of hidden code would be an application's reporting program that also happens to erase certain entries from the audit trail.

An *alteration of authorized code* is an attack similar to a trap door, in which a program that has specified privileges (for instance, the system's administrator account or an application's master user account) is modified to carry out some illicit functions of the attacker's choosing.

Injection attacks

An *injection attack* is one where the attacker is attempting to insert computer instructions into a computer program's input field, in an attempt to trick the target computer into performing functions unintended by the program's designer. These functions can range from displaying sensitive data to allowing the attacker to change or remove data from the system.

Examples of injection attacks include

- ✓ **SQL Injection:** Here, the attacker is injecting SQL statements in an attempt to trick the back-end database server to perform specific functions.
- ✓ **Frame Injection** (also known as *cross-frame scripting*, or *XFS*): Here, the attacker is attempting to load arbitrary code into a browser in order to steal data from other frames present in the browser session.

Cross-site scripting attacks

A *cross-site scripting* attack, commonly known as *XSS*, is one where an attacker is able to inject client-side script into web pages viewed by other intended victims. This attack allows an attacker to bypass security mechanisms present in websites and web browsers.

The two principal types of XSS attacks are non-persistent and persistent attacks. In a typical *non-persistent attack,* the attacker must trick the victim into clicking a malicious URL that contains malicious script, which will be executed on the victim's browser. Such a script could, for instance, steal the victim's session cookies — which could then be used by the attacker to access the victim's session.

In a *persistent attack,* the attacker arranges to store malicious code on a website (such as a message board, or comments in a blog). Then any users who click the malicious link will be executing malicious script on their systems.

Cross-site scripting is known as XSS, because the term CSS was already in common use (CSS stands for *cascading style sheets*, an HTML programming term).

According to Veracode, 68% of web applications contain cross-site scripting vulnerabilities.

Cross-site request forgery

In a *cross-site request forgery (CSRF)* attack, the attacker is attempting to trick a victim into clicking a link that will perform some action that the victim would not otherwise approve.

For example, an attacker creates a web page with images that users can click in order to view larger versions of the images. The attacker could place code on the image such as this example:

```
<img src=http://www.bank.com/transfer?from-
      account=mary&amt=100000&to-account=fred>
```

If victim Mary happens to be logged in to bank.com when she clicks the link, she will initiate a transfer of $100,000 to attacker Fred's account.

A common method used to protect users from CSRF attacks is the inclusion of one-time-use hidden variables (known as a "nonce") on important pages. The website keeps track of these hidden variables; any variation (or repeat) will indicate possible tampering.

Another method used to protect users against CSRF attacks is the inclusion of a secondary approval dialogue for any significant transaction. That way, if the attacker is able to sneak in a CSRF link that the victim clicks, the attack won't be successful unless the victim also approves the transaction.

Escalation of privilege

One technique commonly used by attackers is known as *escalation of privilege*. Here an attacker accesses a system, and then uses any number of attack techniques (such as an injection attack) to increase the attacker's privilege level from (say) that of an ordinary user to that of an administrator. The attacker's logic (which is often correct) is that sensitive or valuable information may be more readily accessible if the attacker can somehow increase his or her privileges on the target system.

Denial of Service

The *Denial of Service* (DoS) attack is an interesting one because the attacker never does gain entry into the targeted computer system — then again, he or she isn't *trying* to get in. Instead, the attacker is trying to make the target system unavailable for its users.

There are two types of DoS attacks. In the first, the attacker floods the victim's system with such a large number of network packets that legitimate users of the system can't reach it. The most successful DoS attacks not only slow down the system, but actually cause it to crash. Some methods of DoS attacks, such as the *SYN attack,* exhaust the system's resources to the point that it can no longer function. True, SYN attacks are old hat, but they reveal a little bit about the creative thinking of the black hats out there.

Bot armies: The power of one

Computer researchers and engineers are familiar with the fact that large communities of computers are very powerful if someone can easily manage and control them. The bad guys haven't overlooked this fact. On the contrary, those on the dark side have a respectable degree of sophistication. Here's how it works: Many viruses and Trojan horses are designed to turn your PC into a remotely controlled *zombie,* or *bot* (short for robot). When a PC is infected with a bot, the bot software communicates back to a server, usually via an IRC (Internet Relay Chat) protocol channel, and registers itself.

The person behind this activity is called a *bot herder.* He or she uses software on a server to control hundreds, thousands, even hundreds of thousands of these bots — called *bot armies* — to do his or her bidding, usually by sending or relaying large volumes of spam, hosting phishing or illegal content websites, or performing DDoS attacks on businesses, governments, or universities.

The second type of DoS attack is one where the attacker creates a specific message that is designed to cause the target system to malfunction and stop running. In this attack, it's usually unnecessary to send large quantities of messages — just a single message that is crafted just right.

The *ping of death* attack (where a malformed or extremely large "ping" packet is sent to the target system) is a good example of a DoS attack.

A form of DoS attack, called *Distributed Denial of Service* (DDoS), occurs when an attacker uses hundreds, or even thousands or tens of thousands, of systems to attack a target simultaneously.

Dictionary attacks

The *dictionary attack* is a method used to crack computer account passwords by using common words found in a dictionary.

Most commonly, a dictionary-attack tool acquires a copy of the UNIX password or shadow file, or the Windows SAM file. The hacker then loads the file on his or her local system and runs a password-cracking program to attempt to discover account passwords by guessing dictionary words and combinations of dictionary words and numbers: for example, *4food*.

This type of attack has prompted companies to require their employees and customers to pick *good* passwords — meaning passwords that consist of random letters interspersed with numbers and special characters: !@#)

(*&^%;[]{}:'"><. So, rather than an easily guessed password such as *Alexis,* a user would use a more difficult-to-guess password such as *Al3x1s**. Such a good password is practically impossible to break with a dictionary attack.

(See also the section, "Brute force," later in this chapter.)

Spoofing

In a *spoofing* attack, the attacker changes the network identity of a computer or program some way so as to trick the targeted system into granting access to the attacker. For instance, a targeted computer may accept Telnet requests only from systems that have specific IP addresses. Knowing this, the attacker can send spoofed TCP/IP packets to the system in an attempt to fool the target system and break in.

In an IP spoofing attack, packets sent from the target system in response to the attacker's packets will not be sent to the attacker, but instead to the actual IP address that the attacker is spoofing (so as to avoid detection, or to make the victim think that an attack is originating from a specific site). In this type of attack, the attacker is essentially flying blind.

Spam

Spam is the scourge of e-mail around the world. At times, it may make up as much as 95 percent of all e-mail on the Internet.

We don't feel that it's especially useful to discuss the methods that spammers use to build their mailing lists in any great detail. Spammers harvest e-mail addresses from newsgroups, and social networking sites; unscrupulous website operators sell e-mail addresses to spammers, and malware harvests e-mail addresses from hacked e-mail accounts. Sometimes spammers just get lucky and guess e-mail addresses, and some of the vile product gets through.

The effects of spam

The important thing to discuss about spam is prevention. You want to block spam for several reasons:

- ✔ **E-mail volume:** Spam clogs e-mail servers, reducing performance and raising costs by requiring larger hard drives to store all that e-mail. The volume of spam also consumes a lot of network bandwidth, stealing resources away from legitimate activities — such as social networking, or checking your stock prices or sports team scores.

✔ **Distraction and clutter:** Because spam can account for such a large volume of e-mail, legitimate e-mails may get deleted in attempts to delete all the spam. Plus, it just takes a lot of time to click the Delete button over and over.

✔ **Malware:** A large proportion of spam contains malware, or links to websites that contain malware, designed to silently poison unprotected computers. Blocking spam reduces your risk of malware infections: If the tempting e-mails aren't in your inbox, you don't have to fight off the urge to click those tantalizing ads about low-cost prescription drugs, sweepstakes winnings, or magical ways to change the size and shape of your body.

Preventing spam

Blocking spam is very much a normal operational activity, like antivirus measures and backups are. You can use several types of anti-spam solutions and find many options available of each type, which translates into low-cost solutions that you can use fairly easily.

The types of spam-blocking solutions include these:

✔ **Centralized appliance:** The dominant method for blocking spam. Easy-to-administer appliances connect to the network, often ahead of the e-mail server, relieving the e-mail server of ever having to store spam e-mail messages in the first place. Most web-based spam-blocking appliances are managed with a web-based interface. Some also filter out malware. Many multifunction security appliances can also perform other functions such as website filtering, intrusion detection, and data leakage prevention.

✔ **Spam-blocking service:** A third-party service receives an organization's e-mail, blocks out the spam, and forwards only the legitimate e-mail to the organization's e-mail server. The organization doesn't have to install anything. The advantage of a spam-blocking service is the complete absence of spam consuming any network resources on the corporate network. Like spam-blocking appliances, spam-blocking services are usually administered through a simple web-based interface.

✔ **Spam-blocking software:** Formerly a favored type of solution but now declining in popularity. This type of solution comes in the form of anti-spam software that runs on the e-mail server, plucking out spam messages when they enter or after they're stored.

✔ **Workstation-based software:** Formerly popular but almost never used anymore.

The most effective spam-blocking solutions are centralized and placed as far ahead of e-mail servers as possible, in order to regain network and system resources stolen by spam, and to simplify administration.

Social engineering

Social engineering is an attack against people as a way of getting access to targeted systems. The classic case of social engineering occurs when a hacker makes a number of telephone calls to various people in an organization and gets a tidbit of information from each one. For instance, he or she can get modem access numbers from one person, IP addresses and system names from another, a user ID from another, and a password reset from a help-desk employee. And voilà, the attacker puts these pieces together to log in to the company's system by using its established remote-access facilities.

Another common social engineering ploy is one in which the attacker, posing as the system or security administrator, tells people to change their passwords to a specified value. The attacker then tries to log in to the system by using that account to see whether any suckers did what he or she asked them to.

Even social engineering has gone high-tech: A good deal of the spam that floods the Internet is in the form of phishing and pharming attacks, described here:

- ✔ **Phishing:** A perpetrator creates genuine-looking e-mail messages that appear to have originated from real, high-value sites, such as online banking. The purpose of the e-mail is to trick the recipient into clicking the hyperlink that takes the user to a realistic-looking login page. When the user inputs his or her credentials, the perpetrator records them and then later uses them to attempt to steal funds from the victim. A typical phishing e-mail is shown in Figure 7-4.

- ✔ **Pharming:** The end result of pharming is very similar to phishing: A user goes to an imposter website whose owner wants to steal users' login credentials. The method of attack, however, is quite different. In a pharming attack, the attacker targets the user's DNS environment so that it returns incorrect values, leading victims to imposter sites. For example, if an attacker can successfully attack an organization's local DNS server, it can redirect all DNS queries for MyBank.com from its real site to a fake site that's run by the attacker.

- ✔ **Spear phishing:** A type of phishing in which the attacker targets certain users or groups of users. For example, if phishers can determine which online financial institutions their potential victims use, those phishers may be able to produce more effective fraud schemes.

✔ **Whaling:** A type of phishing attack that targets senior executives in one or more organizations. For example, officers in an organization can be targeted through a message claiming to be related to a lawsuit or subpoena against the organization.

TrustedBank™

Dear valued customer of TrustedBank,

We have recieved notice that you have recently attempted to withdraw the following amount from your checking account while in another country: $135.25.

If this information is not correct, someone unknown may have access to your account. As a safety measure, please visit our website via the link below to verify your personal information:

http://www.trustedbank.com/general/custverifyinfo.asp

Once you have done this, our fraud department will work to resolve this discrepency. We are happy you have chosen us to do business with.

Thank you,
TrustedBank

Member FDIC © 2005 TrustedBank, Inc.

Figure 7-4:
An example
of a phish-
ing e-mail
message.

A social engineer preys on the human desire to help others. When you receive a phone call from someone who's pleading for assistance, you empathize with the person and want to help. Doesn't it make you feel better to know that you've done your good deed for the day? Social engineers know this and use it to their advantage.

You can learn more about phishing from the Anti-Phishing Work Group at `www.apwg.org`.

Pseudo flaw

A *pseudo flaw* attack is a special form of social engineering in which an attacker, posing as a system or security administrator or vendor, tells unsuspecting users that a security flaw has been discovered on their system and that they should install a certain *patch,* which is usually a Trojan horse.

Figure 7-5 shows a pop-up window from a scareware program that pretends to be anti-spyware when it is actually malware.

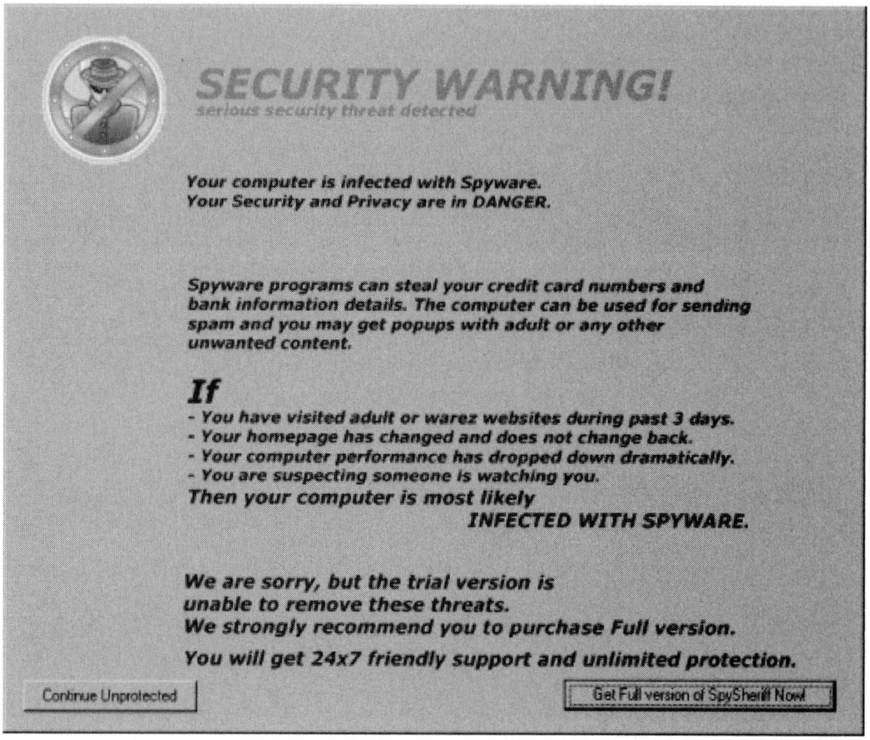

Figure 7-5:
An example of scareware.

Remote maintenance

Organizations need to be especially wary of vendors who need to connect via modem, VPN, or remote desktop connection to their systems or networks in order to troubleshoot a problem or perform maintenance. If the vendor's employee is dishonest, he or she may perform any number of acts that would constitute abuse, at best — hacking, at worst. This person may steal information or services, insert trap doors or logic bombs, or use his or her customer's system to attack other systems in the enterprise or on the Internet.

In all fairness, most vendors have honest intentions when they legitimately need to connect to a customer's computer in order to fix a problem. But a few dishonest employees in these vendor organizations have made this an activity that you should think twice about. Vendors should be able to connect to your systems only at your request, and only for a defined period of time. The privileges that you give to the vendor should be the minimum needed for its employee to quickly get in, fix the problem, and get out.

Be sure to have your vendors and suppliers notify your organization when any of their service personnel leaves their organization. This can alert you to the fact that those who left are no longer authorized to work on your systems.

Maintenance hooks

Legitimate remote maintenance is one thing, but it's quite another for a software developer to bury illicit hooks in software code that permit a program to expose features, functions, or data inappropriately. For instance, if the user enters certain values in data fields, a program could drop into Maintenance mode or Debug mode, thereby exposing internal system information.

Maintenance hooks are trouble when they're undocumented and deliberately buried in software code to intentionally evade detection.

Sniffing and eavesdropping

An intruder (or employee) may devise some means for listening to traffic on the organization's internal network by using a sniffer program. *Sniffer* programs can listen for and capture login sessions, recording user IDs and passwords. Systems that encrypt the login password on the wire aren't necessarily better off in the case of sniffers. Hacking tools can capture the encrypted password and later perform a dictionary or brute force attack against it to discover the password. This process can, however, take months or even years, so encrypted passwords over the network are substantially safer than cleartext password transmission.

Eavesdropping isn't limited to the high-tech approach. One can listen in on conversations in airports, restaurants, and other public places. An intruder can install listening devices in conference rooms, on telephone lines, or in gifts given to the intended victim. ("Here, have this large, attractive lapel pin.")

Traffic analysis and inference

An attacker can analyze network traffic patterns and other types of transmissions in order to make inferences about something that he or she wants to know more about. In this type of attack, the attacker doesn't have access to the *contents* of the transmissions — only their patterns. For instance, the attacker could be in a position to know the workload on a network and thus infer that the network's high utilization from 10:00 p.m. to 1:00 a.m. is the organization performing backups over the network. The attacker can use this information to his or her advantage by attempting to sabotage systems shortly before 10:00 p.m. in order to prevent a backup from occurring. Usually, traffic analysis and inference isn't an end to itself, but part of a bigger plan.

Brute force

As attacks go, *brute force* is the most time-consuming; attackers use it as a last resort when more devious or clever methods fail. Whatever the target, the perpetrator of a brute-force attack repeatedly hits his or her target, making small changes each time, hoping that he or she can eventually get in.

You most often see brute-force attacks in the form of an attacker trying to log in with some user ID and trying every possible password until he or she finds the right one. Most newer computer systems are designed to repel this sort of attack by locking out accounts that have had too many unsuccessful login attempts. An honest user sees this lockout mechanism sometimes when he or she tries to log in to his or her account at work, only to be locked out — and then he or she remembers changing that password the day before. (D'oh!)

Antivirus Software

Antivirus software has (understandably) become so popular that nearly every organization requires its use on all its desktop and server systems. Many manufacturers and integrators of personal computers sold at retail include an antivirus program as standard equipment. Antivirus software on new computers is almost as common as seat belts and air bags on new cars.

Antivirus software (commonly known as *AV software*) operates by intercepting operating system routines that store files and open files. The AV software compares the contents of the file being opened or stored against a list of virus signatures. If the AV software detects a virus, it prevents the file from being opened or saved, usually alerting the user via a pop-up window (which is like a high-tech jack-in-the-box). Enterprise versions of the AV software send an alert to a central monitoring console so that the company's antivirus bureau is alerted and can take evasive action if necessary.

While the number of viruses grows, the antivirus software vendors provide a way for users to update their AV software's list of signatures so that they can defend against the latest viruses. AV software automatically contacts the AV vendor's central computer and downloads a new signature file if the vendor's version is newer than the user's. Enterprise versions of AV software can now push new signature files to all desktop systems and even invoke new scans in real time. AV software now commonly looks for updates one or more times per day.

Heuristics

AV software's new problem is that tens of millions of known viruses have been developed, and over a million are in circulation today. Thus AV software vendors are considering a new approach called *heuristics* to defend against viruses: The AV software detects certain kinds of anomalous behavior (for instance, the replacement of an .exe file with a newer version) instead of using the tedious method of checking all the virus signatures. Most AV products today use both the signature method and heuristics for detecting viruses; everyone (except the virus writers) hopes that someday heuristics become the primary method for virus detection.

Heuristics can solve a number of problems:

- ✔ **Conservation of space:** While the number of viruses grows, signature files grow ever larger, taking more time to download and consuming more space on systems. You don't really have to worry about file size when PC hard drives cost less than $5 per gigabyte, but AV software is making its way onto resource-limited personal digital assistants (PDAs), smartphones, and other lightweight devices that can't store tens of thousands of virus signatures.

- ✔ **Decreased download time:** The rate of virus creation means that you need to download signature files more and more frequently. (Pretty soon, it seems, the Internet will have enough capacity to support only AV signature-file downloads, Facebook, Twitter, YouTube, and porn sites.)

- ✔ **Improved computer performance:** Rather than constantly comparing messages to increasingly larger signature files, the computer's defenses are focused on symptoms rather than if a document does or does not possess a virus signature.

AV software losing its edge

For a while there it appeared that we were winning the virus wars, with antivirus programs doing a good job of getting updates to users quickly and often, and with better detection techniques.

But innovation has its dark side too.

The people writing malware, realizing that antivirus software was doing a better job of detecting them, created some new techniques to evade antivirus software. One very successful technique is to scramble the virus's code each time it was sent to another computer. The result: the "signature" for a single piece of malware can be different on every victim computer. This means (eventually) that every individual malware infection in the world is unique.

With an attack like this, antivirus companies can never keep up. There are, however, other ways of fighting the malware wars:

✔ **Application whitelisting:** Mechanisms on workstations permit only registered applications to execute.

✔ **Data leakage prevention:** Programs and network devices are designed to detect possible data leakage, which may be a result of a malware infection.

✔ **Malware callback detection:** Network devices that listen for signs of malware that is "calling home" to its point of origin.

These techniques will probably be helpful — for a while.

AV popping up everywhere

You can find antivirus software on more than just PC desktops. You also run across it on e-mail servers that scan attachments, as well as on web proxy servers, file servers, and application servers. Even firewalls and spam blockers are getting into the act.

Antivirus software is available for UNIX systems, too, but ironically, the UNIX versions check for PC viruses (not UNIX viruses). Why put antivirus software on UNIX systems? Well, often UNIX systems are used as file servers (with Samba) or web servers — which makes them part of the information conduit between PCs, so why not try to block viruses there, too?

Perpetrators

You often hear the nomenclature of computer menaces refer to hackers, intruders, script kiddies, virus writers, bot herders, and phreakers. Just what sorts of people are these, anyway?

Hackers

These days *hacker* is a broad-brush term implicating almost any person who has computer skills and mouse in hand as a wild-eyed cybervillain. Actually, the *real* hacker is a rare breed indeed: extremely knowledgeable, patient, creative, resourceful, and well aware that knowledge is power. He or she is determined to find a new way to explore and maybe exploit some particular system, protocol, or program. He or she studies the architecture and design of the target in order to better understand how they work, and perhaps find a weakness and exploit it. The reasons for doing so can be complex.

Hackers are often employees with day jobs who experiment after hours. Most hackers are socially responsible and want to discover weaknesses in computer hardware, software, and firmware and help get them fixed before icky, bad people discover them and cause real damage. Some are hired as consultants to ply their skills to test and improve system security.

Many years ago, being a hacker was a badge of honor, associated with intelligence and ingenuity. But in popular culture, the term now carries near-universal connotations of troublemaking and criminal activity.

Script kiddies

Script kiddies are individuals with nowhere near the technical acumen of real hackers. Instead, they acquire programs and scripts developed by hackers and use those ready-made tools to carry out attacks. Frequently, script kiddies don't even know how their attack tools work.

Don't underestimate the power of script kiddies, however. They can cause significant damage to systems and networks if they're determined to attack them. A fool who has a tool may still be a fool — but with the right tool, even a fool can wield a lot of power and do a lot of damage.

Virus writers

Like hackers, *virus writers* — or *VXers* — can span a broad range of expertise. Some virus writers are highly skilled and creative, quite able to engineer an effective virus on their own. But like script kiddies, many virus writers rely on templates and illicit virus cookbooks to create subtle variations of existing viruses.

Bot herders

Bot herders are individuals who establish, grow, and use bot armies to carry out attacks and cause other types of trouble. They may develop their own bot software, but mostly they use bot software developed by others.

Phreakers

The original *phreakers* were people who cracked telephone networks in order to get free long-distance service. Improvements in telephone networks have rendered the original techniques useless, and some phreakers have resorted to outright criminal acts, such as stealing long-distance calling cards.

The term *phreakers* is sometimes used to describe hackers who try to break into systems and services in order to get free services.

Black hats and white hats

These are just terms for the bad guys and the good guys, respectively. There is a Black Hat security conference, and we hear it's interesting. Guess who goes.

Professional perps and organized crime

The U.S. Treasury Department reported that starting in 2006, organized criminal organizations were making more money on cybercrime and online fraud than they did through drug trafficking. That chilling statistic should make you sit up and take notice: You're no longer dealing with angry children, but with deranged adults who have developed criminal enterprises with profiteering and troublemaking as their profession. They have investors, budgets, research and development departments, marketing and sales departments, conferences, and profit sharing. Big money now supports the development of viruses, bots, Trojan horses, and other means for stealing money from organizations, governments, banks, and (especially) the general public!

Prep Test

1 Masquerading as another person in order to obtain information illicitly is known as

- **A** ○ Hacking
- **B** ○ Social engineering
- **C** ○ Extortion
- **D** ○ Exhumation

2 Viruses, rootkits, and Trojan horses are known as

- **A** ○ Maniacal code
- **B** ○ Fractured code
- **C** ○ Infectious code
- **D** ○ Malicious code

3 Antivirus software that detects viruses by watching for anomalous behavior uses what technique?

- **A** ○ Signature matching
- **B** ○ Fleuristics
- **C** ○ Heroistics
- **D** ○ Heuristics

4 A developer, suspecting that he may be fired soon, modifies an important program that will corrupt payroll files long after he is gone. The developer has created a(n)

- **A** ○ Delayed virus
- **B** ○ Logic bomb
- **C** ○ Applet bomb
- **D** ○ Trojan horse

5 A SYN flood is an example of a

- **A** ○ Dictionary attack
- **B** ○ High Watermark attack
- **C** ○ Buffer Overflow attack
- **D** ○ Denial of Service attack

6 The process of recording changes made to systems is known as

A ○ Change Review Board
B ○ System Maintenance
C ○ Change Management
D ○ Configuration Management

7 A system that accumulates knowledge by observing events' inputs and outcomes is known as a(n)

A ○ Expert system
B ○ Neural network
C ○ Synaptic network
D ○ Neural array

8 The logic present in an object is known as

A ○ Encapsulation
B ○ Personality
C ○ Behavior
D ○ Method

9 The restricted environment that Java applets occupy is known as a

A ○ Sandbox
B ○ Workbox
C ○ Trusted Zone
D ○ Instantiation

10 An attacker has placed a URL on a website that, if clicked, will cause malicious javascript to execute on victims' browsers. This is known as a

A ○ Phishing attack
B ○ Script injection attack
C ○ Cross-site scripting attack
D ○ Cross-site request forgery attack

Answers

1 **B.** Social engineering. *Social engineering* is the process of obtaining information from people by tricking them into giving up an important piece of information, such as a modem access number. *Review "System Attack Methods."*

2 **D.** Malicious code. *Malicious code* is the generic term used to describe computer codes used to inflict damage on a computer system. *Review "Malicious code."*

3 **D.** Heuristics. *Heuristics* is the technique used to detect viruses by recognizing anomalous behavior. *Review "Malicious code."*

4 **B.** Logic bomb. A *logic bomb* is a type of malicious code that's designed to cause damage at a predetermined date in the future. *Review "Malicious code."*

5 **D.** Denial of Service attack. These attacks are designed to incapacitate a system by flooding it with traffic. *Review "Denial of Service."*

6 **D.** Configuration Management. This is the process used to record all configuration changes to hardware and software. *Review "Configuration Management."*

7 **B.** Neural network. Neural networks become proficient at predicting outcomes by making large numbers of observations, noting the inputs and results of each. *Review "Neural networks."*

8 **D.** Method. A *method* is the formal name given to business logic — also known as *code* — present in an object. *Review "Object-Oriented Environments."*

9 **A.** Sandbox. This is the name given to the restricted environment in which Java applets reside. *Review "Adding applets to the mix."*

10 **C.** Cross-site scripting attack. In a cross-site scripting attack, the attacker places malicious script language in a URL that will be executed on a victim's browser. *Review "System Attack Methods."*

Chapter 8

Cryptography

. . . .

In This Chapter

▶ Unlocking cryptography and its alternatives

▶ Understanding the differences between symmetric and asymmetric key systems

▶ Getting a grasp on what keys are and how to use them

▶ Keeping online information secure by using cryptography

▶ Knowing how the bad guys can attack an encryption system

. . . .

*T*his is the part where *Good Will Hunting* meets the *Rain Man* and *A Beautiful Mind.* If solving long, complex, theoretical math problems on windowpanes isn't your forte, you'll probably want to read this chapter slowly and carefully — then perhaps read it again.

Cryptography (from the Greek *kryptos,* meaning *hidden,* and *graphia,* meaning *writing*) is the science of encrypting and decrypting communications to make them unintelligible for all but the intended recipient.

The Certified Information Systems Security Professional (CISSP) candidate must have a thorough understanding of the fundamental concepts of cryptography, the basic operation of cryptographic systems, common uses and applications, and methods of attack. The CISSP exam tests the candidate's ability to apply general cryptographic concepts to real-world issues and problems. You don't have to memorize mathematical formulas or the step-by-step operation of various cryptographic systems. However, you should have a firm grasp of cryptographic concepts and technologies, as well as their specific strengths, weaknesses, uses, and applications.

The Role of Cryptography in Information Security

Cryptography can be used to achieve several goals of information security, including confidentiality, integrity, and authentication.

✓ **Confidentiality:** First, cryptography protects the confidentiality (or secrecy) of information. Even when the transmission or storage medium has been compromised, the encrypted information is practically useless to unauthorized persons without the proper keys for decryption.

✓ **Integrity:** Cryptography can also be used to ensure the integrity (or accuracy) of information through the use of hashing algorithms and message digests.

✓ **Authentication:** Finally, cryptography can be used for authentication (and non-repudiation) services through digital signatures, digital certificates, or a Public Key Infrastructure (PKI).

Don't confuse these three points with the C-I-A triad, which we discuss in Chapter 6: The C-I-A triad deals with confidentiality, integrity, and *availability;* cryptography does nothing to ensure availability.

He said, she said: The concept of non-repudiation

To *repudiate* is to deny; *non-repudiation* means that an action (such as an online transaction, e-mail communication, and so on) or occurrence can't be easily denied. Non-repudiation is a related function of identification and authentication (I&A) and accountability. For example, it's difficult for a user to deny sending an e-mail message that was digitally signed with that user's private key. Likewise, it's difficult to deny responsibility for an enterprise-wide outage if the accounting logs positively identify you (from username and strong authentication) as the poor soul who inadvertently issued the write-erase command on the core routers two seconds before everything dropped!

Tales from the crypt-o: A brief history of cryptography

Cryptography dates back over 4,000 years to the ancient Egyptians when hieroglyphs were used not to protect messages but to add mystique.

Around 400 B.C., the Spartans began using a military cryptography system known as the *scytale,* which consisted of a strip of parchment wrapped around a wooden rod of a specified secret length and diameter. The message to be encoded was written on the strip of parchment vertically down the rod and then unwrapped and sent by messenger to the intended recipient. The recipient had an identical rod to wrap the strip of parchment around and decode the message.

Around 50 B.C., Julius Caesar used a substitution cipher to transmit secret messages. This system involved substituting letters of the message with other letters from the same alphabet. For example, a simple encryption scheme may have required the sender to shift each letter three spaces to the right: so,

A = D, B = E, C = F, and so on. The recipient would then shift the letters three spaces to the left to decrypt and read the message.

This system, which uses only a single alphabet to encrypt and decrypt an entire message, is known as a *monoalphabetic substitution.* This system was particularly effective for Caesar because most of the population was illiterate at the time.

In the 15th century, a cryptographic system utilizing concentric disks to provide substitution was used in Italy. In 1790, Thomas Jefferson invented an encryption device by using a stack of 26 individually rotating disks. The Japanese Purple Machine and German Enigma Machine are two examples of cryptographic devices used successfully during World War II — at least, until the Allies cracked the codes. More recently, Quaker Oats developed the Cap'n Crunch Magic Decoder Ring for encrypting and decrypting simple messages!

Cryptography Basics

Cryptography today has evolved into a complex science (some say an art) presenting many great promises and challenges in the field of information security. The basics of cryptography include various terms and concepts, the individual components of the cryptosystem, and the classes and types of ciphers.

The science of crypto

Cryptography is the science of encrypting and decrypting information, such as a private message, to protect its confidentiality, integrity, and/or authenticity. Practitioners of cryptography are known as *cryptographers*.

Cryptanalysis is the science of deciphering (or breaking) ciphertext without the cryptographic key. Practitioners of cryptanalysis are known as *cryptanalysts*.

Cryptology is the science that encompasses both cryptography and cryptanalysis. Practitioners of cryptology are known as *cryptologists*.

Plaintext and ciphertext

A *plaintext* message is a message in its original readable format or a ciphertext message that has been properly decrypted (unscrambled) to produce the original readable plaintext message.

A *ciphertext* message is a plaintext message that has been transformed (encrypted) into a scrambled message that's unintelligible. This term doesn't apply to messages from your boss that may also happen to be unintelligible!

Encryption and decryption

Encryption (or *enciphering*) is the process of converting plaintext communications into ciphertext. *Decryption* (or *deciphering*) reverses that process, converting ciphertext into plaintext. (See Figure 8-1.)

Figure 8-1:
Encryption
and
decryption.

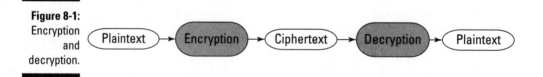

Traffic on a network can be encrypted by using either *end-to-end* or *link encryption*.

End-to-end encryption

With *end-to-end encryption,* packets are encrypted once at the original encryption source and then decrypted only at the final decryption destination. The advantages of end-to-end encryption are its speed and overall security.

However, in order for the packets to be properly routed, only the data is encrypted, not the routing information.

Link encryption

Link encryption requires that each node (for example, a router) has separate key pairs for its upstream and downstream neighbors. Packets are encrypted and decrypted, then re-encrypted at every node along the network path.

The following example in Lab 8-1 and Figure 8-2 illustrates link encryption:

Lab 8-1   Link Encryption

1. **Computer 1 encrypts a message by using Secret Key A, and then transmits the message to Router 1.**

2. **Router 1 decrypts the message by using Secret Key A, re-encrypts the message by using Secret Key B, and then transmits the message to Router 2.**

3. **Router 2 decrypts the message by using Secret Key B, re-encrypts the message by using Secret Key C, and then transmits the message to Computer 2.**

4. **Computer 2 decrypts the message by using Secret Key C.**

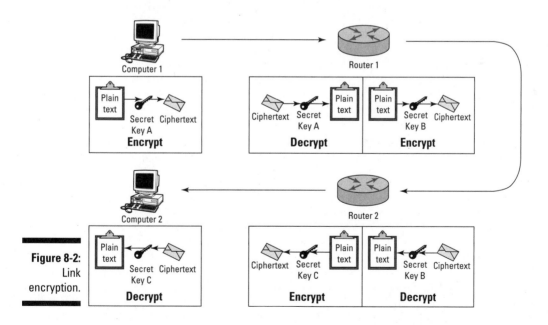

Figure 8-2: Link encryption.

The advantage of using link encryption is that the entire packet (including routing information) is encrypted. However, link encryption has the following two disadvantages:

✔ **Latency:** Packets must be encrypted/decrypted at every node, which creates latency (delay) in the transmission of those packets.

✔ **Inherent vulnerability:** If a node is compromised or a packet's decrypted contents are cached in a node, the message can be compromised.

Putting it all together: The cryptosystem

A *cryptosystem* is the hardware or software implementation that transforms plaintext into ciphertext (encrypting it) and back into plaintext (decrypting it).

An effective cryptosystem must have the following properties:

✔ The encryption and decryption process is efficient for all possible keys within the cryptosystem's keyspace.

A *keyspace* is the range of all possible values for a key in a cryptosystem.

✔ The cryptosystem is easy to use.

✔ The strength of the cryptosystem depends on the secrecy of the *cryptovariables* (or keys), rather than the secrecy of the algorithm.

A *restricted algorithm* refers to a cryptographic algorithm that must be kept secret in order to provide security. Restricted algorithms are not very effective, because the effectiveness depends on keeping the algorithm itself secret rather than the complexity and high number of variable solutions of the algorithm, and therefore are not commonly used today. They are generally used only for applications that require minimal security.

Cryptosystems are typically composed of two basic elements:

✔ **Cryptographic algorithm:** Also called a *cipher,* the cryptographic algorithm details the step-by-step mathematical function used to produce

- Ciphertext (encipher)
- Plaintext (decipher)

✔ **Cryptovariable:** Also called a *key,* the *cryptovariable* is a secret value applied to the algorithm. The strength and effectiveness of the cryptosystem largely depend on the secrecy and strength of the cryptovariable.

Key clustering (or simply *clustering*) occurs when identical ciphertext messages are generated from a plaintext message by using the same encryption algorithm but different encryption keys. Key clustering indicates a weakness in a cryptographic algorithm because it statistically reduces the number of key combinations that must be attempted in a brute force attack.

A *cryptosystem* consists of the cryptographic algorithm (cipher) and the cryptovariable (key), as well as all the possible plaintexts and ciphertexts produced by the cipher and key.

An analogy of a cryptosystem is a deadbolt lock. A deadbolt lock can be easily identified, and its inner working mechanisms aren't closely guarded state secrets. What makes a deadbolt lock effective is the individual key that controls a specific lock on a specific door. However, if the key is weak (imagine only one or two notches on a flat key) or not well protected (left under your doormat), the lock won't protect your belongings. Similarly, if an attacker is able to determine what cryptographic algorithm (lock) was used to encrypt a message, it should still be protected because you're using a strong key (128-bit) that you've kept secret, rather than a six-character password that you wrote on a scrap of paper and left under your mouse pad.

Classes of ciphers

Ciphers are cryptographic transformations. The two main classes of ciphers used in symmetric key algorithms are *block* and *stream* (see the section "Not Quite the Metric System: Symmetric and Asymmetric Key Systems," later in this chapter), which describe how the ciphers operate on input data.

The two main classes of ciphers are block ciphers and stream ciphers.

Block ciphers

Block ciphers operate on a single fixed block (typically 64 bits) of plaintext to produce the corresponding ciphertext. Using a given key in a block cipher, the same plaintext block always produces the same ciphertext block. Advantages of block ciphers compared with stream ciphers are

- ✔ **Reusable keys:** Key management is much easier.
- ✔ **Interoperability:** Block ciphers are more widely supported.

Block ciphers are typically implemented in software.

Stream ciphers

Stream ciphers operate in real time on a continuous stream of data, typically bit by bit. Stream ciphers generally work faster than block ciphers and require less code to implement. However, the keys in a stream cipher are generally used only once (see the sidebar "A disposable cipher: The one-time pad") and then discarded. Key management becomes a serious problem. Using a stream cipher, the same plaintext bit or byte will produce a different ciphertext bit or byte every time it is encrypted. Stream ciphers are typically implemented in hardware.

A disposable cipher: The one-time pad

A *one-time pad* (key) is a keystream (a stream of random or pseudo-random characters) that can be used only once. Considered unbreakable because it's completely random and is used only once and then destroyed, it consists of a pad of the same length as the message to which it's applied. Both the sender and receiver have an identical pad, which is used by the sender to encrypt the message and by the receiver to decrypt the message. This type of cipher is very effective for short messages but is impractical for larger (several megabytes) messages (due to the computing resources required to create unique keystreams for such messages). One-time pads are typically implemented as stream ciphers.

A one-time pad is an example of a stream cipher and is considered unbreakable.

Types of ciphers

The two basic types of ciphers are *substitution* and *transposition*. Both are involved in the process of transforming plaintext into ciphertext.

Most modern cryptosystems use both substitution and permutation to achieve encryption.

Substitution ciphers

Substitution ciphers replace bits, characters, or character blocks in plaintext with alternate bits, characters, or character blocks to produce ciphertext. A classic example of a substitution cipher is one that Julius Caesar used: He substituted letters of the message with other letters from the same alphabet. (Read more about this in the sidebar "Tales from the crypt-o: A brief history of cryptography," earlier in this chapter.) In a simple substitution cipher using the standard English alphabet, a *cryptovariable* (key) is added *modulo 26* to the plaintext message. In modulo 26 addition, the remainder is the final result for any sum equal to or greater than 26. For example, a basic substitution cipher in which the word *BOY* is encrypted by adding three characters using modulo 26 math produces the following result:

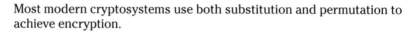

	B	O	Y	PLAINTEXT
	2	15	25	NUMERIC VALUE
+	3	3	3	SUBSTITUTION VALUE
	5	18	2	MODULO 26 RESULT
	E	R	B	CIPHERTEXT

A substitution cipher may be monoalphabetic or polyalphabetic:

- ✔ **Monoalphabetic:** A single alphabet is used to encrypt the entire plaintext message.

- ✔ **Polyalphabetic:** A more complex substitution that uses a different alphabet to encrypt each bit, character, or character block of a plaintext message.

A more modern example of a substitution cipher is the S-boxes (Substitution boxes) employed in the Data Encryption Standard (DES) algorithm. The S-boxes in DES produce a nonlinear substitution (6 bits in, 4 bits out). ***Note:*** Do *not* attempt to sing this to the tune "Shave and a Haircut" to improve the strength of the encryption by hiding any statistical relationship between the plaintext and ciphertext characters.

Transposition (or permutation) ciphers

Transposition ciphers rearrange bits, characters, or character blocks in plaintext to produce ciphertext. In a simple columnar transposition cipher, a message might be read horizontally but written vertically to produce the ciphertext as in the following example:

```
THE QUICK BROWN FOX JUMPS OVER THE LAZY DOG
```

written in 9 columns as

```
THEQUICKB
ROWNFOXJU
MPSOVERTH
ELAZYDOG
```

then transposed (encrypted) vertically as

```
TRMEHOPLEWSAQNOZUFVYIOEDCXROKJTGBUH
```

The original letters of the plaintext message are the same; only the order has been changed to achieve encryption.

DES performs permutations through the use of P-boxes (Permutation boxes) to spread the influence of a plaintext character over many characters so that they're not easily traced back to the S-boxes used in the substitution cipher.

Other types of ciphers include

- ✔ **Codes:** Includes words and phrases to communicate a secret message.

- ✔ **Running (or book) ciphers:** For example, the key is page 137 of *The Catcher in the Rye,* and text on that page is added modulo 26 to perform encryption/decryption.

✔ **Vernam ciphers:** Also known as *one-time pads,* which are keystreams that can be used only once. We discuss these more in the earlier sidebar "A disposable cipher: The one-time pad."

✔ **Concealment ciphers:** These ciphers include *steganography,* which we discuss in the section "Steganography: A picture is worth a thousand (hidden) words," later in this chapter.

Cryptography Alternatives

Technology does provide valid and interesting alternatives to cryptography when a message needs to be protected during transmission. Some useful options are listed in the following sections.

Steganography: A picture is worth a thousand (hidden) words

Steganography is the art of hiding the very existence of a message. It is related to but different from cryptography. Like cryptography, one purpose of steganography is to protect the contents of a message. However, unlike cryptography, the contents of the message aren't encrypted. Instead, the existence of the message is hidden in some other communications medium.

For example, a message may be hidden in a graphic or sound file, in slack space on storage media, in traffic noise over a network, or in a digital image. By using the example of a digital image, the least significant bit (the rightmost bit) of each byte in the image file can be used to transmit a hidden message without noticeably altering the image. However, because the message itself isn't encrypted, if it is discovered, its contents can be easily compromised.

Digital watermarking: The (ouch) low watermark

Digital watermarking is a technique similar (and related) to steganography that can be used to verify the authenticity of an image or data, or to protect the intellectual property rights of the creator. Watermarking is the visible cousin of steganography — no attempt is made to hide its existence. Watermarks have long been used on paper currency and office letterhead or paper stock.

Within the last decade, the use of digital watermarking has become more widespread. For example, to display photo examples on the Internet without risking intellectual property theft, a copyright notice may be prominently imprinted across the image. As with steganography, nothing is encrypted using digital watermarking; the confidentiality of the material is not protected with a watermark.

Not Quite the Metric System: Symmetric and Asymmetric Key Systems

Cryptographic algorithms are broadly classified as either symmetric or asymmetric key systems.

Symmetric key cryptography

Symmetric key cryptography, also known as *symmetric algorithm, secret key, single key,* and *private key* cryptography, uses a single key to both encrypt and decrypt information. Two parties (for our example, Thomas and Richard) can exchange an encrypted message by using the procedure in Lab 8-2:

Lab 8-2	Exchanging an Encrypted Message with Symmetric Key Cryptography

1. **The sender (Thomas) encrypts the plaintext message with a secret key known only to the intended recipient (Richard).**

2. **The sender then transmits the encrypted message to the intended recipient.**

3. **The recipient decrypts the message with the same secret key to obtain the plaintext message.**

In order for an attacker (Harold) to read the message, he must guess the secret key (by using a brute-force attack, for example) or intercept the secret key during the initial exchange.

The following list includes the main disadvantages of symmetric systems:

- ✔ **Distribution:** Secure distribution of secret keys is absolutely required either through out-of-band methods or by using asymmetric systems.

- ✔ **Scalability:** A different key is required for each pair of communicating parties.

> ✔ **Limited functionality:** Symmetric systems can't provide authentication or non-repudiation (see the earlier sidebar "He said, she said: The concept of non-repudiation").

Of course, symmetric systems do have many advantages:

> ✔ **Speed:** Symmetric systems are much faster than asymmetric systems.
>
> ✔ **Strength:** Strength is gained when used with a large key (128 bit, 256 bit, or larger).
>
> ✔ **Availability:** There are many algorithms available for organizations to select and use.

Symmetric key algorithms include Data Encryption Standard (DES), Triple DES (3DES), Advanced Encryption Standard (AES), International Data Encryption Algorithm (IDEA), and Rivest Cipher 5 (RC5).

Symmetric key systems use a shared secret key.

Data Encryption Standard (DES)

In the early 1970s, the National Institute of Standards and Technology (NIST) solicited vendors to submit encryption algorithm proposals to be evaluated by the National Security Agency (NSA) in support of a national cryptographic standard. This new encryption standard was used for private-sector and Sensitive but Unclassified (SBU) government data. In 1974, IBM submitted a 128-bit algorithm originally known as *Lucifer*. After some modifications (the algorithm was shortened to 56 bits and the S-boxes were changed), the IBM proposal was endorsed by the NSA and formally adopted as the Data Encryption Standard. It was published in *Federal Information Processing Standard* (FIPS) PUB 46 in 1977 (updated and revised in 1988 as FIPS PUB 46-1) and *American National Standards Institute* (ANSI) X3.92 in 1981.

DES is a block cipher that uses a 56-bit key.

The DES algorithm is a symmetric (or private) key cipher consisting of an algorithm and a key. The algorithm is a 64-bit block cipher based on a 56-bit symmetric key. (It consists of 56 key bits plus 8 parity bits . . . or think of it as 8 bytes, with each byte containing 7 key bits and 1 parity bit.) During encryption, the original message (plaintext) is divided into 64-bit blocks. Operating on a single block at a time, each 64-bit plaintext block is split into two 32-bit blocks. Under control of the 56-bit symmetric key, 16 rounds of transpositions and substitutions are performed on each individual character to produce the resulting ciphertext output.

A *parity bit* is used to detect errors in a bit pattern. For example, if the bit pattern has 56 key bits (ones and zeros) that add up to an even number, an *odd-parity bit* should be a one, making the total of the bits — including the parity bit — an odd number. For an *even-parity bit*, if the 56 key bits add up to an even number, the parity bit should be a zero, making the total of the bits— including the parity bit — an even number. If an algorithm uses even parity and the resulting bit pattern (including the parity bit) is an odd number, then the transmission has been corrupted.

A *round* is a transformation (permutations and substitutions) that an encryption algorithm performs on a block of plaintext to convert (encrypt) it into ciphertext.

The four distinct modes of operation (the mode of operation defines how the plaintext/ciphertext blocks are processed) in DES are Electronic Code Book, Cipher Block Chaining, Cipher Feedback, and Output Feedback.

The four modes of DES are ECB, CBC, CFB, and OFB. ECB and CBC are the most commonly used.

The original goal of DES was to develop an encryption standard that could be used for 10 to 15 years. Although DES far exceeded this goal, in 1999, the Electronic Frontier Foundation achieved the inevitable, breaking a DES key in only 23 hours.

Electronic Code Book (ECB)

Electronic Code Book (ECB) mode is the native mode for DES operation and normally produces the highest throughput. It is best used for encrypting keys or small amounts of data. ECB mode operates on 64-bit blocks of plaintext independently and produces 64-bit blocks of ciphertext. One significant disadvantage of ECB is that the same plaintext, encrypted with the same key, always produces the same ciphertext. If used to encrypt large amounts of data, it's susceptible to Chosen Text Attacks (CTA) (discussed in the section "Chosen Text Attack (CTA)," later in this chapter) because certain patterns may be revealed.

Cipher Block Chaining (CBC)

Cipher Block Chaining (CBC) mode is the most common mode of DES operation. Like ECB mode, CBC mode operates on 64-bit blocks of plaintext to produce 64-bit blocks of ciphertext. However, in CBC mode, each block is XORed (see the sidebar "The XORcist," later in this chapter) with the ciphertext of the preceding block to create a dependency, or *chain,* thereby producing a more random ciphertext result. The first block is encrypted with a random block known as the *initialization vector* (IV). One disadvantage of CBC mode is that errors propagate. However, this problem is limited to the block in which the error occurs and the block that immediately follows, after which, the decryption resynchronizes.

The XORcist

The *Exclusive Or (XOR) function* is a binary operation applied to two input bits: for example, a plaintext bit and a key bit. If the two bits are equal, the result is 0 (zero). If the two bits aren't equal, the result is 1.

Input A (Plaintext)	Input B (Key)	Output C (Ciphertext)
0	0	0
0	1	1
1	0	1
1	1	0

Cipher Feedback (CFB)

Cipher Feedback (CFB) mode is a stream cipher most often used to encrypt individual characters. In this mode, previously generated ciphertext is used as feedback for key generation in the next keystream. The resulting ciphertext is chained together, which causes errors to be multiplied throughout the encryption process.

Output Feedback (OFB)

Output Feedback (OFB) mode is also a stream cipher very similar to CFB. It is often used to encrypt satellite communications. In this mode, previous plaintext is used as feedback for key generation in the next keystream. Because the resulting ciphertext is not chained together, errors don't spread throughout the encryption process.

Triple DES (3DES)

Triple Data Encryption Standard (3DES) effectively extended the life of the DES algorithm. In Triple DES implementations, a message is encrypted by using one key, encrypted by using a second key, and then again encrypted by using either the first key or a third key.

The use of three separate 56-bit encryption keys produces an effective key length of 168 bits. But Triple DES doesn't just triple the work factor required to crack the DES algorithm (see the sidebar "Work factor: Force × effort = work!" in this chapter). Because the attacker doesn't know whether he or she successfully cracked even the first 56-bit key (pick a number between 0 and 72 quadrillion!) until all three keys are cracked and the correct plaintext is produced, the work factor required is more like $2^{56} \times 2^{56} \times 2^{56}$, or 72 quadrillion x 72 quadrillion x 72 quadrillion. (Don't try this multiplication on a calculator; just trust us on this one.)

You say To-*may*-to, I say To-*mah*-to: 3DES variations

The several variations of Triple DES (3DES) are as follows:

- ✔ DES-EEE2 (Encrypt-Encrypt-Encrypt), using 1st key, 2nd key, 1st key

- ✔ DES-EDE2 (Encrypt-Decrypt-Encrypt), using 1st key, 2nd key, 1st key

- ✔ DES-EEE3 (Encrypt-Encrypt-Encrypt), using 1st key, 2nd key, 3rd key

- ✔ DES-EDE3 (Encrypt-Decrypt-Encrypt), using 1st key, 2nd key, 3rd key

The basic function of Triple DES is sometimes explained like this: The message is encrypted using one key, decrypted using a second key, and again encrypted using the first key. The differences in syntax (and operation) are subtle but important: The second key (in an EDE implementation) doesn't truly decrypt the original message because the output is still gibberish (ciphertext). This variation was developed for backwards compatibility with single DES cryptosystems. Also, you should understand that use of the first key twice (in EDE2 and EEE2) is one common implementation, but use of a third distinct key is also possible (in EDE3 and EEE3).

Double DES wasn't a significant improvement to DES. In fact, by using a Meet-in-the-Middle Attack (see the section "Meet-in-the-Middle Attack," later in this chapter), the work factor required to crack Double DES is only slightly greater than for DES. For this reason, Double DES isn't commonly used.

Using Triple DES would seem enough to protect even the most sensitive data for at least a few lifetimes, but a few problems exist with Triple DES. First, the performance cost is significant. Although Triple DES is faster than many other symmetric encryption algorithms, it's still unacceptably slow and therefore doesn't work with many applications that require high-speed throughput of large volumes of data.

Second, a weakness exists in the implementation that allows a cryptanalyst to reduce the effective key size to 108 bits in a brute force attack. Although a 108-bit key size still requires a significant amount of time to crack (theoretically, several million millennia), it's still a weakness.

Advanced Encryption Standard (AES)

In May 2002, NIST announced the Rijndael Block Cipher as the new standard to implement the *Advanced Encryption Standard (AES),* which replaced DES as the U.S. government standard for encrypting Sensitive but Unclassified data. AES was subsequently approved for encrypting classified U.S. government data up to the Top Secret level (using 192- or 256-key lengths).

See Chapter 6 for more on data classification.

The *Rijndael Block Cipher,* developed by Dr. Joan Daemen and Dr. Vincent Rijmen, uses variable block and key lengths (128, 192, or 256 bits) and between 10 and 14 rounds. It was designed to be simple, resistant to known attacks, and fast. It can be implemented in either hardware or software and has relatively low memory requirements.

AES is based on the Rijndael Block Cipher.

Until recently, the only known successful attacks against AES were *side-channel attacks,* which don't directly attack the encryption algorithm, but instead attack the system on which the encryption algorithm is implemented. Side-channel attacks using cache-timing techniques are most common against AES implementations. In 2009, a theoretical related-key attack against AES was published. The attack method is considered theoretical because, although it reduces the mathematical complexity required to break an AES key, it is still well beyond the computational capability available today.

Blowfish and Twofish Algorithm

The *Blowfish Algorithm* operates on 64-bit blocks, employs 16 rounds, and uses variable key lengths of up to 448 bits. The *Twofish Algorithm,* a finalist in the AES selection process, is a symmetric block cipher that operates on 128-bit blocks, employing 16 rounds with variable key lengths up to 256 bits. Both Blowfish and Twofish were designed by Bruce Schneier (and others) and are freely available in the public domain (neither algorithm has been patented). To date, there are no known successful cryptanalytic attacks against either algorithm.

Rivest Ciphers

Drs. Ron Rivest, Adi Shamir, and Len Adleman invented the RSA algorithm and founded RSA Data Security (RSA = *R*ivest, *S*hamir, *A*dleman). The Rivest Ciphers are a series of symmetric algorithms that include RC2, RC4, RC5, and RC6 (RC1 was never published and RC3 was broken during development):

- ✔ **RC2:** A block-mode cipher that encrypts 64-bit blocks of data by using a variable-length key.

- ✔ **RC4:** A stream cipher (data is encrypted in real time) that uses a variable-length key (128 bits is standard).

- ✔ **RC5:** Similar to RC2, but includes a variable-length key (0 to 2,048 bits), variable block size (32, 64, or 128 bits), and variable number of processing rounds (0 to 255).

- ✔ **RC6:** Derived from RC5 and a finalist in the AES selection process. It uses a 128-bit block size and variable-length keys of 128, 192, or 256 bits.

IDEA Cipher

The *International Data Encryption Algorithm (IDEA)* Cipher evolved from the Proposed Encryption Standard and the Improved Proposed Encryption Standard (IPES) originally developed in 1990. IDEA is a block cipher that operates on 64-bit plaintext blocks by using a 128-bit key. IDEA performs eight rounds on 16-bit sub-blocks and can operate in four distinct modes similar to DES. The IDEA Cipher provides stronger encryption than RC4 and Triple DES, but because it's patented, it's not widely used today. However, the patents are set to expire in various countries between 2010 and 2012. It is currently used in some software applications, including Pretty Good Privacy (PGP) e-mail. (For more on PGP, read "E-mail Security Applications" later in this chapter.) There are currently no known practical cryptanalytic attacks against the IDEA Cipher.

Asymmetric key cryptography

Asymmetric key cryptography (also known as *asymmetric algorithm cryptography* or *public key cryptography*) uses two separate keys: one key to encrypt and a different key to decrypt information. These keys are known as *public* and *private key pairs*. When two parties want to exchange an encrypted message by using asymmetric key cryptography, they follow the steps in Lab 8-3:

Lab 8-3	Exchanging an Encrypted Message with Asymmetric Key Cryptography

1. **The sender (Thomas) encrypts the plaintext message with the intended recipient's (Richard) public key.**

2. **This produces a ciphertext message that can then be transmitted to the intended recipient (Richard).**

3. **The recipient (Richard) then decrypts the message with his private key, known only to him.**

Only the private key can decrypt the message; thus, an attacker (Harold) possessing only the public key can't decrypt the message. This also means that not even the original sender can decrypt the message. This use of an asymmetric key system is known as a *secure message*. A secure message guarantees the confidentiality of the message.

Asymmetric key systems use a public key and a private key.

Secure message format uses the recipient's private key to protect confidentiality.

If the sender wants to guarantee the authenticity of a message (or, more correctly, the authenticity of the sender), he or she can sign the message by using the procedure described in Lab 8-4:

Lab 8-4 Signing a Message to Guarantee Authenticity

1. **The sender (Thomas) encrypts the plaintext message with his own private key.**

2. **This produces a ciphertext message that can then be transmitted to the intended recipient (Richard).**

3. **To verify that the message is in fact from the purported sender, the recipient (Richard) applies the sender's (Thomas's) public key (which is known to every Tom, Dick, and Harry).**

Of course, an attacker can also verify the authenticity of the message. This use of an asymmetric key system is known as an *open message format* because it guarantees only the authenticity, not the confidentiality.

Open message format uses the sender's private key to ensure authenticity.

If the sender wants to guarantee both the confidentiality and authenticity of a message, he or she can do so by using the procedure in Lab 8-5:

Lab 8-5 Guaranteeing Confidentiality and Authenticity of a Message

1. **The sender (Thomas) encrypts the message first with the intended recipient's (Richard's) public key and then with his own private key.**

2. **This produces a ciphertext message that can then be transmitted to the intended recipient (Richard).**

3. **The recipient (Richard) uses the sender's (Thomas's) public key to verify the authenticity of the message, and then uses his own private key to decrypt the message's contents.**

If an attacker intercepts the message, he or she can apply the sender's public key, but then has an encrypted message that he or she can't decrypt without the intended recipient's private key. Thus, both confidentiality and authenticity are assured. This use of an asymmetric key system is known as a *secure and signed message format*.

A secure and signed message format uses the sender's private key and the recipient's public key to protect confidentiality and ensure authenticity.

A public key and a private key are mathematically related, but theoretically, no one can compute or derive the private key from the public key. This property of asymmetric systems is based on the concept of a one-way function. A *one-way function* is a problem that you can easily compute in one direction but not in the reverse direction. In asymmetric key systems, a *trapdoor* (private key) resolves the reverse operation of the one-way function.

Because of the complexity of asymmetric key systems, they are more commonly used for key management or digital signatures than for encryption of bulk information. Often, a *hybrid* system is employed, using an asymmetric system to securely distribute the secret keys of a symmetric key system that's used to encrypt the data.

The main disadvantage of asymmetric systems is their lower speed. Because of the types of algorithms that are used to achieve the one-way hash functions, very large keys are required. (A 128-bit symmetric key has the equivalent strength of a 2,304-bit asymmetric key.) Those large keys, in turn, require more computational power, causing a significant loss of speed (up to 10,000 times slower than a comparable symmetric key system).

However, the many significant advantages of asymmetric systems include

- ✔ **Extended functionality:** Asymmetric key systems can provide both confidentiality and authentication; symmetric systems can provide only confidentiality.

- ✔ **Scalability:** Because symmetric key systems require secret key exchanges between all of the communicating parties, their scalability is limited. Asymmetric key systems, which do not require secret key exchanges, resolve key management issues associated with symmetric key systems, and are therefore more scalable.

Asymmetric key algorithms include RSA, Diffie-Hellman, El Gamal, Merkle-Hellman (Trapdoor) Knapsack, and Elliptic Curve, which we talk about in the following sections.

RSA

In 1978, Drs. Ron Rivest, Adi Shamir, and Len Adleman published the RSA algorithm, which is a *key transport* algorithm based on the difficulty of factoring a number that's the product of two large prime numbers (typically 512 bits). Two users (Thomas and Richard) can securely transport symmetric keys by using RSA as described in Lab 8-6:

Lab 8-6   Securely Transporting Symmetric Keys with RSA

1. **Thomas creates a symmetric key, encrypts it with Richard's public key, and then transmits it to Richard.**

2. **Richard decrypts the symmetric key by using his own private key.**

RSA is an asymmetric key algorithm based on factoring prime numbers.

Diffie-Hellman Key Exchange

In 1976, Drs. Whitfield Diffie and Martin Hellman published a paper, entitled "New Directions in Cryptography," that detailed a new paradigm for secure key exchange based on discrete logarithms. *Diffie-Hellman* is described as a key agreement algorithm. Two users (Thomas and Richard) can exchange symmetric keys by using Diffie-Hellman as described in Lab 8-7:

Lab 8-7   Exchanging Symmetric Keys with Diffie-Hellman

1. **Thomas and Richard obtain each other's public keys.**

2. **Thomas and Richard then combine their own private keys with the public key of the other person, producing a symmetric key that only the two users involved in the exchange know.**

Diffie-Hellman key exchange is vulnerable to Man-in-the-Middle Attacks, in which an attacker (Harold) intercepts the public keys during the initial exchange and substitutes his own private key to create a session key that can decrypt the session. (You can read more about these attacks in the section "Man-in-the-Middle Attack," later in this chapter.) A separate authentication mechanism is necessary to protect against this type of attack, ensuring that the two parties communicating in the session are, in fact, the legitimate parties.

Diffie-Hellman is an asymmetric key algorithm based on discrete logarithms.

El Gamal

El Gamal is an unpatented, asymmetric key algorithm based on the discrete logarithm problem used in Diffie-Hellman (discussed in the preceding section). El Gamal extends the functionality of Diffie-Hellman to include encryption and digital signatures.

Merkle-Hellman (Trapdoor) Knapsack

The *Merkle-Hellman (Trapdoor) Knapsack,* published in 1978, employs a unique approach to asymmetric cryptography. It's based on the problem of determining what items, in a set of items that have fixed weights, can be combined in order to obtain a given total weight. Knapsack was broken in 1982.

Knapsack is an asymmetric key algorithm based on fixed weights.

Elliptic Curve (EC)

In 1985, Neal Koblitz and Victor Miller proposed a new model for asymmetric algorithms based on elliptic curves (EC). Elliptic curves are far more difficult to compute than conventional discrete logarithm problems or factoring prime numbers. (A 160-bit EC key is equivalent to a 1,024-bit RSA key.) The use of smaller keys means that EC is significantly faster than other asymmetric algorithms (and many symmetric algorithms), and can be widely implemented in various hardware applications including wireless devices and smart cards.

Elliptic Curve is more efficient than other asymmetric key systems and many symmetric key systems because it can use a smaller key.

Message Authentication

Message authentication guarantees the authenticity and integrity of a message by ensuring that

- ✔ A message hasn't been altered (either maliciously or accidentally) during transmission.
- ✔ A message isn't a replay of a previous message.
- ✔ The message was sent from the origin stated (it's not a forgery).
- ✔ The message is sent to the intended recipient.

Checksums, CRC-values, and parity checks are examples of basic message authentication and integrity controls. More advanced message authentication is performed by using digital signatures and message digests.

Digital signatures and message digests can provide message authentication.

Digital signatures

The *Digital Signature Standard* (DSS), published by the National Institute of Standards and Technology (NIST) in Federal Information Processing Standard (FIPS) 186-1, specifies two acceptable algorithms in its standard: the RSA Digital Signature Algorithm and the Digital Signature Algorithm (DSA, which is based on a modified El Gamal algorithm). Both algorithms use the SHA-1 Secure Hash Algorithm, which we discuss in the section "Message digests," later in this chapter.

A digital signature is a simple way to verify the authenticity (and integrity) of a message. Instead of encrypting a message with the intended receiver's public key, the sender encrypts it with his or her own private key. The sender's public key properly decrypts the message, authenticating the originator of the message. This process is known as an *open message format* in asymmetric key systems, which we discuss in the section "Asymmetric key cryptography," earlier in this chapter.

Message digests

It's often impractical to encrypt a message with the receiver's public key to protect confidentiality, and then encrypt the entire message again by using the sender's private key to protect authenticity and integrity. Instead, a representation of the encrypted message is encrypted with the sender's private key to produce a digital signature. The intended recipient decrypts this representation by using the sender's public key, and then independently calculates the expected results of the decrypted representation by using the same, known, one-way hashing algorithm. If the results are the same, the integrity of the original message is assured. This representation of the entire message is known as a *message digest*.

To *digest* means to reduce or condense something, and a message digest does precisely that. (Conversely, *indigestion* means to expand . . . like gases . . . how do you spell *relief?*) A message digest is a condensed representation of a message; think *Reader's Digest*. Ideally, a message digest has the following properties:

- ✔ The original message can't be re-created from the message digest.
- ✔ Finding a message that produces a particular digest shouldn't be computationally feasible.
- ✔ No two messages should produce the same message digest (known as a *collision*).
- ✔ The message digest should be calculated by using the entire contents of the original message — it shouldn't be a representation of a representation.

Message digests are produced by using a one-way hash function. There are several types of one-way hashing algorithms (digest algorithms), including MD5, SHA-1, and HMAC.

A *collision* results when two messages produce the same digest or when a message produces the same digest as a different message.

A *one-way function* ensures that the same key can't encrypt and decrypt a message in an asymmetric key system. One key encrypts the message (produces ciphertext), and a second key (the trapdoor) decrypts the message (produces plaintext), effectively reversing the one-way function. A one-way function's purpose is to ensure confidentiality.

A *one-way hashing algorithm* produces a hashing value (or message digest) that can't be reversed; that is, it can't be decrypted. In other words, no trapdoor exists for a one-way hashing algorithm. The purpose of a one-way hashing algorithm is to ensure integrity and authentication.

MD5, SHA-1 and SHA-2, and HMAC are all examples of commonly used message authentication algorithms.

MD family

MD (Message Digest) is a family of one-way hashing algorithms developed by Dr. Ron Rivest that includes MD (obsolete), MD2, MD3 (not widely used), MD4, MD5, and MD6:

- ✔ **MD2:** Developed in 1989 and still widely used today, MD2 takes a variable size input (message) and produces a fixed-size output (128-bit message digest). MD2 is very slow (it was originally developed for 8-bit computers) and is highly susceptible to collisions.

- ✔ **MD4:** Developed in 1990, MD4 produces a 128-bit digest and is used to compute NT-password hashes for various Microsoft Windows operating systems, including NT, XP, and Vista. An MD4 hash is typically represented as a 32-digit hexadecimal number. Several known weaknesses are associated with MD4, and it's also susceptible to collision attacks.

- ✔ **MD5:** Developed in 1991, MD5 is one of the most popular hashing algorithms in use today, commonly used to store passwords and to check the integrity of files. Like MD2 and MD4, MD5 produces a 128-bit digest. Messages are processed in 512-bit blocks, using four rounds of transformation. The resulting hash is typically represented as a 32-digit hexadecimal number. MD5 is also susceptible to collisions and is now considered "cryptographically broken" by the U.S. Department of Homeland Security.

- ✔ **MD6:** Developed in 2008, MD6 uses very large input message blocks (up to 512 *bytes*) and produces variable-length digests (up to 512 bits). MD6 was originally submitted for consideration as the new SHA-3 standard but was eliminated from further consideration after the first round in July 2009. Unfortunately, the first widespread use of MD6 (albeit, unauthorized and illicit) was in the Conficker.B worm in late 2008, shortly after the algorithm was published!

SHA family

Like MD, SHA (Secure Hash Algorithm) is another family of one-way hash functions. The SHA family of algorithms is designed by the U.S. National Security Agency (NSA) and published by NIST. The SHA family of algorithms includes SHA-1 and SHA-2, and one in the oven — SHA-3:

- ✔ **SHA-1:** Published in 1995, SHA-1 takes a variable size input (message) and produces a fixed-size output (160-bit message digest, versus MD5's 128-bit message digest). SHA-1 processes messages in 512-bit blocks and adds padding to a message length, if necessary, to produce a total message length that's a multiple of 512.

- ✔ **SHA-2:** Published in 2001, SHA-2 consists of four hash functions — SHA-224, SHA-256, SHA-384, and SHA-512 — that have digest lengths of 224, 256, 384, and 512 bits, respectively. SHA-2 processes messages in 512-bit blocks for the 224, 256, and 384 variants, and 1,024-bit blocks for SHA-512.

- ✔ **SHA-3:** The new SHA-3 standard is scheduled to be published in 2012.

HMAC

The Hashed Message Authentication Code (or Checksum) (HMAC) further extends the security of the MD5 and SHA-1 algorithms through the concept of a *keyed digest*. HMAC incorporates a previously shared secret key and the original message into a single message digest. Thus, even if an attacker intercepts a message, modifies its contents, and calculates a new message digest, the result doesn't match the receiver's hash calculation because the modified message's hash doesn't include the secret key.

Public Key Infrastructure (PKI)

A *Public Key Infrastructure (PKI)* is an arrangement whereby a central authority stores encryption keys or *certificates* (an electronic document that uses the public key of an organization or individual to establish identity, and a digital signature to establish authenticity) associated with users and systems, thereby enabling secure communications through the integration of digital signatures, digital certificates, and other services necessary to ensure confidentiality, integrity, authentication, non-repudiation, and access control.

The four basic components of a PKI are the Certification Authority, Registration Authority, repository, and archive:

- ✔ **Certification Authority (CA):** The Certification Authority (CA) comprises hardware, software, and the personnel administering the PKI. The CA issues certificates, maintains and publishes status information and Certificate Revocation Lists (CRLs), and maintains archives.

- ✔ **Registration Authority (RA):** The Registration Authority (RA) also comprises hardware, software, and the personnel administering the PKI. It's responsible for verifying certificate contents for the CA.

⊾ **Repository:** A *repository* is a system that accepts certificates and CRLs from a CA and distributes them to authorized parties.

⊾ **Archive:** An *archive* offers long-term storage of archived information from the CA.

Key Management Functions

Like physical keys, encryption keys must be safeguarded. Most successful attacks against encryption exploit some vulnerability in *key management* functions rather than some inherent weakness in the encryption algorithm. The following are the major functions associated with managing encryption keys:

⊾ **Key generation:** Keys must be generated randomly on a secure system, and the generation sequence itself shouldn't provide potential clues regarding the contents of the keyspace. Generated keys shouldn't be displayed in the clear.

⊾ **Key distribution:** Keys must be securely distributed. This is a major vulnerability in symmetric key systems. Using an asymmetric system to securely distribute secret keys is one solution.

⊾ **Key installation:** Key installation is often a manual process. This process should ensure that the key isn't compromised during installation, incorrectly entered, or too difficult to be used readily.

⊾ **Key storage:** Keys must be stored on protected or encrypted storage media, or the application using the keys should include safeguards that prevent extraction of the keys.

⊾ **Key change:** Keys, like passwords, should be changed regularly, relative to the value of the information being protected and the frequency of use. Keys used frequently are more likely to be compromised through interception and statistical analysis. As with a changing of the guard, vulnerabilities inherent to any change must be addressed.

⊾ **Key control:** Key control addresses the proper use of keys. Different keys have different functions and may only be approved for certain levels of classification.

⊾ **Key disposal:** Keys (and any distribution media) must be properly disposed of, erased, or destroyed so that the key's contents are not disclosed, possibly providing an attacker insight into the key management system.

The seven key management issues are generation, distribution, installation, storage, change, control, and disposal.

Key Escrow and Key Recovery

Law enforcement has always been concerned about the potential use of encryption for criminal purposes. To counter this threat, NIST published the Escrowed Encryption Standard (EES) in Federal Information Processing Standards (FIPS) Publication 185 (1994). The premise of the EES is to divide a secret key into two parts and place those two parts into escrow with two separate, trusted organizations. With a court order, the two parts can be obtained by law enforcement officials, the secret key recovered, and the suspected communications decrypted. One implementation of the EES is the Clipper Chip proposed by the U.S. government. The Clipper Chip uses the Skipjack Secret Key algorithm for encryption and an 80-bit secret key.

E-Mail Security Applications

Several applications employing various cryptographic techniques have been developed to provide confidentiality, integrity, authentication, non-repudiation, and access control for e-mail communications.

- **Secure Multipurpose Internet Mail Extensions (S/MIME):** S/MIME is a secure method of sending e-mail incorporated into several popular browsers and e-mail applications. S/MIME provides confidentiality and authentication by using the RSA asymmetric key system, digital signatures, and X.509 digital certificates. S/MIME complies with the Public Key Cryptography Standard (PKCS) #7 format and has been proposed as a standard to the Internet Engineering Task Force (IETF).

- **MIME Object Security Services (MOSS):** MOSS provides confidentiality, integrity, identification and authentication, and non-repudiation by using MD2 or MD5, RSA asymmetric keys, and DES. MOSS has never been widely implemented or used.

- **Privacy Enhanced Mail (PEM):** PEM was proposed as a PKCS-compliant standard by the IETF but has never been widely implemented or used. It provides confidentiality and authentication by using 3DES for encryption, MD2 or MD5 message digests, X.509 digital certificates, and the RSA asymmetric system for digital signatures and secure key distribution.

- **Pretty Good Privacy (PGP):** PGP is a popular e-mail encryption application. It provides confidentiality and authentication by using the IDEA Cipher for encryption and the RSA asymmetric system for digital signatures and secure key distribution. Instead of a central Certificate Authority (CA), PGP uses a *trust model* (in which the communicating parties implicitly trust each other), which is ideally suited for smaller groups to validate user identity (as opposed to a PKI infrastructure, which can be costly and difficult to maintain).

Today two basic versions of PGP software are available: Freeware versions from PGP International at www.pgpi.org, and a commercial version from Symantec Corporation at www.symantec.com. There is also an open-source version, called GPG, available at www.gnupg.org.

Symantec acquired the commercial version of PGP in 2010. Symantec's PGP product line includes a whole disk encryption solution.

PGP is a freeware e-mail security application (free to individuals, not organizations) that uses the IDEA algorithm (symmetric) for encryption and the RSA algorithm (asymmetric) for key distribution and digital signatures.

Internet Security Applications

As with e-mail applications, several protocols, standards, and applications have been developed to provide security for Internet communications and transactions.

Secure Sockets Layer (SSL)/Transport Layer Security (TLS)

The *Secure Sockets Layer* (SSL) protocol, developed by Netscape in 1994, provides session-based encryption and authentication for secure communication between clients and servers on the Internet. SSL operates at the Transport Layer (Layer 4) of the OSI model, is independent of the application protocol, and provides server authentication with optional client authentication. SSL uses the RSA asymmetric key system; IDEA, DES, and 3DES symmetric key systems; and the MD5 hash function. The current version is SSL 3.0. SSL 3.0 was standardized by the IETF in Transport Layer Security (TLS) 1.0 and released in 1999 with only minor modifications to the original SSL 3.0 specification. TLS 1.2 is the most current version of TLS.

See Chapter 5 for a complete discussion of the OSI model.

SSL is most visible to users when used in conjunction with web servers when they serve encrypted pages using the *https* protocol. SSL is also gaining favor as a protocol for Virtual Private Networks (VPNs) used for remote access.

Although it is not as popular as it once was, you should know that the Secure Electronic Transaction (SET) specification is an Internet security application developed jointly by MasterCard and Visa for secure e-commerce (see the sidebar "Secure Electronic Transaction [SET]").

Secure Electronic Transaction (SET)

The *Secure Electronic Transaction* (SET) specification was developed by MasterCard and Visa to provide secure e-commerce transactions by implementing authentication mechanisms while protecting the confidentiality and integrity of cardholder data. SET defines the following features:

✔ **Confidentiality:** Using DES

✔ **Integrity:** Using digital signatures and the RSA asymmetric system

✔ **Cardholder authentication:** Using digital signatures and X.509 digital certificates

✔ **Merchant authentication:** Using digital signatures and X.509 digital certificates

✔ **Interoperability:** Between different hardware and software manufacturers

SET utilizes dual signatures by allowing two pieces of data to be linked and sent to two different entities. SET never won favor in the marketplace and has fallen into disuse.

Secure Hypertext Transfer Protocol (S-HTTP)

Secure Hypertext Transfer Protocol (S-HTTP) is an Internet protocol that provides a method for secure communications with a web server. S-HTTP is a connectionless-oriented protocol that encapsulates data after security properties for the session have been successfully negotiated. It uses symmetric encryption (for confidentiality), message digests (for integrity), and public key encryption (for client-server authentication and non-repudiation). Instead of encrypting an entire session as in SSL, S-HTTP can be applied to individual web documents.

S-HTTP is not widely used, and should not be confused with *https*. See the earlier section on SSL/TLS.

IPSec

Internet Protocol Security (IPSec) is an IETF open standard for secure communications over public IP-based networks, such as the Internet. IPSec ensures confidentiality, integrity, and authenticity by using OSI model Layer 3 (Network) encryption and authentication to provide an end-to-end solution. IPSec operates in two modes:

✔ **Transport Mode:** Only the data is encrypted.

✔ **Tunnel Mode:** The entire packet is encrypted.

See Chapter 5 for more on IPSec.

The two modes of IPSec are Transport mode and Tunnel mode.

The two main protocols used in IPSec are

- ✔ **Authentication Header (AH):** Provides integrity, authentication, and non-repudiation
- ✔ **Encapsulating Security Payload (ESP):** Provides confidentiality (encryption) and limited authentication

Each pair of hosts communicating in an IPSec session must establish a security association (SA).

An *SA* is a one-way connection between two communicating parties; two SAs are required for each pair of communicating hosts. Additionally, each SA supports only a single protocol (AH or ESP). Thus, if both AH and ESP are used between two communicating hosts, a total of four SAs is required. An SA has three parameters that uniquely identify it in an IPSec session:

- ✔ **Security Parameter Index (SPI):** The SPI is a 32-bit string used by the receiving station to differentiate between SAs terminating on that station. The SPI is located within the AH or ESP header.
- ✔ **Destination IP Address:** The destination address could be the end station or an intermediate gateway or firewall, but it must be a unicast address. (See Chapter 5 for more on unicast addresses.)
- ✔ **Security Protocol ID:** Either an AH or ESP association.

In IPSec, a security association (SA) is a one-way connection. You need a minimum of two SAs for two-way communications.

Key management is provided in IPSec by using the Internet Key Exchange (IKE). *IKE* is actually a combination of three complementary protocols: The Internet Security Association and Key Management Protocol (ISAKMP), the Secure Key Exchange Mechanism (SKEME), and the Oakley Key Determination Protocol. IKE operates in three modes: Main mode, Aggressive mode, and Quick mode.

Multi-Protocol Label Switching (MPLS)

Multi-Protocol Label Switching (MPLS) is an extremely fast method for forwarding packets through a network by using labels inserted between Layer 2 and Layer 3 headers in the packet. MPLS is protocol independent and highly scalable, providing Quality of Service (QoS) with multiple Classes of Service (CoS) and secure Layer 3 Virtual Private Network (VPN) tunneling.

Secure Shell (SSH-2)

Secure Shell (SSH-2, or version 2) is used for secure remote access as one alternative to Telnet. It can be used to provide confidentiality, integrity, and authentication. SSH-2 establishes an encrypted tunnel between the SSH client and SSH server and can also authenticate the client to the server. SSH version 1 is also widely used but has inherent vulnerabilities that are easily exploited.

SSH-2 (or simply SSH) is an Internet security application that provides secure remote access.

Wireless Transport Layer Security (WTLS)

The *Wireless Transport Layer Security* (WTLS) protocol provides security services for the Wireless Application Protocol (WAP) commonly used for Internet connectivity by mobile devices. WTLS provides three classes of security:

- ✔ **Class 1:** Anonymous Authentication

- ✔ **Class 2:** Server Authentication Only

- ✔ **Class 3:** Client-Server Authentication: Additional (but somewhat limited) security is provided in WAP through the use of Service Set Identifiers (SSID) and Wired Equivalent Privacy (WEP) Keys. A significant improvement in wireless security incorporates the Extensible Authentication Protocol (EAP), which uses a Remote Authentication Dial-In User Service (RADIUS) server for authentication.

WEP has well-known and easily exploited vulnerabilities that render it largely ineffective. WEP should only be used if other security protocols are not available.

Methods of Attack

Attempts to crack a cryptosystem can be generally classified into four classes of attack methods:

- ✔ **Analytic attacks:** An *analytic attack* uses algebraic manipulation in an attempt to reduce the complexity of the algorithm.

- ✔ **Brute-force attacks:** In a *brute-force* (or *exhaustion*) *attack,* the cryptanalyst attempts every possible combination of key patterns, sometimes utilizing rainbow tables, and specialized or scalable computing architectures. This type of attack can be very time-intensive (up to several hundred million years) and resource-intensive, depending on the length of the key, the speed of the attacker's computer . . . and the lifespan of the attacker.

✔ **Implementation attacks:** *Implementation attacks* attempt to exploit some weakness in the cryptosystem such as vulnerability in a protocol or algorithm.

✔ **Statistical attacks:** A *statistical attack* attempts to exploit some statistical weakness in the cryptosystem, such as a lack of randomness in key generation.

A *rainbow table* is a precomputed table used to reverse cryptographic hash functions in a specific algorithm. Examples of password-cracking programs that use rainbow tables include Ophcrack and RainbowCrack.

The specific attack methods discussed in the following sections employ various elements of the four classes we describe in the preceding list.

The Birthday Attack

The *Birthday Attack* attempts to exploit the probability of two messages producing the same message digest by using the same hash function. It's based on the statistical probability (greater than 50 percent) that in a room containing 23 or more people, 2 people in that room have the same birthday. However, for 2 people in a room to share a specific birthday (such as August 3rd), 253 or more people must be in the room to have a statistical probability of greater than 50 percent (even if one of the birthdays is on February 29).

Work factor: Force —ts effort = work!

Work factor (discussed earlier in this chapter) describes the expenditure required — in terms of time, effort, and resources — to break a cryptosystem. Given enough time, effort, and resources, any cryptosystem can be broken. The goal of all cryptosystems, then, is to achieve a work factor that sufficiently protects the encrypted information against a reasonable estimate of available time, effort, and resources. However, *reasonable* can be difficult to estimate as technology continues to improve rapidly.

Moore's Law is based on an observation by Gordon Moore, one of the founders of Intel, that processing power seems to double about every 18 months. To compensate for Moore's Law, some *really* hard encryption algorithms are used. Today, encrypted information is valuable for perhaps only three months with encryption algorithms that (theoretically) would take several hundred millennia to break; everybody's confident in the knowledge that by tomorrow such a feat will be mere child's play.

Ciphertext Only Attack (COA)

In a *Ciphertext Only Attack (COA)*, the cryptanalyst obtains the ciphertext of several messages, all encrypted by using the same encryption algorithm, but he or she doesn't have the associated plaintext. The cryptanalyst then attempts to decrypt the data by searching for repeating patterns and using statistical analysis. For example, certain words in the English language, such as *the* and *or,* occur frequently. This type of attack is generally difficult and requires a large sample of ciphertext.

Chosen Text Attack (CTA)

In a *Chosen Text Attack* (CTA), the cryptanalyst selects a sample of plaintext and obtains the corresponding ciphertext. Several types of Chosen Text Attacks exist, including Chosen Plaintext, Adaptive Chosen Plaintext, Chosen Ciphertext, and Adaptive Chosen Ciphertext:

- **Chosen Plaintext Attack (CPA):** The cryptanalyst chooses plaintext to be encrypted, and the corresponding ciphertext is obtained.
- **Adaptive Chosen Plaintext Attack (ACPA):** The cryptanalyst chooses plaintext to be encrypted; then based on the resulting ciphertext, he chooses another sample to be encrypted.
- **Chosen Ciphertext Attack (CCA):** The cryptanalyst chooses ciphertext to be decrypted, and the corresponding plaintext is obtained.
- **Adaptive Chosen Ciphertext Attack (ACCA):** The cryptanalyst chooses ciphertext to be decrypted; then based on the resulting ciphertext, he chooses another sample to be decrypted.

Known Plaintext Attack (KPA)

In a *Known Plaintext Attack* (KPA), the cryptanalyst has obtained the ciphertext and corresponding plaintext of several past messages, which he or she uses to decipher new messages.

Man-in-the-Middle Attack

A *Man-in-the-Middle Attack* involves an attacker intercepting messages between two parties on a network and potentially modifying the original message.

Meet-in-the-Middle Attack

A *Meet-in-the-Middle Attack* involves an attacker encrypting known plaintext with each possible key on one end, decrypting the corresponding ciphertext with each possible key, and then comparing the results *in the middle*. Although commonly classified as a brute-force attack, this kind of attack may also be considered an analytic attack because it does involve some differential analysis.

Replay Attack

A *Replay Attack* occurs when a session key is intercepted and used against a later encrypted session between the same two parties. Replay attacks can be countered by incorporating a time stamp in the session key.

Prep Test

1 **The four modes of DES include all the following except**

A ○ ECB

B ○ ECC

C ○ CFB

D ○ CBC

2 **A type of cipher that replaces bits, characters, or character blocks with alternate bits, characters, or character blocks to produce ciphertext is known as a**

A ○ Permutation cipher

B ○ Block cipher

C ○ Transposition cipher

D ○ Substitution cipher

3 **Which of the following is not an advantage of symmetric key systems?**

A ○ Scalability

B ○ Speed

C ○ Strength

D ○ Availability

4 **The Advanced Encryption Standard (AES) is based on what symmetric key algorithm?**

A ○ Twofish

B ○ Knapsack

C ○ Diffie-Hellman

D ○ Rijndael

5 **A message that's encrypted with only the sender's private key, for the purpose of authentication, is known as a(n)**

A ○ Secure message format

B ○ Signed and secure message format

C ○ Open message format

D ○ Message digest

6 **All the following are examples of asymmetric key systems based on discrete logarithms except**

A ○ Diffie-Hellman
B ○ Elliptic Curve
C ○ RSA
D ○ El Gamal

7 **The four main components of a Public Key Infrastructure (PKI) include all the following except**

A ○ Directory Service
B ○ Certification Authority
C ○ Repository
D ○ Archive

8 **Which of the following Internet specifications provides secure e-commerce by using symmetric key systems, asymmetric key systems, and dual signatures?**

A ○ Public Key Infrastructure (PKI)
B ○ Secure Electronic Transaction (SET)
C ○ Secure Sockets Layer (SSL)
D ○ Secure Hypertext Transfer Protocol (S-HTTP)

9 **The minimum number of SAs required for a two-way IPSec session between two communicating hosts using both AH and ESP is**

A ○ 1
B ○ 2
C ○ 4
D ○ 8

10 **An IPSec SA consists of the following parameters, which uniquely identify it in an IPSec session, except**

A ○ Source IP Address
B ○ Destination IP Address
C ○ Security Protocol ID
D ○ Security Parameter Index (SPI)

Answers

1 **B.** ECC. ECC is the Elliptic Curve cryptosystem, an asymmetric algorithm. ECB (Electronic Code Book), CFB (Cipher Feedback), CBC (Cipher Block Chaining), and OFB (Output Feedback) are all valid DES modes of operation. *Review "Data Encryption Standard (DES)."*

2 **D.** Substitution cipher. Transposition ciphers and permutation ciphers rearrange data to produce ciphertext. A block cipher is a type of cipher that operates on a block of data. *Review "Types of ciphers."*

3 **A.** Scalability. Symmetric key systems aren't scalable because of the difficulty of key management between individual pairs of communicating parties. *Review "Symmetric key cryptography."*

4 **D.** Rijndael. The NIST selected the Rijndael Block Cipher as the AES. Twofish was a finalist for the AES standard but wasn't selected. Knapsack and Diffie-Hellman are asymmetric key systems. *Review "Advanced Encryption Standard (AES)."*

5 **C.** Open message format. A secure message is encrypted by using the receiver's public key to achieve confidentiality. A signed and secure message is encrypted with both the receiver's public key and the sender's private key. A one-way hashing function produces a message digest to digitally sign a message for authentication. *Review "Asymmetric key cryptography."*

6 **C.** RSA. RSA is based on factoring large prime numbers. *Review "RSA."*

7 **A.** Directory Service. The four basic components of a PKI are the Certificate Authority (CA), Registration Authority (RA), Repository, and Archive. *Review "Public Key Infrastructure (PKI)."*

8 **B.** Secure Electronic Transaction (SET). Only SET implements the concept of dual signatures for authentication. *Review "Internet Security Applications."*

9 **C.** 4. Four Security Associations (SAs) are required because SAs are simplex (one-way) and an SA is required for each protocol. *Review "IPSec."*

10 **A.** Source IP Address. The Source IP Address isn't included in an SA. *Review "IPSec."*

Chapter 9

Security Architecture and Design

● ●

In This Chapter

▶ Taking a look at computer architecture, including hardware, firmware, and software

▶ Reviewing basic security architecture concepts

▶ Taking account of access control models

▶ Understanding evaluation criteria and certification/accreditation

● ●

C hapters 5 and 7 address network security and software development security, respectively, but the primary focus of this chapter is *systems* security. The system comprises all the guts of a computer system, both literally and figuratively.

We also discuss security *models* in this chapter; security models apply to the inner workings of individual computers, but also to large networks consisting of hundreds or even thousands of computers. Security models are abstract by nature, and they can even be applied to embedded systems, which are small enough to fit on the head of a pin, as well as large systems, such as the global Internet. Security models are generalizations about how security can be used to protect information. Being familiar with these models helps the security professional to better protect information assets in his or her employer's environment.

In this chapter, we discuss basic computer architecture (if you're already CompTIA A+ certified, the following section will be a simple, quick review), security architectures (including important concepts such as the Trusted Computing Base [TCB], open and closed systems, and security modes), access control models, security countermeasures, evaluation criteria, and certification and accreditation.

Computer Architecture

Basic computer (system) *architecture* refers to the structure of a computer system and comprises its hardware, firmware, and software. The architecture of most computers constructed in the past two decades has settled on a model consisting of one or more central processing units (CPUs), memory, and peripheral devices, all connected with a bus (or more than one). Most computers have one or more types of connectors that permit the attachment of storage devices, output devices (such as printers or plotters), human interface devices (such as a keyboard, monitor, and mouse), and communications to local area networks (LANs, WiFi, or Bluetooth). Most computers have a primary software program called its *operating system,* which facilitates most general-purpose or specific uses for the computer. The operating system allows application programs to use the computer's hardware to perform tasks. This architecture is in use in the very smallest computers (even hand-held computers, such as Apple's iPhone), laptop computers, server computers, and mainframe computers and supercomputers.

The CompTIA A+ certification exam covers computer architecture in depth and is an excellent way to prepare for this portion of the CISSP examination.

Hardware

Hardware consists of the physical components in computer architecture. This broad definition of hardware can include keyboards, monitors, printers, and other peripherals. However, in this context, concern yourself with only the main components of the computer architecture itself, which include the CPU, memory, and bus.

CPU

The *CPU* (Central Processing Unit) or microprocessor is the electronic circuitry that performs a computer's arithmetic, logic, and computing functions. As shown in Figure 9-1, the main components of a CPU include

- ✔ **Arithmetic Logic Unit (ALU):** Performs numerical calculations and comparative logic functions, such as `ADD`, `SUBTRACT`, `DIVIDE`, and `MULTIPLY`

- ✔ **Bus Interface Unit (BIU):** Supervises data transfers over the bus system between the CPU and I/O devices

- ✔ **Control Unit:** Coordinates activities of the other CPU components during program execution

- ✔ **Decode Unit:** Converts incoming instructions into individual CPU commands

- **Floating-Point Unit (FPU):** Handles higher math operations for the ALU and control unit

- **Memory Management Unit (MMU):** Handles addressing and cataloging data that's stored in memory and translates logical addressing into physical addressing

- **Pre-Fetch Unit:** Preloads instructions into CPU registers

- **Protection Test Unit (PTU):** Monitors all CPU functions to ensure that they're properly executed

- **Registers:** Hold CPU data, addresses, and instructions temporarily, in special buffers

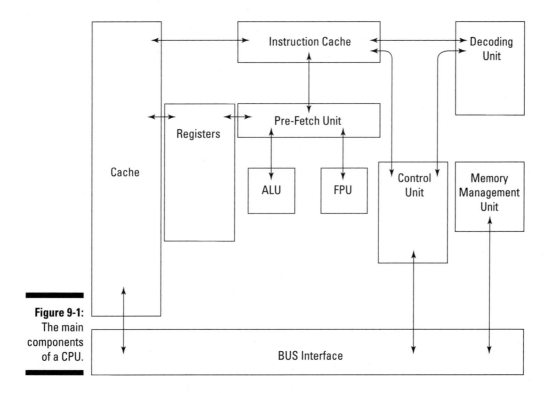

Figure 9-1: The main components of a CPU.

The basic operation of a microprocessor consists of two distinct phases: *fetch* and *execute*. (It's not too different from what your dog does: You throw the stick, and he fetches the stick.) During the fetch phase, the CPU locates and retrieves a required instruction from memory. During the execute phase, the CPU decodes and executes the instruction. These two phases make up a basic *machine cycle* that's controlled by the CPU clock signals. Many complex instructions require more than a single machine cycle to execute.

The four operating states for a computer (CPU) are

- **Operating (or run) state:** The CPU executes an instruction or instructions.
- **Problem (or application) state:** The CPU calculates a solution to an application-based problem. During this state, only a limited subset of instructions (non-privileged instructions) is available.
- **Supervisory state:** The CPU executes a *privileged* instruction, meaning that instruction is available only to a system administrator or other authorized user/process.
- **Wait state:** The CPU hasn't yet completed execution of an instruction and must extend the cycle.

The two basic types of CPU designs used in modern computer systems are

- **Complex-Instruction-Set Computing (CISC):** Can perform multiple operations per single instruction. Optimized for systems in which the fetch phase is the longest part of the instruction execution cycle. CPUs that use CISC include Intel x86, PDP-11, and Motorola 68000.
- **Reduced-Instruction-Set Computing (RISC):** Uses fewer, simpler instructions than CISC architecture, requiring fewer clock cycles to execute. Optimized for systems in which the fetch and execute phases are approximately equal. CPUs that have RISC architecture include Alpha, PowerPC, and SPARC.

Microprocessors are also often described as scalar or superscalar (no, you can't tell which they are by looking at them). A *scalar* processor executes a single instruction at a time. A *superscalar* processor can execute multiple instructions concurrently.

Finally, many systems (microprocessors) are classified according to additional functionality (which must be supported by the installed operating system):

- **Multitasking:** Alternates the execution of multiple subprograms or tasks on a single processor.
- **Multiprogramming:** Alternates the execution of multiple programs on a single processor.
- **Multiprocessing:** Executes multiple programs on multiple processors simultaneously.

Two related concepts are multistate and multiuser systems that, more correctly, refer to operating-system capabilities:

- **Multistate:** The operating system supports multiple operating states, such as single-user and multiuser modes in the UNIX/Linux world and Normal and Safe modes in the Windows world.

✔ **Multiuser:** The operating system can differentiate between users. For example, it provides different shell environments, profiles, or privilege levels for each user, as well as process isolation between users.

An important security issue in multiuser systems involves privileged accounts, and programs or processes that run in a privileged state. Programs such as su (UNIX/Linux) and RunAs (Windows) allow a user to switch to a different account, such as root or administrator, and execute privileged commands in this context. Many programs rely on privileged service accounts to function properly. Utilities such as IBM's Superzap, for example, are used to install fixes to the operating system or other applications.

Bus

The *bus* is a group of electronic conductors that interconnect the various components of the computer, transmitting signals, addresses, and data between these components. Bus structures are organized as follows:

✔ **Data bus:** Transmits data between the CPU, memory, and peripheral devices

✔ **Address bus:** Transmits addresses of data and instructions between the CPU and memory

✔ **Control bus:** Transmits control information (device status) between the CPU and other devices

A computer bus isn't painted yellow, and it doesn't have red flashing lights and a stop sign!

Main memory

Main memory (also known as *main storage*) is the part of the computer that stores programs, instructions, and data. The two basic types of *physical* (or real — as opposed to virtual — more on that later) memory are

✔ **Random Access Memory (RAM):** *Volatile* memory (data is lost if power is removed) is memory that can be directly addressed and whose stored data can be altered. RAM is typically implemented in a computer's architecture as cache memory and primary memory. The two main types of RAM are

- **Dynamic RAM (DRAM):** Must be *refreshed* (the contents rewritten) every two milliseconds because of capacitance decay. Refreshing is accomplished by using multiple clock signals known as multiphase clock signals.

- **Static RAM (SRAM):** Faster than DRAM and uses circuit latches to represent data, so it doesn't need to be refreshed. Because SRAM doesn't need to be refreshed, a single-phase clock signal is used.

✔ **Read-Only Memory (ROM):** *Nonvolatile* memory (data is retained, even if power is removed) is memory that can be directly addressed but whose stored data can't be easily altered. ROM is typically implemented in a computer's architecture as firmware (which we discuss in the following section). Variations of ROM include

- **Programmable Read-Only Memory (PROM):** This type of ROM can't be rewritten.

- **Erasable Programmable Read-Only Memory (EPROM):** This type of ROM is erased by shining ultraviolet light into the small window on the top of the chip. (No, we aren't kidding.)

- **Electrically Erasable Programmable Read-Only Memory (EEPROM):** This type of ROM was one of the first that could be changed without UV light. Also known as Electrically Alterable Read-Only Memory (EAROM).

- **Flash Memory:** This type of memory is used in USB thumb drives.

Be sure you don't confuse the term "main storage" with the storage provided by hard drives.

Secondary memory

Secondary memory (also known as *secondary storage*) is a variation of these two basic types of physical memory. It provides dynamic storage on nonvolatile magnetic media such as hard drives, solid-state drives, or tape drives (which are considered *sequential memory* because data can't be directly accessed — instead, you must search from the beginning of the tape). *Virtual memory* (such as a paging file, swap space, or swap partition) is a type of secondary memory that uses both installed physical memory and available hard-drive space to present a larger apparent memory space to the CPU than actually exists in main storage.

Two important security concepts associated with memory are the protection domain (also called protected memory) and memory addressing.

A *protection domain* prevents other programs or processes from accessing and modifying the contents of address space that's already been assigned to another active program or process. This protection can be performed by the operating system or implemented in hardware. The purpose of a protection domain is to protect the memory space assigned to a process so that no other process can read from the space or alter it. The memory space occupied by each process can be considered private.

Memory space describes the amount of physical memory available in a computer system (for example, 2 GB), whereas *address space* specifies where memory is located in a computer system (a memory address). *Memory addressing* describes the method used by the CPU to access the contents of memory. A *physical* memory address is a hard-coded address assigned to physically installed memory. It can only be accessed by the operating system that maps physical addresses to virtual addresses. A *virtual* (or *symbolic*) memory address is the address used by applications (and programmers) to specify a desired location in memory. Common virtual memory addressing modes include

- ✔ **Base addressing:** An address used as the origin for calculating other addresses.
- ✔ **Absolute addressing:** An address that identifies a location without reference to a base address — or it may be a base address itself.
- ✔ **Indexed addressing:** Specifies an address relative to an index register. (If the index register changes, the resulting memory location changes.)
- ✔ **Indirect addressing:** The specified address contains the address to the final desired location in memory.
- ✔ **Direct addressing:** Specifies the address of the final desired memory location.

Don't confuse the concepts of virtual memory and virtual addressing. *Virtual memory* combines physical memory and hard drive space to create more apparent memory (or *memory space*). *Virtual addressing* is the method used by applications and programmers to specify a desired location in physical memory.

Firmware

Firmware is a program or set of computer instructions stored in the physical circuitry of ROM memory. These types of programs are typically changed infrequently or not at all. In servers and user workstations, firmware usually stores the initial computer instructions that are executed when the server or workstation is powered on; the firmware starts the CPU and other onboard chips, and establishes communications by using the keyboard, monitor, network adaptor, and hard drive. The firmware retrieves blocks of data from the hard drive that are then used to load and start the operating system.

A computer's BIOS is a common example of firmware. *BIOS*, or Basic Input-Output System, contains instructions needed to start a computer when it's first powered on, initialize devices, and load the operating system from secondary storage such as a hard drive.

Firmware is also found in devices such as digital cameras, DSL routers, and MP3 players.

Firmware is typically stored on one or more ROM chips on a computer's *motherboard* (the main circuit board containing the CPU(s), memory, and other circuitry).

Software

Software includes the operating system and programs or applications that are installed on a computer system. We cover software security in Chapter 7.

Operating systems

A computer *operating system* (OS) is the software that controls the workings of a computer, enabling the computer to be used. The operating system can be thought of as a logical platform, through which other programs can be run to perform work.

The main components of an operating system are

- ✔ **Kernel:** The core component of the operating system that allows processes, control of hardware devices, and communications to external devices and systems to run.

- ✔ **Device drivers:** Software modules used by the kernel to communicate with internal and external devices that may be connected to the computer.

- ✔ **Tools:** Independent programs that perform specific maintenance functions, such as filesystem repair or network testing. Tools can be run automatically or manually.

The operating system controls a computer's resources. The main functions of the operating system are

- ✔ **Process management:** Sets up an environment in which multiple independent processes (programs) can run.

- ✔ **Resource management:** Controls access to all available resources, using schemes that may be based on priority or efficiency.

- ✔ **I/O device management:** Controls communication to all devices that are connected to the computer, including hard drives, printers, monitors, keyboard, mouse, and so on.

- ✔ **Memory management:** Controls the allocation and access to main memory (RAM), allocating it to processes, as well as general uses such as disk caching.

- ✔ **File management:** Controls the file systems that are present on hard drives and other types of devices, and performs all file operations on behalf of individual processes.

- ✔ **Communications management:** Controls communications on all available communications media on behalf of processes.

Virtualization

A *virtual machine* is a software implementation of a computer, enabling many running copies of an operating system to execute on a single running computer without interfering with each other. Virtual machines are typically controlled by a *hypervisor,* a software program that allocates resources for each resident operating system (called a *guest*).

A hypervisor serves as an operating system for multiple operating systems. One of the strengths of virtualization is that the resident operating system has little or no awareness of the fact that it's running as a guest — instead, it may believe that it has direct control of the computer's hardware. Only your system administrator knows for sure.

Security in the Cloud

Cloud computing is the new technology buzzword. *Clouds* are OSs running on the Internet, available for rent as services, in whatever quantity is needed at the time. These elastic environments provide the resources you need, on demand. *The Cloud* is another term for this way of looking at the Internet, often represented by a cartoonlike drawing of a cloud in network diagrams.

Cloud computing is nothing more than leased, running operating systems, available online when you need them. Are they secure? Well, they *can* be. Several aspects of security apply to cloud computing, including

✔ **Policies, procedures, and standards.** Management and use of cloud-based computing resources should — just as with traditional infrastructures — be based on top-down policies and standards. Clouds are no place to play.

✔ **Hardening.** This mainstay security concept belongs as much in the Cloud as it does wherever else an operating system, database, or network service is found. System hardening is discussed later in this chapter.

✔ **Access control.** Equally important at network, system, database, and application layers. Centralization is the key to controlling access.

✔ **Change and Configuration Management.** No matter who owns systems in the Cloud, changes must be controlled, and configurations centrally managed.

✔ **Application security.** Just as on dedicated systems, applications require all standard security controls and safeguards to keep them — and the data they access — safe.

✔ **Cloud fabric security.** Whatever glue is holding the Cloud together — virtualization, grids, chewing gum — that layer must be tightly controlled and well managed so that threats cannot be allowed to exploit any vulnerabilities that can result in compromised systems.

Most of this sounds like traditional security management. That's no accident. There's nothing new under the sun, including cloud computing and whatever is just over the horizon. Security professionals will need to stay abreast of security developments in cloud computing, even if their organization isn't using cloud computing. Some developments in cloud security may translate into new or changed issues in traditional computing environments.

High quality standards for cloud computing — for cloud service providers as well as organizations using cloud services — can be found at the Cloud Security Alliance (`www.cloudsecurityalliance.org`) and the European Network and Information Security Agency (ENISA — `www.enisa.europa.eu`).

Security Architecture

Basic concepts related to security architecture include the Trusted Computing Base (TCB), open and closed systems, protection rings, security modes, and recovery procedures.

Trusted Computing Base (TCB)

A *Trusted Computing Base* (TCB) is the entire complement of protection mechanisms within a computer system (including hardware, firmware, and software) that's responsible for enforcing a security policy. A *security perimeter* is the boundary that separates the TCB from the rest of the system.

A Trusted Computing Base (TCB) is the total combination of protection mechanisms within a computer system (including hardware, firmware, and software) that's responsible for enforcing a security policy.

Access control is the ability to permit or deny the use of an *object* (a passive entity, such as a system or file) by a *subject* (an active entity, such as an individual or a process).

Access control is the ability to permit or deny the use of an object (a system or file) by a subject (an individual or a process).

A *reference monitor* is a system component that enforces access controls on an object. Stated another way, a reference monitor is an abstract machine that mediates all access to an object by a subject.

A reference monitor is a system component that enforces access controls on an object.

A *security kernel* is the combination of hardware, firmware, and software elements in a Trusted Computing Base that implements the reference monitor concept. Three requirements of a security kernel are that it must

- ✔ Mediate all access
- ✔ Be protected from modification
- ✔ Be verified as correct

A *security kernel* is the combination of hardware, firmware, and software elements in a Trusted Computing Base (TCB) that implements the reference monitor concept.

Open and closed systems

An *open system* is a vendor-independent system that complies with a published and accepted standard. This compliance with open standards promotes interoperability between systems and components made by different vendors. Additionally, open systems can be independently reviewed and evaluated, which facilitates identification of bugs and vulnerabilities and the rapid development of solutions and updates. Examples of open systems include the Linux operating system, the Open Office desktop productivity system, and the Apache web server.

A *closed system* uses proprietary hardware and/or software that may not be compatible with other systems or components. Source code for software in a closed system isn't normally available to customers or researchers. Examples of closed systems include the Microsoft Windows operating system, Oracle database management system, and Apple iTunes.

Protection rings

The concept of protection rings implements multiple concentric domains with increasing levels of trust near the center. The most privileged ring is identified as Ring 0 and normally includes the operating system's security kernel. Additional system components are placed in the appropriate concentric ring according to the principle of least privilege. (For more on this topic, read Chapter 10.) The MIT MULTICS operating system implements the concept of protection rings in its architecture.

Security modes

A system's *security mode of operation* describes how a system handles stored information at various classification levels. Several security modes of operation, based on the classification level of information being processed on a system and the clearance level of authorized users, have been defined. These designations are typically used for U.S. military and government systems, and include

✔ **Dedicated:** All authorized users must have a clearance level equal to or higher than the highest level of information processed on the system and a valid need-to-know.

✔ **System High:** All authorized users must have a clearance level equal to or higher than the highest level of information processed on the system, but a valid need-to-know isn't necessarily required.

✔ **Multilevel:** Information at different classification levels is stored or processed on a *trusted computer system* (a system that employs all necessary hardware and software assurance measures and meets the specified requirements for reliability and security). Authorized users must have an appropriate clearance level, and access restrictions are enforced by the system accordingly.

✔ **Limited access:** Authorized users aren't required to have a security clearance, but the highest level of information on the system is Sensitive but Unclassified (SBU).

A trusted computer system is a system with a Trusted Computing Base (TCB).

Security modes of operation generally come into play in environments that contain highly sensitive information, such as government and military environments. Most private and education systems run in *multilevel mode,* meaning they contain information at all sensitivity levels.

See Chapter 6 for more on security clearance levels.

Recovery procedures

A hardware or software failure can potentially compromise a system's security mechanisms. Security designs that protect a system during a hardware or software failure include

✔ **Fault-tolerant systems:** These systems continue to operate after the failure of a computer or network component. The system must be capable of detecting and correcting — or circumventing — a fault.

✔ **Fail-safe systems:** When a hardware or software failure is detected, program execution is terminated, and the system is protected from compromise.

✔ **Fail-soft (resilient) systems:** When a hardware or software failure is detected, certain noncritical processing is terminated, and the computer or network continues to function in a degraded mode.

✔ **Failover systems:** When a hardware or software failure is detected, the system automatically transfers processing to a component, such as a clustered server.

See Chapter 10 for more information on resilient techniques including clustering, high availability, and fault tolerance.

Vulnerabilities in security architectures

Unless detected (and corrected) by an experienced security analyst, many weaknesses may be present in a system and permit exploitation, attack, or malfunction. We discuss the most important problems in the following list:

- **Covert channels:** Unknown, hidden communications that take place within the medium of a legitimate communications channel.

- **Rootkits:** By their very nature, rootkits are designed to subvert system architecture by inserting themselves into an environment in a way that makes it difficult or impossible to detect. For instance, some rootkits run as a hypervisor and change the computer's operating system into a guest, which changes the basic nature of the system in a powerful but subtle way. We wouldn't normally discuss malware in a chapter on computer and security architecture, but rootkits are a game-changer that warrants mention: They use various techniques to hide themselves from the target system.

- **Race conditions:** Software code in multiprocessing and multiuser systems, unless very carefully designed and tested, can result in critical errors that are difficult to find. A *race condition* is a flaw in a system where the output or result of an activity in the system is unexpectedly tied to the timing of other events. The term *race condition* comes from the idea of two events or signals that are racing to influence an activity.

  The most common race condition is the time-of-check-to-time-of-use bug caused by changes in a system between the checking of a condition and the use of the results of that check. For example, two programs that both try to open a file for exclusive use may both open the file, even though only one should be able to.

- **State attacks:** Web-based applications use session management to distinguish users from one another. The mechanisms used by the web application to establish sessions must be able to resist attack. Primarily, the algorithms used to create session identifiers must not permit an attacker from being able to steal session identifiers, or guess other users' session identifiers. A successful attack would result in an attacker taking over another user's session, which can lead to the compromise of confidential data, fraud, and monetary theft.

- **Emanations:** The unintentional emissions of electromagnetic or acoustic energy from a system can be intercepted by others and possibly used to illicitly obtain information from the system. A common form of unde-sired emanations is radiated energy from CRT (cathode-ray tube) com-puter monitors. A third party can discover what data is being displayed on a CRT by intercepting radiation emanating from the display adaptor or monitor from as far as several hundred meters. A third party can also eavesdrop on a network if it has one or more un-terminated coaxial cables in its cable plant.

Security Countermeasures

In security architecture, many countermeasures are needed to make an environment more secure. In this section, we discuss several concepts that will help a designer be able to design a more secure environment. A security specialist can also use these principles to help recognize and distinguish secure environments from those that are less so.

Defense in depth

Defense in depth is a security architecture concept that describes a strategy for resisting attacks. A system that employs a defense in depth will have two or more layers of protective controls that are designed to protect the system or data stored there.

An example defense-in-depth architecture would consist of a database protected by several components:

- ✔ Screening router
- ✔ Firewall
- ✔ Intrusion prevention system
- ✔ Hardened operating system
- ✔ OS-based network access filtering

All the layers listed here help to protect the database. In fact, each one of them by itself offers nearly complete protection. But when considered together, all these controls offer a varied (in effect, deeper) defense, hence the term *defense in depth*.

Defense in depth refers to the use of multiple layers of protection.

System hardening

Most types of information systems, including computer operating systems, have several general-purpose features that make it easy to set up the systems. But systems that are exposed to the Internet should be "hardened," or configured according to the following concepts:

- ✔ Remove all unnecessary components
- ✔ Remove all unnecessary accounts

✔ Close all unnecessary network listening ports

✔ Change all default passwords to complex, difficult to guess passwords

✔ All necessary programs should run at the lowest possible privilege

✔ Security patches should be installed as soon as they are available

The Center for Internet Security has an especially nice collection of system hardening standards. You can find these at www.cisecurity.org.

Heterogeneous environment

Rather than containing systems or components of a single type, a *heterogeneous environment* contains a variety of different types of systems. Contrast an environment that consists only of Windows 2008 servers and the latest SQL Server and IIS Server, to a more complex environment that contains Windows, Linux, and Solaris servers with Microsoft SQL Server, MySQL, and Oracle databases.

The advantage of a heterogeneous environment is its variety of systems; for one thing, the various types of systems probably won't possess common vulnerabilities, which makes them harder to attack.

The weakness of a *homogeneous environment* (one where all of the systems are the same) is its uniformity. If a weakness in one of the systems is discovered, all systems may have the weakness. If one of the systems is attacked and compromised, all may be attacked and compromised.

You can liken homogeneity to a herd of animals; if they are genetically identical, then they may all be susceptible to a disease that could wipe out the entire herd. If they are genetically diverse, then perhaps some will be able to survive the disease.

System resilience

The *resilience* of a system is a measure of its ability to keep running, even under less-than-ideal conditions.

Resilience can mean a lot of different things. Here are some examples.

✔ **Filter malicious input.** System can recognize and reject input that may be an attack. Examples of suspicious input include what you get typically in an injection attack, buffer-overflow attack, or Denial of Service attack.

✔ **Redundant components.** System contains redundant components that permit the system to continue running even when hardware failures or malfunctions occur. Examples of redundant components include multiple power supplies, multiple network interfaces, redundant storage techniques such as RAID, and redundant server architecture techniques such as clustering.

System resilience is described in more detail in Chapter 10.

✔ **Maintenance hooks:** Hidden, undocumented features in software programs that are intended to inappropriately expose data or functions for illicit use. We discuss this topic in Chapter 7.

✔ **Security countermeasures:** Knowing that systems are subject to frequent or constant attack, systems architects need to include several security countermeasures in order to minimize system vulnerability. Such countermeasures include

- Revealing as little information about the system as possible. For example, don't permit the system to ever display the version of operating system, database, or application software that's running.

- Limiting access to only those persons who must use the system in order to fulfill needed organizational functions.

- Disabling unnecessary services in order to reduce the number of attack targets.

- Using strong authentication in order to make it as difficult as possible for outsiders to access the system.

TEMPEST in a teapot?

The U.S. military conducted a series of experiments to determine whether emanations from computer equipment would reveal activities taking place. These experiments were controlled through a project named TEMPEST. Standards have been developed in the U.S. and other NATO countries that provide three levels of protection, depending upon the distance between a potential attacker and a target system. The Level I standard is for systems with only 1 meter of safe distance; Level II is for systems with 20 meters; Level III is for systems with 100 meters of safe distance between systems and potential attackers. Systems can be certified to these standards in the U.S. and other NATO countries.

Security Models

Security models help us to understand the sometimes-complex security mechanisms in information systems. Security models illustrate simple concepts that we can use when analyzing an existing system or designing a new one.

In this section we describe the time-honored concepts of confidentiality, integrity, and availability (known together as *CIA*, or the *CIA Triad*), and access control models.

Confidentiality

Confidentiality refers to the concept that information and functions should be accessed only by authorized subjects. This is usually accomplished through several means, including

- ✓ **Access and authorization:** Ranging from physical access to facilities containing computers, to user account access and role-based access controls, the objective here is to make sure that only those persons with proper business authorization are permitted to access information.

- ✓ **Vulnerability management:** This includes everything from system hardening to patch management and the elimination of vulnerabilities from web applications. What we're trying to avoid here is any possibility that someone can attack the system and get to the data.

- ✓ **Sound system design:** The overall design of the system excludes unauthorized subjects from access to protected data.

- ✓ **Sound data management practices:** The organization has established processes that define the use of the information it manages or controls.

These characteristics work together to ensure that secrets remain secrets.

Integrity

Integrity refers to the concept that information in a system will arrive correctly and maintain that correctness throughout its lifetime. Systems housing the information will reject attempted changes by unauthorized parties or unauthorized means. The characteristics of data whose integrity is intact are:

- ✔ Completeness
- ✔ Timeliness
- ✔ Accuracy
- ✔ Validity

Some of the measures taken to ensure data integrity are

- ✔ **Authorization:** This refers to whether data has proper authorization to enter a system. The integrity of a data record includes whether it should even be in the system.
- ✔ **Input control:** This includes verifying that the new data entering the system is in the proper format and in the proper range.
- ✔ **Access control:** This is used to control who (and what) is permitted to change the data.
- ✔ **Output control:** This includes verifying that the data leaving the system is in the proper format.

All of these steps help to ensure that the data in a system has the highest possible quality.

Availability

Availability refers to the concept that a system (and the data within it) will be accessible when users want to use it. The characteristics of a system that determine its availability include:

- ✔ **Resilient hardware design:** Features may include redundant power supplies, network adaptors, processors and other components. These help to ensure that a system will keep running even if some of its internal components fail.
- ✔ **Resilient software:** The operating system and other software components need to be designed and configured to be as reliable as possible.
- ✔ **Resilient architecture:** We're talking big picture here. In addition to resilient hardware design, we would suggest that other components have redundancy including routers, firewalls, switches, telecommunications circuits, and whatever other items may otherwise be single points of failure.
- ✔ **Sound configuration management and Change Management processes:** Availability includes not only the components of the system itself, but is also reliant on good system management practices. After all, availability means avoiding unscheduled downtime, which is often a consequence of sloppy configuration management and Change Management practices.

The CIA Triad includes the top three principles of information protection: Confidentiality, Integrity, and Availability.

Access Control Models

Models are used to express access control requirements in a theoretical or mathematical framework that precisely describes or quantifies real access control systems. Common access control models include Bell-LaPadula, Access Matrix, Take-Grant, Biba, Clark-Wilson, Information Flow, and Non-interference.

Bell-LaPadula, Access Matrix, and Take-Grant models address confidentiality of stored information. Biba and Clark-Wilson address integrity of stored information.

Bell-LaPadula

Published in 1973, the Bell-LaPadula model was the first formal confidentiality model of a mandatory access control system. (We discuss mandatory and discretionary access controls in Chapter 4.) It was developed for the U.S. Department of Defense (DoD) to formalize the DoD multilevel security policy. As we discuss in Chapter 6, the DoD classifies information based on sensitivity at three basic levels: Confidential, Secret, and Top Secret. In order to access classified information (and systems), an individual must have access (a clearance level equal to or exceeding the classification of the information or system) and need-to-know (legitimately in need of access to perform a required job function). The Bell-LaPadula model implements the access component of this security policy.

Bell-LaPadula is a state machine model that addresses only the confidentiality of information. The basic premise of Bell-LaPadula is that information can't flow downward. This means that information at a higher level is not permitted to be copied or moved to a lower level. Bell-LaPadula defines the following two properties:

- ✔ **Simple security property (ss property):** A subject can't read information from an object that has a higher sensitivity label than the subject (also known as *no read up,* or *NRU*).

- ✔ ***-property (star property):** A subject can't write information to an object that has a lower sensitivity label than the subject (also known as *no write down,* or *NWD*).

Bell-LaPadula also defines two additional properties that give it the flexibility of a discretionary access control model:

- **Discretionary security property:** This property determines access based on an *Access Matrix* — more on that model in the following section.

- **Trusted subject:** A trusted subject is an entity that can violate the *-property but not its intent.

A *state machine* is an abstract model used to design computer programs; the state machine illustrates which "state" the program will be in at any time.

Access Matrix

An *Access Matrix model,* in general, provides object access rights (read/write/execute, or R/W/X) to subjects in a discretionary access control (DAC) system. An Access Matrix consists of access control lists (columns) and capability lists (rows). See Table 9-1 for an example.

Table 9-1	An Access Matrix Example		
Subject/Object	*Directory: H/R*	*File: Personnel*	*Process: LPD*
Thomas	Read	Read/Write	Execute
Lisa	Read	Read	Execute
Harold	None	None	None

Take-Grant

Take-Grant systems specify the rights that a subject can transfer to or from another subject or object. These rights are defined through four basic operations: create, revoke, take, and grant.

Biba

Published in 1977, the Biba integrity model (sometimes referred to as Bell-LaPadula upside down) was the first formal integrity model. Biba is a lattice-based model that addresses the first goal of integrity: ensuring that modifications to data aren't made by unauthorized users or processes. (See Chapter 6 for a complete discussion of the three goals of integrity.) Biba defines the following two properties:

- **Simple integrity property:** A subject can't read information from an object that has a lower integrity level than the subject (also called *no read down*).

- ***-integrity property (star integrity property):** A subject can't write information to an object that has a higher integrity level than the subject (also known as *no write up*).

Clark-Wilson

Published in 1987, the *Clark-Wilson integrity model* establishes a security framework for use in commercial activities, such as the banking industry. Clark-Wilson addresses all three goals of integrity and identifies special requirements for inputting data based on the following items and procedures (see Chapter 6 for more on the three goals of integrity):

- ✔ **Unconstrained data item (UDI):** Data outside the control area, such as input data.

- ✔ **Constrained data item (CDI):** Data inside the control area. (Integrity must be preserved.)

- ✔ **Integrity verification procedures (IVP):** Checks validity of CDIs.

- ✔ **Transformation procedures (TP):** Maintains integrity of CDIs.

The Clark-Wilson integrity model is based on the concept of a *well-formed transaction,* in which a transaction is sufficiently ordered and controlled so that it maintains internal and external consistency.

Information Flow

An *Information Flow model* is a type of access control model based on the flow of information, rather than on imposing access controls. Objects are assigned a security class and value, and their direction of flow @md from one application to another or from one system to another — is controlled by a security policy. This model type is useful for analyzing covert channels, through detailed analysis of the flow of information in a system, including the sources of information and the paths of flow.

Non-interference

A *Non-interference model* ensures that the actions of different objects and subjects aren't seen by (and don't interfere with) other objects and subjects on the same system.

Evaluation Criteria

Evaluation criteria provide a standard for quantifying the security of a computer system or network. These criteria include the Trusted Computer System Evaluation Criteria (TCSEC), Trusted Network Interpretation (TNI), European Information Technology Security Evaluation Criteria (ITSEC), and the Common Criteria.

Trusted Computer System Evaluation Criteria (TCSEC)

The Trusted Computer System Evaluation Criteria (TCSEC), commonly known as the *Orange Book,* is part of the Rainbow Series developed for the U.S. DoD by the National Computer Security Center (NCSC) in 1983. (The current issue was published in 1985.) It's the formal implementation of the Bell-LaPadula model. The evaluation criteria were developed to achieve the following objectives:

- **Measurement:** Provides a metric for assessing comparative levels of trust between different computer systems.

- **Guidance:** Identifies standard security requirements that vendors must build into systems to achieve a given trust level.

- **Acquisition:** Provides customers a standard for specifying acquisition requirements and identifying systems that meet those requirements.

The four basic control requirements identified in the Orange Book are

- **Security policy:** The rules and procedures by which a trusted system operates. Specific TCSEC requirements include

  - **Discretionary access control (DAC):** Owners of objects are able to assign permissions to other subjects. Read more about this requirement in Chapter 4.

  - **Mandatory access control (MAC):** Permissions to objects are managed centrally by an administrator. Read more about this requirement in Chapter 4.

  - **Object reuse:** Protects confidentiality of objects that are reassigned after initial use. For example, a deleted file still exists on storage media; only the file allocation table (FAT) and first character of the file have been modified. Thus residual data may be restored, which describes the problem of *data remanence.* Object-reuse requirements define procedures for actually erasing the data.

  - **Labels:** Sensitivity labels are required in MAC-based systems. (Read more about information classification in Chapter 6.) Specific TCSEC labeling requirements include integrity, export, and subject/object labels.

- **Assurance:** Guarantees that a security policy is correctly implemented. Specific TCSEC requirements (listed here) are classified as *operational assurance requirements:*

  - **System architecture:** TCSEC requires features and principles of system design that implement specific security features.

  - **System integrity:** Hardware and firmware operate properly and are tested to verify proper operation.

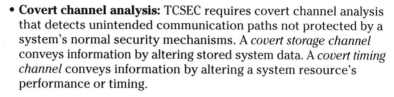

- **Covert channel analysis:** TCSEC requires covert channel analysis that detects unintended communication paths not protected by a system's normal security mechanisms. A *covert storage channel* conveys information by altering stored system data. A *covert timing channel* conveys information by altering a system resource's performance or timing.

  A systems or security architect must understand covert channels and how they work in order to prevent the use of covert channels in the system environment.

- **Trusted facility management:** The assignment of a specific individual to administer the security-related functions of a system. Closely related to the concepts of *least privilege, separation of duties,* and *need-to-know,* which we discuss in Chapters 6 and 10.

- **Trusted recovery:** Ensures that security isn't compromised in the event of a system crash or failure. This process involves two primary activities: failure preparation and system recovery, which we discuss in Chapter 10.

- **Security testing:** Specifies required testing by the developer and the National Computer Security Center (NCSC).

- **Design specification and verification:** Requires a mathematical and automated proof that the design description is consistent with the security policy.

- **Configuration management:** Identifying, controlling, accounting for, and auditing all changes made to the Trusted Computing Base (TCB) during the design, development, and maintenance phases of a system's life cycle.

- **Trusted distribution:** Protects a system during transport from a vendor to a customer.

✔ **Accountability:** The ability to associate users and processes with their actions. Specific TCSEC requirements include

- **Identification and authentication (I&A):** Systems need to track who performs what activities. We discuss this topic in Chapter 4.

- **Trusted Path:** A direct communications path between the user and the Trusted Computing Base (TCB) that doesn't require interaction with untrusted applications or operating-system layers.

- **Audit:** Recording, examining, analyzing, and reviewing security-related activities in a trusted system, which we discuss in Chapters 4, 10, and 12.

✔ **Documentation:** Specific TCSEC requirements include

- **Security Features User's Guide (SFUG):** User's manual for the system.

- **Trusted Facility Manual (TFM):** System administrator's and/or security administrator's manual.

- **Test documentation:** According to the TCSEC manual, this documentation must be in a position to "show how the security mechanisms were tested, and results of the security mechanisms' functional testing."

- **Design documentation:** Defines system boundaries and internal components, such as the Trusted Computing Base (TCB).

The Orange Book defines four major hierarchical classes of security protection and numbered subclasses (higher numbers indicate higher security):

✔ **D:** Minimal protection

✔ **C:** Discretionary protection (C1 and C2)

✔ **B:** Mandatory protection (B1, B2, and B3)

✔ **A:** Verified protection (A1)

These classes are further defined in Table 9-2.

Table 9-2		TCSEC Classes
Class	**Name**	**Sample Requirements**
D	Minimal protection	Reserved for systems that fail evaluation.
C1	Discretionary protection (DAC)	System doesn't need to distinguish between individual users and types of access.
C2	Controlled access protection (DAC)	System must distinguish between individual users and types of access; object reuse security features required.
B1	Labeled security protection (MAC)	Sensitivity labels required for all subjects and storage objects.
B2	Structured protection (MAC)	Sensitivity labels required for all subjects and objects; trusted path requirements.
B3	Security domains (MAC)	Access control lists (ACLs) are specifically required; system must protect against covert channels.
A1	Verified design (MAC)	Formal Top-Level Specification (FTLS) required; configuration management procedures must be enforced throughout entire system life cycle.
Beyond A1		Self-protection and reference monitors are implemented in the Trusted Computing Base (TCB). TCB verified to source-code level.

You don't need to know specific requirements of each TCSEC level for the CISSP exam, but you should know at what levels DAC and MAC are implemented and the relative trust levels of the classes, including numbered subclasses.

Major limitations of the Orange Book include that

- ✔ It addresses only confidentiality issues. It doesn't include integrity and availability.
- ✔ It isn't applicable to most commercial systems.
- ✔ It emphasizes protection from unauthorized access, despite statistical evidence that many security violations involve insiders.
- ✔ It doesn't address networking issues.

Trusted Network Interpretation (TNI)

Part of the Rainbow Series, like TCSEC (discussed in the preceding section), Trusted Network Interpretation (TNI) addresses confidentiality and integrity in trusted computer/communications network systems. Within the Rainbow Series, it's known as the *Red Book.*

Part I of the TNI is a guideline for extending the system protection standards defined in the TCSEC (the *Orange Book*) to networks. Part II of the TNI describes additional security features such as communications integrity, protection from denial of service, and transmission security.

European Information Technology Security Evaluation Criteria (ITSEC)

The European Information Technology Security Evaluation Criteria (ITSEC) was developed during the late 1980s, and the current issue was published in 1991. Unlike TCSEC, ITSEC addresses confidentiality, integrity, and availability, as well as evaluating an entire system, defined as a *Target of Evaluation* (TOE), rather than a single computing platform.

ITSEC evaluates *functionality* (security objectives, or *why;* security-enforcing functions, or *what;* and security mechanisms, or *how*) and *assurance* (effectiveness and correctness) separately. The ten functionality (F) classes and seven evaluation (E) (assurance) levels are listed in Table 9-3.

Table 9-3   ITSEC Functionality (F) Classes and Evaluation (E) Levels mapped to TCSEC levels

(F) Class	(E) Level	Description
NA	E0	Equivalent to TCSEC level D
F-C1	E1	Equivalent to TCSEC level C1
F-C2	E2	Equivalent to TCSEC level C2
F-B1	E3	Equivalent to TCSEC level B1
F-B2	E4	Equivalent to TCSEC level B2
F-B3	E5	Equivalent to TCSEC level B3
F-B3	E6	Equivalent to TCSEC level A1
F-IN	NA	TOEs with high integrity requirements
F-AV	NA	TOEs with high availability requirements
F-DI	NA	TOEs with high integrity requirements during data communication
F-DC	NA	TOEs with high confidentiality requirements during data communication
F-DX	NA	Networks with high confidentiality and integrity requirements

You don't need to know specific requirements of each ITSEC level for the CISSP exam, but you should know how the basic functionality levels (F-C1 through F-B3) and evaluation levels (E0 through E6) correlate to TCSEC levels.

Common Criteria

The Common Criteria for Information Technology Security Evaluation (usually just called *Common Criteria*) is an international effort to standardize and improve existing European and North American evaluation criteria. The final draft was published in 1997, and the Common Criteria has been adopted as an international standard in ISO 15408. The Common Criteria defines eight *evaluation assurance levels* (EALs), which are listed in Table 9-4.

Table 9-4			The Common Criteria
Level	*TCSEC Equivalent*	*ITSEC Equivalent*	*Description*
EAL0	NA	NA	Inadequate assurance
EAL1	NA	NA	Functionally tested
EAL2	C1	E1	Structurally tested
EAL3	C2	E2	Methodically tested and checked
EAL4	B1	E3	Methodically designed, tested, and reviewed
EAL5	B2	E4	Semi-formally designed and tested
EAL6	B3	E5	Semi-formally verified design and tested
EAL7	A1	E6	Formally verified design and tested

You don't need to know specific requirements of each Common Criteria level for the CISSP exam, but you should understand the basic evaluation hierarchy (EAL0 through EAL7, in order of increasing levels of trust).

System Certification and Accreditation

System *certification* is a formal methodology for comprehensive testing and documentation of information system security safeguards, both technical and nontechnical, in a given environment by using established evaluation criteria (the TCSEC).

Accreditation is an official, written approval for the operation of a specific system in a specific environment, as documented in the certification report. Accreditation is normally granted by a senior executive or Designated Approving Authority (DAA). The term *DAA* is used in the U.S. military and government. A DAA is normally a senior official, such as a commanding officer.

System certification and accreditation must be updated when any changes are made to the system or environment, and they must also be periodically re-validated, which typically happens every three years.

The certification and accreditation process has been formally implemented in U.S. military and government organizations as the Defense Information Technology Security Certification and Accreditation Process (DITSCAP) and National Information Assurance Certification and Accreditation Process (NIACAP), respectively. These important processes are used to make sure that a new (or changed) system has the proper design and operational characteristics, and that it's suitable for a specific task.

DITSCAP

The Defense Information Technology Security Certification and Accreditation Process (DITSCAP) formalizes the certification and accreditation process for U.S. DoD information systems through four distinct phases:

- **Definition:** Security requirements are determined by defining the organization and system's mission, environment, and architecture.
- **Verification:** Ensures that a system undergoing development or modification remains compliant with the System Security Authorization Agreement (SSAA), which is a baseline security-configuration document.
- **Validation:** Confirms compliance with the SSAA.
- **Post-Accreditation:** Represents ongoing activities required to maintain compliance, and address new and evolving threats, throughout a system's life cycle.

NIACAP

The National Information Assurance Certification and Accreditation Process (NIACAP) formalizes the certification and accreditation process for U.S. government national security information systems. NIACAP consists of four phases (Definition, Verification, Validation, and Post-Accreditation) that generally correspond to the DITSCAP phases. Additionally, NIACAP defines three types of accreditation:

- **Site accreditation:** All applications and systems at a specific location are evaluated.
- **Type accreditation:** A specific application or system for multiple locations is evaluated.
- **System accreditation:** A specific application or system at a specific location is evaluated.

DCID 6/3

The Director of Central Intelligence Directive 6/3 is the process used to protect sensitive information that's stored on computers used by the U.S. Central Intelligence Agency (CIA).

Prep Test

1 The four CPU operating states include all the following except

A ○ Operating

B ○ Problem

C ○ Wait

D ○ Virtual

2 *A computer system that alternates execution of multiple subprograms on a single processor* describes what type of system?

A ○ Multiprogramming

B ○ Multitasking

C ○ Multiuser

D ○ Multiprocessing

3 An address used as the origin for calculating other addresses describes

A ○ Base addressing

B ○ Indexed addressing

C ○ Indirect addressing

D ○ Direct addressing

4 The four main functions of the operating system include all the following except

A ○ Process management

B ○ BIOS management

C ○ I/O device management

D ○ File management

5 *The total combination of protection mechanisms within a computer system, including hardware, firmware, and software, which is responsible for enforcing a security policy* defines

A ○ Reference monitor

B ○ Security kernel

C ○ Trusted Computing Base

D ○ Protection domain

6 *A system that continues to operate following failure of a network component describes which type of system?*

A ○ Fault-tolerant

B ○ Fail-safe

C ○ Fail-soft

D ○ Failover

7 **Which of the following access control models addresses availability issues?**

A ○ Bell-LaPadula

B ○ Biba

C ○ Clark-Wilson

D ○ None of the above

8 **The four basic control requirements identified in the Orange Book include all the following except**

A ○ Role-based access control

B ○ Discretionary access control

C ○ Mandatory access control

D ○ Object reuse

9 **The purpose of session management in a web application is**

A ○ To prevent Denial of Service attacks

B ○ To collect session-based security metrics

C ○ To control the number of concurrent sessions

D ○ To protect sessions from unauthorized access

10 **Which of the following ITSEC classification levels is equivalent to TCSEC level B3?**

A ○ E3

B ○ E4

C ○ E5

D ○ E6

Answers

1 **D.** Virtual. The four CPU operating states are operating (or run), problem (or application), supervisory, and wait. *Review "CPU."*

2 **B.** Multitasking. A multiprogramming computer alternates execution of multiple programs on a single processor. A multiuser computer supports several users. A multiprocessing computer executes multiple programs on multiple processors. *Review "CPU."*

3 **A.** Base addressing. Indexed addressing specifies an address relative to an index register. Indirect addressing specifies the address of the desired location. Direct addressing specifies the desired location. *Review "Memory."*

4 **B.** BIOS management. The four main functions of an OS are process management, I/O device management, memory management, and file management. The system BIOS operates independently of the OS. *Review "Software."*

5 **C.** Trusted Computing Base. A reference monitor enforces access controls on an object. A security kernel implements the reference monitor concept. A protection ring is a security concept that implements the principle of least privilege. *Review "Trusted Computing Base (TCB)."*

6 **A.** Fault-tolerant. A fail-safe system terminates program execution. A fail-soft system continues functioning in a degraded mode. A failover system automatically switches to a hot backup. *Review "Recovery procedures."*

7 **D.** None of the above. Bell-LaPadula addresses confidentiality issues. Biba and Clark-Wilson address integrity issues. *Review "Access Control Models."*

8 **A.** Role-based access control. The four basic control requirements identified in the Orange Book are discretionary access control, mandatory access control, object reuse, and labels. *Review "Trusted Computer System Evaluation Criteria (TCSEC)."*

9 **D.** To protect sessions from unauthorized access. Session management, usually implemented through cookies, hidden variables, or URL variables, is used to track individual application user sessions. *Review "Vulnerabilities in security architectures."*

10 **C.** E5. E3 is equivalent to TCSEC level B1, E4 to B2, and E6 to A1. *Review "European Information Technology Security Evaluation Criteria (ITSEC)."*

Chapter 10

Security Operations

In This Chapter

▶ Using administrative management and control

▶ Managing security operations concepts and controls

▶ Knowing your threats and countermeasures

▶ Understanding auditing and audit trails

▶ Making monitoring a priority

*T*he Security Operations domain introduces several essential concepts. Fortunately, it also overlaps other domains, such as Information Security Governance and Risk Management, Access Control, and Business Continuity and Disaster Recovery Planning.

What do you need to know about the Security Operations domain? We let the official (ISC)² CISSP study guide answer that question: "The candidate will be expected to know the resources that must be protected, the privileges that must be restricted, the control mechanisms available, the potential for abuse of access, the appropriate controls, and the principles of good practice."

This chapter covers administrative management and control, security operations concepts and management, security threats and countermeasures, security auditing, audit trails, and security monitoring — everything you need to know about the Security Operations domain (not to be confused with the concept of *need-to-know,* which we also cover in this chapter)!

Administrative Management and Control

An organization needs clearly documented policies and procedures in order to facilitate the use and protection of information. There are numerous conceptual best practices for protecting the business and its important information assets. These best practices all have to do with how people — not technology — work together to support the business.

This is collectively known as *administrative management and control.*

Job requirements and qualifications

Even before posting a "Help Wanted" sign (Do people still do that?!) or an ad on a job search website, an employer should ensure that the position to be filled is clearly documented and contains a complete description of the job requirements, the qualifications, and the scope of responsibilities and authority.

The job (or position) description should be created as a collaborative effort between the hiring manager — who fully understands the functional requirements of the specific position to be filled — and the human resources manager — who fully understands the applicable employment laws and organizational requirements to be addressed.

Having a clearly documented job (or position) description can benefit an organization for many reasons:

- ✔ The hiring manager knows (and can clearly articulate) exactly what skills a certain job requires.
- ✔ The human resources manager can pre-screen job applicants quickly and accurately.
- ✔ Potential candidates can ensure they apply only for positions for which they're qualified, and they can properly prepare themselves for interviews (for example, by matching their skills and experiences to the specific requirements of the position).
- ✔ After the organization fills the position, the position description helps to reduce confusion about what the organization expects from the new employee and provides objective criteria for evaluating performance.

See Chapter 6 for more information on job descriptions.

Background checks and verification

An organization should conduct background checks and verify application information for all potential employees and contractors. This process can help to expose any undesirable or unqualified candidates. For example

- A previous criminal conviction may immediately disqualify a candidate from certain positions within an organization.

- Even when the existence of a criminal record itself doesn't automatically disqualify a candidate, if the candidate fails to disclose this information in the job application or interview, it should be a clear warning sign for a potential employer.

- Some positions that require a U.S. government security clearance are available only to U.S. citizens.

- A candidate's credit history should be examined if the position has significant financial responsibilities or handles high-value assets, or if a high opportunity for fraud exists.

- It has been estimated that as many as 40 percent of job applicants "exaggerate the truth" on their résumés and applications. Common sources of omitted, exaggerated, or outright misleading information include employment dates, salary history, education, certifications, and achievements. Although the information itself may not be disqualifying, a dishonest applicant should not be given the opportunity to become a dishonest employee.

Most background checks require the written consent of the applicant and disclosure of certain private information (such as the applicant's Social Security number). Private information obtained for the purposes of a background check, as well as the results of the background check, must be properly handled and safeguarded in accordance with applicable laws and the organization's records retention and destruction policies.

Background checks and verification can include the following information:

- Criminal record
- Citizenship
- Credit history
- Employment history
- Education
- Certifications and licenses
- Union and association membership

See Chapter 6 for more information on background checks and security clearances.

Separation of duties and responsibilities

The concept of *separation* (or *segregation*) *of duties and responsibilities* ensures that no single individual has complete authority and control of a critical system or process. This practice promotes security in the following ways:

- ✔ **Reduces opportunities for fraud or abuse:** In order for fraud or abuse to occur, two or more individuals must collude or be complicit in the performance of their duties.

- ✔ **Reduces mistakes:** Because two or more individuals perform the process, mistakes are less likely to occur or mistakes are more quickly detected and corrected.

- ✔ **Reduces dependence on individuals:** Critical processes are accomplished by groups of individuals or teams. Multiple individuals should be trained on different parts of the process (for example, through job rotation, discussed in the following section) to help ensure that the absence of an individual doesn't unnecessarily delay or impede successful completion of a step in the process.

Here are some common examples of separation of duties and responsibilities within organizations:

- ✔ A bank assigns the first three numbers of a six-number safe combination to one employee and the second three numbers to another employee. A single employee isn't permitted to have all six numbers, so a lone employee is unable to gain access to the safe and steal its contents.

- ✔ An accounting department might separate record entry and internal auditing functions, or accounts payable and check disbursing functions.

- ✔ A system administrator is responsible for setting up new accounts and assigning permissions, which a security administrator then verifies.

- ✔ A programmer develops software code, but a separate individual is responsible for testing and validation, and yet another individual is responsible for loading the code on production systems.

- ✔ Destruction of classified materials may require two individuals to complete or witness the destruction.

- ✔ Disposal of assets may require an approval signature by the office manager and verification by building security.

In smaller organizations, separation of duties and responsibilities can some-times be difficult to implement because of limited personnel and resources.

Job rotation

Job rotation (or *rotation of duties*) is another effective security control that gives many benefits to an organization. Similar to the concept of separation of duties and responsibilities, job rotations involve regularly (or randomly) transferring key personnel into different positions or departments within an organization, with or without notice. Job rotations accomplish several impor-tant organizational objectives:

- **Reduce opportunities for fraud or abuse.** Regular job rotations can accomplish this objective in the following two ways:

  - People hesitate to set up the means for periodically or routinely stealing corporate information because they know that they could be moved to another shift or task at almost any time.

  - People don't work with each other long enough to form collusive relationships that could damage the company.

- **Eliminate single points of failure.** By ensuring that numerous people within an organization or department know how to perform several different job functions, an organization can reduce dependence on indi-viduals and thereby eliminate single points of failure when an individual is absent, incapacitated, no longer employed with the organization, or otherwise unavailable to perform a critical job function.

- **Promote professional growth.** Through cross-training opportunities, job rotations can help an individual's professional growth and career devel-opment, and reduce monotony and/or fatigue.

Job rotations can also include changing workers' workstations and work loca-tions, which can also keep would-be saboteurs off balance.

As with the practice of separation of duties, small organizations can have dif-ficulty implementing job rotations.

Mandatory vacations

Requiring employees to take one or more weeks of their vacation in a single block of time gives the organization an opportunity to uncover potential fraud or abuse. Employees engaging in illegal or prohibited activities are sometimes reluctant to be away from the office, concerned that these activities will be discovered in their absence. This may occur as a result of an actual audit or investigation, or when someone else performing that person's normal day-to-day functions in their absence uncovers an irregularity. Less ominously, mandatory vacations may help in other ways:

✔ Reduce individual stress and therefore reduce opportunities for mistakes or coercion by others.

✔ Discover inefficient processes when a substitute performs a job function more quickly or discovers a better way to get something done.

✔ Reveal single points of failure and opportunities for job rotation (and separation of duties and responsibilities) when a process or job function idles because the only person who knows how to perform that function is lying on a beach somewhere.

Need-to-know

The concept of *need-to-know* states that only people with a valid need to know certain information in order to perform their job functions, should have access to that information. In addition to having a need-to-know, an individual must have an appropriate security clearance level in order for access to be granted. Conversely, an individual with the appropriate security clearance level, but without a need-to-know, should not be granted access.

One of the most difficult challenges in managing need-to-know is the use of controls that enforce need-to-know. Also, information owners need to be able to distinguish *I need-to-know* from *I want-to-know, I-want-to-feel-important*, and *I'm-just-curious*.

Need-to-know is a closely related concept to least privilege, discussed in the next section, and can help organizations implement the concept of least privilege in a practical manner.

Least privilege

Least privilege is closely related to need-to-know, but least privilege applies more to functionality than to access of data. The *principle of least privilege* is that persons should have the capability to perform only the tasks (or have access to only the data) that are required to perform their primary jobs, and no more.

Accumulation of privileges

In many organizations, people frequently transfer between jobs and/or departments (see the earlier section on job rotations). Along the way, they'll need new access and privileges to do their new jobs. Far too often, organizational security processes do not adequately ensure that access rights that are no longer required by an individual are actually revoked. Instead, individuals accumulate privileges, and over a period of many years an employee can have far more access and privileges than they need. We call this *accumulation of privileges,* and it's a real problem for organizations — sort of the antithesis of least privilege!

To give an individual more privileges and access than required invites trouble. Offering the capability to perform more than the job requires may become a temptation that results, sooner or later, in an abuse of privilege.

For example, giving a user full permissions on a network share, rather than just read and modify rights to a specific directory, opens the door not only for abuse of those privileges (for example, reading or copying other sensitive information on the network share) but also for costly mistakes (accidentally deleting a file — or the entire directory!). As a starting point, organizations should approach permissions with a "deny all" mentality, then add needed permissions as required.

Least privilege is also closely related to separation of duties and responsibilities, described in the section "Separation of duties and responsibilities," earlier in this chapter. Distributing the duties and responsibilities for a given job function among several people means that those individuals require fewer privileges on a system or resource.

The principle of least privilege states that people should have the fewest privileges necessary to allow them to perform their tasks.

User monitoring

Monitoring the activities of an organization's users, particularly those who have special (for example, administrator) privileges, is another important security practice.

User monitoring can include casual or direct observation, analysis of security logs, inspection of workstation hard drives, random drug testing (in certain job functions and in accordance with applicable privacy laws), audits of attendance and building access records, review of call logs and transcripts, and other activities.

User monitoring, and its purposes, should be fully addressed in an organization's written policy manuals. Information systems should display a login warning that clearly informs the user that their activities may be monitored and for what purposes. The login warning should also clearly indicate who owns the information and information assets processed on the system or network, and that the user has *no expectation of privacy* with regard to information stored or processed on the system. The login process should require users to affirmatively acknowledge the login warning by clicking OK or I Agree in order to gain access to the system.

An organization should conduct user monitoring in accordance with its written policies and applicable laws. Also, only personnel authorized to do so (such as security, legal, or human resources) should perform this monitoring, and only for authorized purposes.

Termination of employment

Employees who violate security policies (or any organizational policies for that matter) are subject to disciplinary action that may include termination. Usually termination is a last resort, but it may be necessary if an employee has a history of security problems.

It is vital to lock down or revoke local and remote access for a terminated employee as soon as possible, especially in cases where the employee is being fired or laid off. The potential consequences associated with continued access by an angry employee are serious enough to warrant emergency procedures for immediate termination of access. We discuss hiring and termination practices in greater detail in Chapter 6.

Security Operations Concepts

The topic of security operations covers a wide variety of concepts, which we describe in the following sections. The common theme among these concepts is protecting the confidentiality, integrity, and availability of information assets. Information is protected through controls and the reduction of threats and vulnerabilities.

Avoiding single points of failure

A *single point of failure* is any part of a system, process, or network whose failure can cause the whole system to become unavailable. The technical lexicon is full of strategies and solutions that attempt to address single points of failure: *reliable systems design, high-availability (HA), clustering, mirroring, virtualization,* and more.

How virtualization makes high-availability a reality

Server virtualization is a rapidly growing and popular trend that has come of age in recent years. Virtualization allows organizations to build more resilient, highly efficient, cost-effective technology infrastructures to better support their business-critical systems and applications. Popular virtualization solutions include VMware vSphere and Microsoft Hyper-V. Although virtualization has many, many benefits, here's a quick look at the high-availability benefit.

Virtual systems can be replicated or "moved" between separate physical systems, often without interrupting server operations or network connectivity. This can be accomplished over a local area network (LAN) when two physical servers (hosting multiple virtual servers) share common storage (a storage-area network [SAN]). For example, if Physical Server #1 fails, all the virtual servers on that physical server can be quickly "moved" to Physical Server #2. Or, in an alternate scenario, if a virtual server on Physical Server #1 reaches a pre-defined performance threshold (such as processor, memory, or bandwidth utilization), the virtual server can be "moved" — automatically and seamlessly — to Physical Server #2.

For business continuity or disaster recovery purposes, virtual servers can also be pre-staged in separate geographic locations, ready to be activated or "booted up" when needed. Using a third-party application, critical applications and data can be continuously replicated to a disaster recovery site or secondary data-center in near real-time, so that normal business operations can be restored as quickly as possible.

In reality, any system, process, or network has numerous single points of failure. To the extent possible, effective security planning attempts to identify and eliminate these single points of failure and thereby avoid a self-inflicted denial of service because of a weak architecture.

When conducting security planning for any new or existing system, process, or network, try brainstorming to identify as many possible single points of failure as you can. Consider the following examples:

- ✔ **Systems:** Does the system have redundant power supplies and cooling fans? What about separate power sources? Are hard drives configured for RAID? Are components hot-swappable? Can (and should) the system be clustered or virtualized? Can data be replicated to another system/location in real time?

- ✔ **Networks:** Do your routers and firewalls fail over automatically? Do they fail back? Do your routers have multiple paths available to your network destinations? Do you have multiple service providers? Do they share the same network POPs (points-of-presence)? What happens if the connection to your telecommunication provider's central office is cut? Do your multiple telecommunication providers' networks go through the same telecommunications hotel?

A *telecommunications* (or *telecom*) *hotel* is a facility that houses equipment belonging to many different telecommunications companies.

✔ **Processes:** Do your personnel security policies and practices *create* single points of failure? Perhaps you've instituted a separation of duties and responsibilities, but you haven't established a corresponding rotation of duties and responsibilities. If this situation sounds familiar, you may actually be causing a process to rely on a single *person* — that's a single point of failure! Do you have contingency processes in place in case a primary system, process, or person isn't available?

"Failure is not an option" was the famous resolution that set NASA engineers to solving the dire system troubles aboard the Apollo XIII moon flight. In a typical network, failure is *always* a possibility that must be addressed. The accompanying sidebar lays out some of the essential concepts for doing so.

Handling sensitive information

Sensitive information such as financial records, employee data, and information about customers must be clearly marked, properly handled and stored, and appropriately destroyed in accordance with established organizational policies, standards, and procedures:

✔ **Marking:** How an organization identifies sensitive information, whether electronic or hard copy. For example, a marking might read PRIVILEGED AND CONFIDENTIAL. See Chapter 6 for a more detailed discussion of data classification.

✔ **Handling:** The organization should have established procedures for handling sensitive information. These procedures detail how employees can transport, transmit, and use such information, as well as any applicable restrictions.

✔ **Storage and Backup:** Similar to handling, the organization must have procedures and requirements specifying how sensitive information must be stored and backed up.

✔ **Destruction:** Sooner or later, an organization must destroy a document that contains sensitive information. The organization must have procedures detailing how to destroy sensitive information that has been previously retained, regardless of whether the data is in hard copy or saved as an electronic file.

Records retention

Most organizations are bound by various laws to collect and store certain information, as well as to keep it for specified periods of time. An organization must be aware of legal requirements and ensure that it's in compliance with all applicable regulations.

Failure is not an option . . . ?

When a control failure results in a state that permits no accesses, that state is known as a *fail-safe* or *fail-closed* condition. When a control failure results in a state that permits all accesses, it is known as a *fail-open* condition. Related to these terms, a *fail-over* condition results when a primary control has failed and a secondary control becomes active, thereby eliminating a single point of failure. Finally, a *fail-back* condition results when a previously failed primary control is restored. The primary control again becomes active, and the secondary control goes back to a standby or passive state.

Records retention policies should cover any electronic records that may be located on file servers, document management systems, databases, e-mail systems, archives, and records management systems, as well as paper copies and backup media stored at off-site facilities.

Organizations that want to retain information longer than required by law should firmly establish why such information should be kept longer. Nowadays, just having information can be a liability, so this should be the exception rather than the norm.

At the opposite end of the records retention spectrum, many organizations now destroy records (including backup media) as soon as legally permissible in order to limit the scope (and cost) of any *future* discovery requests or litigation. Before implementing any such draconian retention policies that severely restrict your organization's retention periods, you should fully understand the negative implications such a policy has for your disaster recovery capabilities. Also, consult with your organization's legal counsel to ensure that you're in full compliance with all applicable laws and regulations.

 Although extremely short retention policies and practices may be prudent for limiting future discovery requests or litigation, they're *illegal* for limiting pending discovery requests or litigation (or even records that you have a reasonable expectation may become the subject of future litigation). In such cases, don't destroy pertinent records — otherwise you go to jail. You go directly to jail! You don't pass Go, you don't collect $200, and (oh, yeah) you don't pass the CISSP exam, either — or even remain eligible for CISSP certification!

Threats and Countermeasures

Plenty of threats, if carried out, could cause damage to the organization. We discuss some of these threats in the following sections.

Errors and Omissions

Errors and Omissions (E&O) is an insurance term that describes strategic and tactical errors that an organization can face, whether by *commission* (performing an action) or *omission* (failure to perform an action). In addition to general liability coverage, insurance companies also sell Errors and Omissions insurance. Errors and Omissions liability is also known as *professional liability*.

An example of Errors and Omissions is an error that prevents a company from delivering goods or services per the terms of a contract.

Organizations can prevent some Errors and Omissions through product reviews and quality control processes. For example, an accounting firm can implement systems that help to prevent calculation errors, and a medical transcription organization may implement access control systems to prevent the accidental disclosure of information.

Fraud

Fraud is defined as any deceptive or misrepresented activity that results in illicit personal gain. Workers who have detailed knowledge of business processes and/or insider access to information are in a particularly good position to defraud their employers.

Some examples of fraud include

- ✔ Writing bad checks
- ✔ Lying about personal information in order to receive a product or service for which the person isn't entitled

You can best counter fraud by using controls and processes to ensure that people aren't misrepresenting themselves or the information that they assert. Generally, you use controls that attempt to confirm information.

Other countermeasures may include establishing a fraud detection capability to ensure that employees and customers aren't trying to cheat the organization out of goods, services, or cash. A *fraud detection system* analyzes transactions and provides a list of possibly fraudulent transactions that security and systems professionals within the organization can review.

Organizations also need to examine their business processes and the roles and responsibilities of key personnel executing those processes. Among other things, business processes should make defrauding the organization through *collusion* difficult — meaning that employees can't easily work together for their illicit personal gain. See our discussion in the sections "Separation of duties and responsibilities" and "Job rotation," both earlier in this chapter.

Hackers and crackers

Hackers are (by their own account, anyway) computer enthusiasts who enjoy discovering the intricacies of computers and programming languages, and they can often be considered experts. The term *hacker* has been associated more with individuals who break into computer systems and networks in order to cause disruption or steal information. Hackers insist that those malicious individuals are known as *crackers*. Whatever you call them, you need to prevent them from accessing your systems and data for malicious or unauthorized purposes.

As long as the world is filled with hackers (and crackers), malicious code and viruses will remain important security risks that you must guard against. Viruses, worms, and Trojan horses are all examples of malicious code. We cover these topics in detail in Chapter 7.

Industrial espionage

Industrial espionage is the act of obtaining proprietary or confidential information in order to pass it to a competitor. Espionage is difficult to prevent, but you can deter such activity with visible audit trails and access controls.

Loss of physical and infrastructure support

Loss of physical and infrastructure support is a broad category that represents the kinds of actions that result in a data processing operation losing its physical facilities and/or supporting infrastructure. These actions include, but aren't limited to, interruptions in public utilities or events that result in the closure or evacuation of a building. We discuss this topic in depth in Chapter 11.

Malware

Malware is malicious code or software that typically damages or disables, takes control of, or steals information from a computer system. Malware broadly includes

✔ **adware:** Pop-up advertising programs that are commonly installed with freeware or shareware.

✔ **backdoors:** Malicious code that enables an attacker to bypass normal authentication to gain access to a compromised system.

✔ **bootkits:** A kernel-mode variant of a rootkit, commonly used to attack computers that are protected by full-disk encryption.

✔ **logic bombs:** Malicious code that is activated when a specified condition is met, such as a particular date or event.

✔ **rootkits:** Malicious code that provides privileged (root-level) access to a computer.

✔ **spyware:** Malicious software that collects information without the user's knowledge, and/or interferes with the operation of a computer (such as redirecting a web browser or installing additional malware).

✔ **Trojan horses:** Malicious software that masquerades as a legitimate program.

✔ **viruses:** Malicious code that requires a user to perform a specific action to become active, such as clicking an executable (`.exe`) attachment or a malicious website link.

✔ **worms:** Malicious code that is spread rapidly across networks without any user interaction required to activate the worm. Worms typically exploit known vulnerabilities and flaws that have not been patched.

Bots, botnets, and APTs: Not so groovy, baby!

No, we're not talking about fembots here, and APT doesn't stand for Austin Powers Trilogy! Bots, botnets, and *advanced persistent threats* (APTs) are sophisticated threat infrastructures that use malware to attack computers and networks.

A *bot* is an individual machine (such as a desktop or laptop computer, smartphone, or tablet) that has been infected with malware and is under the control of an attacker (known as a *bot-herder*). *Botnets* are networks that consist of thousands, hundreds of thousands, and even millions of bots worldwide. Botnets typically have many command-and-control servers distributed all over the Internet, which gives the botnet a resilient, distributed infrastructure. Individual bots can be updated or their functionality can be completely changed by the command-and-control servers. Botnets are sometimes classified as spamming botnets, DDoS botnets, or financial botnets, among others.

APTs are targeted intrusions, usually perpetrated by a group with significant resources (such as organized crime or a rogue nation-state), that use sophisticated botnets to attack a specific target, such as an enterprise or government network.

Sabotage

Sabotage is the deliberate destruction of property, which could include physical or information assets. This is best deterred and detected with highly visible audit trails, and it is best prevented with strict physical and logical access controls.

Theft

Theft involves taking property from its owner without the owner's consent. A wide variety of controls can deter and prevent theft, including locks, alarm systems, cameras, audit trails (in the case of information theft), and identifying marks on equipment.

Unlike the theft of physical assets, such as computers, you can find detecting data theft very difficult. When someone steals data, *that data is right where you left it;* the thief has simply made an unauthorized copy of the data and moved it to a secret location.

Security Controls

Controls are steps in processes — or components in information systems — that enforce compliance with business or security rules. Technology can enforce a control, or an individual may perform a manual step or procedure.

The major types of controls are

- ✔ **Preventive controls:** Used to prevent errors and unauthorized actions.
- ✔ **Detective controls:** Used to detect errors and unauthorized activities.
- ✔ **Corrective controls:** Used to reverse or minimize the impact of errors and unauthorized events. These are also known as *recovery controls.*
- ✔ **Automatic controls:** Those that automatically enforce a security policy.
- ✔ **Manual controls:** Those that must be proactively performed in order to enforce a security policy.

All the controls discussed in the following sections fall into these categories. A control is preventive, detective, or corrective; also, the control is either automatic or manual.

Operations controls are the processes and procedures that protect business operations and information. The major operations controls are

- ✔ Resource protection
- ✔ Privileged entity controls
- ✔ Change controls
- ✔ Media controls
- ✔ Administrative controls
- ✔ Trusted recovery

The following sections delve into each operations control in more detail.

Resource protection

Resource protection is the broad category of controls that protect information assets and information infrastructure. The resources that require protection include

- ✔ **Communications hardware and software:** Routers, switches, firewalls, load balancers, multiplexers, fax machines, Virtual Private Network (VPN) servers, and so on, as well as the software that these devices use
- ✔ **Computers and their storage systems:** All corporate servers and client workstations, storage area networks (SANs), network-attached storage (NAS), direct-attached storage (DAS), near-line and offline storage systems, and backup devices
- ✔ **Business data:** All stored information, such as financial data, sales and marketing information, personnel and payroll data, customer and supplier data, proprietary product or process data, and intellectual property
- ✔ **System data:** Operating systems, utilities, user IDs and password files, audit trails, and configuration files
- ✔ **Backup media:** Tapes, removable disks, and off-site replicated disk systems
- ✔ **Software:** Application source code, programs, tools, libraries, vendor software, and other proprietary software

Privileged entity controls

Privileged entity controls are the mechanisms, generally built into computer operating systems, which give privileged access to hardware, software, and data. In UNIX and Windows, the controls that permit privileged functions reside in the operating system.

Change controls

Change controls are the people-operated processes that govern architectural and configuration changes in a production environment. Instead of just making changes to systems and the way that they relate to each other, change control is a formal process of proposal, design, review, approval, implementation, and recordkeeping.

The two prevalent forms of change controls are Change Management and Configuration Management:

- **Change Management** is the approval-based process that ensures that only approved changes are implemented.

- **Configuration Management** is the control that records all of the soft configuration (settings and parameters in the operating system, database, and application) and software changes that are performed with approval from the Change Management process.

See Chapter 7 for more on Change and Configuration Management.

Patch and vulnerability management

On a daily basis, flaws are discovered in server and desktop operating systems, database management systems, and various other applications. Many of these flaws are security vulnerabilities that could permit an attacker to access sensitive data or critical functions. Patch management is closely associated with configuration management and change control processes.

To perform patch management, follow these basic steps:

1. Retrieve security advisories from vendors and third-party organizations.

2. Perform risk analysis on each advisory to determine its applicability and risk to your organization.

3. Develop a plan to either install the security patch or to perform another workaround, if any is available.

You should base your decision on which solution best eliminates the vulnerability.

4. Test the security patch or workaround in a test environment.

This process involves making sure that stated functions still work properly and that no unexpected side-effects arise as a result of installing the patch or workaround.

5. Install the security patch in the production environment.

6. Verify that the patch is properly installed and that systems still perform properly.

7. Update all relevant documentation to include any changes made or patches installed.

Configuration Management is the process (or processes) of actively managing the configuration of every system, device, and application and thoroughly documenting those configurations.

Media controls

Media controls refer to a broad category of controls that are used to manage information classification and physical media. Information classification refers to the tasks of marking information according to its sensitivity, as well as the subsequent handling, storage, transmission, and disposal procedures that accompany each classification level. Physical media is similarly marked; likewise, controls specify handling, storage, and disposal procedures.

Administrative controls

Administrative controls are the family of controls that includes least privilege, separation of duties, and rotation of duties. These controls form the basis of many processes, as well as access control and function control methodologies.

Trusted recovery

Trusted recovery is concerned with the processes and procedures that support the hardware or software recovery of a system. Specifically, the confidentiality and integrity of the information stored on and the functions served by a system being recovered must be preserved at all times.

The primary problem with system recovery is that a system may be operated briefly in maintenance or single-user mode in which all the software controls protecting the operating system and business data may not be functioning.

Organizations should have well-defined processes and procedures for system recovery to ensure that no inappropriate disclosure or leakage of sensitive information can occur.

Security Auditing and Due Care

Auditing is the process of examining systems and/or business processes to ensure that they've been properly designed and are being properly used. Audits are frequently performed by an independent third-party or an autonomous group within the organization. This helps to ensure that the audit results are accurate and are not biased because of organizational politics or other circumstances.

Audits are frequently performed to ensure an organization is in compliance with business or security policies and other requirements that the business may be subject to. These policies and requirements can include government laws and regulations, legal contracts, and industry or trade group standards and best practices.

Business-critical systems need to be subject to regular audits as dictated by regulatory, contractual, or trade group requirements.

Due care requires that an organization operate using good business practices — usually a set of standards formally or informally stated by industry trade groups. An organization can be liable if it fails to exercise due care (see Chapter 12 for more on due care).

Audit Trails

Audit trails are the auxiliary records that are created which record transactions and other events. Of the many reasons for having audit trails, here are a few:

- **Enforcement of accountability:** Employees tend to be more accountable for their actions when they know that audit trails capture the details of those actions.

- **Investigation:** Investigators who need to trace the actions of an individual's activities can rely on audit trails to see what that person did.

- **Event reconstruction:** Analysts may need to understand and reconstruct a complex event. Without audit trails, event reconstruction could be an exercise in futility.

- **Problem identification:** Audit trails can help an analyst or engineer identify and rectify the root cause of a problem.

Audit or audit trail?

To *audit* is an activity, and an *audit* is the output of the activity — the verification of accuracy of an application or system.

An *audit trail* is a record of events, without regard to correctness or accuracy of the event. It just reports an event.

Anatomy of an audit record

The basic components of an audit record are

- ✔ **Date and time:** When the event occurred
- ✔ **Who:** The person who performed the event
- ✔ **Where:** The location at which the person performed the event (for instance, which terminal or workstation the person used during the event)
- ✔ **Details:** Information about the event (such as original and changed settings)

Types of audit trails

Audit trails (also known as *audit logs* or just *logs*) come in several shapes and sizes. They include myriad log files and formats, such as cryptic `sendmail` logs and `syslog` entries, system login records, network trace logs, and transaction logs from applications.

Audit trails lack one important feature: consistency of format. It's as though everyone who ever wrote a program that generates an audit log crawled into a cave and invented his own audit log file format.

How to go looking for trouble

After you set up your audit logs and have the operating system tools, utilities, and applications logging events, how do you differentiate between normal activities and events that indicate real trouble?

Audit trails — the justification for time synchronization

System and network administrators have long recognized the value in synchronizing the time-of-day clocks in their systems with recognized standards, such as the U.S. National Bureau of Standards (NBS) atomic clock. Although this synchronization may just seem like a cool 007 thing to do, systems really do need to have their time-of-day clocks synchronized to within fractions of a second.

Imagine a situation in which you're trying to piece together a complex set of events that took place on several computers. The order in which events take place on several systems is highly significant. But what if the time-of-day clocks on these systems are several seconds or minutes apart? If the systems' clocks aren't synchronized, you can find it difficult, if not impossible, to determine the actual order in which events occurred.

This is really a two-fold problem. First, how do you determine whether an audit log entry is a routine event or an event indicating a problem? Second, how do you parse (or analyze) all of the information that is collected? It is often more practical to perform random sampling of the various log files on a regular basis so that you know the information is being properly collected and can recognize when something is wrong (for example, a log file that is normally only a few kilobytes in size suddenly grows to several megabytes).

Most modern operating systems and software applications lack the tools to parse audit logs and send appropriate messages to your pager, mobile phone, or e-mail inbox. However, many third-party software packages can collect and parse this information, and wake you up in the middle of the night when something really bad is happening.

Problem management and audit trails

So what do you do when you see trouble brewing in the audit logs? Follow these steps:

1. **Determine whether the audit trail entry indicates genuine trouble or whether the entry is a false-positive.**

   If the entry is a false-positive, then create an exception (if your auditing application allows it) and document the nature of the event. If real trouble exists, determine the appropriate response and, if the situation warrants, sound the alarm and rally the troops.

2. **Conduct a root cause analysis.**

   Audit trails are used to troubleshoot and reconstruct events, and root cause analysis is ideal in this situation. The analysis should lead to resolution of the problem — and eventually, the capability to prevent the problem in the future.

Without the audit trail, you're groping in the dark (a bad thing in the security business) — clueless as to what happened, and clueless as to how to prevent it from happening again.

Retaining audit logs

Many administrators forget to consider the many, *many* gigabytes of audit logs produced every day by a firewall or an intrusion detection system (IDS), but they find out soon enough when the system runs out of disk space — or worse yet, log files that you actually need for an investigation are overwritten by newer log files.

We can't tell you how long you should keep your audit logs, but it would be irresponsible for you to just chuck 'em without finding out from someone authoritative how long they should be kept. In many industries, audit log retention ultimately becomes a legal issue (complying with federal, state, and local laws), especially with applications. Find out how long audit logs need to be kept, and then figure out how to keep them.

Protection of audit logs

The integrity of audit logs is an absolute necessity, and this is another one of those difficult situations that may keep you up at night.

Audit logs must be protected against sabotage and other attacks that would prevent audit logs from properly and reliably recording events.

Here's the problem: Audit logs are usually just data files on a computer. A determined person who wants to cause trouble and/or erase his tracks is going to look around for the audit logs and try to alter them. Do you really think you can absolutely prevent this? No way. But you can come close.

With some creativity, you can utilize a few techniques on the really important audit logs, such as writing them directly to a sequential access device (tape drive) or a write-only device (CD-ROM), or sneaking them off the subject system over the network to another system.

None of these techniques is foolproof, but these methods can make it more difficult for determined intruders (or malicious insiders) to cause the kind of trouble that they have in mind.

Audit logging can also be the source of a Denial of Service (DoS) attack. For example, an intruder or insider who wants to perform some illicit, usually audited, transaction(s) is naturally worried about the audit log recording his dirty deed. However, he can launch a DoS attack on the audit log: Either he can perform thousands (or millions) of transactions or he can consume disk space in some other way to cause the audit-trail mechanism to run out of available disk space. After the audit-logging mechanism is gagged, the intruder can transact away, and the audit log won't record a thing, unless the system is designed to stop processing transactions if it is unable to write audit-log entries.

Here we circle back to the idea that protecting audit logs is vitally important. If they're disk-based, you need some mechanism in place that can move them quickly off the system in case an intruder tries to destroy them.

Monitoring

Monitoring covers much wider ground than just periodic or constant inspection of audit logs. Monitoring includes the following activities:

- ✔ Penetration testing
- ✔ Intrusion detection
- ✔ Violation processing
- ✔ Keystroke monitoring
- ✔ Traffic and trend analysis
- ✔ Facilities monitoring

The following sections give the skinny on each monitoring activity.

Penetration testing

Penetration testing (*pen testing* for short) is the general term that describes the use of tools to discover and identify logical and physical security vulnerabilities.

See Chapter 4 for more information on penetration testing.

Penetration testing techniques include

- ✔ **Port scanning:** A *port scan* is a tool that communicates over the network with one or more target systems on various Transmission Control Protocol/Internet Protocol (TCP/IP) ports. A port scan can discover the presence of ports that you should probably deactivate (because they serve no useful or necessary purpose on a particular system) or upgrade/patch (because of a software vulnerability that could lead to a break-in). Some examples of port-scanning tools include Nessus, SATAN, and Nmap.

- ✔ **Vulnerability scanning:** Similar to port scanning, *vulnerability scanning* is a means of identifying exploitable vulnerabilities in a system. You most often use such vulnerability-scanning tools to ensure that web-based applications, operating systems, and databases don't have any vulnerabilities that might permit an attacker to compromise a system or database.

✔ **Packet sniffing:** A *packet sniffer* is a tool that captures all TCP/IP packets on a network, not just those being sent to the system or device doing the sniffing. An Ethernet network is a shared-media network (see Chapter 5), which means that any or all devices on the local area network (LAN) can (theoretically) view all packets. However, switched-media LANs are more prevalent today and sniffers on switched-media LANs generally pick up only packets intended for the device running the sniffer.

A network adapter that operates in *promiscuous mode* accepts all packets, not just the packets destined for the system, and sends them to the operating system.

✔ **War dialing:** Hackers use war dialing to sequentially dial all phone numbers in a range to discover any active modems. The hacker then attempts to compromise any connected systems or networks via the modem connection.

✔ **War driving:** War driving is the 21st-century version of war dialing: Someone uses a laptop computer equipped with a wireless LAN card and literally drives around a densely populated area, looking to discover unprotected (or poorly protected) wireless LANs.

✔ **Radiation monitoring:** *Radio frequency (RF) emanations* describe the electromagnetic radiation emitted by computers and network devices. *Radiation monitoring* is similar to packet sniffing and war driving in that someone uses sophisticated equipment to try to determine what data is being displayed on monitors, transmitted on LANs, or processed in computers.

✔ **Dumpster diving:** Dumpster diving is low-tech penetration testing at its best (or worst), and is exactly what it sounds like. Dumpster diving can sometimes be an extraordinarily fruitful way to obtain information about an organization. Organizations in highly competitive environments also need to be concerned about where their recycled paper goes.

✔ **Eavesdropping:** Eavesdropping is as low-tech as dumpster diving, but a little less (physically) dirty. Basically an *eavesdropper* takes advantage of one or more persons who are talking or using a computer — and paying little attention to whether someone else is listening to their conversations or watching them work with discreet over-the-shoulder glances. (The technical term for the latter is *shoulder surfing*.)

✔ **Social engineering:** If eavesdropping is passive, then *social engineering* is the *active* way of getting information from workers. It involves such low-tech tactics as an attacker pretending to be a support technician, then calling an employee and asking for their password. You'd think most people would be smart enough not to fall for this, but people are people (and Soylent Green is people)! We cover this topic in more detail in Chapter 7.

Packet sniffing isn't all bad

Packet sniffing isn't just a tool used by hackers to pick up user IDs and passwords from the LAN. Packet sniffing has legitimate uses, as well. Primarily, you can use it as a diagnostic tool to troubleshoot network devices, such as a firewall (to see whether the desired packets get through), routers, switches, and virtual LANs (VLANs).

The obvious danger of the packet sniffer falling into the wrong hands is that it provides the capability to capture user IDs and passwords. Equally perilous is the fact that packet sniffers are next to impossible to detect on a network.

Intrusion detection and prevention

Intrusion detection is the technique used to detect unauthorized activity on a network. An intrusion detection system is frequently called an *IDS*. The two types of IDSs used today are

- *Network-based* **intrusion detection (NIDS):** Consists of a separate device attached to a LAN that listens to all network traffic by using various methods (which we describe later in this section) to detect anomalous activity.

- *Host-based* **intrusion detection (HIDS):** This is really a subset of network-based IDS, in which only the network traffic destined for a particular host is monitored.

Both network- and host-based IDSs use a couple of methods:

- **Signature-based:** A *signature-based* IDS compares network traffic that is observed with a list of patterns in a signature file. A signature-based IDS detects any of a known set of attacks, but if an intruder is able to change the patterns that he uses in his attack, then his attack may be able to slip by the IDS without being detected. The other downside of signature-based IDS is that the signature file must be periodically updated.

- **Anomaly-based:** An *anomaly-based* IDS monitors all the traffic over the network and builds traffic profiles. Over time, the IDS will report deviations from the profiles that it has built. The upside of anomaly-based IDSs is that there are no signature files to periodically update. The downside is that you may have a high volume of false-positives. Behavior-based and heuristics-based IDSs are similar to anomaly-based IDSs and share many of the same advantages. Rather than detecting anomalies to normal traffic patterns, behavior-based and heuristics-based systems attempt to recognize and learn potential attack patterns.

Intrusion detection doesn't stop intruders, but intrusion prevention does . . . or, at least, it slows them down. *Intrusion prevention systems* (IPSs) are newer and more common systems than IDSs, and IPSs are designed to detect *and block* intrusions. An intrusion prevention system is simply an IDS that can take action, such as dropping a connection or blocking a port, when an intrusion is detected.

Intrusion detection looks for known attacks and/or anomalous behavior on a network or host.

See Chapter 5 for more on intrusion detection and intrusion prevention systems.

Violation analysis

Violation analysis is the science of examining activity and audit logs to discover inappropriate activities. Violation analysis uses *clipping levels,* which are the thresholds that differentiate violations from non-events.

For example, users on a particular system sometimes type in their passwords incorrectly, so a few errors are allowed. But wisely, you set a clipping level of four failed login attempts per hour. Whenever a user has fewer than four failed attempts, everything's cool. But when the clipping level is exceeded, then a violation has occurred. In this example, the violation may indicate that someone is trying to break in to the system by guessing passwords.

Keystroke monitoring

Keystroke monitoring records all input activities on a terminal or workstation. Keystroke monitoring writes large volumes of data to log files; you may find it difficult to hide, and ethical issues exist regarding the privacy rights of the person or people whose activities you monitor at this level of scrutiny.

Use keystroke monitoring with care — perhaps only as an aid for an active investigation.

Traffic and trend analysis

Traffic analysis and *trend analysis* are the techniques used to make inferences about the activities of an individual or an organization, based on the type and volume of traffic on a network. For instance, a dramatic rise in network traffic at 2:00 a.m. might be an indication of backups or batch processing.

Hackers use traffic and trend analysis, too. You can read more about this topic in Chapter 7.

Facilities monitoring

No monitoring plan is complete without some physical monitoring capabilities. A few methods are

- ✔ Watching the logs of buildings with card-key access control to see whether doors are being propped open or if people are attempting to enter restricted areas
- ✔ Monitoring unmanned entrances and other locations with closed-circuit television (CCTV) monitoring systems
- ✔ Staffing key locations with security guards
- ✔ Installing and monitoring security alarm sensors on doors and windows, and motion sensors in areas not normally manned

Responding to events

So, through your foresight and leadership (and the excellent book that you're reading right now), your organization has full security monitoring capabilities. What do you do when one of the monitoring systems indicates that a security event is unfolding? How can you recognize that something's up and respond appropriately?

The process of detecting, responding, and fixing a problem is known as *problem management* or *incident management*.

Like Business Continuity Planning and Disaster Recovery Planning (which we talk about in Chapter 11), security event recognition requires advance planning:

- ✔ **Monitoring personnel:** Who's monitoring which events, audit logs, and other facilities?
- ✔ **Initial response:** What are the first steps to be performed when a suspicious event is noticed? Written procedures would be a good idea here.
- ✔ **Confirmation:** Who performs this task, and how does he or she do it? Someone needs to determine whether the event is a false alarm.
- ✔ **Notification:** How will the appropriate persons or the affected community be notified? Who bears this responsibility? Presuming that someone is using the system generating the alarm, key personnel and/or the user community may need to be notified in the event that the event will continue to unfold and interrupt service.

✔ **Escalation:** Who defines which senior managers need to be notified and when? If the event crosses predetermined thresholds, you may need to notify higher levels of management.

✔ **Resolution:** How do you plan a resolution? Most of the time, someone needs to *do* something to manage the event, such as shutting down and rebooting a server, locking a user account, suspending a service, or any number of other actions.

✔ **Event reporting:** Will there be standard reporting formats, and by what means will reports be delivered? How various events will be reported needs to be worked out in advance, too.

✔ **Event review:** How do you plan to review the event in terms of action and prevention? At the conclusion of the event, stakeholders need to discuss the event to determine whether the response was appropriate and whether the organization can avoid the event (or ones like it) in the future.

✔ **Security Violations:** All known security violations should be documented, and a root-cause analysis should be performed in order to determine whether any changes in processes or technology are needed.

Security incident response is no longer a nice-to-have luxury. Security regulations often require a formal incident response capability. This entails setting up a response and communication plan, and training key individuals who will know what to do should a security incident occur.

We discuss this topic further in Chapter 12.

Security event resolution

How should an organization define *resolution* of a security event? Is it when the affected system's functionality has been restored? Is it when the perpetrator has been identified? Is it after any architecture or process changes designed to prevent a repeat of the event have been put into place? Each organization will need to get its arms around this so that both senior management and the security group will have a clear understanding of what is meant by the term *resolution*.

Prep Test

1 **The two types of intrusion detection are**

A ○ Attack-based systems and response-based systems
B ○ Signature-based systems and anomaly-based systems
C ○ Knowledge-based systems and scripture-based systems
D ○ Passive monitoring systems and active monitoring systems

2 **Recording data traveling on a network is known as**

A ○ Promiscuous mode
B ○ Packet sniffing
C ○ Packet snoring
D ○ Packing sneaking

3 **Which of the following is NOT an example of penetration testing?**

A ○ Radiation monitoring
B ○ War driving
C ○ Port scanning
D ○ War diving

4 **Trusted recovery is concerned with**

A ○ The ability of a system to be rebuilt
B ○ The vulnerability of a system while it's being rebuilt
C ○ The ability of a system to rebuild itself
D ○ The willingness of a system to rebuild itself

5 **The third-party inspection of a system is known as a(n)**

A ○ Confidence check
B ○ Integrity trail
C ○ Audit trail
D ○ Audit

6 One of the primary concerns with long-term audit log retention is

A ○ Whether anyone will be around who can find them
B ○ Whether any violations of privacy laws have occurred
C ○ Whether anyone will be around who understands them
D ○ Whether any tape/disk drives will be available to read them

7 The required operating state of a network interface on a system running a sniffer is

A ○ Open mode
B ○ Promiscuous mode
C ○ Licentious mode
D ○ Pretentious mode

8 Filling a system's hard drive so that it can no longer record audit records is known as a(n)

A ○ Audit lock-out
B ○ Audit exception
C ○ Denial of Facilities attack
D ○ Denial of Service attack

9 An investigator who needs to have access to detailed employee event information may need to use

A ○ Keystroke monitoring
B ○ Intrusion detection
C ○ Keystroke analysis
D ○ Trend analysis

10 Which of the following is NOT true about a signature-based IDS?

A ○ It reports a low number of false-positives.
B ○ It requires periodic updating of its signature files.
C ○ It reports a high number of false-positives.
D ○ It can't detect anomalies based on trends.

Answers

1 **B.** Signature-based systems and anomaly-based systems. The two types of IDS systems are signature-based and anomaly-based. *Review "Intrusion detection and prevention."*

2 **B.** Packet sniffing. Packet sniffing is the technique used to record network traffic. *Review "Penetration testing."*

3 **D.** War diving. War diving isn't a testing technique, but radiation monitoring, war driving, and port scanning are. *Review "Penetration testing."*

4 **B.** The vulnerability of a system while it's being rebuilt. Most operating systems in single-user mode lack the security controls present in a system that's fully operational. *Review "Security Controls."*

5 **D.** Audit. An audit is an inspection of a system or process. *Review "Security Auditing and Due Care."*

6 **D.** Whether any tape/disk drives will be available to read them. The challenge with audit log retention is choosing a medium that will be readable many years in the future. *Review "Retaining audit logs."*

7 **B.** Promiscuous mode. Promiscuous mode is the term that describes the state of a system that's accepting all packets on the network, not just those packets destined for the system. *Review "Penetration testing."*

8 **D.** Denial of Service attack. Filling a system's hard drive is one way to launch a Denial of Service attack on an audit log mechanism. Filling the hard drive prevents the mechanism from being able to write additional entries to the log. *Review "Protection of audit logs."*

9 **A.** Keystroke monitoring. Keystroke monitoring records every key press and mouse movement. *Review "Keystroke monitoring."*

10 **C.** It reports a high number of false-positives. Signature-based IDSs generally have a low number of false-positives. *Review "Intrusion detection and prevention."*

Security Operations

Chapter 11

Business Continuity and Disaster Recovery Planning

*B*usiness Continuity Planning (BCP) and Disaster Recovery Planning (DRP) work hand in hand to provide an organization with the means to continue and recover business operations when a disaster strikes. BCP and DRP are intensive and highly detailed planning initiatives, each one resulting in important-looking three-ring binders filled with business continuation and recovery procedures that every participant can put on his or her bookshelf.

Business Continuity Planning and Disaster Recovery Planning exist for one reason: Bad things happen. Organizations that want to survive a disastrous event need to make formal and extensive plans — contingency plans to keep the business running and recovery plans to return operations to normal.

Keeping a business operating during a disaster can be like juggling with one arm tied behind your back (we first thought of plate-spinning and one-armed paper hangers, but most of our readers are probably too young to understand these). You'd better plan in advance how you're going to do it, and practice! It could happen at night, you know (one-handed juggling in the dark is a lot harder).

Defining Disastrous Events

An amazing variety of disasters can beset an organization's business operations. They fall into two main categories: natural and man-made.

After reading the following sections, you should no longer be skeptical about the need for Business Continuity Planning and Disaster Recovery Planning.

Regardless of whether a disaster is natural or man-made, a disaster can disrupt business operations. We discuss how in the section "How disasters affect businesses," later in this chapter.

Natural disasters

In many cases, formal methodologies are used to predict the likelihood of a particular disaster. For example, *50-year flood plain* is a term that you've probably heard to describe the maximum physical limits of a river flood that's likely to occur once in a 50-year period. The likelihood of each of the following disasters depends greatly on local and regional geography:

- Fires and explosions
- Earthquakes
- Storms (snow, ice, hail, prolonged rain, wind, dust, solar)
- Floods
- Hurricanes, typhoons, and cyclones
- Volcanoes and lava flows
- Tornadoes
- Landslides
- Avalanches
- Tsunamis
- Pandemics

Many of these occurrences may have secondary effects; often these secondary effects have a bigger impact on business operations, sometimes in a wider area than the initial disaster (for instance, a landslide in a rural area can topple power transmission lines, which results in a citywide blackout). Some of these effects are

- **Utility outages:** Electric power, natural gas, water, and so on
- **Communications outages:** Telephone, cable, wireless, TV, and radio

✔ **Transportation outages:** Road, airport, train, and port closures

✔ **Evacuations/unavailability of personnel:** From both home and work locations

Man-made disasters

As if natural disasters weren't enough, several other events can disrupt business operations, all as a result of deliberate and accidental acts:

✔ **Accidents:** Hazardous materials spills, power outages, communications failures, and floods due to water supply accidents

✔ **Crime and mischief:** Arson, vandalism, and burglary

✔ **War and terrorism:** Bombings, sabotage, and other destructive acts

✔ **Cyber attacks/cyber warfare:** Denial of Service (DoS) attacks, malware, data destruction, and similar acts

✔ **Civil disturbances:** Riots, demonstrations, strikes, sickouts, and other such events

---

Disaster recovery planning and terrorist attacks

The 2001 terrorist attacks in New York, Washington, D.C., and Pennsylvania — and the subsequent collapse of the World Trade Center buildings — had Disaster Recovery Planning and Business Continuity Planning officials all over the world scrambling to update their plans.

This kind of planning is still a highly relevant topic more than a decade later. The attacks redefined the limits of extreme, deliberate acts of destruction. Previously, the most heinous attacks imaginable were large-scale bombings such as the 1993 attack on the World Trade Center or the 1995 bombing of the Alfred P. Murrah Federal Building in Oklahoma City.

The collapse of the World Trade Center towers resulted in the loss of life of 40 percent of the employees of the Sandler O'Neill & Partners investment bank. Bond broker Cantor Fitzgerald lost 658 employees in the attack — nearly its entire workforce. The sudden loss of a large number of employees had rarely been figured into BCP and DRP plans before. Businesses suddenly had to figure into contingency and recovery plans the previously unheard-of scenario, "What do we do if significant numbers of employees are suddenly lost?"

Traditional BCP and DRP plans nearly always assumed that a business still had plenty of workers around to keep the business rolling; those insiders might be delayed by weather or other events, but eventually they'd be back to continue running the business. The attacks on September 11, 2001, changed all that forever. Organizations need to include the possibility of the loss of a significant portion of their workforces into their business continuity plans. They owe this to their constituents and to their investors.

How disasters affect businesses

Disasters can affect businesses in a lot of ways — some obvious, and others not so obvious.

- ✔ **Damage to business buildings.** Disasters can damage or destroy a building or make it uninhabitable.

- ✔ **Damage to business records.** Along with damaging a building, a disaster may damage a building's contents, including business records, whether they are in the form of paper, microfilm, or electronic.

- ✔ **Damage to business equipment.** A disaster may be capable of damaging business equipment including computers, copiers, and all sorts of other machinery. Anything electrical or mechanical from calculators to nuclear reactors can be damaged in a disaster.

- ✔ **Damage to communications.** Disasters can damage common carrier facilities including telephone networks (both landline and cellular), data networks, even wireless and satellite-based systems. Even if a business's buildings and equipment are untouched by a disaster, communications outages can be crippling. Further, damaged communications infrastructure in other cities can be capable of knocking out many businesses' voice and data networks (the September 11, 2001, attacks had an immediate impact on communications over a wide area of the northeastern U.S.; a number of telecommunications providers had strategic regional facilities there).

- ✔ **Damage to public utilities.** Power, water, natural gas, and steam services can be damaged by a disaster. Even if a business's premises are undamaged, a utility outage can cause significant business disruption.

- ✔ **Damage to transportation systems.** Freeways, railroads, and airports can all be damaged in a disaster. Damaged transportation infrastructure in other regions (where customers, partners, and suppliers are located, for instance) can cripple organizations dependent on the movement of materials, goods, or customers.

- ✔ **Injuries and loss of life.** Violent disasters in populated areas often cause casualties. When employees, contractors, or customers are killed or injured, businesses are affected in negative ways: there may be fewer customers or fewer available employees to deliver goods and services. Losses don't need to be the employees or customers themselves; when family members are injured or in danger, employees will usually stay home to care for them and return to work only when those situations have stabilized.

- ✔ **Indirect damage: suppliers and customers.** If a disaster strikes a region where key suppliers or customers are located, the effect on businesses can be almost as serious as if the business itself suffered damage.

The list above may not be complete, but hopefully it will get you thinking about all the ways a disaster can affect your organization.

How BCP and DRP Work Together

Business Continuity Planning and Disaster Recovery Planning are two sides of the same coin. Each springs into action when a disaster strikes. But they do have different goals:

- **BCP:** Business Continuity Planning deals with keeping business operations running — perhaps in another location or by using different tools and processes — after a disaster has struck.
- **DRP:** Disaster Recovery Planning deals with restoring normal business operations after the disaster takes place.

While the Business Continuity team is busy keeping business operations running via one of possibly several contingency plans, the Disaster Recovery team members are busy restoring the original facilities and equipment so that they can resume normal operations.

Here's an analogy. Two boys kick a big anthill — a disaster for the ant colony. Some of the ants scramble to save the eggs and the food supply; that's Ant City business continuity. Other ants work on rebuilding the anthill; that's Ant City disaster recovery. Both teams work to ensure the anthill's survival, but each team has its own role to play.

BCP and DRP projects have these common elements:

- **Identification of critical business functions:** The Business Impact Assessment and Vulnerability Assessment (discussed in the section "Conducting the Business Impact Assessment," later in this chapter) identify these functions.
- **Identification of possible disaster scenarios:** The planning team identifies all the likely man-made and natural disaster scenarios, ranked by probability and impact to the organization.
- **Experts:** People who understand the organization's critical business processes.

The similarities end with this list. The BCP project concentrates on *continuing* business operations, whereas the DRP project focuses on *recovering* the original business functions. Although both plans deal with the long-term survival of the business, they involve different activities. When a significant disaster occurs, both activities kick into gear at the same time, keeping vital business functions running (BCP) and getting things back to normal as soon as possible (DRP).

Planning for pandemics

In the last hundred years (and indeed, in all of recorded history before the 20th century), several pandemics have swept through the world. A *pandemic* is a rapid spread of a new disease for which few people have natural immunity. Large numbers of people may fall ill, resulting in high rates of absenteeism; supplier slow-downs; and shortages in materials, goods, and services. Some pandemics have a high mortality rate — many people die.

Contingency planning for a pandemic requires a different approach from that for other types of disasters. When a disaster such as an earthquake, hurricane, or volcano occurs, help in many forms soon comes pouring into the region to help repair transportation, communications, and other vital services. Organizations can rely on outsourced help or operations in other regions to keep critical operations running. But in a pandemic, no outside help may be available,

and much larger regions may be affected. In general, a pandemic can induce a global slow-down in manpower, supplies, and services, as well as a depressed demand for most goods and services. Whole national economies can grind to a near-halt.

Businesses affected by a pandemic should expect high rates of absenteeism for extended periods of time. Local or regional municipalities may impose quarantines and travel restrictions, which slows the movement of customers and supplies. Schools may be closed for extended periods of time, which could require working parents to stay at home. Businesses should plan on operating only the most critical business processes, and they may have to rely on cross-trained staff because some of the usual staff members may be ill, or unwilling or unable to travel to work.

COOPeration is the key

Like many disciplines based in technology, BCP and DRP are also changing rapidly. One new approach is COOP, or Continuity of Operations, which is a blending of BCP and DRP into a single mission: keeping the organization running after a disaster.

If you are interested in learning more, an excellent reference for added information on COOP is the FEMA (U.S. Federal Emergency Management Agency) guide IS-547, Introduction to COOP, which is available at `www.training.fema.gov/EMIWeb/IS/IS547lst.asp`.

Understanding BCP Project Elements

Before a BCP project can begin, everyone on the project team has to make and understand some basic definitions and assumptions. These critical items include

✔ **Senior management support:** The development of a Business Continuity Plan is time consuming, with no immediate or tangible *return on investment* (ROI). If you want a successful BCP project, you need the support of the organization's senior management, including adequate budget, manpower, and visible statements backing the project. Senior management needs to make explicit statements identifying the responsible parties, as well as the importance of the BCP project, budget, priorities, urgency, and timing.

✔ **Senior management involvement:** Senior management can't just bless the BCP project. Because senior managers and directors may have implicit and explicit responsibility for the organization's ability to recover from a disaster, senior management needs to have a degree of direct involvement in the BCP effort. The careers that these people save may be their own.

✔ **Project team membership:** Which people do you want to put on the BCP project team? The team must represent all relevant functions and business units. Many of the team members probably have their usual jobs, too, so the team needs to develop a realistic timeline for how quickly the BCP project can make progress.

✔ **Who brings the donuts:** Because it's critical that BCP meetings are well attended, quality donuts are an essential success component.

A BCP project typically has four components: scope determination, the Business Impact Assessment, the Business Continuity Plan, and implementation. We discuss each of these components in the following sections.

BCP and DRP: A simple illustration

Here's a scenario: A business is a delivery service that has one delivery truck, which delivers goods around the city.

Business Continuity Planning deals with keeping the delivery service running in case something happens to the truck, presumably with a backup truck, substitute drivers, maps to get around traffic jams, and other contingencies to keep the delivery function running.

Disaster Recovery Planning, on the other hand, deals with fixing the original delivery truck, which might involve making repairs or even buying/leasing a new truck.

Determining BCP Scope

The success and effectiveness of a Business Continuity Plan depends greatly on whether senior management and the project team properly define its scope. Business processes and technology can muddy the waters and make this task difficult. For instance, distributed systems dependence on at least some desktop systems for vital business functions expands the scope beyond core functions. Geographically dispersed companies — often the result of mergers — complicate matters as well.

Also, large companies are understandably more complex. The boundaries between where a function begins and ends are oftentimes fuzzy and sometimes poorly documented and not well understood.

Political pressures can influence the scope of the BCP as well. A department that *thinks* it's vital, but which falls outside the BCP scope, may lobby to be included in the BCP. Everybody wants to be important (and some just want to *appear* to be important). You need senior management support of scope (what the project team *really* needs to include and what it doesn't) to put a stop to the political games.

Scope creep (what happens when a project's scope grows beyond the original intent) can become *scope leap* if you have a weak or inexperienced BCP project team. For the success of the project, strong leaders must make rational decisions about the scope of the project. Remember, you can change the scope of BCP projects in later iterations of the project.

The project team needs to find a balance between too narrow a scope, which makes the plan ineffective, and too wide a scope, which makes the plan too cumbersome.

Conducting the Business Impact Assessment

The *Business Impact Assessment* (BIA) describes the impact that a disaster is expected to have on business operations. This important early step in Business Continuity Planning helps an organization figure out which business processes are more resilient and which are more fragile.

A disaster's impact includes quantitative and qualitative effects. The *quantitative impact* is generally financial, such as loss of revenue or output of production. The *qualitative impact* has more to do with the delivery of goods and/or services.

Any Business Impact Assessment worth its salt needs to perform the following tasks well:

- ✔ Perform a Vulnerability Assessment
- ✔ Carry out a Criticality Assessment — determining how critically important a particular business function is to the ongoing viability of the organization
- ✔ Determine the Maximum Tolerable Downtime
- ✔ Establish recovery targets
- ✔ Determine resource requirements

You can get the scoop on these activities in the following sections.

Vulnerability Assessment

Often, a BIA includes a *Vulnerability Assessment* that helps get a handle on obvious and not-so-obvious weaknesses in business critical systems. A Vulnerability Assessment has quantitative (financial) and qualitative (operational) sections, similar to a Risk Assessment, which is covered in detail in Chapter 6.

The purpose of a Vulnerability Assessment is to determine the impact — both quantitative and qualitative — of the loss of a critical business function.

Quantitative losses include

- ✔ Loss of revenue
- ✔ Loss of operating capital
- ✔ Loss because of personal liabilities
- ✔ Increase in expenses
- ✔ Penalties because of violations of business contracts
- ✔ Violations of laws and regulations (which can result in legal costs such as fines and civil penalties)

Qualitative losses include loss of

- ✔ Service quality
- ✔ Competitive advantages
- ✔ Customer satisfaction
- ✔ Market share
- ✔ Prestige and reputation

The Vulnerability Assessment identifies *critical support areas,* which are business functions that, if lost, would cause irreparable harm to the business by jeopardizing critical business processes or the lives and safety of personnel. The Vulnerability Assessment should carefully study critical support areas to identify the resources that those areas require to continue functioning.

Quantitative losses include an increase in operating expenses because of any higher costs associated with executing the contingency plan. In other words, planners need to remember to consider operating costs that may be higher during a disaster situation.

Criticality Assessment

The BCP team should inventory all high-level business functions (for example, customer support, order processing, returns, cash management, accounts receivable, payroll, and so on) and rank them in order of criticality. The team should also describe the impact of a disruption to each function on overall business operations.

The team members need to estimate the duration of a disaster event to effectively prepare the Criticality Assessment. Project team members need to consider the impact of a disruption based on the length of time that a disaster impairs critical business functions. You can see the vast difference in business impact of a disruption that lasts one minute, compared to one hour, one day, one week, or longer. Generally, the criticality of a business function depends on the degree of impact that its impairment has on the business.

Planners need to consider disasters that occur at different times in the business cycle, whatever that might be for an organization. Response to a disaster at the busiest time of the month (or year) may vary quite a bit from response at other times.

Identifying key players

Although you can consider a variety of angles when evaluating vulnerability and criticality, commonly you start with a high-level organization chart. (Hip people call this chart the *org chart*). In most companies, the major functions pretty much follow the structure of the organization.

Following an org chart helps the BCP project team consider all the steps in a critical process. Walk through the org chart, stopping at each manager's or director's position and asking, "What does he do?", "What does she do?", and "Who files the TPS reports?" This mental stroll can help jog your memory, and help you better see all the parts of the organization's big picture.

Remembering payroll

Organizations that inventory and categorize their business processes usually look outward to the goods and services that they provide to their customers. During a disaster-related crisis, organizations that survive have effective contingency plans for these processes.

But some organizations overlook internal services that support ongoing operations. An important example is payroll. Some disasters can last weeks or even months while organizations rebuild their goods and services delivery. If you don't have payroll high on the list of processes to recover, employees could find themselves going without a paycheck for quite a while. An organization in this position may find itself losing the people it needs to get normal operations running again, which could precipitate a secondary disaster that has long-term consequences.

A retail organization that we're familiar with has an interesting contingency plan for paying its branch-office employees. Branch managers are authorized to pay their employees a fixed amount of cash each week if the organization's payroll system stops functioning. When automated payroll systems are restored, the cash payments are entered into the system, so that payroll records for each employee will be accurate.

When you're cruising an org chart to make sure that it covers all areas of the organization, you may easily overlook outsourced functions that might not show up in the org chart. For instance, if your organization outsources accounts payable (A/P) functions, you might miss this detail if you don't see it on an org chart. Okay, you'd probably notice the absence of *all* A/P. But if your organization outsources only part of A/P — say, a group that detects and investigates A/P fraud (looking for payment patterns that suggest the presence of phony payment requests) — your org chart probably doesn't include that vital function.

Establishing Maximum Tolerable Downtime

An extension of the Criticality Assessment (which we talk about in the section "Criticality Assessment," earlier in this chapter) is a statement of Maximum Tolerable Downtime (MTD —also known as Maximum Tolerable Period of Disruption or MTPD) for each critical business function. *Maximum Tolerable Downtime* is the maximum period of time that a critical business function can be inoperative before the company incurs significant and long-lasting damage.

For example, imagine that your favorite online merchant — a bookseller, an auction house, or an online trading company — goes down for an hour, a day, or a week. At some point, you have to figure that a prolonged disruption sinks the ship, meaning the business can't survive. Determining MTD involves figuring out at what point the organization suffers permanent, measurable loss as a result of a disaster. Online retailers know that even shorter outages may mean that some customers will switch brands and take their business elsewhere.

Make the Maximum Tolerable Downtime assessment a major factor in determining the criticality — and priority — of business functions. A function that can withstand only two hours of downtime obviously has a higher priority than another function that can withstand several days of downtime.

Maximum Tolerable Downtime is a measure of the longest period of time that a critical business function can be disrupted without suffering unacceptable consequences, perhaps threatening the actual survivability of the organization.

Establish recovery targets

When you establish the Criticality Assessment and Maximum Tolerable Downtime for each business process (which we talk about in the preceding sections), the planning team can establish recovery targets. These targets represent the period of time from the onset of a disaster until critical processes have resumed functioning.

Two primary recovery targets are usually established for each business process: a Recovery Time Objective and Recovery Point Objective. We discuss these targets in the following sections.

How bad does it have to be?

Establishing reasonable Maximum Tolerable Downtime (MTD) values can be difficult. The issue here is similar to pain threshold and the actual effects of a disaster. Early on, we used to say that an MTD value was valid when its magnitude was sufficient to cause the complete failure of a business. Now we believe that's too high a threshold; after all, some organizations won't actually fail even in a huge disaster: for example, local governments and religious institutions won't go out of business and disappear from the landscape.

So what's a reasonable measure of MTD? It depends on your particular organization and situation, but here are some ideas:

✔ Threshold of public outcry

✔ Loss of a certain number of market-share points

✔ Loss of a certain percentage of constituents

✔ Loss of life

You need to identify a reasonable threshold of MTD — short of your organization ceasing to exist, but something more reasonable, such as a significant loss of business or loss of confidence in your organization.

Recovery Time Objective

A *Recovery Time Objective* (RTO) is the maximum period of time in which a business process must be restored after a disaster.

An organization without a DR plan that suffers a serious disaster, such as an earthquake or hurricane, could experience an RTO of one to two weeks or more. An organization could possibly need this length of time to select a new location for processing data, purchase new systems, load application software and data, and resume processing. An organization that can't tolerate such a long outage needs to establish a shorter RTO and determine the level of investments required to meet that target.

Recovery Point Objective

A *Recovery Point Objective* (RPO) is the maximum period of time in which data might be lost if a disaster strikes.

The traditional schedule for backing up data is once per day. If a disaster occurs before backups are done, the organization can lose an entire day's worth of information. This is because system and data recovery are often performed using the last good set of backups. An organization that requires a shorter RPO needs to figure out a way to make copies of transaction data more frequently than once per day.

Here are some examples of how organizations might establish their RPOs:

- ✔ **Keyed Invoices.** An accounts payable department opens the mail and manually keys in the invoices that it receives from its suppliers. Data entry clerks spend their entire day inputting invoices. If a disaster occurs before backups are run at the end of the business day (and if that disaster requires the organization to rebuild systems from backup tapes), those clerks have to redo that whole day's worth of data entry.

- ✔ **Online orders:** A small business develops an online web application that customers can use to place orders. At the end of each day, the Orders department runs a program that prints out all the day's orders, and the Shipping department fills those orders on the following day. If a disaster occurs at any time during the day, the business loses all online orders placed since the previous day's backup.

If you establish the Maximum Tolerable Downtime for processes such as the ones in the preceding list as less than one business day, the organization needs to take some steps to save online data more than once per day.

Many organizations consider off-site backup media storage, where backup tapes are transported off-site as frequently as every day, or where electronic vaulting to an offsite location is performed several times each day. An event such as a fire can destroy computers as well as backup media if it is nearby.

How the Recovery Time Objective and Recovery Point Objective work together

RPO and RTO targets are different measures of recovery for a system, but they work together. When the team establishes proposed targets, the team members need to understand how each target works.

At first glance, you might think that RPO should be a shorter time than RTO (or maybe the other way around). In fact, different businesses and applications present different business requirements that might make RPO less than RTO, equal to RTO, or greater than RTO. Here are some examples:

- **RPO greater than RTO:** A business can recover an application in 4 hours (RTO), and it has a maximum data loss (RPO) of 24 hours. So, if a disaster occurs, the business can get the application running again in 4 hours, but data recovered in the system consists of data entered prior to 24 hours before the incident took place.

- **RPO equal to RTO:** A business can recover an application in 12 hours (RTO), with a maximum data loss of 12 hours (RPO). You can probably imagine this scenario: An application mirrors (or replicates) data to a backup system in real-time. If a disaster occurs, the disaster recovery team requires 12 hours to start the backup system. After the team gets the system running, the business has data from until 12 hours in the past — the time when the primary system failed.

- **RPO less than RTO:** The disaster recovery team can recover an application in 4 hours (RTO), with a maximum data loss of 1 hour (RPO). How can this situation happen? Maybe a back-office transaction-posting application, which receives and processes data from order-processing applications, fails. If the back-office application is down for 4 hours, data coming from the order-processing applications may be buffered someplace else, and when the back-office application resumes processing, it can then receive and process the waiting input data.

Defining Resource Requirements

The *Resource Requirements* portion of the BIA is a listing of the resources that an organization needs in order to continue operating each critical business function. In an organization that has finite resources (which is pretty much every organization), the most critical functions get first pick, and the lower-priority functions get the leftovers.

Understanding what resources are required to support a business process helps the project team to figure out what the contingency plan for that process needs to contain, and how the process can be operated in Emergency mode and then recovered.

The high cost of rapid recovery

Disaster recovery teams often establish ambitious Recovery Point and Recovery Time Objectives for systems in a DRP project. Teams working on recovery objectives need to understand that *the speed of recovery is directly proportional to its cost.*

For instance, a DRP project team decides to make the RPO for an application two hours. To meet that goal, the organization has to purchase new storage systems, plus an expensive data connection from the main processing center to the backup processing center. But the cost of so

short an RPO may not be warranted. The project team needs to understand the cost of downtime (in dollars per hour or per day) versus the cost of recovery. For instance, if the cost of downtime for an application is $40,000 per hour and a two-hour RPO requires a $500,000 investment in equipment and a $20,000-per-month expense, then the investment may be warranted. If, however, the cost of downtime for the application is $500 per hour, then the organization doesn't need this level of investment and should establish a longer RPO.

Examples of required resources include

- ✔ **Systems and applications:** In order for a business process to continue operating, it may require one or more IT systems or applications — not only the primary supporting application, but also other systems and applications that the primary application requires in order to continue functioning.

- ✔ **Suppliers and partners:** Many business processes require a supply of materials or services from outside organizations, without which the business process can't continue operating.

- ✔ **Key personnel:** Most business processes require a number of specifically trained or equipped staff members — or contingent workers such as contractors or personnel from another company — to run business processes and operate systems.

- ✔ **Business equipment:** Anything from PBXs to copiers, postage machines, POS (point-of-sale) machines, red Swingline staplers, and any other machinery required to support critical business processes.

When you identify required resources for complex business processes, you may want to identify additional information about each resource, including resource owners, criticality, and dependencies.

Identifying the Elements of a Business Continuity Plan

A complete Business Continuity Plan consists of several components that handle not only the continuation of critical business functions, but also all the functions and resources that support those critical functions.

Emergency response

Emergency response teams must be identified for every possible type of disaster. These response teams need written procedures and checklists to keep critical business functions operating.

Written procedures are vital for two reasons. First, the people who perform critical functions after a disaster may not be familiar with them: They may not usually perform those functions. (During a disaster, the people who ordinarily perform the function may be unavailable.) Second, the team probably needs to use different procedures and processes for performing the critical functions during a disaster than they would under normal conditions. Also, the circumstances surrounding a disaster might have people feeling out-of-sorts; having a written procedure guides them into action (kind of like the "break glass" instructions on some fire alarms, in case you forget what to do).

Damage assessment

When a disaster strikes, experts need to be called in to inspect the premises and determine the extent of the damage. Typically, you need experts who can assess building damage, as well as damage to any special equipment and machinery.

Depending on the nature of the disaster, you may have to perform damage assessment in stages. A first assessment may involve a quick walkthrough to look for obvious damage, followed by a more time-consuming and detailed assessment to look for problems that you don't see right away.

Damage assessments determine whether an organization can still use buildings and equipment, whether they can use those items after some repairs, or whether they must abandon those items altogether.

Personnel safety

In any kind of disaster, the safety of personnel is the highest priority, ahead of buildings, equipment, computers, backup tapes, and so on. Personnel safety is critical not only because of the intrinsic value of human life, but also because people — not physical assets — make the business run.

Personnel notification

The Business Continuity Plan must have some provisions for notifying all affected personnel that a disaster has occurred. An organization needs to establish multiple methods for notifying key business-continuity personnel in case public communications infrastructures are interrupted.

Not all disasters are obvious: A fire or broken water main is a local event, not a regional one. And in an event such as a tornado or flood, employees who live even a few miles away may not know the condition of the business. Consequently, the organization needs a plan for communicating with employees, no matter what the situation.

Throughout a disaster and the recovery from it, management must be given regular status reports as well as updates on crucial tactical issues so that management can align resources to support critical business operations that function on a contingency basis. For instance, a manager of a corporate Facilities department can loan equipment that critical departments need so that they can keep functioning.

Backups and off-site storage

Things go wrong with hardware and software, resulting in wrecked or unreachable data. When it's gone, it's gone! Thus IT departments everywhere make copies of their critical data on tapes, removable discs, or external storage systems.

These backups must be performed regularly, usually once per day. The backup media must also be stored off-site in the event that the facility housing the original systems is damaged. Having backup tapes *in* the data center may be convenient for doing a quick data restore but of little value if backup tapes are destroyed along with their respective systems.

For systems with large amounts of data, that data must be well *understood* in order to determine what kinds of backups need to be performed (full, differential, and incremental) and how frequently. Consider these factors:

> ✔ The time that it takes to perform backups
>
> ✔ The effort required to restore data
>
> ✔ The procedures for restoring data from backups, compared with other methods for recovering the data

For example, consider whether you can restore application software from backup tapes more quickly than by installing them from their release media (the original CD-ROMs or downloaded install files). Just make sure you can recover your configuration settings if you re-install software from release media. Also, if a large part of the database is static, do you really need to back it all up every day?

You must choose off-site storage of backup media and other materials (documentation, and so on) carefully. Factors to consider include survivability of the off-site storage facility, as well as the distance from the off-site facility to the data center, airports, and alternate processing sites. The facility needs to be close enough so that media retrieval doesn't take too long (*how* long depends on the organization's recovery needs), but not so close that the facility becomes involved in the same natural disaster as the business.

Remote backup services are a viable alternative to off-site backup media storage. Broadband Internet access makes it possible to back up critical data to a backup service provider — often faster than magnetic tapes can be returned from an off-site facility and data recovered from them.

The end of magnetic tape?

Magnetic tape has been the backup medium of choice since the 1960s. Gradually improving in reliability, capacity, and throughput, magtape has hung in there as the mainstay of backup. But, the era of magnetic tape may be nearing its end.

The *linear access* property of magtape means you have to read all the way through a tape to know its contents and to restore data that may be near the end. In addition, magnetic tape is somewhat fragile, and it is less tolerant of defects at higher storage densities.

Commercially viable alternatives to magnetic tape are emerging. Among them:

✔ *Virtual Tape Library (VTL).* This is really just disk-based storage; a VTL has the appearance of magnetic tape to backup programs. In a hot-pluggable RAID array, you could take these disks and send them offsite.

✔ *Replication.* An organization with two or more processing centers can consider replicating data from one location to another.

✔ *Remote backup.* If data sets aren't too large and if Internet bandwidth is sufficient, data can be backed up to a remote processing center or one of several organizations that provide "backup as a service" capabilities.

In comparison to these methods, proven but linear and relatively magnetic tape may soon be a part of the great data-processing museum in the sky.

Some organizations have one or more databases so large that the organizations literally can't (or, at any rate, don't) back them up to tape. Instead, they keep one or more replicated copies of their databases on other computers in other cities. BCP planners need to consider this possibility when developing continuity plans.

The purpose of off-site media storage is to ensure that up-to-date data is available in the event that systems in the primary data center are damaged.

Software escrow agreements

Your organization should consider *software escrow agreements* (wherein the software vendor sends a copy of its software code to a third-party escrow organization for safekeeping) with the software vendors whose applications support critical business functions. In the event that an insurmountable disaster (which could include bankruptcy) strikes the software vendor, your organization must consider all options for the continued maintenance of those critical applications, including in-house support.

External communications

The Corporate Communications, External Affairs, and (if applicable) Investor Relations departments should all have plans in place for communicating the facts about a disaster to the press, customers, and public. You need contingency plans for these functions if you want the organization to continue communicating to the outside world. Open communication during a disaster is vital so that customers, suppliers, and investors don't panic (which they might do if they don't know the true extent of the disaster).

The emergency communications plan needs to take into account the possibility that some corporate facilities or personnel may be unavailable. Thus you need to keep even the data and procedures related to the communications plan safe so that they're available in any situation.

Utilities

Data-processing facilities that support time-critical business functions must keep running in the event of a power failure. Although every situation is different, the principle remains the same: The BCP team must determine for what period of time the data-processing facility must be able to continue operating without utility power. A power engineer can find out the length of typical (we don't want to say *routine*) power outages in your area and crunch the numbers to arrive at the mean time of outages. By using that information, as well as an inventory of the data center's equipment and environmental equipment, you can determine whether the organization needs an uninterruptible power supply (UPS) alone, or a UPS *and* an electric generator.

A business can use uninterruptible power supplies (UPSs) and emergency electric generators to provide electric power during prolonged power outages. A UPS is also good for a controlled shutdown, if the organization is better off having their systems powered off during a disaster.

In a really long power outage (more than a day or two), it is also essential to have a plan for the replenishment of generator fuel.

Logistics and supplies

The BCP team needs to study _every aspect_ of critical functions that must be made to continue in a disaster. Every resource that's needed to sustain the critical operation must be identified and then considered against every possible disaster scenario to determine what special plans must be made. For instance, if a business operation relies upon a just-in-time shipment of materials for its operation and an earthquake has closed the region's only highway (or airport or sea/lake port), then alternative means for acquiring those materials must be determined in advance. Or, perhaps an emergency ration of those materials needs to be stockpiled so that the business function can continue uninterrupted.

Fire and water protection

Many natural disasters disrupt public utilities, including water supplies or delivery. In the event that a disaster has interrupted water delivery, new problems arise. Your facility may not be allowed to operate without the means for fighting a fire, should one occur.

In many places, businesses could be ordered to close if they can't prove that they can effectively fight a fire using other means, such as FM-200 inert gas. Then again, if water supplies have been interrupted, you have other issues to contend with, such as drinking water and water for restrooms. Without water, you're hosed!

We discuss fire protection in more detail in Chapter 13.

Documentation

Any critical business function must be able to continue operating after a disaster strikes. And to make sure you can sustain operations, you need to make available all relevant documentation for every piece of equipment, as well as every critical process and procedure that the organization performs in a given location.

Don't be lulled into taking for granted the emerging trend of hardware and software products that don't come with any documentation. Many vendors deliver their documentation *only* over the Internet, or they charge extra for a hard copy. But many types of disasters may disrupt Internet communications, thereby leaving an operation high and dry with no instructions for how to use and manage tools or applications.

At least one set of hard copy (or CD-ROM soft copy) documentation (including your Business Continuity Plan and Disaster Recovery Plan) should be stored at the same off-site storage facility that stores the organization's backup tapes. It would also be smart to issue soft copies of BCP and DRP documentation to all relevant personnel on USB storage devices (with encryption if needed).

Continuity and recovery documentation must exist in hard copy in the event that it's unavailable via electronic means.

Data processing continuity planning

Data processing facilities are so vital to businesses today that a lot of emphasis is placed on them. Generally this comes down to these variables: where and how the business will continue to sustain its data processing functions.

Because data centers are so expensive and time-consuming to build, better business sense dictates having an alternate processing site available. The types of sites are

- **Cold site:** A *cold site* is basically an empty computer room with environmental facilities (UPS; heating, ventilation, and air conditioning [HVAC]; and so on) but no computing equipment. This is the least-costly option, but more time is required to assume a workload because computers need to be brought in from somewhere and set up, and data and applications need to be loaded. Connectivity to other locations also needs to be installed.

- **Warm site:** A *warm site* is basically a cold site, but with computers and communications links already in place. In order to take over production operations, you must load the computers with application software and business data.

- **Hot site:** Indisputably the most expensive option, you equip a *hot site* with the same computers as the production system, with application changes, operating system changes, and even patches kept in sync with their live production-system counterparts. You even keep business data up-to-date at the hot site by using some sort of mirroring or transaction replication. Because the organization trains its staff in how to operate the organization's business applications (and staff members have documentation), the operations staff knows what to do to take over data processing operations at a moment's notice.

- **Reciprocal site:** Your organization and another organization sign a *reciprocal agreement* in which you both pledge the availability of your organization's data center in the event of a disaster. Back in the day, when data centers were rare, many organizations made this sort of arrangement, but it's fallen out of favor in recent years.

- **Multiple data centers:** Larger organizations can consider the option of running daily operations out of two or more regional data centers that are hundreds (or more) of miles apart. The advantage of this arrangement is that the organization doesn't have to make arrangements with outside vendors for hot/warm/cold sites, and the organization's staff is already onsite and familiar with business and computer operations.

A hot site provides the most rapid recovery capability, but it also costs the most because of the effort required to maintain its readiness.

Table 11-1 compares these options side by side.

Table 11-1	Data Processing Continuity Planning Site Comparison			
Feature	**Hot Site**	**Warm Site**	**Cold Site**	**Multiple Data Centers**
Cost	Highest	Medium	Low	No additional
Computer-equipped	Yes	Yes	No	Yes

Feature	Hot Site	Warm Site	Cold Site	Multiple Data Centers
Connectivity-equipped	Yes	Yes	No	Yes
Data-equipped	Yes	No	No	Yes
Staffed	Yes	No	No	Yes
Typical lead time to readiness	Minutes to hours	Hours to days	Days to weeks	Minutes to hours or longer

Developing the BC Plan

After you define the scope of the BCP project and develop the Business Impact Assessment (BIA), Criticality Assessment, and Maximum Tolerable Downtimes (MTDs), you know

- ✔ What portion of the organization is included in the plan.

- ✔ Of this portion of the organization, which business functions are so critical that the business would fail if these functions were interrupted for long (or even short) periods of time.

- ✔ The general degree of impact on the business when one of the critical functions fails. This idea comes from quantitative and qualitative data.

The hard part of the Business Continuity Planning project begins now: You need to develop the strategy for continuing each critical business function when disasters occur, which is known as the *Continuity Strategy*.

When you develop a Continuity Strategy, you must set politics aside and look at the excruciating details of critical business functions. You need strong coffee, several pizzas, buckets of Rolaids, and cool heads.

Making your BCP project a success

For the important and time-consuming Continuity Strategy phase of the project, you need to follow these guidelines:

- ✔ **Call things like you see them.** No biases. No angles. No politics. No favorites. No favors. You're trying to save the business before the disaster strikes.

✔ **Build smaller teams of experts.** Each critical business function should have teams dedicated to just that function. That team's job is to analyze just one critical business function and figure out how you can keep it functioning despite a disaster of some sort. Pick the right people for each team — people who *really* understand the details of the business process that they're examining.

✔ **Brainstorm.** Proper brainstorming considers all ideas, even silly ones (up to a point). Even a silly-sounding idea can lead to a *good* idea.

✔ **Have teams share results with each other.** Teams working on individual continuity strategies can get ideas from each other. Each team can share highlights of its work over the past week or two. Some of the things that they say may spark ideas in other teams. You can improve the entire effort by holding these sharing sessions.

✔ **Don't encourage competition or politics in or between teams.** Don't pit teams against each other. Identifying success factors isn't a zero-sum game: Everyone needs to do an excellent job.

✔ **Retain a BCP mentor/expert.** If your organization doesn't have experienced business continuity planners on staff, you need to bring in a consultant — someone who has helped develop plans for other organizations. Even more important than that, make sure the consultant you hire has been on the scene when disaster struck a business he or she was consulting for and has seen a BCP in action.

Simplifying large or complex critical functions

Some critical business functions may be too large and complex to examine in one big chunk. You can break down those complex functions into smaller components, perhaps like this:

✔ **People:** Has the team identified the critical people — or more appropriately, the critical sub-functions — required to keep the function running?

✔ **Facilities:** In the event that the function's primary facilities are unavailable, where can the business perform the function?

✔ **Technology:** What hardware, software, and other computing/network components support the critical function? If parts or all of these components are unavailable, what other equipment can support the critical business functions? Do you need to perform the functions any differently?

✔ **Miscellaneous:** What supplies, other equipment, and services do you need to support the critical business function?

Getting amazing things done

It is amazing what you can accomplish if you don't care who gets the credit. Nowhere is this truer in business than in Business Continuity Planning. A BCP project is a setting where people will jostle for power, influence, and credit.

These forces must be neutralized. Business Continuity Planning should be apolitical, meaning differences and personal agendas are set aside. Only then is there a reasonable chance of success. The business, and its employees and customers, deserve nothing less.

Analyzing processes is like disassembling Tinkertoy houses — you have to break them down to the level of their individual components. You really *do* need to understand each step in even the largest processes in order to be able to develop good continuity plans for them.

If a team that analyzes a large complex business function breaks it into groups, such as the groups in the preceding list, the team members need to get together frequently to ensure that their respective strategies for each group eventually become a cohesive whole. Eventually these groups need to come back together and integrate their separate materials into one complete plan.

Documenting the strategy

Now for the part that everyone loves: documentation. The details of the continuity plans for each critical function must be described in minute detail, step by step by step.

Why? The people who develop the strategy may very well *not* be the people who execute it. The people who develop the strategy may change roles in the company or change jobs altogether. Or the scope of an actual disaster may be wide enough that the critical personnel just aren't available. Any skeptics should consider September 11 and the impact that this disaster had on a number of companies that lost practically every*one* and every*thing*.

Best practices for documenting Business Continuity Plans exist. For this reason, you may want to have an expert around. For $300 an hour, a consultant can spend a couple of weeks developing templates. But watch out — your consultant might just download templates from a BCP website, tweak them a little bit, and spend the rest of his or her time playing Angry Birds. To be sure you get a peach of a consultant, do the old-fashioned things: check his references, ask for work samples, see if he has a decent Facebook page. (We're pretty sure we're kidding about that last one.)

Why hire an expert?

Most people don't do Business Continuity Planning for a living. Although you may be the expert in your particular business processes, you don't necessarily know all the angles of contingency planning.

Turn this question around for a minute: What would you think if an IT shop developed a security strategy without having a security expert's help? Do you think they'd have a sound, viable strategy?

The same argument fits equally well with BCP.

For the remaining skeptics, do yourself a favor: Hire a BCP expert for just a short time to help validate your framework and plan. If your expert says that your plan is great, then you can consider it money well spent to confirm your suspicions. If the consultant says that your plan needs help, ask for details on where and how. Then, you can decide whether to rework and improve your plan.

When disaster strikes, it's too late to wish that you had a good Business Continuity Plan.

Implementing the Business Continuity Plan

It is an accomplishment indeed when the BCP documentation has been written, reviewed, edited, and placed into three-ring binders. However, the job isn't yet done. The Business Continuity Plan needs senior management buy-in, the plan must be announced and socialized throughout the organization, and one or more persons must be dedicated to keeping the plan up-to-date. Oh yeah, and the plan needs to be tested!

Securing senior management approval

After the entire plan has been documented and reviewed by all stakeholders, it's time for senior management to examine it and approve it. Not only must senior management approve the plan, but senior management must also *publicly* approve it. By "public" we don't mean the general public; instead, we mean that senior management should make it well known inside the business that they support the Business Continuity Planning process.

Senior management's approval is needed so that all affected and involved employees in the organization understand the importance of emergency planning.

Promoting organizational awareness

Everyone in the organization needs to know about the plan and his or her role in it. You may need to establish training for potentially large numbers of people who need to *be there* when a disaster strikes.

All employees in the organization must know about the Business Continuity Plan.

Maintaining the plan

No, the plan isn't finished. It has just begun! Now the BCP *person* (the project team members by this time have collected their commemorative denim shirts, mugs, and mouse pads, and have moved on to other projects) needs to periodically *chase* The Powers That Be to make sure that they know about all significant changes to the environment.

In fact, if the BCP person has any leadership left at this point in the process, he or she needs to start attending the Change Control Board (or whatever that company calls it) meetings and to jot down notes that may mean that some detail in a BCP document may need some changes.

The Business Continuity Plan is easier to modify than it is to create out of thin air. Once or twice each year, someone knowledgeable needs to examine the detailed strategy and procedure documents in the BCP to make sure that they'll still work — and update them if necessary.

Disaster Recovery Planning

As we describe in the section "How BCP and DRP Work Together," earlier in this chapter, the planning for both Disaster Recovery and Business Continuity have common roots. Both need to assemble similar project teams, both need executive sponsorship and support, and both must identify critical business processes.

Disaster Recovery Planning and Business Continuity Planning are both vital activities that can ensure an organization's survival. BCP and DRP fit hand-in-glove (although we're not sure which is the hand and which is the glove — it probably doesn't matter).

Here, the similarities end. In the following sections, we discuss the development and implementation of the Disaster Recovery Plan.

Developing a Disaster Recovery Plan

Although the BCP folks develop a plan to keep business operations rolling, the DRP people develop a plan to restore the damaged facility (or facilities) so that the critical business functions can operate in their original location(s).

Preparing for emergency response

Emergency response teams must be prepared for every possible scenario. Members of these teams need a variety of specialized training to deal with such things as water and smoke damage, structural damage, flooding, and hazardous materials.

You must document all the types of responses so that the response teams know what to do. The emergency response documentation consists of two major parts: how to respond to each type of incident, and the most up-to-date facts about the facilities and equipment that the organization uses.

In other words, you want your teams to know how to deal with water damage, smoke damage, structural damage, hazardous materials, and many other things. Your teams also need to know everything about every company facility: Where to find utility entrances, electrical equipment, HVAC equipment, fire control, elevators, communications, data closets, and so on; which vendors maintain and service them; and so on. And you need experts who know about the materials and construction of the buildings themselves. Those experts might be your own employees, outside consultants, or a little of both.

It is the DRP team's responsibility to identify the experts needed for all phases of emergency response.

Responding to an emergency branches into two activities: salvage and recovery. Tangential to this is preparing financially for the costs associated with salvage and recovery.

Salvage

The salvage team is concerned with restoring full functionality to the damaged facility. This restoration includes several activities:

- ✔ **Damage assessment:** Arrange a thorough examination of the facility to identify the full extent and nature of the damage. Frequently, outside experts, such as structural engineers, perform this inspection.

- ✔ **Salvage assets:** Remove assets, such as computer equipment, records, furniture, inventory, and so on, from the facility.

✔ **Cleaning:** Thoroughly clean the facility to eliminate smoke damage, water damage, debris, and more. Outside companies that specialize in these services frequently perform this job.

✔ **Restoring the facility to operational readiness:** Complete repairs, and restock and reequip the facility to return it to pre-disaster readiness. At this point, the facility is ready for business functions to resume there.

The salvage team is primarily concerned with the restoration of a facility and its return to operational readiness.

Recovery

Recovery comprises equipping the BCP team (yes, the BCP team — recovery involves both BCP and DRP) with any logistics, supplies, or coordination in order to get alternate functional sites up and running. This activity should be heavily scripted, with lots of procedures and checklists in order to ensure that every detail is handled.

Financial readiness

The salvage and recovery operations can cost a lot of money. The organization must prepare for potentially large expenses (at least several times the normal monthly operating cost) to restore operations to the original facility.

Financial readiness can take several forms, including

✔ **Insurance:** An organization may purchase an insurance policy that pays for the replacement of damaged assets and perhaps even some of the other costs associated with conducting emergency operations.

✔ **Cash reserves:** An organization may set aside cash to purchase assets for emergency use, as well as to use for emergency operations costs.

✔ **Line of credit:** An organization may establish a line of credit, prior to a disaster, to be used to purchase assets or pay for emergency operations should a disaster occur.

✔ **Pre-purchased assets:** An organization may choose to purchase assets to be used for disaster recovery purposes in advance, and store those assets at or near a location where they will be utilized in the event of a disaster.

✔ **Letters of agreement:** An organization may wish to establish legal agreements that would be enacted in a disaster. These may range from use of emergency work locations (such as nearby hotels), use of fleet vehicles, appropriation of computers used by lower-priority systems, and so on.

✔ **Standby assets:** An organization can use existing assets as items to be re-purposed in the event of a disaster. For example, a computer system that is used for software testing could be quickly re-used for production operations if a disaster strikes.

Not only response, but also prevention

On the surface, Disaster Recovery Planning may appear to be all about cleaning up and restoring business operations after a hurricane, tornado, or flood. However, the DRP project can add considerable value to the organization if it also points out things that put the business at risk in the first place. For instance, the DRP team may discover a design flaw in a building that makes it more vulnerable to damage during a flood. The planning team can make a recommendation outlining the necessary repairs that would reduce the likelihood of flood damage, resulting in less downtime and lower repair costs. Such foresight could reduce the impact that a disaster would have, thereby making recovery that much easier.

Notifying personnel

The Disaster Recovery Plan team needs to have communication plans prepared in advance of any disaster. Employees need to be notified about closed facilities and any special work instructions (such as an alternate location to report for work). The planning team needs to realize that one or more of the usual means of communications may have also been adversely affected by the same event that damaged business facilities. For example, if a building has been damaged, the voice-mail system that people would try to call into so that they could check messages and get workplace status might not be working.

Organizations need to anticipate the effects of a disaster when considering emergency communications. For instance, you need to establish in advance two or more ways to locate each important staff member. These ways may include landlines, cell phones, spouses' cell phones, and alternate contact numbers (such as neighbors or relatives).

Mobile text messaging (also known as SMS or Short Messaging Service) is often a reliable means of communication even when cellphone communications systems are congested.

Many organizations' emergency operations plans include the use of audio conference bridges so that personnel can discuss operational issues hour by hour throughout the event. Instead of relying on a single provider (which you might not be able to reach because of communications problems or because it's affected by the same disaster), organizations should have a second (and maybe even a third) audio conference provider established. Emergency communications documentation needs to include dial-in information for both (or all three) conference systems.

Facilitating external communications

The corporate departments that communicate with customers, investors, government, and the media are equipped with pretty much the same information as for Business Continuity Planning. There are really no differences in logistical planning for external communications between DRP and BCP. See the section "External communications," earlier in this chapter for a summary of communications with external entities.

Maintaining physical and logical security

Looting and vandalism sometimes occur after significant disastrous events. The organization must be prepared to deploy additional guards, as well as erect temporary fencing and other physical barriers in order to protect its physical assets until damaged facilities are secured and law and order are restored. And we're not just concerned with physical assets: personnel (if any are present) require protection too.

When developing DR plans, keep in mind the need to protect information from unauthorized access as well as accidental or deliberate damage. The security controls used in main production systems need to be implemented on recovery systems as well. These controls will probably include

- Access controls
- Authorization
- Audit logging
- Intrusion detection
- Firewalls
- Encryption (including data in motion, as well as data at rest)
- Backup
- Physical access controls
- Environmental controls
- Personnel controls (background checks, security training, and so on)

We discuss these controls throughout this entire book.

Information that resides on disaster recovery systems is the same data that resides on normal production systems, so you must protect it by using the same or similar controls.

Personnel safety

The safety of personnel needs to be addressed, as there are often personnel working in areas with damage and safety issues, usually right after a disaster, during salvage and damage assessment.

An organization's number-one priority is the safety of its personnel.

Testing the Disaster Recovery Plan

By the time that an organization has completed a DRP, it's probably spent hundreds of man-hours and possibly tens (or hundreds) of thousands of dollars on consulting fees. You'd think that after making this big of an investment, any organization would want to test its DRP to make sure that it works when a real emergency strikes.

The following sections outline five methods available for testing the Disaster Recovery Plan.

Checklist

A *checklist test* is a detailed review of DRP documents, performed by individuals working on their own. The purpose of a checklist test is to identify inaccuracies, errors, and omissions in DRP documentation.

It's easy to coordinate this type of test, because each person who performs the test does it when his or her schedule permits (provided they complete it before any deadlines).

By itself, a document review is an insufficient way to test a DRP; however, it's a logical starting place. Perform one or more of the other tests soon after you do the checklist test.

Structured walkthrough

A structured walkthrough is a team approach to the checklist test. Here, several business and technology experts in the organization gather to "walk" through the BCP plan documents. A moderator or facilitator leads participants to discuss each step in BCP documents so that they can identify issues and opportunities for making documents more accurate and complete. Group discussions usually help to identify issues that people will not find when working on their own. Often the participants want to perform the review in a fancy mountain or oceanside retreat, where they can think much more clearly.

During a structured walkthrough, the facilitator writes down "parking lot" issues (items to be considered at a later time, written down now so they will not be forgotten) on a whiteboard or flipchart while the group identifies those issues. These are action items that will serve to make improvements to BCP documents. Each action item needs to have an accountable person assigned, as well as a completion date, so that the action items will be completed in a reasonable time. Depending upon the extent of the changes, a follow-up walkthrough may need to be conducted at a later time.

A structured walkthrough usually requires two to eight hours or more to complete.

Simulation

In a *simulation,* all the designated disaster recovery personnel practice going through the motions associated with a real recovery. In a simulation, the team doesn't actually perform any recovery or alternate processing.

An organization that plans to perform a simulation test appoints a facilitator who develops a disaster scenario, using a type of disaster that's likely to occur in the region. For instance, an organization in San Francisco might choose an earthquake scenario, and an organization in Miami could choose a hurricane.

In a simple simulation, the facilitator reads out announcements as if they're news briefs. Such announcements describe an unfolding scenario and can also include information about the organization's status at the time. An example announcement might read like this:

> It is 8:15 a.m. local time, and a magnitude 7.1 earthquake has just occurred, fifteen miles from company headquarters. Building One is heavily damaged and some people are seriously injured. Building Two (the one containing the organization's computer system) is damaged and personnel are unable to enter the building. Electric power is out, and the generator has not started because of an unknown problem that may be earthquake related. Executives Jeff Finsch and Sarah Brewer (CIO and CFO) are backpacking on the Appalachian Trail and cannot be reached.

The disaster-simulation team, meeting in a conference room, discusses emergency response procedures and how the response might unfold. They consider the conditions described to them and identify any issues that could impact an actual disaster response.

The simulation facilitator makes additional announcements throughout the simulation. Just like in a real disaster, the team doesn't know everything right away — instead, news trickles in. In the simulation, the facilitator reads scripted statements that, um, simulate the way that information flows in a real disaster.

A more realistic simulation can be held at the organization's emergency response center, where some resources that support emergency response may be available. Another idea is to hold the simulation on a day that is not announced ahead of time, so that responders will be genuinely surprised and possibly be less prepared to respond.

Remember to test your backup media to make sure that you can actually restore data from backups!

Parallel

A *parallel test* involves performing all the steps of a real recovery, except that you keep the real, live production systems running. The actual production systems run in parallel with the disaster recovery systems. The parallel test is very time-consuming, but it does test the accuracy of the applications because analysts compare data on the test recovery systems with production data.

The technical architecture of the target application determines how a parallel test needs to be conducted. The general principle of a parallel test is that the *disaster recovery system* (meaning the system that remains on standby until a real disaster occurs, at which time, the organization presses it into production service) runs process work at the same time that the primary system continues its normal work. Precisely *how* this is accomplished depends on technical details. For a system that operates on batches of data, those batches can be copied to the DR system for processing there, and results can be compared for accuracy and timeliness.

Highly interactive applications are more difficult to test in a strictly parallel test. Instead, it might be necessary to record user interactions on the live system and then "play back" those interactions using an application testing tool. Then responses, accuracy, and timing can be verified after the test to verify whether the DR system worked properly.

While a parallel test may be difficult to set up, its results can provide a good indication of whether disaster recovery systems will perform during a disaster. Also, the risks associated with a parallel test are low, since a failure of the DR system will not impact real business transactions.

The parallel test includes loading data onto recovery systems without taking production systems down.

Interruption (or cutover)

An *interruption test* (sometimes known as a "cutover" test) is similar to a parallel test except that in an interruption test, a function's primary systems are actually shut off or disconnected. An interruption test is the *ultimate* test of a disaster recovery plan because one or more of the business's critical functions actually depends upon the availability, integrity, and accuracy of the recovery systems.

An interruption test should be performed only after successful walkthroughs and at least one parallel test. In an interruption test, backup systems are processing the full production workload and all primary and ancillary functions including:

- ✔ User access
- ✔ Administrative access
- ✔ Integrations to other applications
- ✔ Support
- ✔ Reporting
- ✔ . . . And whatever else the main production environment needs to support

An interruption test is the ultimate test of the ability for a disaster recovery system to perform properly in a real disaster, but it's also the test with the highest risk.

Creating competitive advantage

Every problem can be transformed into an opportunity. The problem of having to invest valuable resources in planning for events that may never occur can be put to some good use in improving the business.

In capitalist economies, most organizations must compete for business. Two of the ways that they compete are by offering better services, and by telling their customers (and potential customers) that their services are superior to those of their competitors.

One of the ways that organizations can leverage their investment in BCP and DRP is to tell their customers that this makes their products and services better. Organizations would create marketing messages that describe characteristics that are a byproduct of BCP and DRP planning, primarily improvements in customer service that is free of interruptions caused by disasters.

Organizations that provide Internet-based services can use this competitive advantage to boast a higher level of availability than would be possible from a single-location entity. Customers that require continuous availability may be likelier to select an organization with an effective DRP and BCP program than one that does not.

Prep Test

1 The longest period of time that a business can survive without a critical function is called

A ○ Downtime Tolerability Period

B ○ Greatest Tolerable Downtime

C ○ Maximum Survivable Downtime

D ○ Maximum Tolerable Downtime

2 Which of the following is *not* a natural disaster?

A ○ Avalanche

B ○ Stock market crash

C ○ Fire

D ○ Water supply storage drought

3 The impact of a disaster on business operations is contained in

A ○ Local newspapers and online media

B ○ The Business Impact Assessment

C ○ The Operations Impact Assessment

D ○ The Vulnerability Assessment

4 The decision whether to purchase an emergency generator is based on

A ○ Wholesale electric rates

B ○ Retail electric rates

C ○ The duration of a typical outage

D ○ The income rate of affected systems

5 The purpose of a UPS is

A ○ To provide instantaneous power cutover when utility power fails

B ○ A lower cost for overnight shipping following a disaster

C ○ The need to steer an unresponsive vehicle after it's moving again

D ○ To restore electric power within 24 hours

6 The Business Impact Assessment

A ○ Describes the impact of disaster recovery planning on the budget

B ○ Describes the impact of a disaster on business operations

C ○ Is a prerequisite to the Vulnerability Assessment

D ○ Is the first official statement produced after a disaster

7 **To maximize the safety of backup media, it should be stored**

   A ○ At a specialized off-site media storage facility

   B ○ At the residences of various senior managers

   C ○ In the operations center in a locked cabinet

   D ○ Between 50°F and 60°F

8 **An alternate information-processing facility with all systems, patches, and data mirrored from live production systems is known as a**

   A ○ Warm site

   B ○ Hot site

   C ○ Recovery site

   D ○ Mutual Aid Center

9 **The greatest advantage of a cold site is**

   A ○ It can be built nearly anywhere

   B ○ Its high responsiveness

   C ○ Its low cost

   D ○ Its close proximity to airports

10 **The most extensive test for a Disaster Recovery Plan**

   A ○ Has dual failover

   B ○ Is a waste of paper

   C ○ Is known as a parallel test

   D ○ Is known as an interruption test

Answers

1 **D.** Maximum Tolerable Downtime. This is the term that describes the maximum period of time that a business function can suspend operations and the company can still survive. *Review "Conducting the Business Impact Assessment."*

2 **B.** Stock market crash. A stock market crash is a man-made (non-natural) disaster. *Review "Defining Disastrous Events."*

3 **B.** Business Impact Assessment. The BIA describes the impact that a disaster will have on business operations. *Review "Conducting the Business Impact Assessment."*

4 **C.** The duration of a typical outage. The average and worst-case duration of electrical power outages help to determine whether a business should purchase an emergency generator. *Review "BCP Recovery Plan Development."*

5 **A.** To provide instantaneous power cutover when utility power fails. A UPS provides continuous electric power to all equipment connected to it. *Review "Identifying the Elements of a Business Continuity Plan."*

6 **B.** Describes the impact of a disaster on business operations. A Business Impact Assessment (BIA) contains quantitative and qualitative estimates of the impact of a disaster. *Review "Conducting the Business Impact Assessment."*

7 **A.** At a specialized off-site media storage facility. Such a specialized facility is designed to withstand most disastrous events. *Review "Identifying the Elements of a Business Continuity Plan."*

8 **B.** Hot site. Although a hot site is the most expensive to build and maintain, it provides the greatest possible performance. *Review "Identifying the Elements of a Business Continuity Plan."*

9 **C.** Its low cost. Cold sites are inexpensive, but they're the slowest to set up and get running. *Review "Identifying the Elements of a Business Continuity Plan."*

10 **D.** Is known as an interruption test. The interruption test performs an actual failover of applications to the servers. *Review "Testing the Disaster Recovery Plan."*

Chapter 12

Legal, Regulations, Investigations, and Compliance

- -

In This Chapter

▶ Understanding major categories and types of laws

▶ Knowing the major categories of computer crime

▶ Identifying U.S. and international laws that pertain to information security

▶ Handling investigations, forensics, evidence, and incident response

- -

Similar to police officers, information security professionals are expected to determine when a computer crime has occurred, secure the crime scene, and collect any evidence — to protect and to serve! In order to perform these functions effectively, the CISSP candidate must know what a computer crime is, how to conduct an investigation and collect evidence, and understand what laws may have been violated.

Furthermore, CISSP candidates are expected to be familiar with the laws and regulations that are relevant to information security throughout the world and in various industries. This could include national laws, local laws, and any laws that pertain to the types of activities performed by organizations.

Major Types and Classifications of Law

Our discussion of the major types and classifications of law consists of U.S. and international law, including many key concepts and terms that you need to understand for the CISSP exam.

Common law

Common law (also known as *case law*) originated in medieval England, and is derived from the decisions (or *precedents*) of judges. Common law is based on the doctrine of *stare decisis* ("let the decision stand") and is often codified by statutes. Under the common law system of the United States, three major categories of laws are defined at the federal and state levels: *criminal*, *civil* (or *tort*), and *administrative* (or *regulatory*) laws.

Criminal law

Criminal law defines those crimes committed against society, even when the actual victim is a business or individual(s). Criminal laws are enacted to protect the general public. As such, in the eyes of the court, the victim is incidental to the greater cause.

Criminal penalties

Penalties under criminal law have two main purposes:

- ✔ **Punishment:** Penalties may include jail/prison sentences, probation, fines, and/or financial restitution to the victim.

- ✔ **Deterrence:** Penalties must be severe enough to dissuade any further criminal activity by the offender or anyone else considering a similar crime.

Burden of proof under criminal law

To be convicted under criminal law, a judge or jury must believe *beyond a reasonable doubt* that the defendant is guilty. Therefore the burden of proof in a criminal case rests firmly with the prosecution.

Classifications of criminal law

Criminal law has two main classifications, depending on severity, such as type of crime/attack or total loss in dollars:

- ✔ **Felony:** More serious crimes, normally resulting in jail/prison terms of more than one year.

- ✔ **Misdemeanor:** Less serious crimes, normally resulting in fines or jail/prison terms of less than one year.

Civil law

Civil (tort) law addresses wrongful acts committed against an individual or business, either willfully or negligently, resulting in damage, loss, injury, or death.

Civil penalties

Unlike criminal penalties, civil penalties don't include jail or prison terms. Instead, civil penalties provide financial restitution to the victim:

- ✔ **Compensatory damages:** Actual damages to the victim, including attorney/legal fees, lost profits, investigative costs, and so on

- ✔ **Punitive damages:** Determined by a jury and intended to punish the offender

✔ **Statutory damages:** Mandatory damages determined by law and assessed for violating the law

Burden of proof under civil law

Convictions under civil law are typically easier to obtain than under criminal law because the burden of proof is much less. To be convicted under civil law, a jury must believe *based upon the preponderance of the evidence* that the defendant is guilty. This simply means that the available evidence leads the judge or jury to a conclusion of guilt.

Liability and due care

The concepts of liability and due care are germane to civil law cases, but they're also applicable under administrative law, which we discuss in the following section.

The standard criteria for assessing the legal requirements for implementing recommended safeguards is to evaluate the cost of the safeguard and the estimated loss from the corresponding threat, if realized. If the cost is less than the estimated loss and the organization doesn't implement a safeguard, then a legal liability may exist. This is based on the principle of *proximate causation,* in which an action taken or not taken was part of a sequence of events that resulted in negative consequences.

Under the Federal Sentencing Guidelines, senior corporate officers may be personally liable if their organization fails to comply with applicable laws. Such individuals must follow the prudent man (or person) rule, which requires them to perform their duties:

✔ In good faith

✔ In the best interests of the enterprise

✔ With the care and diligence that ordinary, prudent people in a similar position would exercise under similar circumstances

The concepts of *due care* and *due diligence* are related but distinctly different:

✔ **Due care:** The conduct that a reasonable person exercises in a given situation, which provides a standard for determining negligence. In the practice of information security, due care relates to the steps that individuals or organizations take to perform their duties and implement security best practices.

✔ **Due diligence:** The prudent management and execution of due care. It's most often used in legal and financial circles to describe the actions that an organization takes to research the viability and merits of an investment or merger/acquisition opportunity. In the context of information security, due diligence commonly refers to risk identification and risk management practices, not only in the day-to-day operations of an organization, but also in the case of technology procurement, as well as mergers and acquisitions.

Lawyer-speak

Although the information in this sidebar is not tested on the CISSP examination, it may come in handy when you're attempting to learn the various laws and regulations in this domain. You'll find it helpful to know the correct parlance (fancy-speak for *jargon*) used. For example:

18 U.S.C. § 1030 (1986) (the Computer Fraud and Abuse Act of 1986) refers to Section 1030 in Title 18 of the 1986 edition of the United States Code, not "18 University of Southern California squiggly-thingy 1030 (1986)."

Federal statutes and administrative laws are usually cited in the following format:

- **The title number:** Titles are grouped by subject matter.

- **The abbreviation for the code:** For example, *U.S.C.* is United States Code; *C.F.R.* is Code of Federal Regulations

- **The section number:** *§* means "The Word Formerly Known as Section."

- **The year of publication:** Listed in parentheses.

Other important abbreviations to understand include

- **Fed. Reg.:** Federal Register.

- **Fed. R. Evid.:** Federal Rules of Evidence.

- **PL:** Public Law.

- **§§:** Sections; for example, 18 U.S.C. §§ 2701–11 refers to sections 2701 through 2711.

- **v.:** versus; for example, United States v. Moore. *Note:* The rest of the civilized world understands *vs.* to mean *versus* and *v.* to mean *version* or *volume,* but you need to remember two important points: Lawyers aren't part of the civilized world, and they apparently charge by the letter (as well as by the minute).

Another important aspect of due care is the principle of *culpable negligence.* If an organization fails to follow a standard of due care in the protection of its assets, the organization may be held culpably negligent. In such cases, jury awards may be adjusted accordingly, and the organization's insurance company may be required to pay only a portion of any loss — the organization may get stuck paying the rest of the bill!

Administrative law

Administrative (regulatory) laws define standards of performance and conduct for major industries (including banking, energy, and healthcare), organizations, and officials. These laws are typically enforced by various government agencies, and violations may result in financial penalties and/or imprisonment.

International law

Given the global nature of the Internet, it's often necessary for many countries to cooperate in order to bring a computer criminal to justice. But because practically every country in the world has its own unique legal system, such cooperation is always difficult and often impossible. As a starting point, many countries disagree on exactly what justice is. Other problems include

- **Lack of universal cooperation:** We can't answer the question, "Why can't we all just get along?" but we can tell you that it's highly unlikely that a 14-year-old hacker in some remote corner of the world will commit some dastardly crime that unites us all in our efforts to take him down, bringing about a lasting world peace.

- **Different interpretations of laws:** What's illegal in one country (or even in one state in the U.S.) isn't necessarily illegal in another.

- **Different rules of evidence:** This problem can encompass different rules for obtaining and collecting evidence, as well as different rules for admissibility of evidence.

- **Low priority:** Different nations have different views regarding the seriousness of computer crimes; and in the realm of international relations, computer crimes are usually of minimal concern.

- **Outdated laws and technology:** Related to the low-priority problem. Technology varies greatly throughout the world, and many countries (not only the Third World countries) lag far behind others. For this reason and many others, computer crime laws are often a low priority and aren't kept current. This problem is further exacerbated by the different technical capabilities of the various law enforcement agencies that may be involved in an international case.

- **Extradition:** Many countries don't have extradition treaties and won't extradite suspects to a country that has different or controversial practices, such as capital punishment. Although capital punishment for a computer crime may sound extreme, recent events and the threat of cyberterrorism make this a very real possibility.

Besides common law systems (which we talk about in the section "Common law," earlier in this chapter, other countries throughout the world use legal systems including

- **Civil law systems:** Not to be confused with U.S. civil law, which is based on common law. *Civil law* systems use constitutions and statutes exclusively and aren't based on precedent. The role of a judge in a civil law system is to interpret the law. Civil law is the most widespread type of law system used throughout the world.

✔ **Religious (or customary) law systems:** Derived from religious beliefs
and values. Common religious law systems include *Sharia* in Islam,
Halakha in Judaism, and Canon law in Christianity.

✔ **Pluralistic (or mixed) law systems:** Combinations of various systems,
such as civil and common law, civil and religious law, and common and
religious law.

Major Categories of Computer Crime

Computer crime consists of any criminal activity in which computer systems
or networks are used as tools. Computer crime also includes crimes in which
computer systems are targeted, or in which computers are the scene of the
crime committed. That's a pretty wide spectrum.

The real world, however, has difficulty dealing with computer crimes. Several
reasons why computer crimes are hard to cope with include

✔ **Lack of understanding:** In general, legislators, judges, attorneys, law
enforcement officials, and jurors don't understand the many different
technologies and issues involved in a computer crime.

✔ **Inadequate laws:** Laws are slow to change, and fail to keep pace with
rapidly evolving new technology.

✔ **Multiple roles of computers in crime:** These roles include crimes committed *against* a computer (such as hacking into a system and stealing
information) and crimes committed *by using* a computer (such as using
a system to launch a Distributed Denial of Service attack).Computers
may also *support* criminal enterprises, where criminals use computers
for crime-related recordkeeping or communications.

Computer crimes are often difficult to prosecute for the reasons we just
listed, and also because of the following issues:

✔ **Lack of tangible assets:** Traditional rules of property often don't apply in
a computer crime case. However, property rules have been extended in
many countries to include electronic information. Computing resources,
bandwidth, and data (in the form of magnetic particles) are often the only
assets at issue. These can be very difficult to quantify and assign a value
to. The asset valuation process, which we discuss in Chapter 6, can provide vital information for valuing electronic information.

✔ **Rules of evidence:** Often, original documents aren't available in a computer crime case. Most evidence in such a case is considered hearsay
evidence (which we discuss later in the upcoming section "Hearsay

rule") and must meet certain requirements to be admissible in court. Often, evidence is a computer itself, or data on its hard drive.

✔ **Lack of evidence:** Many crimes are difficult to prosecute because law enforcement agencies lack the skills or resources to even *identify* the perpetrator, much less gather sufficient evidence to bring charges and successfully prosecute. Frequently, skilled computer criminals use a long trail of compromised computers through different countries in order to make it as difficult as possible for even diligent law enforcement agencies to identify them.

✔ **Definition of loss:** A loss of confidentiality or integrity of data goes far beyond the normal definition of loss in a criminal or civil case.

✔ **Location of perpetrators:** Often, the people who commit computer crimes against specific organizations do so from locations outside of the victim's country. Computer criminals do this, knowing that even if they make a mistake and create discoverable evidence that identifies them, the victim's country law enforcement agencies will have difficulty apprehending the criminal.

✔ **Criminal profiles:** Computer criminals often aren't hardened criminals and may include the following:

- **Juveniles:** Juvenile laws in many countries aren't taken seriously and are inadequate to deter crime. A busy prosecutor is unlikely to pursue a low-profile crime committed by a juvenile that results in a three-year probation sentence for the offender.

- **Trusted individuals:** Many computer criminals are individuals who hold a position of trust within a company and have no prior criminal record. Such an individual likely can afford a dream team for legal defense, and a judge may be inclined to levy a more lenient sentence for the first-time offender. However, recent corporate scandals in the U.S. have set a strong precedent for punishment at the highest levels.

Computer crimes are often classified under one of the following six major categories:

✔ Business attacks

✔ Financial attacks

✔ "Fun" attacks

✔ Grudge attacks

✔ Ideological attacks

✔ Military and intelligence attacks

✔ Terrorist attacks

Business attacks

Businesses are increasingly the targets of computer and Internet attacks. These attacks include competitive intelligence gathering, Denial of Service, and other computer-related attacks. Businesses can be inviting targets for an attacker due to

- ✔ **Lack of expertise:** Despite heightened security awareness, a shortage of qualified security professionals still exists, particularly in private enterprise.
- ✔ **Lack of resources:** Businesses often lack the resources to prevent, or even detect, attacks against their systems.
- ✔ **Lack of reporting or prosecution:** Because of public relations concerns and the inability to prosecute computer criminals because of either a lack of evidence or a lack of properly handled evidence, the majority of business attacks still go unreported.

The cost to businesses can be significant, including loss of trade secrets or proprietary information, loss of revenue, and loss of reputation.

Financial attacks

Banks, large corporations, and e-commerce sites are the targets of financial attacks, all of which are motivated by greed. Financial attacks may seek to steal or embezzle funds, gain access to online financial information, extort individuals or businesses, or obtain the personal credit card numbers of customers.

"Fun" attacks

"Fun" attacks are perpetrated by thrill-seekers and script kiddies who are motivated by curiosity or excitement. Although these attackers may not intend to do any harm or use any of the information that they access, they're still dangerous and their activities are still illegal.

These attacks can also be relatively easy to detect and prosecute. Because the perpetrators are often *script kiddies* (hackers who use scripts or programs written by other hackers because they don't have programming skills themselves) or otherwise-inexperienced hackers, they may not know how to cover their tracks effectively.

Also, because no real harm is normally done nor intended against the system, it may be tempting (although ill-advised) for a business to prosecute the individual and put a positive public relations spin on the incident. You've seen the film at 11:00: "We quickly detected the attack, prevented any harm to our network, and prosecuted the responsible individual; our security is *unbreak-able!*" Such action, however, will likely motivate others to launch a more serious and concerted grudge attack against the business.

Many computer criminals in this category only seek notoriety. Although it's one thing to brag to a small circle of friends about defacing a public website, the wily hacker who appears on CNN reaches the next level of hacker celebrity-dom. These twisted individuals want to be caught to revel in their 15 minutes of fame.

As we discuss in Chapter 7, *script kiddies* are novice hackers or less experienced (not too salty) crackers. Typically, script kiddies are new to the dark side — and perhaps don't realize just how dark (and illegal) the dark side really is. Script kiddies lack true hacking or programming skills, so they must rely on freely available tools that others have created and distributed on the Internet, and they often don't know or understand how much damage they may actually do to a system or network.

Grudge attacks

Grudge attacks are targeted at individuals or businesses, and the attacker is motivated by a desire to take revenge against a person or organization. A disgruntled employee, for example, may steal trade secrets, delete valuable data, or plant a *logic bomb* (a type of malware, see Chapters 7 and 10) in a critical system or application.

Fortunately, these attacks (at least in the case of a disgruntled employee) can be easier to prevent or prosecute than many other types of attacks because:

- ✔ The attacker is often known to the victim.
- ✔ The attack has a visible impact that produces a viable evidence trail.
- ✔ Most businesses (already sensitive to the possibility of wrongful-termination suits) have well-established termination procedures.
- ✔ Specific laws (such as the U.S. Economic Espionage Act of 1996, which we discuss in the section "U.S. Economic Espionage Act of 1996," later in this chapter) provide very severe penalties for such crimes.

Ideological attacks

Ideological attacks — commonly known as "hacktivism" — have become increasingly common in recent years. Hacktivists typically target businesses or organizations to protest a controversial position that does not agree with their own ideology. These attacks typically take the form of Distributed Denial-of-Service (DDoS) attacks, but can also include data theft. For example, the U.S. Senate and many businesses — including the Sony PlayStation Network — were targeted in 2011 and early 2012 because of their support for the Stop Online Piracy Act (SOPA).

Military and intelligence attacks

Military and intelligence attacks are perpetrated by criminals, traitors, or foreign intelligence agents seeking classified law enforcement or military information. Such attacks may also be carried out by governments during times of war and conflict.

Terrorist attacks

Terrorism exists at many levels on the Internet. In April 2001, during a period of tense relations between China and the U.S. (resulting from the crash landing of a U.S. Navy reconnaissance plane on Hainan Island), Chinese hackers (in this case, cyberterrorists) launched a major effort to disrupt critical U.S. infrastructure, which included U.S. government and military systems.

Following the terrorist attacks against the U.S. on September 11, 2001, the general public became painfully aware of the extent of terrorism on the Internet. Terrorist organizations and cells use online capabilities to coordinate attacks, transfer funds, harm international commerce, disrupt critical systems, disseminate propaganda, recruit new members, and gain useful information about developing techniques and instruments of terror, including nuclear, biological, and chemical weapons.

Types of Laws Relevant to Computer Crimes

Given the difficulties in defining and prosecuting computer crimes, many prosecutors seek to convict computer criminals on more traditional criminal statutes, such as theft, fraud, extortion, and embezzlement. Intellectual property rights and privacy laws, in addition to specific computer crime laws, also exist to protect the general public and assist prosecutors.

The CISSP candidate should understand that because of the difficulty in prosecuting computer crimes, prosecutors often use more traditional criminal statutes, intellectual property rights, and privacy laws to convict criminals. In addition, you should also realize that specific computer crime laws do exist.

Intellectual property

Intellectual property is protected by U.S. law under one of four classifications:

- ✔ Patents
- ✔ Trademarks
- ✔ Copyrights
- ✔ Trade secrets

Intellectual property rights worldwide are agreed upon, defined, and enforced by various organizations and treaties, including the World Intellectual Property Organization (WIPO), World Customs Organization (WCO), World Trade Organization (WTO), United Nations Commission on International Trade Law (UNCITRAL), European Union (EU), and Trade-Related Aspects of Intellectual Property Rights (TRIPs).

Licensing violations are among the most prevalent examples of intellectual property rights infringement. Other examples include plagiarism, software piracy, and corporate espionage.

Patents

A *patent,* as defined by the U.S. Patent and Trademark Office (PTO) is "the grant of a property right to the inventor." A patent grant confers upon the owner (either an individual or a company) "the right to exclude others from making, using, offering for sale, selling, or importing the invention." In order to qualify for a patent, an invention must be novel, useful, and not obvious. An invention must also be tangible — an idea cannot be patented. Examples of computer-related objects that may be protected by patents are computer hardware and physical devices in firmware.

A patent is granted by the U.S. PTO for an invention that has been sufficiently documented by the applicant and that has been verified as original by the PTO. A U.S. patent is generally valid for 20 years from the date of application and is effective only within the U.S., including territories and possessions. Patent applications must be filed with the appropriate patent office in various countries throughout the world to receive patent protection in that country. The owner of the patent may grant a license to others for use of the invention or its design, often for a fee.

U.S. patent (and trademark) laws and rules are covered in 35 U.S.C. and 37 C.F.R., respectively. The Patent Cooperation Treaty (PCT) provides some international protection for patents. More than 130 countries worldwide have adopted the PCT. Patent infringements are not prosecuted by the U.S. PTO. Instead, the holder of a patent must enforce their patent rights through the appropriate legal system.

Patent grants were previously valid for only 17 years, but have recently been changed, for newly granted patents, to 20 years.

Trademark

A *trademark,* as defined by the U.S. PTO, is "any word, name, symbol, or device, or any combination, used, or intended to be used, in commerce to identify and distinguish the goods of one manufacturer or seller from goods manufactured or sold by others." Computer-related objects that may be protected by trademarks include corporate brands and operating system logos. U.S. Public Law 105–330, the Trademark Law Treaty Implementation Act, provides some international protection for U.S. registered trademarks.

Copyright

A *copyright* is a form of protection granted to the authors of "original works of authorship," both published and unpublished. A copyright protects a tangible form of expression rather than the idea or subject matter itself. Under the original Copyright Act of 1909, publication was generally the key to obtaining a federal copyright. However, the Copyright Act of 1976 changed this requirement, and copyright protection now applies to any original work of authorship immediately, from the time that it's created in a tangible form. Object code or documentation are examples of computer-related objects that may be protected by copyrights.

Copyrights can be registered through the Copyright Office of the Library of Congress, but a work doesn't need to be registered to be protected by copyright. Copyright protection generally lasts for the lifetime of the author plus 70 years.

Trade secret

A *trade secret* is proprietary or business-related information that a company or individual uses and has exclusive rights to. To be considered a trade secret, the information must meet the following requirements:

- ✔ **Must be genuine and not obvious:** Any unique method of accomplishing a task would constitute a trade secret, especially if it is backed up by copyrighted, patented, or proprietary software or methods that give that organization a competitive advantage.

- ✔ **Must provide the owner a competitive or economic advantage and, therefore, have value to the owner:** For example, Google's search algorithms — the "secret sauce" that makes it popular with users (and therefore advertisers) — aren't universally known. Some secrets are protected.

- ✔ **Must be reasonably protected from disclosure:** This doesn't mean that it must be kept absolutely and exclusively secret, but the owner must exercise due care in its protection.

Software source code or firmware code are examples of computer-related objects that an organization may protect as trade secrets.

Privacy and data protection laws

Privacy and data protection laws are enacted to protect information collected and maintained on individuals from unauthorized disclosure or misuse. Privacy laws are one area in which the United States lags behind many others, particularly, the European Union (EU), which has defined restrictive privacy regulations that prohibit the transfer of personal information to countries (including the United States) that don't equally protect such information. The EU privacy rules include the following requirements about personal data and records:

- ✓ **Must be collected fairly and lawfully.**
- ✓ **Must only be used for the purposes for which it was collected and only for a reasonable period of time.**
- ✓ **Must be accurate and kept up to date.**
- ✓ **Must be accessible to individuals who request a report on personal information held about themselves.**
- ✓ **Individuals must have the right to have any errors in their personal data corrected.**
- ✓ **Personal data can't be disclosed to other organizations or individuals unless authorized by law or consent of the individual.**
- ✓ **Transmission of personal data to locations where equivalent privacy protection cannot be assured is prohibited.**

Several important pieces of privacy and data protection legislation include the Federal Privacy Act, the Health Insurance Portability and Accountability Act (HIPAA), the Health Information Technology for Economic and Clinical Health Act (HITECH), and the Gramm-Leach-Bliley Act (GLBA) in the United States, and the Data Protection Act (DPA) in the United Kingdom. Finally, the Payment Card Industry Data Security Standard (PCI DSS) is an example of an industry policing itself — without the need for government laws or regulations.

U.S. Federal Privacy Act of 1974, 5 U.S.C. § 552A

The Federal Privacy Act of 1974 protects records and information maintained by U.S. government agencies about U.S. citizens and lawful permanent residents. Except under certain specific conditions, no agency may disclose any record about an individual "except pursuant to a written request by, or with the prior written consent of, the individual to whom the record pertains." The Privacy Act also has provisions for access and amendment of an individual's records by that individual, except in cases of "information compiled in reasonable anticipation of a civil action or proceeding." The Privacy Act provides individual penalties for violations, including a misdemeanor charge and fines up to $5,000.

Although the Federal Privacy Act of 1974 pre-dates the Internet as we know it today, don't dismiss its relevance. The provisions of the Privacy Act are as important as ever and remain in full force and effect today.

U.S. Health Insurance Portability and Accountability Act (HIPAA) of 1996, PL 104–191

HIPAA was signed into law effective August 1996. The HIPAA legislation provided Congress three years from that date to pass comprehensive health privacy legislation. When Congress failed to pass legislation by the deadline, the Department of Health and Human Services (HHS) received the authority to develop the privacy and security regulations for HIPAA. In October 1999, HHS released proposed HIPAA privacy regulations entitled "Privacy Standards for Individually Identifiable Health Information," which took effect in April 2003. HIPAA security standards were subsequently published in February 2003 and took effect in April 2003. Organizations that must comply with HIPAA regulations are referred to as *covered entities* and include

- ✔ **Payers (or health plan):** An individual or group health plan that provides — or pays the cost of — medical care; for example, insurers

- ✔ **Healthcare clearinghouses:** A public or private entity that processes or facilitates the processing of nonstandard data elements of health information into standard data elements, such as data warehouses

- ✔ **Health providers:** A provider of medical or other health services, such as hospitals, HMOs, doctors, specialists, dentists, and counselors

Civil penalties for HIPAA violations include fines of $100 per incident, up to $25,000 per provision, per calendar year. Criminal penalties include fines up to $250,000 and potential imprisonment of corporate officers for up to ten years. Additional state penalties may also apply.

In 2009, Congress passed additional HIPAA provisions as part of the American Recovery and Reinvestment Act of 2009, requiring covered entities to publicly disclose security breaches involving personal information. (See the section "Disclosure laws" later in this chapter for a discussion of disclosure laws.)

U.S. Health Information Technology for Economic and Clinical Health Act (HITECH) of 2009

The HITECH Act, passed as part of the American Recovery and Reinvestment Act of 2009, broadens the scope of HIPAA compliance to include the business associates of HIPAA covered entities. These include third-party administrators, pharmacy benefit managers for health plans, claims processing/billing/transcription companies, and persons performing legal, accounting and administrative work.

Another highly important provision of the HITECH Act promotes and, in many cases, funds the adoption of electronic health records (EHRs), in order to increase the effectiveness of individual medical treatment, improve efficiency in the U.S. healthcare system, and reduce the overall cost of healthcare.

Anticipating that the widespread adoption of EHRs will increase privacy and security risks, the HITECH Act introduces new security and privacy-related requirements.

In the event of a breach of "unsecured protected health information," the HITECH Act requires covered entities to notify the affected individuals and the Secretary of the U.S. Department of Health and Human Services (HHS). The regulation defines *unsecured protected health information (PHI)* as PHI that is not secured through the use of a technology or methodology to render it unusable, unreadable, or indecipherable to unauthorized individuals.

The notification requirements vary according to the amount of data breached

- ✔ A data breach affecting more than 500 people must be reported imme-diately to the HHS, major media outlets and individuals affected by the breach, and must be posted on the official HHS website.

- ✔ A data breach affecting fewer than 500 people must be reported to the individuals affected by the breach, and to the HHS secretary on an annual basis.

Finally, the HITECH Act also requires the issuance of technical guidance on the technologies and methodologies "that render protected health informa-tion unusable, unreadable, or indecipherable to unauthorized individuals". The guidance specifies data destruction and encryption as actions that render PHI unusable if it is lost or stolen. PHI that is encrypted and whose encryption keys are properly secured provides a "safe harbor" to covered entities and does not require them to issue data-breach notifications.

U.S. Gramm-Leach-Bliley Financial Services Modernization Act, PL 106-102

Gramm-Leach-Bliley (known as GLBA) opened up competition among banks, insurance companies, and securities companies. GLBA also requires financial institutions to better protect their customers' personally identifiable informa-tion (PII) with three rules:

- ✔ **Financial Privacy Rule:** Requires each financial institution to provide information to each customer regarding the protection of customers' private information.

- ✔ **Safeguards Rule:** Requires each financial institution to develop a formal written security plan that describes how the institution will protect its customers' PII.

- ✔ **Pretexting Protection:** Requires each financial institution to take pre-cautions to prevent attempts by social engineers to acquire private information about institutions' customers.

Civil penalties for GLBA violations are up to $100,000 for each violation. Furthermore, officers and directors of financial institutions are personally liable for civil penalties of not more than $10,000 for each violation.

U.K. Data Protection Act

Passed by Parliament in 1998, the U.K. Data Protection Act (DPA) applies to any organization that handles sensitive personal data about living persons. Such data includes

✔ Names

✔ Birth and anniversary dates

✔ Addresses, phone numbers, and e-mail addresses

✔ Racial or ethnic origins

✔ Political opinions and religious (or similar) beliefs

✔ Trade or labor union membership

✔ Physical or mental condition

✔ Sexual orientation or lifestyle

✔ Criminal or civil records or allegations

The DPA applies to electronically stored information, but certain paper records used for commercial purposes may also be covered. The DPA consists of eight privacy and disclosure principles as follows:

✔ "Personal data shall be processed fairly and lawfully and [shall not be processed unless certain other conditions (set forth in the Act) are met]."

✔ "Personal data shall be obtained only for one or more specified and lawful purposes, and shall not be further processed in any manner incompatible with that purpose or those purposes."

✔ "Personal data shall be adequate, relevant, and not excessive in relation to the purpose or purposes for which they are processed."

✔ "Personal data shall be accurate and, where necessary, kept up-to-date."

✔ "Personal data processed for any purpose or purposes shall not be kept for longer than is necessary for that purpose or those purposes."

✔ "Personal data shall be processed in accordance with the rights of data subjects under this Act."

✔ "Appropriate technical and organizational measures shall be taken against unauthorized or unlawful processing of personal data and against accidental loss or destruction of, or damage to, personal data."

> ✔ "Personal data shall not be transferred to a country or territory outside the European Economic Area unless that country or territory ensures an adequate level of protection for the rights and freedoms of data subjects in relation to the processing of personal data."

DPA compliance is enforced by the Information Commissioner's Office (ICO), an independent official body. Penalties generally include fines which may also be imposed against the officers of a company.

Payment Card Industry Data Security Standard (PCI DSS)

Although not (yet) a legal mandate, the Payment Card Industry Data Security Standard (PCI DSS) is one example of an effective industry initiative for mandating and enforcing security standards. PCI DSS applies to any business worldwide that transmits, processes, or stores payment card (meaning credit card) transactions to conduct business with customers — whether that business handles thousands of credit card transactions a day or a single transaction a year. Compliance is mandated and enforced by the payment card brands (American Express, MasterCard, Visa, and so on) and each payment card brand manages its own compliance program.

Although PCI DSS is an industry standard rather than a legal mandate, many states are beginning to introduce legislation that would make PCI compliance (or at least compliance with certain provisions) mandatory for organizations that do business in that state.

PCI DSS requires organizations to submit an annual self-assessment and network scan, or to complete an onsite PCI data security assessments and quarterly network scans. The actual requirements depend on the number of payment card transactions handled by an organization and other factors, such as previous data loss incidents.

PCI DSS version 2.0 consists of six core principles, supported by 12 accompanying requirements, and more than 200 specific procedures for compliance. These include

> ✔ **Principle 1:** Build and maintain a secure network:
>
> > • **Requirement 1:** Install and maintain a firewall configuration to protect cardholder data.
> >
> > • **Requirement 2:** Don't use vendor-supplied defaults for system passwords and other security parameters.
>
> ✔ **Principle 2:** Protect cardholder data:
>
> > • **Requirement 3:** Protect stored cardholder data.
> >
> > • **Requirement 4:** Encrypt transmission of cardholder data across open, public networks.

✔ **Principle 3:** Maintain a vulnerability management program:

- **Requirement 5:** Use and regularly update antivirus software.

- **Requirement 6:** Develop and maintain secure systems and applications.

✔ **Principle 4:** Implement strong access control measures:

- **Requirement 7:** Restrict access to cardholder data by business need-to-know.

- **Requirement 8:** Assign a unique ID to each person who has computer access.

- **Requirement 9:** Restrict physical access to cardholder data.

✔ **Principle 5:** Regularly monitor and test networks:

- **Requirement 10:** Track and monitor all access to network resources and cardholder data.

- **Requirement 11:** Regularly test security systems and processes.

✔ **Principle 6:** Maintain an information security policy:

- **Requirement 12:** Maintain a policy that addresses information security.

Penalties for non-compliance are levied by the payment card brands and include not being allowed to process credit card transactions, fines up to $25,000 per month for minor violations, and fines up to $500,000 for violations that result in actual lost or stolen financial data.

Disclosure laws

In an effort to combat identity theft, many U.S. states have passed disclosure laws that compel organizations to publicly disclose security breaches that may result in the compromise of personal data.

Although these laws typically include statutory penalties, the damage to an organization's reputation and the potential loss of business — caused by the public disclosure requirement of these laws — can be the most significant and damaging aspect to affected organizations. Thus, public disclosure laws shame organizations into implementing more effective information security policies and practices to lessen the risk of a data breach occurring in the first place.

By requiring organizations to notify individuals of a data breach, disclosure laws fulfill a secondary purpose — allowing potential victims to take defensive or corrective action to help avoid or minimize the damage resulting from identity theft.

California Security Breach Information Act (SB-1386)

Passed in 2003, the California Security Breach Information Act (SB-1386) was the first U.S. state law to require organizations to notify all affected individuals "in the most expedient time possible and without unreasonable delay, consistent with the legitimate needs of law enforcement," if their confidential or personal data is lost, stolen, or compromised, unless that data is encrypted.

The law is applicable to any organization that does business in the state of California — even a single customer or employee in California. An organization is subject to the law even if it doesn't directly do business in California (for example, if it stores personal information about California residents for another company).

Other U.S. states have quickly followed suit, and 46 states, the District of Columbia, Puerto Rico, and the U.S. Virgin Islands now have public disclosure laws. However, these laws aren't necessarily consistent from one state to another, nor are they without flaws and critics.

For example, until early 2008, Indiana's Security Breach Disclosure and Identity Deception law (HEA 1101) did not require an organization to disclose a security breach "if access to the [lost or stolen] device is protected by a *password* [emphasis added] that has not been disclosed." Indiana's law has since been amended and is now one of the toughest state disclosure laws in effect, requiring public disclosure unless "all personal information . . . is protected by encryption."

Finally, a provision in California's and Indiana's disclosure laws, as well as in most other states' laws, allows an organization to avoid much of the cost of disclosure if the cost of providing such notice would exceed $250,000 or if more than 500,000 individuals would need to be notified. Instead, a substitute notice, consisting of e-mail notifications, conspicuous posting on the organization's website, and notification of major statewide media, is permitted.

Data Accountability and Trust Act (DATA)

Introduced in the U.S. House of Representatives as H.R.4127 in October 2005 (then subsequently re-introduced as H.R.2221 in April 2009), the Data Accountability and Trust Act (DATA) has yet to become U.S. law at the time we write this book. However, it would be idealistic to believe that four years of congressional debate and passionate lobbying will not result in the passage of a new federal law. And because four years of work has resulted in more than just a crafty acronym, it is important to understand the potential impact of this federal disclosure law as currently proposed.

DATA would supersede the various state laws already in effect, and although this federal law would provide more consistency, the net effect would be to weaken many state disclosure laws because of specific provisions within

DATA. For example, various definitions in DATA may create large loopholes in the federal law, statutory penalties may lessen both the compensatory and punitive effect of the law, and substitute notification guidelines may completely nullify the deterrent effect of disclosure laws.

Computer crime and information security laws

Important international computer crime and information security laws that the CISSP candidate should be familiar with include

- ✔ U.S. Computer Fraud and Abuse Act of 1986
- ✔ U.S. Electronic Communications Privacy Act of 1986
- ✔ U.S. Computer Security Act of 1987
- ✔ U.S. Federal Sentencing Guidelines of 1991 (not necessarily specific to computer crime, but certainly relevant)
- ✔ U.S. Economic Espionage Act of 1996
- ✔ U.S. Child Pornography Prevention Act of 1996
- ✔ USA PATRIOT Act of 2001
- ✔ U.S. Sarbanes-Oxley Act of 2002
- ✔ U.S. CAN-SPAM Act of 2003
- ✔ The Council of Europe's Convention on Cybercrime of 2001
- ✔ The Computer Misuse Act of 1990 (U.K.)
- ✔ Cybercrime Act of 2001 (Australia)

U.S. Computer Fraud and Abuse Act of 1986, 18 U.S.C. § 1030 (as amended)

In 1984, the first U.S. federal computer crime law, the U.S. Computer Fraud and Abuse Act, was passed. This intermediate act was narrowly defined and somewhat ambiguous. The law covered

- ✔ Classified national defense or foreign relations information
- ✔ Records of financial institutions or credit reporting agencies
- ✔ Government computers

The U.S. Computer Fraud and Abuse Act of 1986 enhanced and strengthened the 1984 law, clarifying definitions of criminal fraud and abuse for federal computer crimes and removing obstacles to prosecution.

The Act established two new felony offenses for the unauthorized access of *federal interest* computers and a misdemeanor for unauthorized trafficking in computer passwords:

- ✔ **Felony 1:** Unauthorized access, or access that exceeds authorization, of a federal interest computer to further an intended fraud, shall be punishable as a felony [Subsection (a)(4)].

- ✔ **Felony 2:** Altering, damaging, or destroying information in a federal interest computer or preventing authorized use of the computer or information, that causes an aggregate loss of $1,000 or more during a one-year period or potentially impairs medical treatment, shall be punishable as a felony [Subsection (a)(5)].

  This provision was stricken in its entirety and replaced with a more general provision, which we discuss later in this section.

- ✔ **Misdemeanor:** Trafficking in computer passwords or similar information if it affects interstate or foreign commerce or permits unauthorized access to computers used by or for the U.S. government [Subsection (a)(6)].

The Act defines a *federal interest computer* (actually, the term was changed to *protected computer* in the 1996 amendments to the Act) as either a computer

- ✔ "[E]xclusively for the use of a financial institution or the United States government, or, in the case of a computer not exclusively for such use, used by or for a financial institution or the United States government and the conduct constituting the offense affect that use by or for the financial institution or the government"

- ✔ "[W]hich is used in interstate or foreign commerce or communication"

Several minor amendments to the U.S. Computer Fraud and Abuse Act were made in 1988, 1989, and 1990, and more significant amendments were made in 1994, 1996 (by the Economic Espionage Act of 1996), and 2001 (by the USA PATRIOT Act of 2001). The Act, in its present form, establishes seven specific computer crimes. In addition to the three that we discuss in the preceding list, these crimes include the following five provisions (we discuss subsection [a][5] in its current form in the following list):

- ✔ Unauthorized access, or access that exceeds authorization, to a computer that results in *disclosure of U.S. national defense or foreign relations information* [Subsection (a)(1)].

- ✔ Unauthorized access, or access that exceeds authorization, to a protected computer to *obtain any information on that computer* [Subsection (a)(2)].

- ✔ Unauthorized access to a protected computer, or access that exceeds authorization, to a protected computer that *affects the use* of that computer by or for the U.S. government [Subsection (a)(3)].

✔ Unauthorized access to a protected computer causing damage or reckless damage, or *intentionally transmitting malicious code* which causes damage to a protected computer [Subsection (a)(5), as amended].

✔ Transmission of interstate or foreign commerce communication *threatening to cause damage* to a protected computer for the purpose of extortion [Subsection (a)(7)].

In the section "USA PATRIOT Act of 2001," later in this chapter, we discuss major amendments to the U.S. Computer Fraud and Abuse Act of 1986 (as amended) that Congress introduced in 2001.

The U.S. Computer Fraud and Abuse Act of 1986 is *the* major computer crime law currently in effect. The CISSP exam likely tests your knowledge of the Act in its original 1986 form, but you should also be prepared for revisions to the exam that may cover the more recent amendments to the Act.

U.S. Electronic Communications Privacy Act (ECPA) of 1986

The ECPA complements the U.S. Computer Fraud and Abuse Act of 1986 and prohibits eavesdropping, interception, or unauthorized monitoring of wire, oral, and electronic communications. However, the ECPA does provide specific statutory exceptions, allowing network providers to monitor their networks for legitimate business purposes if they notify the network users of the monitoring process.

The ECPA was amended extensively by the USA PATRIOT Act of 2001. These changes are discussed in the upcoming "USA PATRIOT Act of 2001" section.

The U.S. Electronic Communications Privacy Act (ECPA) provides the legal basis for network monitoring.

U.S. Computer Security Act of 1987

The U.S. Computer Security Act of 1987 requires federal agencies to take extra security measures to prevent unauthorized access to computers that hold sensitive information. In addition to identifying and developing security plans for sensitive systems, the Act requires those agencies to provide security-related awareness training for their employees. The Act also assigns formal government responsibility for computer security to the National Institute of Standards and Technology (NIST) for information security standards, in general, and to the National Security Agency (NSA) for cryptography in classified government/military systems and applications.

U.S. Federal Sentencing Guidelines of 1991

In November 1991, the United States Sentencing Commission published Chapter 8, "Federal Sentencing Guidelines for Organizations," of the U.S. Federal Sentencing Guidelines. These guidelines establish written standards of conduct for organizations, provide relief in sentencing for organizations that have demonstrated due diligence, and place responsibility for due care on senior management officials with penalties for negligence, including fines of up to $290 million.

U.S. Economic Espionage Act of 1996

The U.S. Economic Espionage Act (EEA) of 1996 was enacted to curtail industrial espionage, particularly when such activity benefits a foreign entity. The EEA makes it a criminal offense to take, download, receive, or possess trade secret information that's been obtained without the owner's authorization. Penalties include fines of up to $10 million, up to 15 years in prison, and forfeiture of any property used to commit the crime. The EEA also enacted the 1996 amendments to the U.S. Computer Fraud and Abuse Act, which we talk about in the section "U.S. Computer Fraud and Abuse Act of 1986, 18 U.S.C. § 1030 (as amended)," earlier in this chapter.

U.S. Child Pornography Prevention Act of 1996

The U.S. Child Pornography Prevention Act (CPPA) of 1996 was enacted to combat the use of computer technology to produce and distribute pornography involving children, including adults portraying children.

USA PATRIOT Act of 2001

Following the terrorist attacks against the United States on September 11, 2001, the USA PATRIOT Act of 2001 (Uniting and Strengthening America by Providing Appropriate Tools Required to Intercept and Obstruct Terrorism Act) was enacted in October 2001 and renewed in March 2006. (Many provisions originally set to expire have since been made permanent under the renewed Act.) This Act takes great strides to strengthen and amend existing computer crime laws, including the U.S. Computer Fraud and Abuse Act and the U.S. Electronic Communications Privacy Act (ECPA), as well as to empower U.S. law enforcement agencies, if only temporarily. U.S. federal courts have subsequently declared some of the Act's provisions unconstitutional. The sections of the Act that are relevant to the CISSP exam include

- ✔ **Section 202 — Authority to Intercept Wire, Oral, and Electronic Communications Relating to Computer Fraud and Abuse Offenses:** Under previous law, investigators couldn't obtain a wiretap order for violations of the Computer Fraud and Abuse Act. This amendment authorizes such action for felony violations of that Act.

- ✔ **Section 209 — Seizure of Voice-Mail Messages Pursuant to Warrants:** Under previous law, investigators could obtain access to e-mail under the ECPA but not voice-mail, which was covered by the more restrictive wiretap statute. This amendment authorizes access to voice-mail with a search warrant rather than a wiretap order.

- ✔ **Section 210 — Scope of Subpoenas for Records of Electronic Communications:** Under previous law, subpoenas of electronic records were restricted to very limited information. This amendment expands the list of records that can be obtained and updates technology-specific terminology.

- ✔ **Section 211 — Clarification of Scope:** This amendment governs privacy protection and disclosure to law enforcement of cable, telephone, and Internet service provider records.

- ✔ **Section 212 — Emergency Disclosure of Electronic Communications to Protect Life and Limb:** Prior to this amendment, no special provisions existed that allowed a communications provider to disclose customer information to law enforcement officials in emergency situations, such as an imminent crime or terrorist attack, without exposing the provider to civil liability suits from the customer.

- ✔ **Section 214 — Pen Register and Trap and Trace Authority under FISA (Foreign Intelligence Surveillance Act):** Clarifies law enforcement authority to trace communications on the Internet and other computer networks, and it authorizes the use of a pen/trap device nationwide, instead of limiting it to the jurisdiction of the court.

A *pen/trap device* refers to a *pen register* that shows outgoing numbers called from a phone and a *trap and trace device* that shows incoming numbers that called a phone. Pen registers and trap and trace devices are collectively referred to as pen/trap devices because most technologies allow the same device to perform both types of traces (incoming and outgoing numbers).

- ✔ **Section 217 — Interception of Computer Trespasser Communications:** Under previous law, it was permissible for organizations to monitor activity on their own networks but not necessarily for law enforcement to assist these organizations in monitoring, even when such help was specifically requested. This amendment allows organizations to authorize persons "acting under color (pretense or appearance) of law" to monitor trespassers on their computer systems.

- ✔ **Section 220 — Nationwide Service of Search Warrants for Electronic Evidence:** Removes jurisdictional issues in obtaining search warrants for e-mail. For an excellent example of this problem, read *The Cuckoo's Egg: Tracking a Spy Through the Maze of Computer Espionage,* by Clifford Stoll (Doubleday).

- ✔ **Section 814 — Deterrence and Prevention of Cyberterrorism:** Greatly strengthens the U.S. Computer Fraud and Abuse Act, including raising the maximum prison sentence from 10 years to 20 years.

- ✔ **Section 815 — Additional Defense to Civil Actions Relating to Preserving Records in Response to Government Requests:** Clarifies the "statutory authorization" (government authority) defense for violations of the ECPA.

✔ **Section 816 — Development and Support of Cybersecurity Forensic Capabilities:** Requires the Attorney General to establish regional computer forensic laboratories, maintain existing laboratories, and provide forensic and training capabilities to Federal, State, and local law enforcement personnel and prosecutors.

The USA PATRIOT Act of 2001 changes many of the provisions in the computer crime laws, particularly the U.S. Computer Fraud and Abuse Act, which we discuss in the section "U.S. Computer Fraud and Abuse Act of 1986, 18 U.S.C. § 1030 (as amended)," later in this chapter; and the Electronic Communications Privacy Act of 1986, which we detail in the section "U.S. Electronic Communications Privacy Act (ECPA) of 1986," earlier in this chapter. As a security professional, you must keep abreast of current laws and affairs to perform your job effectively.

U.S. Sarbanes-Oxley Act of 2002 (SOX)

In the wake of several major corporate and accounting scandals, SOX was passed in 2002 to restore public trust in publicly held corporations and public accounting firms by establishing new standards and strengthening existing standards for these entities including auditing, governance, and financial disclosures.

SOX established the Public Company Accounting Oversight Board (PCAOB), which is a private-sector, nonprofit corporation responsible for overseeing auditors in the implementation of SOX. PCAOB's "Accounting Standard 2" recognizes the role of information technology as it relates to a company's internal controls and financial reporting. The Standard identifies the responsibility of Chief Information Officers (CIOs) for the security of information systems that process and store financial data, and it has many implications for information technology security and governance.

U.S. CAN-SPAM Act of 2003

The U.S. CAN-SPAM Act (Controlling the Assault of Non-Solicited Pornography and Marketing Act) establishes standards for sending commercial e-mail messages, charges the U.S. Federal Trade Commission (FTC) with enforcement of the provision, and provides penalties that include fines and imprisonment for violations of the Act.

Directive 95/46/EC on the protection of personal data (1995, EU)

In 1995, the European Parliament ratified this essential legislation that protects personal information for all European citizens. The directive states that personal data should not be processed at all, except when certain conditions are met.

A legitimate concern about the disposition of European citizens' personal data when it leaves computer systems in Europe and enters computer systems in the U.S. led to the creation of the Safe Harbor program (discussed in the following section).

Safe Harbor (1998)

In an agreement between the European Union and the U.S. Department of Commerce in 1998, the U.S. Department of Commerce developed a certification program called *Safe Harbor.* This permits U.S.-based organizations to certify themselves as properly handling private data belonging to European citizens.

The Council of Europe's Convention on Cybercrime (2001)

The Convention on Cybercrime is an international treaty, currently signed by more than 40 countries (the U.S. ratified the treaty in 2006), requiring criminal laws to be established in signatory nations for computer hacking activities, child pornography, and intellectual property violations. The treaty also attempts to improve international cooperation with respect to monitoring, investigations, and prosecution.

The Computer Misuse Act 1990 (U.K.)

The Computer Misuse Act 1990 (U.K.) defines three criminal offenses related to computer crime: unauthorized access (whether successful or unsuccessful), unauthorized modification, and hindering authorized access (Denial of Service).

Cybercrime Act 2001 (Australia)

The Cybercrime Act 2001 (Australia) establishes criminal penalties, including fines and imprisonment, for people who commit computer crimes (including unauthorized access, unauthorized modification, or Denial of Service) with intent to commit a serious offense.

Investigations

Computer forensics is the science of conducting a computer crime investigation to determine what has happened and who is responsible, and to collect legally admissible evidence for use in a computer crime case.

The purpose of an *investigation* is to determine what happened and who is responsible, and to collect evidence. Incident handling is done to determine what happened, contain and assess damage, and restore normal operations.

Closely related to, but distinctly different from, investigations is incident handling (or response). Incident handling is discussed in detail later in this chapter.

Investigations and incident handling must often be conducted simultaneously in a well-coordinated and controlled manner to ensure that the initial actions of either activity don't destroy evidence or cause further damage to the organization's assets. For this reason, it's important that Computer Incident (or Emergency) Response Teams (CIRT or CERT, respectively) be properly trained and qualified to secure a computer-related crime scene or incident while preserving evidence. Ideally, the CIRT includes individuals who will actually be conducting the investigation.

An analogy to this would be an example of a police patrolman who discovers a murder victim. It's important that the patrolman quickly assesses the safety of the situation and secures the crime scene; but at the same time, he must be careful not to destroy any evidence. The homicide detective's job is to gather and analyze the evidence. Ideally, but rarely, the homicide detective would be the individual who discovers the murder victim, allowing her to assess the safety of the situation, secure the crime scene, and begin collecting evidence. Think of yourself as a *CSI*-SSP!

Evidence

Evidence is information presented in a court of law to confirm or dispel a fact that's under contention, such as the commission of a crime. A case can't be brought to trial without sufficient evidence to support the case. Thus, properly gathering evidence is one of the most important and most difficult tasks of the investigator.

The types of evidence, rules of evidence, admissibility of evidence, chain of custody, and the evidence life cycle make up the main elements that the CISSP exam may cover in the Investigations portion of this domain.

Types of evidence

Sources of legal evidence that you can present in a court of law generally fall into one of four major categories:

- **Direct evidence:** Oral testimony or a written statement based on information gathered through a witness's five senses (in other words, an eyewitness account) that proves or disproves a specific fact or issue.

- **Real (or physical) evidence:** Tangible objects from the actual crime, such as the tools or weapons used and any stolen or damaged property. May also include visual or audio surveillance tapes generated during or after the event. Physical evidence from a computer crime is rarely available.

✔ **Documentary evidence:** Includes originals and copies of business records, computer-generated and computer-stored records, manuals, policies, standards, procedures, and log files. Most evidence presented in a computer crime case is documentary evidence. The *hearsay rule* (which we discuss in the section "Hearsay rule," later in this chapter) is an extremely important test of documentary evidence that must be understood and applied to this type of evidence.

✔ **Demonstrative evidence:** Used to aid the court's understanding of a case. Opinions are considered demonstrative evidence and may be either *expert* (based on personal expertise and facts) or *non-expert* (based on facts only). Other examples of demonstrative evidence include models, simulations, charts, and illustrations.

Other types of evidence that may fall into one or more of the above major categories include

✔ **Best evidence:** Original, unaltered evidence, which is preferred by the court over secondary evidence. Read more about this evidence in the section "Best evidence rule," later in this chapter.

✔ **Secondary evidence:** A duplicate or copy of evidence, such as a tape backup, screen capture, or photograph.

✔ **Corroborative evidence:** Supports or substantiates other evidence presented in a case.

✔ **Conclusive evidence:** Incontrovertible and irrefutable — you know, the smoking gun.

✔ **Circumstantial evidence:** Relevant facts that you can't directly or conclusively connect to other events, but about which a reasonable person can make a reasonable inference.

Rules of evidence

Important rules of evidence for computer crime cases include the best evidence rule and the hearsay evidence rule. The CISSP candidate must understand both of these rules and their applicability to evidence in computer crime cases.

Best evidence rule

The best evidence rule, defined in the Federal Rules of Evidence, states that "to prove the content of a writing, recording, or photograph, the original writing, recording, or photograph is [ordinarily] required."

However, the Federal Rules of Evidence define an exception to this rule as "[i]f data are stored in a computer or similar device, any printout or other output readable by sight, shown to reflect the data accurately, is an 'original'."

Thus, data extracted from a computer — if that data is a fair and accurate representation of the original data — satisfies the best evidence rule and may normally be introduced into court proceedings as such.

Hearsay rule

Hearsay evidence is evidence that's not based on personal, first-hand knowledge of a witness, but rather comes from other sources. Under the Federal Rules of Evidence, hearsay evidence is normally not admissible in court. This rule exists to prevent unreliable testimony from improperly influencing the outcome of a trial.

Business records, including computer records, have traditionally, and perhaps mistakenly, been considered hearsay evidence by most courts because these records cannot be proven accurate and reliable. One of the most significant obstacles for a prosecutor to overcome in a computer crime case is seeking the admission of computer records as evidence.

A prosecutor may be able to introduce computer records as best evidence, rather than hearsay evidence, which we discuss in the preceding section.

Several courts have acknowledged that the hearsay rules are applicable to *computer-stored* records containing human statements but are not applicable to *computer-generated* records untouched by human hands.

Perhaps the most successful and commonly applied test of admissibility for computer records, in general, has been the *business records exception,* established in the Federal Rules of Evidence, for records of regularly conducted activity, meeting the following criteria:

- ✔ Made at or near the time that the act occurred
- ✔ Made by a person who has knowledge of the business process or from information transmitted by a person who has knowledge of the business process
- ✔ Made and relied on during the regular conduct of business, as verified by the custodian or other witness familiar with the records' use
- ✔ Kept for motives that tend to assure their accuracy
- ✔ In the custody of the witness on a regular basis (as required by the chain of evidence)

The chain of evidence establishes accountability for the handling of evidence throughout the evidence life cycle. See the section "Chain of custody and the evidence life cycle" later in this chapter.

Admissibility of evidence

Because computer-generated evidence can sometimes be easily manipulated, altered, or tampered with, and because it's not easily and commonly understood, this type of evidence is usually considered suspect in a court of law. In order to be admissible, evidence must be

- ✔ **Relevant:** It must tend to prove or disprove facts that are relevant and material to the case.

- ✔ **Reliable:** It must be reasonably proven that what is presented as evidence is what was originally collected and that the evidence itself is reliable. This is accomplished, in part, through proper evidence handling and the chain of custody. (We discuss this in the upcoming section "Chain of custody and the evidence life cycle.")

- ✔ **Legally permissible:** It must be obtained through legal means. Evidence that's not legally permissible may include evidence obtained through the following means:

  - **Illegal search and seizure:** Law enforcement personnel must obtain a prior court order; however, non–law enforcement personnel, such as a supervisor or system administrator, may be able to conduct an authorized search under some circumstances.

  - **Illegal wiretaps or phone taps:** Anyone conducting wiretaps or phone taps must obtain a prior court order.

  - **Entrapment or enticement:** *Entrapment* encourages someone to commit a crime that the individual may have had no intention of committing. Conversely, *enticement* lures someone toward certain evidence (a honey pot, if you will) after that individual has already committed a crime. Enticement isn't necessarily illegal, but it does raise certain ethical arguments and may not be admissible in court.

  - **Coercion:** Coerced testimony or confessions are not legally permissible. Coercion involves compelling a person to involuntarily provide evidence through the use of threats, violence (torture), bribery, trickery, or intimidation.

  - **Unauthorized or improper monitoring:** Active monitoring must be properly authorized and conducted in a standard manner; users must be notified that they may be subject to monitoring.

Chain of custody and the evidence life cycle

The *chain of custody* (or *chain of evidence*) provides accountability and protection for evidence throughout its entire life cycle and includes the following information, which is normally kept in an evidence log:

✔ **Persons involved *(Who)*:** Identify any and all individual(s) who discovered, collected, seized, analyzed, stored, preserved, transported, or otherwise controlled the evidence. Also identify any witnesses or other individuals present during any of the above actions.

✔ **Description of evidence *(What)*:** Ensure that all evidence is completely and uniquely described.

✔ **Location of evidence *(Where)*:** Provide specific information about the evidence's location when it is discovered, analyzed, stored, or transported.

✔ **Date/Time *(When)*:** Record the date and time that evidence is discovered, collected, seized, analyzed, stored, or transported. Also, record date and time information for any evidence log entries associated with the evidence.

✔ **Methods used *(How)*:** Provide specific information about how evidence is discovered, collected, stored, preserved, or transported.

Any time that evidence changes possession or is transferred to a different media type, it must be properly recorded in the evidence log to maintain the chain of custody.

Law enforcement officials must strictly adhere to chain of custody requirements, and this adherence is highly recommended for anyone else involved in collecting or seizing evidence. Security professionals and incident response teams must fully understand and follow the chain of custody, no matter how minor or insignificant a security incident may initially appear.

Even properly trained law enforcement officials sometimes make crucial mistakes in evidence handling. Most attorneys won't understand the technical aspects of the evidence that you may present in a case, but they will definitely know evidence-handling rules and will most certainly scrutinize your actions in this area. Improperly handled evidence, no matter how conclusive or damaging, will likely be inadmissible in a court of law.

The *evidence life cycle* describes the various phases of evidence, from its initial discovery to its final disposition.

The evidence life cycle has the following five stages:

✔ Collection and identification

✔ Analysis

✔ Storage, preservation, and transportation

✔ Presentation in court

✔ Return to victim (owner)

The following sections tell you more about each stage.

Collection and identification

Collecting evidence involves taking that evidence into custody. Unfortunately, evidence can't always be collected and must instead be seized. Many legal issues are involved in seizing computers and other electronic evidence. The publication *Searching and Seizing Computers and Obtaining Evidence in Criminal Investigations (January 2001),* published by the U.S. Department of Justice (DOJ) Computer Crime and Intellectual Property Section (CCIPS), provides comprehensive guidance on this subject. Find this publication available for download at www.cybercrime.gov.

In general, law enforcement officials can search and/or seize computers and other electronic evidence under any of four circumstances:

- **Voluntary or consensual:** The owner of the computer or electronic evidence can freely surrender the evidence.

- **Subpoena:** A court issues a subpoena to an individual, ordering that individual to deliver the evidence to the court.

- **Search warrant or Writ of Possession:** A *search warrant* is issued to a law enforcement official by the court, allowing that official to search and seize specific evidence. A *Writ of Possession* is a similar order issued in civil cases.

- **Exigent circumstances:** If probable cause exists and the destruction of evidence is imminent, that evidence may be searched or seized without a warrant.

When evidence is collected, it must be properly marked and identified. This ensures that it can later be properly presented in court as actual evidence gathered from the scene or incident. The collected evidence must be recorded in an evidence log with the following information:

- A **description** of the particular piece of evidence including any specific information, such as make, model, serial number, physical appearance, material condition, and preexisting damage.

- The **name(s)** of the person(s) who discovered and collected the evidence

- The exact **date and time**, **specific location**, and **circumstances** of the discovery/collection.

Additionally, the evidence must be marked, using the following guidelines:

- **Mark the evidence:** If possible without damaging the evidence, mark the actual piece of evidence with the collecting individual's initials, the date, and the case number (if known). Seal the evidence in an appropriate container and again mark the container with the same information.

✔ **Or use an evidence tag:** If the actual evidence cannot be marked, attach an evidence tag with the same information as above, seal the evidence and tag in an appropriate container, and again mark the container with the same information.

✔ **Seal the evidence:** Seal the container with evidence tape and mark the tape in a manner that will clearly indicate any tampering.

✔ **Protect the evidence:** Use extreme caution when collecting and marking evidence to ensure that it's not damaged. If you're using plastic bags for evidence containers, be sure that they're static free.

Always collect and mark evidence in a consistent manner so that you can easily identify evidence and describe your collection and identification techniques to an opposing attorney in court, if necessary.

Analysis

Analysis involves examining the evidence for information pertinent to the case. Analysis should be conducted with extreme caution, by properly trained and experienced personnel only, to ensure the evidence is not altered, damaged, or destroyed.

Storage, preservation, and transportation

All evidence must be properly stored in a secure facility and preserved to prevent damage or contamination from various hazards, including intense heat or cold, extreme humidity, water, magnetic fields, and vibration. Evidence that's not properly protected may be inadmissible in court, and the party responsible for collection and storage may be liable. Care must also be exercised during transportation to ensure that evidence is not lost, temporarily misplaced, damaged, or destroyed.

Presentation in court

Evidence to be presented in court must continue to follow the chain of custody and be handled with the same care as at all other times in the evidence life cycle. This process continues throughout the trial until all testimony related to the evidence is completed and the trial is over.

Return to victim (owner)

After the conclusion of the trial or other disposition, evidence is normally returned to its proper owner. However, under some circumstances, certain evidence may be ordered destroyed, such as contraband, drugs, or drug paraphernalia. Any evidence obtained through a search warrant is legally under the control of the court, possibly requiring the original owner to petition the court for its return.

Conducting investigations

A computer crime investigation should begin immediately upon report of an alleged computer crime or incident. Any incident should be handled, at least initially, as a computer crime investigation until a preliminary investigation determines otherwise.

The CISSP candidate should be familiar with the general steps of the investigative process:

1. **Detect and contain a computer crime.**

   Early detection is critical to a successful investigation. Unfortunately, computer crimes usually involve passive or reactive detection techniques (such as the review of audit trails and accidental discovery), which often leave a cold evidence trail. Containment minimizes further loss or damage. The CIRT, which we discuss in the following section, is the team that is normally responsible for conducting an investigation. The CIRT should be notified (or activated) as quickly as possible after a computer crime is detected or suspected.

2. **Notify management.**

   Management must be notified of any investigations as soon as possible. Knowledge of the investigations should be limited to as few people as possible, on a need-to-know basis. Out-of-band communications methods (reporting in person) should be used to ensure that an intruder does not intercept sensitive communications about the investigation.

3. **Conduct a preliminary investigation.**

   This preliminary investigation determines whether a crime actually occurred. Most incidents turn out to be honest mistakes rather than criminal conduct. This step includes reviewing the complaint or report, inspecting damage, interviewing witnesses, examining logs, and identifying further investigation requirements.

4. **Determine whether the organization should disclose that the crime occurred.**

   First, and most importantly, determine whether law requires the organization to disclose the crime or incident. Next, by coordinating with a public relations or public affairs official of the organization, determine whether the organization wants to disclose this information.

5. **Conduct the investigation.**

   Conducting the investigation involves three activities:

   a. **Identify potential suspects.**

      Potential suspects include insiders and outsiders to the organization. One standard discriminator to help determine or eliminate potential suspects is the MOM test: Did the suspect have the

Motive, Opportunity, and Means? The Motive might relate to financial gain, revenge, or notoriety. A suspect had Opportunity if he or she had access, whether as an authorized user for an unauthorized purpose or as an unauthorized user — due to the existence of a security weakness or vulnerability — for an unauthorized purpose. And Means relates to whether the suspect had the necessary tools and skills to commit the crime.

b. Identify potential witnesses.

Determine whom you want interviewed and who conducts the interviews. Be careful not to alert any potential suspects to the investigation; focus on obtaining facts, not opinions, in witness statements.

c. Prepare for search and seizure.

Identify the types of systems and evidence that you plan to search or seize, designate and train the search and seizure team members (normally members of the Computer Incident Response Team, or CIRT), obtain and serve proper search warrants (if required), and determine potential risk to the system during a search and seizure effort.

6. Report your findings.

The results of the investigation, including evidence, should be reported to management and turned over to proper law enforcement officials or prosecutors, as appropriate.

MOM stands for Motive, Opportunity, and Means.

Incident handling (or response)

Incident response begins before an incident actually occurs. Preparation is the key to a quick and successful response. A well-documented and regularly practiced incident response plan ensures effective preparation. The plan should include

- ✔ **Response procedures:** Include detailed procedures that address different contingencies and situations.

- ✔ **Response authority:** Clearly define roles, responsibilities, and levels of authority for all members of the Computer Incident Response Team (CIRT).

- ✔ **Available resources:** Identify people, tools, and external resources (consultants and law enforcement agents) that are available to the CIRT. Training should include use of these resources, when possible.

- ✔ **Legal review:** The incident response plan should be evaluated by appropriate legal counsel to determine compliance with applicable laws and to determine whether they're enforceable and defensible.

Incident response generally follows these steps:

1. **Determine whether a security incident has occurred.**

   This process is similar to the Detection and Containment step in the investigative process (discussed in the preceding section) and includes defining what constitutes a security incident for your organization. Upon determination that an incident has occurred, it's important to immediately begin detailed documentation of every action taken throughout the incident response process. You should also identify the appropriate alert level. (Ask "Is this an isolated incident or a system-wide event?" and "Has personal or sensitive data been compromised?" and "What laws may have been violated?") The answers will help you determine who to notify and whether or not to activate the entire incident response team or only certain members.

2. **Notify the appropriate people about the incident.**

   This step and the specific procedures associated with it are identical to the Notification of Management step in the investigative process, but also include the Disclosure Determination step from the investigative process. All contact information should be documented before an incident, and all notifications and contacts during an incident should be documented in the incident log.

3. **Contain the incident (or damage).**

   Again, this step is similar to the Detection and Containment step in the investigative process. The purpose of this step is to minimize further loss or damage. You may need to eradicate a virus, deny access, and disable services.

4. **Assess the damage.**

   This assessment includes determining the scope and cause of damage, as well as the responsible (or liable) party.

5. **Recover normal operations.**

   This step may include rebuilding systems, repairing vulnerabilities, improving safeguards, and restoring data and services. Do this step in accordance with a Business Continuity Plan (BCP) that properly identifies priorities for recovery.

6. **Evaluate incident response effectiveness.**

   This final phase of an incident response plan involves identifying the lessons learned — which should include not only what went wrong, but also what went right.

Investigations and incident response follow similar steps but have different purposes: The distinguishing characteristic of an investigation is the gathering of evidence for possible prosecution, whereas incident response focuses on containing the damage and returning to normal operations.

Professional Ethics

Ethics (or moral values) help to describe what you should do in a given situation based on a set of principles or values. Ethical behavior is important to maintaining credibility as an information security professional and is a requirement for maintaining your CISSP certification. An organization often defines its core values (along with its mission statement) to help ensure that its employees understand what is acceptable and expected as they work to achieve the organization's mission, goals, and objectives.

Ethics are not easily discerned, and a fine line often hovers between ethical and unethical activity. Unethical activity doesn't necessarily equate to illegal activity. And what may be acceptable in some organizations, cultures, or societies may be unacceptable or even illegal in others.

Ethical standards can be based on a common or national interest, individual rights, laws, tradition, culture, or religion. One helpful distinction between laws and ethics is that laws define what we *must* do and ethics define what we *should* do.

Many common fallacies abound about computers and the Internet, which contribute to this gray area:

- ✔ **The Computer Game Fallacy:** Any system or network that's not properly protected is fair game.

- ✔ **The Law-Abiding Citizen Fallacy:** If no physical theft is involved, an activity really isn't stealing.

- ✔ **The Shatterproof Fallacy:** Any damage done will have a limited effect.

- ✔ **The Candy-from-a-Baby Fallacy:** It's so easy, it can't be wrong.

- ✔ **The Hacker's Fallacy:** Computers provide a valuable means of learning that will, in turn, benefit society.

    The problem here lies in the distinction between *hackers* and *crackers*. Although both may have a genuine desire to learn, crackers do it at the expense of others.

- ✔ **The Free Information Fallacy:** Any and all information should be free and thus can be obtained through any means.

Almost every recognized group of professionals defines a code of conduct or standards of ethical behavior by which its members must abide. For the CISSP, it is the (ISC)² Code of Ethics. The CISSP candidate must be familiar with the (ISC)² Code of Ethics and Request for Comments (RFC) 1087 "Ethics and the Internet" for professional guidance on ethics (and information that you need to know for the exam).

(ISC)² Code of Ethics

As a requirement for (ISC)² certification, all CISSP candidates must subscribe to and fully support the (ISC)² Code of Ethics. Intentionally or knowingly violating any provision of the (ISC)² Code of Ethics may subject you to a peer review panel and revocation of your hard-earned CISSP certification.

The (ISC)² Code of Ethics consists of a mandatory preamble and four mandatory canons. The canons are listed in order of precedence, thus any conflicts should be resolved in the order presented below:

1. Protect society, the commonwealth, and the infrastructure.
2. Act honorably, honestly, justly, responsibly, and legally.
3. Provide diligent and competent service to principals.
4. Advance and protect the profession.

Additional prescriptive guidance is provided for each of the canons on the (ISC)² website at www.isc2.org. You should carefully review the (ISC)² Code of Ethics and the prescriptive guidance provided on the (ISC)² website prior to taking the CISSP exam.

Internet Architecture Board (IAB) — Ethics and the Internet (RFC 1087)

Published by the Internet Architecture Board (IAB) (www.iab.org) in January 1989, RFC 1087 characterizes as unethical and unacceptable any activity that purposely

- ✔ "Seeks to gain unauthorized access to the resources of the Internet."
- ✔ "Disrupts the intended use of the Internet."
- ✔ "Wastes resources (people, capacity, computer) through such actions."
- ✔ "Destroys the integrity of computer-based information."
- ✔ "Compromises the privacy of users."

Other important tenets of RFC 1087 include

- ✔ "Access to and use of the Internet is a privilege and should be treated as such by all users of [the] system."

> ✔ "Many of the Internet resources are provided by the U.S. Government. Abuse of the system thus becomes a Federal matter above and beyond simple professional ethics."
>
> ✔ "Negligence in the conduct of Internet-wide experiments is both irresponsible and unacceptable."
>
> ✔ "In the final analysis, the health and well-being of the Internet is the responsibility of its users who must, uniformly, guard against abuses which disrupt the system and threaten its long-term viability."

Computer Ethics Institute (CEI)

The Computer Ethics Institute (CEI; http://computerethicsinstitute.org) is a nonprofit research, education, and public policy organization originally founded in 1985 by the Brookings Institution, IBM, the Washington Consulting Group, and the Washington Theological Consortium. CEI members include computer science and information technology professionals, corporate representatives, professional industry associations, public policy groups, and academia.

CEI's mission is "to provide a moral compass for cyberspace." It accomplishes this mission through computer-ethics educational activities that include publications, national conferences, membership and certificate programs, a case study repository, the Ask an Ethicist online forum, consultation, and (most famously) its "Ten Commandments of Computer Ethics," which has been published in 23 languages (presented here in English):

1. Thou shalt not use a computer to harm other people.

2. Thou shalt not interfere with other people's computer work.

3. Thou shalt not snoop around in other people's files.

4. Thou shalt not use a computer to steal.

5. Thou shalt not use a computer to bear false witness.

6. Thou shalt not use or copy software for which you have not paid.

7. Thou shalt not use other people's computer resources without authorization.

8. Thou shalt not appropriate other people's intellectual output.

9. Thou shalt think about the social consequences of the program you write.

10. Thou shalt use a computer in ways that show consideration and respect.

Prep Test

1 Penalties for conviction in a civil case can include

- **A** ○ Imprisonment
- **B** ○ Probation
- **C** ○ Fines
- **D** ○ Community service

2 Possible damages in a civil case are classified as all the following except

- **A** ○ Compensatory
- **B** ○ Punitive
- **C** ○ Statutory
- **D** ○ Financial

3 Computer attacks motivated by curiosity or excitement describe

- **A** ○ "Fun" attacks
- **B** ○ Grudge attacks
- **C** ○ Business attacks
- **D** ○ Financial attacks

4 Intellectual property includes all the following except

- **A** ○ Patents and trademarks
- **B** ○ Trade secrets
- **C** ○ Copyrights
- **D** ○ Computers

5 Under the Computer Fraud and Abuse Act of 1986 (as amended), which of the following is not considered a crime?

- **A** ○ Unauthorized access
- **B** ○ Altering, damaging, or destroying information
- **C** ○ Trafficking child pornography
- **D** ○ Trafficking computer passwords

6 Which of the following is not considered one of the four major categories of evidence?

- **A** ○ Circumstantial evidence
- **B** ○ Direct evidence
- **C** ○ Demonstrative evidence
- **D** ○ Real evidence

7 In order to be admissible in a court of law, evidence must be

A ○ Conclusive

B ○ Relevant

C ○ Incontrovertible

D ○ Immaterial

8 What term describes the evidence-gathering technique of luring an individual toward certain evidence after that individual has already committed a crime; is this considered legal or illegal?

A ○ Enticement/Legal

B ○ Coercion/Illegal

C ○ Entrapment/Illegal

D ○ Enticement/Illegal

9 In a civil case, the court may issue an order allowing a law enforcement official to seize specific evidence. This order is known as a(n)

A ○ Subpoena

B ○ Exigent circumstances doctrine

C ○ Writ of Possession

D ○ Search warrant

10 When should management be notified of a computer crime?

A ○ After the investigation has been completed

B ○ After the preliminary investigation

C ○ Prior to detection

D ○ As soon as it has been detected

Answers

1 **C.** Fines. Fines are the only penalty a jury can award in a civil case. The purpose of a fine is financial restitution to the victim. *Review "Civil penalties."*

2 **D.** Financial. Although damages in a civil case are of a financial nature, they are classified as compensatory, punitive, and statutory. *Review "Civil penalties."*

3 **A.** "Fun" attacks. Grudge attacks are motivated by revenge. Business attacks may be motivated by a number of factors, including competitive intelligence. Financial attacks are motivated by greed. *Review "Major Categories of Computer Crime."*

4 **D.** Computers. Patents and trademarks, trade secrets, and copyrights are all considered intellectual property and are protected by intellectual property rights. Computers are considered physical property. *Review "Intellectual property."*

5 **C.** Trafficking child pornography. The Child Pornography Prevention Act (CPPA) of 1996 addresses child pornography. Review *"U.S. Child Pornography Prevention Act of 1996."*

6 **A.** Circumstantial evidence. Circumstantial evidence is a type of evidence, but it's not considered one of the four main categories of evidence. In fact, circumstantial evidence may include circumstantial, direct, or demonstrative evidence. *Review "Types of evidence."*

7 **B.** Relevant. The tests for admissibility of evidence include relevance, reliability, and legal permissibility. *Review "Admissibility of evidence."*

8 **A.** Enticement/Legal. Entrapment is the act of encouraging someone to commit a crime that the individual may have had no intention of committing. Coercion involves forcing or intimidating someone to testify or confess. Enticement does raise certain ethical arguments but isn't normally illegal. *Review "Admissibility of evidence."*

9 **C.** Writ of Possession. A subpoena requires the owner to deliver evidence to the court. The exigent circumstances doctrine provides an exception to search-and-seizure rules for law enforcement officials in emergency or dangerous situations. A search warrant is issued in criminal cases. *Review "Collection and identification."*

10 **D.** As soon as it has been detected. Management should be informed of a computer crime as soon as it has been detected. Management needs to be aware of, and support, investigations and other activities that follow the detection of the crime.

Chapter 13

Physical (Environmental) Security

· ·

In This Chapter

▶ Recognizing threats to physical security

▶ Planning your site and facility design

▶ Identifying physical (environmental) security controls

▶ Using physical security concepts and controls to protect your facilities

· ·

*I*f you've already read Chapter 4, you may recall our analogy that castles are normally built in a strategic location with concentric towering walls. But what makes a location strategic, and how high is towering? Exactly where should you position the battlements and bastions? Who should guard the entrance, and what are the procedures for raising and lowering the draw-bridge? And what should you do after all the burning and pillaging? These questions fall into the realm of the Physical (Environmental) Security domain.

For the Physical (Environmental) Security domain of the Common Body of Knowledge (CBK), the Certified Information Systems Security Professional (CISSP) candidate must fully understand the various threats to physical secu-rity; the elements of site- and facility-requirements planning and design; the various physical security controls, including access controls, technical con-trols, environmental and life safety controls, and administrative controls; as well as how to support the implementation and operation of these controls, as covered in this chapter.

 Many CISSP candidates underestimate the physical security domain. As a result, exam scores are often lowest in this domain. Although much of the information in this domain may seem to be common sense, the CISSP exam does ask very specific and detailed questions about this domain, and many candidates lack practical experience in fighting fires!

Physical Security Threats

Threats to physical security come in many forms, including natural disas-ters, emergency situations, and man-made threats. All possible threats must be identified in order to perform a complete and thorough risk analysis and develop an appropriate and effective control strategy. Some of the more common threats to physical security include

✔ **Fire:** Threats from fire can be potentially devastating and lethal. Proper precautions, preparation, and training not only help limit the spread of fire and damage, but more important, can also save lives. *Saving human lives is the first priority in any life-threatening situation.* Other hazards associated with fires include smoke, explosions, building collapse, release of toxic materials or vapors, and water damage.

For a fire to burn, it requires three elements: heat, oxygen, and fuel. These three elements are sometimes referred to as the *fire triangle.* (See Figure 13-1.) Fire suppression and extinguishing systems fight fires by removing one of these three elements or by temporarily breaking up the chemical reaction between these three elements (separating the fire triangle). Fires are classified according to the fuel type, as listed in Table 13-1.

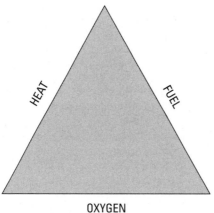

Figure 13-1:
A fire needs these three elements to burn.

Table 13-1   Fire Classes and Suppression/Extinguishing Methods

Class	Description (Fuel)	Extinguishing Method
A	Common combustibles, such as paper, wood, furniture, and clothing	Water or soda acid
B	Burnable fuels, such as gasoline or oil	CO_2, soda acid, or Halon (We discuss these methods in the section "Suppression systems," later in this chapter.)

Class	Description (Fuel)	Extinguishing Method
C	Electrical fires, such as computers or electronics	CO_2 or Halon (**Note:** The most important step to fight a fire in this class: Turn off electricity first!)
D	Special fires, such as chemical or grease fires	May require total immersion or other special techniques

Saving human lives is the first priority in any life-threatening situation.

You must be able to describe Class A, B, and C fires and their primary extinguishing methods. Class D is less common, and the CISSP exam doesn't ask about it.

✔ **Water:** Water damage (and damage from liquids, in general) can occur from many different sources, including pipe breakage, firefighting efforts, leaking roofs, spilled drinks, flooding, and tsunamis. Wet computers and other electrical equipment pose a potentially lethal hazard.

✔ **Vibration and movement:** Causes may include earthquakes, landslides, and explosions. Equipment may also be damaged by sudden or severe vibrations, falling objects, or equipment racks tipping over. More seriously, vibrations or movement may weaken structural integrity, causing a building to collapse.

✔ **Severe weather:** Includes hurricanes, tornadoes, high winds, severe thunderstorms and lightning, rain, snow, sleet, and ice. Such forces of nature may cause fires, water damage and flooding, structural damage, loss of communications and utilities, and personnel hazards.

✔ **Electricity:** Sensitive equipment can be damaged or affected by various electrical hazards and anomalies, including

  • **Electrostatic discharge (ESD):** The ideal humidity range for computer equipment is 40 to 60 percent. Higher humidity causes condensation and corrosion. Lower humidity increases the potential for ESD (static electricity). A static charge of as little as 40V (volts) can damage sensitive circuits, and 2,000V can cause a system shutdown. The minimum discharge that can be felt by humans is 3,000V, and electrostatic discharges of over 25,000V are possible — so if you can feel it, it's a problem for your equipment!

  The ideal humidity range for computer equipment is 40 to 60 percent.

  • **Electrical noise:** Includes Electromagnetic Interference (EMI) and Radio Frequency Interference (RFI). EMI is generated by the different charges between the three electrical wires (hot, neutral, and ground) and can be *common-mode noise* (caused by hot and ground) or *traverse-mode noise* (caused by a difference in power between the hot and neutral wires). RFI is caused by electrical components, such as fluorescent lighting and electric cables. A *transient* is a momentary line-noise disturbance.

- **Electrical anomalies:** These anomalies include the ones listed in Table 13-2.

Table 13-2	Electrical Anomalies
Electrical Event	*Definition*
Blackout	Total loss of power
Fault	Momentary loss of power
Brownout	Prolonged drop in voltage
Sag	Short drop in voltage
Inrush	Initial power rush
Spike	Momentary rush of power
Surge	Prolonged rush of power

You may want to come up with some meaningless mnemonic for the list in Table 13-2, such as "Bob Frequently Buys Shoes In Shoe Stores," because you need to know these terms for the CISSP exam.

- **Lightning strikes:** Approximately 10,000 fires are started every year by lightning strikes in the United States alone, despite the fact that only 20 percent of all lightning ever reaches the ground. Lightning can heat the air in immediate contact with the stroke to 54,000° Fahrenheit (F), which translates to 30,000° Celsius (C), and lightning can discharge 100,000 amperes of electrical current. Now *that's* an inrush!

It's not the volts that kill — it's the amps!

- **Magnetic fields:** Monitors and storage media can be permanently damaged or erased by magnetic fields.

✔ **Sabotage/terrorism/war/theft/vandalism:** Both internal and external threats must be considered. A heightened security posture is also prudent during certain other disruptive situations — including labor disputes, corporate downsizing, hostile terminations, bad publicity, demonstrations/protests, and civil unrest.

✔ **Equipment failure:** Equipment failures are inevitable. Maintenance and support agreements, ready spare parts, and redundant systems can mitigate the effects.

✔ **Loss of communications and utilities:** Including voice and data; electricity; and heating, ventilation, and air conditioning (HVAC). Loss of communications and utilities may happen because of any of the factors discussed in the preceding bullets, as well as human errors and mistakes.

✔ **Personnel loss:** Can happen because of illness, injury, death, transfer, labor disputes, resignations, and terminations. The negative effects of a personnel loss can be mitigated through good security practices, such as documented procedures, job rotations, cross-training, and redundant functions. (See Chapters 6 and 10 for complete discussions of these practices.)

Site and Facility Design Considerations

Astute organizations involve security professionals during the design, planning, and construction of new or renovated locations and facilities. Proper site- and facility-requirements planning during the early stages of construction helps ensure that a new building or data center is adequate, safe, and secure — all of which can help an organization avoid costly situations later.

The principles of Crime Prevention Through Environmental Design (CPTED) have been widely adopted by security practitioners in the design of public and private buildings, offices, communities, and campuses since CPTED was first published in 1971. CPTED focuses on designing facilities by using techniques such as unobstructed areas, creative lighting, and functional landscaping, which help to naturally deter crime through positive psychological effects. By making it difficult for a criminal to hide, gain access to a facility, escape a location, or otherwise perpetrate an illegal and/or violent act, such techniques may cause a would-be criminal to decide against attacking a target or victim, and help to create an environment that's perceived as (and that actually is) safer for legitimate people who regularly use the area. CPTED is comprised of three basic strategies:

✔ **Natural access control:** Uses security zones (or *defensible space*) to limit or restrict movement and differentiate between public, semi-private, and private areas that require differing levels of protection. For example, this natural access control can be accomplished by limiting points of entry into a building and using structures such as sidewalks and lighting to guide visitors to main entrances and reception areas. *Target hardening* complements natural access controls by using mechanical and/or operational controls, such as window and door locks, alarms, picture identification requirements, and visitor sign-in/out procedures.

Fixing broken windows in NYC

CPTED is the multi-disciplinary culmination of a number of works from criminologists, archaeologists, social psychologists, and many others that began in the 1960s. One of its tenets, the Broken Windows theory, was successfully put to the test by Mayor Rudy Giuliani in the early 1990s on a large scale — New York City! Mayor Giuliani's crime-fighting initiatives included cleaning vandalized subway rail cars, citing subway fare jumpers and other minor offenders, and clearing the streets of public nuisances — drunks and New York's infamous "squeegee men." These efforts demoralized and discouraged gang members and vandals who saw their subway "artwork" quickly eradicated, led to an increase in arrests because many fare jumpers and other minor offenders also had more serious criminal backgrounds, and created a safer environment for New York City's residents, commuters, and tourists. The significant reduction in crime that resulted from these and other unconventional crime-fighting methods has had a positive and enduring impact.

✔ **Natural surveillance:** Reduces criminal threats by making intruder activity more observable and easily detected. Natural surveillance can be accomplished by maximizing visibility and activity in strategic areas, for example, by placing windows to overlook streets and parking areas, landscaping to eliminate hidden areas and create clear lines of sight, installing open railings on stairways to improve visibility, and using numerous low-intensity lighting fixtures to eliminate shadows and reduce security-camera glare or blind spots (particularly at night).

✔ **Territorial reinforcement:** Creates a sense of pride and ownership, which causes intruders to more readily stand out and encourages people to report suspicious activity, instead of ignoring it. Territorial reinforcement is accomplished through maintenance activities (picking up litter, cleaning up graffiti, repairing broken windows, and replacing light bulbs), assigning individuals responsibility for an area or space, placing amenities (such as benches and water fountains) in common areas, and displaying prominent signage (where appropriate). It can also include scheduled activities, such as corporate-sponsored beautification projects and company picnics.

Choosing a secure location

Location, location, location! Although, to a certain degree, this bit of conventional business wisdom may be less important to profitability in the age of e-commerce, it's still a critical factor in physical security. Important factors when considering a location include

✔ **Climatology and natural disasters:** Although an organization is unlikely to choose a geographic location solely based on the likelihood of hurricanes or earthquakes, these factors must be considered when designing a safe and secure facility. Other related factors may include flood plains, the location of evacuation routes, and the adequacy of civil and emergency preparedness.

✔ **Local considerations:** Is the location in a high-crime area? Are hazards nearby, such as hazardous materials storage, railway freight lines, or flight paths for the local airport? Is the area heavily industrialized (will air and noise pollution, including vibration, affect your systems)?

✔ **Visibility:** Will your employees and facilities be targeted for crime, terrorism, or vandalism? Is the site near another high-visibility organization that may attract undesired attention? Is your facility located near a government or military target? Keeping a low profile is generally best because you avoid unwanted and unneeded attention; avoid external building markings, if possible.

✔ **Accessibility:** Consider local traffic patterns, convenience to airports, proximity to emergency services (police, fire, and medical facilities), and availability of adequate housing. For example, will on-call employees have to drive for an hour to respond when your organization needs them?

✔ **Utilities:** Where is the facility located in the power grid? Is electrical power stable and clean? Is sufficient fiber optic cable already in place to support telecommunications requirements?

✔ **Joint tenants:** Will you have full access to all necessary environmental controls? Can (and should) physical security costs and responsibilities be shared between joint tenants? Are other tenants potential high-visibility targets? Do other tenants take security as seriously as your organization?

Designing a secure facility

Many of the physical and technical controls that we discuss in the section "Physical (Environmental) Security Controls" later in this chapter, should be considered during the initial design of a secure facility. Doing so often helps reduce the costs and improves the overall effectiveness of these controls. Other building design considerations include

✔ **Exterior walls:** Ideally, exterior walls should be able to withstand high winds (tornadoes and hurricanes/typhoons) and reduce electronic emanations that can be detected and used to re-create high-value data (for example government or military data). If possible, exterior windows should be avoided throughout the building, particularly on lower levels. Metal bars over windows or reinforced windows on lower levels may be necessary. Any windows should be *fixed* (meaning you can't open them), shatterproof, and sufficiently opaque to conceal inside activities.

✔ **Interior walls:** Interior walls adjacent to secure or restricted areas must extend from the floor to the ceiling (through raised flooring and drop ceilings) and must comply with applicable building and fire codes. Walls adjacent to storage areas (such as closets containing janitorial supplies, paper, media, or other flammable materials) must meet minimum fire ratings, which are typically higher than for other interior walls. Ideally, Kevlar (bulletproof) walls should protect the most sensitive areas.

✔ **Floors:** Flooring (both slab and raised) must be capable of bearing loads in accordance with local building codes (typically 150 pounds per square foot). Additionally, raised flooring must have a nonconductive surface and be properly grounded to reduce personnel safety risks.

✔ **Ceilings:** Weight-bearing and fire ratings must be considered. Drop ceilings may temporarily conceal intruders and small water leaks; conversely, stained drop-ceiling tiles can reveal leaks while temporarily impeding water damage.

✔ **Doors:** Doors and locks must be sufficiently strong and well-designed to resist forcible entry, and they need a fire rating equivalent to adjacent walls. Emergency exits must remain unlocked from the inside and should also be clearly marked, as well as monitored or alarmed. Electronic lock mechanisms and other access control devices should fail open (unlock) in the event of an emergency to permit people to exit the building. Many doors swing out to facilitate emergency exiting; thus door hinges are located on the outside of the room or building. These hinges must be properly secured to prevent an intruder from easily lifting hinge pins and removing the door.

✔ **Lighting:** Exterior lighting for all physical spaces and buildings in the security perimeter (including entrances and parking areas) should be sufficient to provide safety for personnel, as well as to discourage prowlers and casual intruders.

✔ **Wiring:** All wiring, conduits, and cable runs must comply with building and fire codes, and be properly protected. Plenum cabling must be used below raised floors and above drop ceilings because PVC-clad cabling releases toxic chemicals when it burns.

A *plenum* is the vacant area above a drop ceiling or below a raised floor. A fire in these areas can spread very rapidly and can carry smoke and fumes to other areas of a burning building. For this reason, non-PVC-coated cabling, known as *plenum cabling*, must be used in these areas.

- **Electricity and HVAC:** Electrical load and HVAC requirements must be carefully planned to ensure that sufficient power is available in the right locations and that proper climate ranges (temperature and humidity) are maintained. We discuss additional controls in the section "Environmental and life safety controls," later in this chapter.

- **Pipes:** Locations of shutoff valves for water, steam, or gas pipes should be identified and appropriately marked. Drains should have *positive flow,* meaning they carry drainage away from the building.

Physical (Environmental) Security Controls

Physical (environmental) security controls include a combination of physical access controls, technical controls, environmental and life safety controls, fire detection and suppression, and administrative controls.

Physical access controls

Physical access controls consist of the systems and techniques used to restrict access to a security perimeter and provide boundary protection, including fencing, security guards, dogs, locks, storage areas, security badges, and biometric access controls.

Fencing

Fencing is the primary means for securing an outside perimeter or external boundary and an important element of physical security that the CISSP candidate must know for the exam. Fencing provides physical access control and includes fences, gates, turnstiles, and mantraps. The main disadvantages of fencing are cost and appearance. General height requirements for fencing are listed in Table 13-3.

Table 13-3	General Fencing Height Requirements
Height	**General Effect**
3–4 ft (1m)	Deters casual trespassers
6–7 ft (2m)	Too high to climb easily
8 ft (2.4m) + three-strand barbed wire	Deters more determined intruders

Mantraps

A *mantrap* is a method of physical access control that consists of a double set of locked doors or turnstiles. The mantrap may be guarded or monitored, may require a different level of access to pass through each door or in a different direction (for example, exit may be permitted at all times, but entry after normal business hours is restricted to only certain people). In more advanced systems, the mantrap may have a weight-sensing floor to prevent more than one person from passing through at the same time.

Security guards

Throughout history, guards have provided physical security for many different situations and environments. You might think that modern surveillance equipment, biometric access controls, and intrusion detection systems (IDSs) would have diminished the role of security guards, but these tools have actually increased the need for skilled physical-security personnel who are capable of operating advanced technology and applying discerning judgment. The major advantages of security guards include

- ✔ **Discernment:** Guards can apply human judgment to different situations.
- ✔ **Visibility:** Guards provide a visible deterrent, response, and control capability.
- ✔ **Multiple functions:** Guards can also perform reception and visitor escort functions.

Some disadvantages include

- ✔ **Unpredictability:** Pre-employment screening and bonding doesn't necessarily assure reliability or integrity.
- ✔ **Imperfections:** Along with human judgment comes the element of human error.
- ✔ **Cost:** Maintaining a full-time security force (including training) or outsourcing these functions can be very expensive.

The main advantage of security guards is their ability to use human judgment when responding to different situations.

Guard dogs

Like human guards, dogs also provide a highly visible deterrent, response, and control capability. Additionally, guard dogs are typically more loyal and reliable than humans, with more acute sensory abilities (smell and hearing). However, the use of guard dogs is typically restricted to an outside security perimeter. Other considerations include

- ✔ Limited judgment capability
- ✔ Cost and maintenance
- ✔ Potential liability issues

Locks

Doors, windows, and other access points into secure or sensitive areas need to be protected. One of the simplest ways to accomplish this protection is by using a lock. The three basic types of locks are

- ✔ **Preset:** Basic mechanical locks that consist of latches, cylinders, and deadbolts; each requires a particular key to open it.
- ✔ **Programmable:** Mechanical (such as dial combination or five-key push-button) or electronic (cipher lock or keypad). *Shoulder surfing,* a social-engineering technique commonly used against these types of locks, involves casually observing an authorized individual entering an access code.
- ✔ **Electronic:** These locks utilize an electronic key (similar to the fancy keys found on expensive cars) that functions like both a hybrid smart card (covered in the section "Security badges," later in this chapter) and a physical key.

Storage areas

Storage areas that contain spare equipment and parts, consumables, and deliveries should be locked and controlled to help prevent theft. Additionally, you should be aware of any hazardous materials being stored in such areas, as well as any environmental factors or restrictions that may affect the contents of the storage area.

Security badges

Security badges (or access cards) are used for identification and authentication of authorized personnel entering a secure facility or area.

A *photo identification card* (also referred to as a *dumb card*) is a simple ID card that has a facial photograph of the bearer. Typically, no technology is embedded in these cards for authentication purposes, so a security guard determines whether to allow the bearer to enter.

Smart cards are digitally encoded cards that contain an integrated chip (IC) or magnetic stripe (possibly in addition to a photo). Various types of smart cards include

- **Magnetic stripe:** The most basic type of smart card. Information is encoded in a magnetic stripe. Common examples include credit cards and automatic teller machine (ATM) cards.

- **Optical-coded:** Similar to, but more reliable than, a magnetic stripe card. Information is encoded in a laser-burned lattice of digital dots. These types of smart cards are becoming more common on U.S. state driver's licenses.

- **Smart card:** Contains printed electrical contacts on the card surface; electric circuit smart cards are true smart cards in that they do more than just identify the user and carry limited personal information, they actually contain information that permits the user to perform a job function and are commonly used for logical access control to computer systems.

- **Proximity card:** Doesn't require the bearer to physically insert the card into the reader. Instead, the reader senses the card in the general area and takes the appropriate action. The three common types of system-sensing proximity cards are

  - **Passive:** These cards don't contain any sort of electrical power supply (such as a battery). They use the electromagnetic field transmitted by the reader to transmit access information (identification).

  - **Field-powered:** These devices contain active electronics, an RF transmitter, and power supply on the card.

  - **Transponders:** Both the card and reader contain a transceiver, control logic, and battery. The reader transmits an interrogating signal (challenge), causing the card to transmit an access code (response).

Although more common in technical access controls, smart cards can also provide two-factor authentication in physical access control systems by requiring the user to enter a personal identification number (PIN) or password, or by incorporating an authentication token or other challenge-response mechanism.

See Chapter 4 for a complete description of the different types of access controls. Smart cards, and their associated access control systems, can be programmed to permit multilevel access, restrict access to certain periods (days and times), and log access information.

Smart card is used as a general term to describe any security badge or access card that has built-in identification and authentication features, such as embedded technology. This may be as simple as a magnetic stripe on an ID card that's swiped through a card reader. However, in the Access Control domain, a *smart card* refers to a very specific, highly specialized type of access card: A magnetic stripe doesn't qualify.

Biometric access controls

Biometrics provide the only absolute method for positively identifying an individual based on some unique physiological or behavioral characteristic of that individual (something you are). We discuss biometrics extensively in Chapter 4. Although biometrics in the Physical (Environmental) Security domain refers to *physical* access control devices (rather than *logical* access control devices, as in the Access Control domain), the underlying concepts and technologies are the same. The major biometric systems in use today include

- Finger scan
- Hand geometry
- Retina pattern
- Iris pattern
- Voice recognition
- Signature dynamics

The accuracy of a biometric system is normally stated as a percentage, in the following terms:

- **False Reject Rate (FRR) or Type I error:** Authorized users who are incorrectly denied access
- **False Accept Rate (FAR) or Type II error:** Unauthorized users who are incorrectly granted access
- **Crossover Error Rate (CER):** The point at which the FRR equals the FAR

Technical controls

Technical controls include monitoring and surveillance, intrusion detection systems (IDSs), and alarms that alert personnel to physical security threats and allow them to respond appropriately.

Surveillance

Visual surveillance systems include photographic and electronic equipment that provides detective and deterrent controls. When used to monitor or record live events, they're a detective control. The visible use of these systems also provides a deterrent control.

Electronic systems such as closed-circuit television (CCTV) can extend and improve the monitoring and surveillance capability of security guards. Photographic systems, including recording equipment, record events for later analysis or as evidence for disciplinary action and prosecution.

Intrusion detection

Intrusion detection in the physical security domain refers to systems that detect attempts to gain unauthorized physical access to a building or area. Modern intrusion detection systems (IDSs) commonly use the following types of sensors:

- ✔ **Photoelectric sensors:** A grid of visible or infrared light is projected over the protected area. If a beam of light within the grid is disturbed, an alarm sounds.

- ✔ **Dry contact switches and metallic tape:** These systems are inexpensive and commonly used along a perimeter or boundary on door and window frames. For example, if the circuit switch is opened or the metallic tape broken, an alarm sounds.

- ✔ **Motion detectors:** Three categories of motion detectors are

  - **Wave pattern:** Generates a low-frequency, ultrasonic, or microwave field over a protected area up to 10,000 square feet (3,000 square meters). Any motion changes the frequency of the reflected wave pattern, causing an alarm to sound.

  - **Capacitance:** Monitors an electrical field for changes in electrical capacitance caused by motion. This type of motion detector is typically used for spot protection within a few inches of a protected object.

  - **Audio:** A *passive system* (meaning it doesn't generate a wave pattern or electrical field) triggered by any abnormal sound. This type of device generates a lot of false alarms and should be used only in areas that have low ambient noise.

Don't confuse intrusion detection systems (IDSs) used to detect physical intruders in the Physical (Environmental) Security domain with network-based and host-based intrusion detection systems (IDSs) (discussed in Chapters 5 and 10) used to detect cyber-intruders.

Alarms

Alarms are activated when a certain condition is detected. Examples of systems employing alarms include fire and smoke detectors, motion sensors and intrusion detection systems (IDSs), metal and explosives detectors, access control systems (physical and logical), detectors geared towards certain environmental conditions (standing water, for instance), and climate-control monitoring systems.

Alarm systems should have separate circuitry and a backup power source. *Line supervision,* comprising technology and processes used to detect attempts to tamper with or disable an alarm system, should also be implemented.

The five general types of alarm systems are

- ✔ **Local systems:** An audible alarm sounds on the local premises. These systems require a *local response capability,* meaning someone must call the police/fire department and/or respond directly.

- ✔ **Central station systems:** Operated and monitored by private security organizations connected directly to the protected site via leased or dial-up lines.

- ✔ **Proprietary systems:** Similar to central station systems, but operated and monitored directly on the premises.

- ✔ **Auxiliary station systems:** These systems — which require prior authorization — use local municipal police or fire circuits to transmit an alarm to the appropriate police or fire headquarters. These systems are typically used in conjunction with one of the systems discussed in the preceding bullets (particularly central station systems) to improve response capabilities.

- ✔ **Remote station systems:** These systems are similar to auxiliary station systems, except they don't use police and fire circuits, and also don't necessarily send the alarm to a police or fire department. An automatic dial-up fire alarm that dials a local police or fire department and plays a prerecorded message is an example of a remote station system.

Environmental and life safety controls

These controls are necessary for maintaining a safe and acceptable operating environment for computers and personnel. These controls include electrical power, HVAC, smoke detection, and fire detection and suppression.

Electrical power

General considerations for electrical power include having one or more dedicated feeders from one or more utility substations or power grids, as well as ensuring that adequate physical access controls are implemented for electrical distribution panels and circuit breakers. An Emergency Power Off (EPO) switch should be installed near major systems and exit doors to shut down power in case of fire or electrical shock. Additionally, a backup power source should be established, such as a diesel or natural-gas power generator. Backup power should only be provided for critical facilities and systems, including emergency lighting, fire detection and suppression, mainframes and servers (and certain workstations), HVAC, physical access control systems, and telecommunications equipment.

Although natural gas can be a cleaner alternative than diesel for backup power, in terms of air and noise pollution, it's generally not acceptable for emergency life systems (such as emergency lighting and fire protection systems) because the fuel source (natural gas) can't be locally stored, so the system relies instead on an external fuel source that must be supplied by pipelines.

Protective controls for electrostatic discharge (ESD), discussed in the earlier section "Physical Security Threats," include

- ✔ Maintain proper humidity levels (40 to 60 percent).
- ✔ Ensure proper grounding.
- ✔ Use anti-static flooring, anti-static carpeting, and floor mats.

Protective controls for electrical noise include

- ✔ Install power line conditioners.
- ✔ Ensure proper grounding.
- ✔ Use shielded cabling.

Using an Uninterruptible Power Supply (UPS) is perhaps the most important protection against electrical anomalies. A UPS provides clean power to sensitive systems and a temporary power source during electrical outages (blackouts, brownouts, and sags); this power supply must be sufficient to properly shut down the protected systems. *Note:* A UPS shouldn't be used as a backup power source. A UPS — even a building UPS — is designed to provide temporary power, typically for 5 to 30 minutes, in order to give a backup generator time to start up or to allow a controlled and proper shutdown of protected systems.

Surge protectors and surge suppressors provide only minimal protection for sensitive computer systems, and they're more commonly (and dangerously) used to overload an electrical outlet or as a daisy-chained extension cord. The protective circuitry in most of these units costs less than one dollar (compare the cost of a low-end surge protector with that of a 6-foot extension cord), and you get what you pay for — these glorified extension cords provide only minimal spike protection. True, a surge protector does provide more protection than nothing at all, but don't be lured into complacency by these units — check them regularly for proper use and operation, and don't accept them as a viable alternative to a UPS.

HVAC

Heating, ventilation, and air conditioning (HVAC) systems maintain the proper environment for computers and personnel. HVAC-requirements planning involves complex calculations based on numerous factors, including the average BTUs (British Thermal Units) produced by the estimated computers and personnel occupying a given area, the size of the room, insulation characteristics, and ventilation systems.

The ideal temperature range for computer equipment is between 50 and 80°F (10 and 26°C). At temperatures as low as 100°F (38°C), magnetic storage media can be damaged.

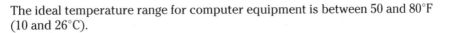

The ideal temperature range for computer equipment is between 50 and 80°F (10 and 26°C).

The ideal humidity range for computer equipment is between 40 and 60 percent. Higher humidity causes condensation and corrosion. Lower humidity increases the potential for ESD (static electricity).

Doors and side panels on computer equipment racks should be kept closed (and locked, as a form of physical access control) to ensure proper airflow for cooling and ventilation. When possible, empty spaces in equipment racks (such as a half-filled rack or gaps between installed equipment) should be covered with blanking panels to reduce hot and cold air mixing between the hot side (typically the power-supply side of the equipment) and the cold side (typically the front of the equipment); such mixing of hot and cold air can reduce the efficiency of cooling systems.

Heating and cooling systems should be properly maintained, and air filters should be cleaned regularly to reduce dust contamination and fire hazards.

Most gas-discharge fire suppression systems automatically shut down HVAC systems prior to discharging, but a separate Emergency Power Off (EPO) switch should be installed near exits to facilitate a manual shutdown in an emergency.

Ideally, HVAC equipment should be dedicated, controlled, and monitored. If the systems aren't dedicated or independently controlled, proper liaison with the building manager is necessary to ensure that everyone knows who to call when there are problems. Monitoring systems should alert the appropriate personnel when operating thresholds are exceeded.

Fire detection and suppression

Fire detection and suppression systems are some of the most essential life safety controls for protecting facilities, equipment, and (most important) human lives.

Detection systems

The three main types of fire detection systems are

- **Heat-sensing:** These devices sense either temperatures exceeding a predetermined level *(fixed-temperature detectors)* or rapidly rising temperatures *(rate-of-rise detectors)*. Fixed-temperature detectors are more common and exhibit a lower false-alarm rate than rate-of-rise detectors.

- **Flame-sensing:** These devices sense either the flicker (or pulsing) of flames or the infrared energy of a flame. These systems are relatively expensive but provide an extremely rapid response time.

- **Smoke-sensing:** These devices detect smoke, one of the by-products of fire. The four types of smoke detectors are

  - **Photoelectric:** Sense variations in light intensity

  - **Beam:** Similar to photoelectric; sense when smoke interrupts beams of light

  - **Ionization:** Detect disturbances in the normal ionization current of radioactive materials

  - **Aspirating:** Draw air into a sampling chamber to detect minute amounts of smoke

The three main types of fire detection systems are heat-sensing, flame-sensing, and smoke-sensing.

Suppression systems

The two primary types of fire suppression systems are

- **Water sprinkler systems:** Water extinguishes fire by removing the heat element from the fire triangle, and it's most effective against Class A fires. Water is the primary fire-extinguishing agent for all business environments. Although water can potentially damage equipment, it's one of the most effective, inexpensive, readily available, and least harmful (to humans) extinguishing agents available. The four variations of water sprinkler systems are

  - **Wet-pipe (or closed-head):** Most commonly used and considered the most reliable. Pipes are always charged with water and ready for activation. Typically, a fusible link in the nozzle melts or ruptures, opening a gate valve that releases the water flow. Disadvantages include flooding because of nozzle or pipe failure and because of frozen pipes in cold weather.

- **Dry-pipe:** No standing water in the pipes. At activation, a clapper valve opens, air is blown out of the pipe, and water flows. This type of system is less efficient than the wet pipe system but reduces the risk of accidental flooding; the time delay provides an opportunity to shut down computer systems (or remove power), if conditions permit.

- **Deluge:** Operates similarly to a dry-pipe system but is designed to deliver large volumes of water quickly. Deluge systems are typically not used for computer-equipment areas.

- **Preaction:** Combines wet- and dry-pipe systems. Pipes are initially dry. When a heat sensor is triggered, the pipes are charged with water, and an alarm is activated. Water isn't actually discharged until a fusible link melts (as in wet-pipe systems). This system is recommended for computer-equipment areas because it reduces the risk of accidental discharge by permitting manual intervention.

The four main types of water sprinkler systems are wet-pipe, dry-pipe, deluge, and preaction.

✔ **Gas discharge systems:** Gas discharge systems may be portable (such as a CO_2 extinguisher) or fixed (beneath a raised floor). These systems are typically classified according to the extinguishing agent that's employed. These agents include

- **Carbon dioxide (CO_2):** CO_2 is a commonly used colorless, odorless gas that extinguishes fire by removing the oxygen element from the fire triangle. (Refer to Figure 13-1.) CO_2 is most effective against Class B and C fires. Because it removes oxygen, its use is potentially lethal and therefore best suited for unmanned areas or with a delay action (that includes manual override) in manned areas.

  CO_2 is also used in portable fire extinguishers, which should be located near all exits and within 50 feet (15 meters) of any electrical equipment. All portable fire extinguishers (CO_2, water, and soda acid) should be clearly marked (listing the extinguisher type and the fire classes it can be used for) and periodically inspected. Additionally, all personnel should receive training in the proper use of fire extinguishers.

- **Soda acid:** Includes a variety of chemical compounds that extinguish fires by removing the fuel element (suppressing the flammable components of the fuel) of the fire triangle. (Refer to Figure 13-1.) Soda acid is most effective against Class A and B fires. It is not used for Class C fires because of the highly corrosive nature of many of the chemicals used.

- **Gas-discharge:** Gas-discharge systems suppress fire by separating the elements of the fire triangle (a chemical reaction); they are most effective against Class B and C fires. (Refer to Figure 13-1.) Inert gases don't damage computer equipment, don't leave liquid or solid residue, mix thoroughly with the air, and spread extremely quickly. However, these gases in concentrations higher than 10 percent are harmful if inhaled, and some types degrade into toxic chemicals (hydrogen fluoride, hydrogen bromide, and bromine) when used on fires that burn at temperatures above 900°F (482°C).

Halon used to be the gas of choice in gas-discharge fire suppression systems. However, because of Halon's ozone-depleting characteristics, the Montreal Protocol of 1987 prohibited the further production and installation of Halon systems (beginning in 1994) and encouraging the replacement of existing systems. Acceptable replacements for Halon include FM-200 (most effective), CEA-410 or CEA-308, NAF-S-III, FE-13, Argon or Argonite, and Inergen.

Halon is an ozone-depleting substance. Acceptable replacements include FM-200, CEA-410 or CEA-308, NAF-S-III, FE-13, Argon or Argonite, and Inergen.

Administrative controls

These controls include the policies and procedures necessary to ensure that physical access controls, technical controls, and environmental and life safety controls are properly implemented and achieve an overall physical security strategy.

Restricted areas

Areas in which sensitive information is handled or processed should be formally designated as restricted areas, with additional security controls implemented. Restricted areas should be clearly marked, and all employees should know the difference between authorized and unauthorized personnel — specifically, how to detect whether someone on the premises is authorized.

Visitors

Visitor policies and escort requirements should be clearly defined in the organizational security policy. Any visitor should be required to present proper identification to a security guard or receptionist, sign a visitor log, complete a nondisclosure agreement (when appropriate), and wear a conspicuous badge that both identifies him or her as a visitor and clearly indicates whether an escort is required (often done with color-coded badges). If an escort is required, the assigned escort should be identified by name and held responsible for the visitor at all times while that visitor is on the premises.

Personnel Privacy

Organizations need to clearly define their privacy policy for employees. Work and personal lives have become increasingly commingled in our "always-connected" world and individual expectations of privacy on the job may not be consistent with the security needs of the organization. Organizations that actively monitor their networks and connected devices — including personal devices used in the workplace — must ensure that employees are aware of and consent to workplace monitoring and that their privacy rights are understood.

Safety

Organizations need to implement appropriate safeguards to create a safe working environment for all employees. Additionally, organizations need to ensure that employees are aware of increased risks when traveling, such as crime, duress, terrorism, and accidents, and that they know the appropriate safeguards to ensure their personal safety and to protect both personal and company property.

Audit trails and access logs

Audit trails and access logs are detective controls that provide a record of events. These records can be analyzed for unauthorized access attempts and patterns of abuse; they can also potentially be used as evidence. We cover audit trails in Chapter 10.

Asset classification and control

Asset classification and control, particularly physical inventories, are an important detective control. The proliferation of desktop PCs, notebooks, smartphones, tablets, and wireless devices has made theft a very common and difficult physical security threat to counter. An accurate inventory helps identify missing equipment and may potentially be used as evidence.

Emergency procedures

Emergency procedures must be clearly documented, readily accessible (often posted in appropriate areas), periodically updated, and routinely practiced (in training and drills). Additional copies may also be kept at secure off-site facilities. Emergency procedures should include emergency system shutdown procedures, evacuation plans and routes, and a Business Continuity Plan/Disaster Recovery Plan (BCP/DRP). (We cover BCP/DRP in Chapter 11.)

General housekeeping

Good housekeeping practices are an important aspect of physical security controls. Implementing and enforcing a no-smoking policy helps reduce not only potential fire hazards, but also contamination of sensitive systems. Cleaning dust and ventilation systems helps maintain a cleaner computing environment and also reduces static electricity and fire hazards. Keeping work areas clean and trash emptied reduces potential fire hazards (by removing combustibles) and also helps identify and locate sensitive information that may have been improperly or carelessly handled.

Pre-employment and post-employment procedures

These procedures include background and reference checks, obtaining security clearances, granting access, and termination procedures. These procedures are covered extensively in Chapters 6 and 10.

Bringing It All Together

After you understand the various threats to physical security and the tools and countermeasures available, consider where these controls may need to be implemented in your organization.

At the organization's perimeter, which may include adjacent buildings or grounds, parking lots, and possibly a moat — well, that's a stretch — physical security threats may include fire, water, vibration and movement, severe weather, sabotage and vandalism, and loss of communications or utilities.

And, of course, you were involved in the initial site selection and facility design planning when your building was built so you have no problem securing the perimeter, right? Well, for the other 99 percent of people who weren't so fortunate and have to address physical security in a preexisting location and facility, begin by assessing which threats are most relevant — and how to mitigate associated risks. Consider recommending physical security controls at the perimeter, such as fencing, security guards, dogs, surveillance, and alarms, when applicable. If these controls already exist, ensure that they're adequate and assessed regularly. If physical security isn't part of your responsibility, ensure that you have a good working relationship with whoever is responsible. Know who to call in an emergency (fire, police, and utilities) and don't be a stranger — establish working relationships with these professionals *before* you need their help! Recommend appropriate security technologies that support physical and environmental security controls.

Interior security deals with . . . the inside of your facility! Many of the same physical security threats that affect the perimeter also affect the interior, but often in very different ways. A fire can be a far more life-threatening emergency inside a facility than outside. Water damage may come from sources other than a flash flood, such as your own fire suppression system.

Again, under ideal circumstances, your employer's interior designer consulted with a CISSP, but more often than not, you have some work to do in this area as well! Consider the various aspects of the facility when you recommend interior controls, including the interior walls, ceilings, floors, doors, and storage areas. And don't forget the lighting, electrical wiring, physical cabling, ventilation systems, and pipes.

Various controls for interior security may include locks, restricted areas, security badges, biometric access controls, surveillance, intrusion detection, motion detectors, alarms, and fire detection and suppression systems.

Operations, facility and equipment security involve addressing many of the same threats as interior security and supporting many of the same security controls and countermeasures, but with a specific focus on how these threats may adversely affect your business and computer operations. Administrative controls, such as designating restricted areas, visitor policies, audit trails and access logs, and asset classification and control, are particularly important.

Prep Test

1 The three elements of the fire triangle necessary for a fire to burn include all the following except

- A ○ Fuel
- B ○ Oxygen
- C ○ Heat
- D ○ Nitrogen

2 Electrical fires are classified as what type of fire and use what extinguishing methods?

- A ○ Class B; CO_2 or soda acid
- B ○ Class B; CO_2 or FM-200
- C ○ Class C; CO_2 or FM-200
- D ○ Class A; water or soda acid

3 A prolonged drop in voltage describes what electrical anomaly?

- A ○ Brownout
- B ○ Blackout
- C ○ Sag
- D ○ Fault

4 What type of cabling should be used below raised floors and above drop ceilings?

- A ○ CAT-5
- B ○ Plenum
- C ○ PVC
- D ○ Water-resistant

5 In order to deter casual trespassers, fencing should be a minimum height of

- A ○ 1 to 3 feet
- B ○ 3 to 4 feet
- C ○ 6 to 7 feet
- D ○ 8 feet or higher

6 Three types of intrusion detection systems (IDSs) used for physical security include photoelectric sensors, dry contact switches, and which of the following?

A ○ Motion detectors
B ○ Anomaly-based
C ○ Host-based
D ○ Network-based

7 A water sprinkler system in which no water is initially present in the pipes and which, at activation, delivers a large volume of water describes what type of system?

A ○ Wet-pipe
B ○ Dry-pipe
C ○ Deluge
D ○ Preaction

8 Portable CO_2 fire extinguishers are classified as what type of extinguishing system?

A ○ Gas-discharge systems
B ○ Water sprinkler systems
C ○ Deluge systems
D ○ Preaction systems

9 Which of the following extinguishing agents fights fires by separating the elements of the fire triangle, rather than by simply removing one element?

A ○ Water
B ○ Soda acid
C ○ CO_2
D ○ FM-200

10 Production of Halon has been banned for what reason?

A ○ It is toxic at temperatures above 900°F.
B ○ It is an ozone-depleting substance.
C ○ It is ineffective.
D ○ It is harmful if inhaled.

Answers

1 **D.** Nitrogen. The fire triangle consists of fuel, oxygen, and heat. *Review "Physical Security Threats."*

2 **C.** Class C; CO_2 or FM-200. Class B fires consist of burnable fuels and are extinguished by using CO_2, soda acid, or FM-200. Class A fires consist of common combustible materials. *Review "Physical Security Threats."*

3 **A.** Brownout. A blackout is a total loss of power, a sag is a short drop in voltage, and a fault is a momentary loss of power. *Review "Physical Security Threats."*

4 **B.** Plenum. Cat 5 cabling can be either plenum or PVC-coated. PVC cabling releases toxic vapors when burned. Both PVC and plenum coatings are water resistant. *Review "Designing a secure facility."*

5 **B.** 3 to 4 feet. Fencing of 1 to 3 feet might deter a toddler or a duck! 6 to 7 feet is too high to climb easily. Eight-foot-tall or higher fencing (that includes three-strand barbed wire at the top) can deter a more determined intruder. *Review "Fencing."*

6 **A.** Motion detectors. Anomaly-based, host-based, and network-based systems are types of intrusion detection systems (IDSs) used for computer systems and networks. *Review "Intrusion detection."*

7 **C.** Deluge. A wet-pipe system always has water present in the pipes. A dry-pipe system is similar to a deluge system but doesn't deliver a large volume of water. A preaction system combines elements of both wet- and dry-pipe systems. *Review "Suppression systems."*

8 **A.** Gas-discharge systems. Water sprinkler systems are fixed systems that discharge water. Deluge and preaction systems are types of water sprinkler systems. *Review "Suppression systems."*

9 **D.** FM-200. Water fights fires by removing the heat element. Soda acid fights fires by suppressing the fuel element. CO_2 fights fires by removing the oxygen element. *Review "Suppression systems."*

10 **B.** It is an ozone-depleting substance. Halon does release toxic chemicals at temperatures above 900°F and is harmful if inhaled in concentrations greater than 10 percent, but its production wasn't banned for these reasons. *Review "Suppression systems."*

Part III
The Part of Tens

The 5th Wave   By Rich Tennant

"We sort of have our own way of mentally preparing our people to take the CISSP exam."

In this part . . .

Ya know 'em, ya love 'em. These short chapters include ten key ideas apiece that can help make your exam and certification experience be a successful one. Read the chapter title, and then savor the wisdom on the pages.

Chapter 14

Ten (Okay, Eight) Test Preparation Tips

● ●

*S*o much information, so little time! In this chapter, we recommend nine tips for helping you prepare for that special day. (No, not *that* special day; read *Wedding Planning For Dummies,* by Marcy Blum and Laura F. Kaiser [Wiley], for that one.) We're talking about the CISSP exam here.

Get a Networking Certification First

The Telecommunications and Network Security domain is the most comprehensive domain tested on the Certified Information Systems Security Professional (CISSP) exam. Although its purpose is to test your security knowledge, you must have a complete understanding of telecommunications and networking basics. For this reason, we strongly advise that you earn a networking certification, such as the CompTIA Network+ or the Cisco Certified Network Associate (CCNA), before attempting the CISSP exam. (For more information on these certifications, see www.comptia.org and www.cisco.com, respectively.) An additional benefit is that you then have another valuable technical certification in high demand within the computer industry.

If you already have one of these certifications, you should find most of the information in the Telecommunications and Network Security domain to be very basic. In this case, a quick review that focuses on security concepts (particularly methods of attack) should be sufficient for this domain. We dedicate Chapter 5 of this book to the Telecommunications and Network Security domain.

If you haven't taken a computer-based examination before, getting a networking certification first will also help familiarize you with the testing center location and environment, as well as the general format of computer-based exams. You can take a generic practice computer-based exam to get used to how they work, at www.pearsonvue.com or a CISSP practice computer-based exam at www.dummies.com/go/cisspfd4e.

Register NOW!

Go online and register for the CISSP exam at www.pearsonvue.com/isc2/ — NOW!

Committing yourself to a test date is the best cure for procrastination, especially because the test costs $599 (U.S.)! Setting your date can help you plan and focus your study efforts.

Make a 60-Day Study Plan

After you register for the CISSP exam, commit yourself to a 60-day study plan. Of course, your work experience and professional reading should span a much greater period, but for your final preparations leading up to the CISSP exam, plan on a 60-day period of intense study.

Exactly how intensely you study depends on your personal experience and learning ability, but plan on a minimum of 2 hours a day for 60 days. If you're a slow learner or reader, or perhaps find yourself weak in many areas, plan on 4 to 6 hours a day and more on the weekends. Regardless, try to stick to the 60-day plan. If you feel that you need 360 hours of study, you might be tempted to spread this out over a 6-month period for 2 hours a day. But committing to 6 months of intense study is much harder (on you, as well as your family and friends) than committing to 2 months. In the end, you'll find yourself studying only as much as you would have in a 60-day period.

Get Organized and READ!

A wealth of security information is available for the CISSP candidate. However, studying everything is impractical. Instead, get organized, determine your strengths and weaknesses, and then READ!

Begin by downloading the free, official *CISSP Candidate Information Bulletin* from the (ISC)² website (www.isc2.org). This bulletin provides a good outline of the subjects on which you'll be tested.

Next, read this book, take the practice exam, and review the materials on the Dummies website (www.dummies.com/go/cisspfd4e). *CISSP For Dummies,* 4th Edition, is written to provide the CISSP candidate with an excellent overview of all the broad topics covered on the CISSP exam.

Next, focus on the areas that you identify as your weakest. Read or review additional references — the (ISC)² website lists numerous resources at `https://resourceguide.isc2.org`.

Finally, in the last week before your exam, go through all your selected study materials at least once. Review or read *CISSP For Dummies,* 4th Edition, one more time, as well as your personal study notes, and complete as many practice questions as you can.

Taking the time to make flash cards and review them each day during slow times — such as when riding the bus or train — is a great way to help you study. You not only learn through repetition (looking at the cards over and over), but by making the cards themselves.

Join a Study Group

You can find strength in numbers. Joining a study group or creating your own can help you stay focused and provide a wealth of information from the broad perspectives and experiences of other security professionals. You can find a study group, discussion forums, and many other helpful resources at `www.cccure.org`.

Also, your local (ISC)² chapter or a chapter of the Information Systems Security Association (ISSA) may be sponsoring CISSP study groups. You can find their contact information at `www.issa.org`.

Take Practice Exams

No practice exams are available that exactly duplicate the CISSP exam. And forget about brain dumps (actual test questions and answers that others have unscrupulously posted on the Internet) — in addition to possibly being wrong, brain dumps violate the CISSP exam's non-disclosure agreement. However, many resources are available for practice questions. You may find some practice questions too hard, others too easy, and some just plain irrelevant. Despite that, the repetition of practice questions can help reinforce important information that you need to know in order to successfully answer questions on the CISSP exam. For this reason, we recommend taking as many practice exams as possible and using the results to help you focus on your weak areas. Use the Practice Test on the Dummies website (`www.dummies.com/go/cisspfd4e`), and try the CISSP Quizzes on the CISSP Open Study Group website (`www.cccure.org`).

Take a CISSP Review Seminar

You can take an official (ISC)² CISSP Review or Live OnLine Seminar. The Review seminar is an intense, five-day session that definitely has you eating, drinking, and sleeping CISSP after you finish. Like the exam, the review seminars can be quite expensive and might require some travel. Similarly, the Live OnLine seminar gives you the same benefits of the Review seminar on a computer, without the exotic travel. Schedules and additional information are available at www.isc2.org.

Take a Breather

The day before the exam, relax and plan for a comfortable night's rest. If you've been cramming for the exam, set your study materials aside the day before the exam. At that point, you either know the material or you don't!

Chapter 15

Ten Test-Day Tips

. . . .

*W*ell, your big day has finally arrived. After months of study and mind-numbing stress, you cram all night before the exam, skip breakfast because you're running late, and then forget everything you know because you have a splitting headache for the next six hours while sitting for your exam! That isn't exactly a recipe for success — but the following ten test day tips can definitely get you on the right track.

Get a Good Night's Rest

The night before the exam isn't the time to do any last-minute cramming. Studies have proven that a good night's rest is essential to doing well on an exam. Have a nice dinner (we recommend going for some carbohydrates and avoiding anything spicy), and then get to bed early. Save the all-night party for the day after the exam.

Dress Comfortably

You should dress in attire that's comfortable — remember, this is a six-hour exam. It's also a good idea to dress in layers — the exam room could be warmer or cooler than you're used to.

Eat a Good Breakfast

Mountain Dew and donuts: because breakfast is the most important meal of the day! Seriously, though, even if you're not a breakfast person, try to get something down before sitting for the CISSP exam. No extra time is allotted for lunch breaks, so plan on eating a good, healthy, hearty breakfast.

Arrive Early

Absolutely, *under no circumstances,* do you want to arrive late for this exam. Make sure that you know where the testing center is located, what the traffic is like at that time of the day, and where you can park. You may even want to do a dry run before the test day to be sure you know what delays you might encounter (particularly if you're not familiar with the area where the exam is being administered).

Bring a Photo ID

The testing center will verify your identity when you arrive for your exam. You need to bring your driver's license, government-issued ID, or passport — these are the only forms of ID that are accepted.

Bring Snacks and Drinks

Check with your testing center (`http://pearsonvue.com/isc2/`) regarding their rules about consuming snacks and drinks in the testing area. If they are permitted, bring a small bag that holds enough food and drink to get you through the exam. A *big* bottle of water is essential. Also, consider bringing a soda and some snacks, a sandwich, energy bars — whatever you like to snack on that replenishes and renews you without making you too thirsty.

Bring Prescription and Over-the-Counter Medications

Again, check with your testing center and notify the test administrator if you're taking any prescription medication that must be taken during the exam (for example, one dose every four hours — remember, this is a six-hour exam!). Nothing can ruin your chances of succeeding on the CISSP exam like a medical emergency! Also, consider bringing some basic over-the-counter meds, such as acetaminophen or antacids, to eliminate any annoying inconveniences such as headaches, heartburn, or a gastrointestinal malady. A box of tissues might also be appropriate — if you have a cold or you feel like crying when you see the exam!

Leave Your Cell Phone and Pager Behind

This is the one day that your office is going to have to do without you. Turn off your smartphone, cell phone, pager, miscellaneous mobile devices, digital watch alarms, and anything else that goes *beep*. Even better, leave it all locked and hidden in your car or at home.

Take Frequent Breaks

Six hours is a long time. Be sure to get up and walk around during the exam. We recommend taking a short, five-minute break every hour during the exam. Eat a snack, go to the restroom, walk around, stretch, crack your knuckles, or whatever (breathe?) . . . and then get back to the task at hand. You might even incorporate breaks into your test-taking strategy. For example, answer 50 questions and then take a short break.

Also, if you find your mind wandering or you have trouble focusing, take a break. Burnout and fatigue can lead to careless mistakes or indifference. If you feel these symptoms coming on, take a break.

But be careful not to overdo your breaks. Stick to frequent but short breaks, and you'll be fine.

Guess — as a Last Resort

Guessing is a desperate approach to test-taking, but it can be effective when all else fails. An unanswered question is definitely wrong, so don't leave any questions unanswered. If you must guess, try to eliminate as many obviously wrong answers as possible. If you can eliminate two possible choices, you have a 50/50 chance of getting the answer right. Another strategy for guessing is to count up the total number of A, B, C, and D answers you've already identified. Most (although not all) multiple-choice tests, should have a fairly even distribution of answers.

Chapter 16

Ten More Sources for Security Certifications

● ●

*M*any professional and technical security certifications that are available can either help you prepare for Certified Information Systems Security Professional (CISSP) certification or complement the CISSP certification. In this chapter, we list several other security certifications.

ASIS International

> www.asisonline.org

Formerly the American Society for Industrial Security, ASIS International offers the Certified Protection Professional (CPP) certification for security professionals who have a bachelor's degree and seven years of security experience (including three years in a security management position), or nine years of security experience (three years in a security management position) if the professional doesn't have a bachelor's degree. The CPP exam consists of 200 multiple-choice questions in the following subject areas:

- ✔ Security Principles and Practices
- ✔ Business Principles and Practices
- ✔ Legal Aspects
- ✔ Personnel Security
- ✔ Physical Security
- ✔ Information Security
- ✔ Crisis Management
- ✔ Investigations

Check Point

www.checkpoint.com

The Check Point Certified Professional Program provides product-focused certifications based on one of the most popular firewall products on the market today: Check Point FireWall-1. Certifications include

✔ Check Point Certified Security Administrator (CCSA)

✔ Check Point Certified Security Expert (CCSE)

Cisco

www.cisco.com

Earning a certification as a Cisco security specialist demonstrates proficiency in designing, installing, and supporting Cisco security products. Cisco security certifications include:

✔ Cisco ASA Specialist

✔ Cisco Firewall Security Specialist

✔ Cisco IOS Security Specialist

✔ Cisco IPS Specialist

✔ Cisco Network Admission Control Specialist

✔ Cisco Security Sales Specialist

✔ Cisco Security Solutions and Design Specialist

✔ Cisco VPN Security Specialist

✔ Cisco Web Security Field Engineer Specialist

Finally, the mother of all certifications, the *crème de la crème* . . . the Cisco Certified Internetworking Expert (CCIE) offers a security track that requires satisfactory completion of a two-hour written exam and an eight-hour hands-on lab. The CCIE makes the reality show *Survivor* look easy!

CompTIA

www.comptia.org

CompTIA — the Computing Technology Industry Association — provides industry-supported, vendor-neutral certifications that test a candidate's understanding of basic foundation skills and core competencies in a given subject area. Although deemed entry-level by many, CompTIA certifications nonetheless provide a valuable and trusted certification in any technical career path.

CompTIA exams also have the advantage — at least in the realm of vendor-neutral security certifications — of being readily available and relatively inexpensive. Security topics covered on the 100-question Security+ exam include

- ✔ Systems Security
- ✔ Network Infrastructure
- ✔ Access Control
- ✔ Assessments and Audits
- ✔ Cryptography
- ✔ Organizational Security

CWNP

www.cwnp.com

CWNP (Certified Wireless Network Professional) offers vendor neutral enterprise WiFi career certifications. Certified Wireless Security Professional (CWSP) is a professional-level certification for network engineers. Earning the CWNP certification requires the candidate to pass two exams: Wireless LAN Administration (PW0-104) and Wireless LAN Security (PW0-204).

DRI International

www.drii.org

Disaster Recovery Institute International (DRII) provides four levels of certification in Business Continuity and Disaster Recovery Planning, including

- ✔ **Associate Business Continuity Professional (ABCP):** For individuals who have limited industry experience (less than two years) but have at least entry-level proficiency in Business Continuity Planning.

- ✔ **Certified Functional Continuity Professional (CFCP):** For individuals who have a demonstrated knowledge and experience of more than two years and can demonstrate practical experience in three of the Professional Practices areas (listed later in this section).

- ✔ **Certified Business Continuity Professional (CBCP):** For individuals who have a demonstrated knowledge and experience of more than two years and can demonstrate practical experience in five of the Professional Practices areas (listed later in this section).

- ✔ **Master Business Continuity Professional (MBCP):** For individuals who have a demonstrated knowledge and experience of more than five years and can demonstrate practical experience in seven of the Professional Practices areas (listed later in this section). This certification also requires completion of a directed research paper or a 3½-hour case-study exam for an additional $250 fee.

The multiple-choice exam is administered at various locations and dates throughout the year. The exam tests the candidate's knowledge in ten subject areas covered in the Professional Practices for Business Continuity Planners document:

- ✔ Program Initiation and Management
- ✔ Risk Evaluation and Control
- ✔ Business Impact Analysis
- ✔ Developing Business Continuity Strategies
- ✔ Emergency Response and Operations
- ✔ Developing and Implementing Business Continuity Plans
- ✔ Awareness and Training Programs

✔ Business Continuity Plan Exercise, Audit, and Maintenance

✔ Public Relations and Crisis Communications

✔ Coordination with External Agencies

EC-Council

www.eccouncil.org

The International Council of E-Commerce Consultants offers numerous security certifications at various levels, including

✔ Certified Ethical Hacker (C|EH)

✔ Computer Hacking Forensic Investigator (C|HFI)

✔ EC-Council Certified Security Analyst (E|CSA)

✔ Licensed Penetration Tester (L|PT)

✔ EC-Council Network Security Administrator (E|NSA)

✔ Certified Chief Information Security Officer (C|CISO)

ISACA

www.isaca.org

The Information Systems Audit and Control Association (ISACA) administers the Certified Information Systems Auditor (CISA), Certified Information Security Manager (CISM), Certified in Risk and Information Systems Control (CRISC), and Certified in the Governance of Enterprise Information Technology (CGEIT) certifications. These certifications are helpful for professionals who work in organizations subject to various security regulations including Sarbanes-Oxley, Health Insurance Portability and Accountability Act (HIPAA), Gramm-Leach-Bliley Act (GLBA), and the Payment Card Industry Data Security Standard (PCI DSS).

CISA

The 200-question multiple-choice CISA exam, offered biannually in June and December, covers the following six job-practice areas:

- ✔ Information Systems Audit Process
- ✔ Information Technology Governance
- ✔ Systems and Infrastructure Lifecycle Management
- ✔ Information Technology Service Delivery and Support
- ✔ Protection of Information Assets
- ✔ Business Continuity and Disaster Recovery

Minimum requirements for CISA certification include five years of current work experience (meaning within the past ten years or within five years of passing the exam) in the fields of Information Systems auditing, control, assurance, or security.

CISM

The 200-question multiple-choice CISM exam, offered biannually in June and December, covers the following five job-practice areas:

- ✔ Information Security Governance
- ✔ Information Risk Management
- ✔ Information Security Program Development
- ✔ Information Security Program Management
- ✔ Incident Management & Response

Minimum requirements for CISM certification include five years of current work experience (within the past ten years or within five years of passing the exam) in the field of information security. Of the five years of experience, at least three years must be in an information security management role.

CRISC

The four-hour, 200-question multiple-choice CRISC exam, offered biannually in June and December, covers the following five job-practice areas:

- ✔ Risk Identification, Assessment, and Evaluation
- ✔ Risk Response

✔ Risk Monitoring

✔ Information Systems Control Design and Implementation

✔ IS Control Monitoring and Maintenance

The minimum requirements for CRISC include three years of work experience in at least three of the domains just listed.

CGEIT

The 120-question multiple-choice CGEIT exam, offered biannually in June and December, covers the following six job-practice areas:

✔ IT Governance Framework

✔ Strategic Alignment

✔ Value Delivery

✔ Risk Management

✔ Resource Management

✔ Performance Measurement

Minimum requirements for CGEIT certification include five years of current work experience (within the past ten years or within five years of passing the exam), including specific evidence of management, advisory, or oversight experience associated with the governance of the IT-related contribution to the enterprise.

(ISC)²

```
www.isc2.org
```

In addition to the CISSP certification, the International Information Systems Security Certifications Consortium (ISC)² offers the Systems Security Certified Practitioner (SSCP), Certified Secure Software Lifecycle Professional (CSSLP), and Certification and Accreditation Professional (CAP) certifications.

SSCP

Developed in 1998, the SSCP certifies network and systems administrators who implement security policies, standards, and procedures. The SSCP tests the candidate's knowledge in seven domains that comprise the Information Systems Security Administrator Common Body of Knowledge (CBK):

- ✔ Access Controls
- ✔ Analysis and Monitoring
- ✔ Cryptography
- ✔ Malicious Code
- ✔ Networks and Telecommunications
- ✔ Risk, Response, and Recovery
- ✔ Security Operations and Administration

Similar in format to the CISSP exam, the SSCP exam is a paper-based, 125-question, multiple-choice examination. You have three hours to complete the exam. A minimum of one year of related work experience in at least one of the seven domains is required.

CSSLP

The CSSLP is designed to address security deficiencies in the software life cycle, as evidenced by the fact that most security breaches are related to applications security. The CSSLP is for any stakeholder in the software life cycle who has at least four years of experience. Potential candidates include

- ✔ Top management
- ✔ Business unit heads
- ✔ IT managers
- ✔ Security specialists
- ✔ Application owners
- ✔ Developers and coders
- ✔ Project managers and team leaders
- ✔ Technical architects
- ✔ Quality assurance managers
- ✔ Business analysts
- ✔ Industry group delivery heads
- ✔ Client-side program managers
- ✔ Auditors

The CSSLP CBK focuses on building security into the software development life cycle (SDLC) and consists of the following domains:

- Secure Software Concepts
- Secure Software Requirements
- Secure Software Design
- Secure Software Implementation/Coding
- Secure Software Testing
- Software Acceptance
- Software Deployment, Operations, Maintenance, and Disposal

CAP

The CAP certification is for candidates in U.S. state and local governments, and for civilians in the commercial job market, who are responsible for formally certifying and accrediting security in information systems. Candidates have job positions such as authorizing officials, system or information owners, information system security officers (ISSOs), and senior system managers. CAP candidates must have a minimum of two years of direct, full-time systems security certification and accreditation in one or more of the following five CAP domains:

- Understanding the Purpose of Certification
- Initiation of the System Authorization Process
- Certification Phase
- Accreditation Phase
- Continuous Monitoring Phase

CISSP concentrations

(ISC)^2 also offers three CISSP concentrations:

- **ISSAP (Information Systems Security Architecture Professional):** For CISSPs who have at least two years of experience in security architecture. The six CBK domains are
  - Access Control Systems and Methodology
  - Cryptography
  - Physical Security Integration

- Requirements Analysis and Security Standards, Guidelines, and Criteria

- Technology-Related Business Continuity and Disaster Recovery Planning

- Telecommunications and Network Security

✔ **ISSEP (Information Systems Security Engineering Professional):** Developed in cooperation with the U.S. National Security Agency (NSA) for systems security engineering professionals. The four CBK domains include

- Certification and Accreditation

- Systems Security Engineering

- Technical Management

- U.S. Government Information Assurance Regulations

✔ **ISSMP (Information Systems Security Management Professional):** For CISSPs who have at least two years of management experience, specifically in the areas of project management, risk management, security awareness program development and management, or Business Continuity Planning management at an enterprise-wide level. The five included CBK domains are

- Business Continuity Planning (BCP), Disaster Recovery Planning (DRP), and Continuity of Operations Planning (COOP)

- Enterprise Security Management Practices

- Enterprise-Wide System Development Security

- Law, Investigations, Forensics, and Ethics

- Overseeing Compliance of Operations Security

SANS/GIAC

```
www.sans.org
www.giac.org
```

The Global Information Assurance Certification (GIAC) was founded by the SANS (Systems Administration, Networking, and Security) Institute in 1999. GIAC certification is a more technical and hands-on certification than the CISSP certification. Candidates for GIAC certification must first complete a written practical assignment. Assignments that receive a passing grade are posted on the SANS website and qualify the individual to take a technical certification to complete GIAC certification. GIAC currently offers more than 20 individual certifications in the following six broad categories:

- ✔ Security Administration
- ✔ Forensics
- ✔ Management
- ✔ Audit
- ✔ Software Security
- ✔ Legal

Chapter 17

Ten Security Websites

. . . .

*Y*ou can find literally hundreds (if not thousands) of security websites on the Internet. The list that we came up with for this Part of Tens chapter is therefore by no means complete. Security websites come in many flavors (including Black Hat and White Hat), and certainly some websites are better than others, with more being developed every day. This chapter gives you a brief list of sites that you may find useful, both while you prepare for the CISSP exam and while you do your job as a security professional. Please explore these sites (and bookmark them, if you're so inclined) and continue your never-ending quest for knowledge.

CISSP Open Study Guide

www.cccure.org

The CISSP Open Study Guide website includes many valuable study resources for the CISSP candidate, such as study guides, downloads, study presentations, online quizzes, books, news, and access to numerous study groups and discussion forums.

Carnegie Mellon SEI CERT Coordination Center

www.cert.org

The Carnegie Mellon Software Engineering Institute (SEI) Computer Emergency Response Team (CERT) Coordination Center includes information about vulnerabilities and fixes, incidents, and security practices and evaluations; offers survivability research and analysis; and provides training and education resources.

Common Vulnerabilities and Exposures

```
http://cve.mitre.org
```

The Common Vulnerabilities and Exposures (CVE) is a list, maintained by the MITRE Corporation, of standardized names for vulnerabilities and other information security exposures. You can download the CVE dictionary – which contains publicly known information security vulnerabilities and exposures – from this website.

Dark Reading

```
www.darkreading.com
```

Dark Reading is an excellent portal for current security-related news and information on a number of security topics. Join their security discussions, subscribe to RSS feeds, and follow their blogs to keep current on the latest in security and data protection.

(ISC)²

```
www.isc2.org
```

The (ISC)² website is not only the most important website for CISSP candidates — it's where you download the Candidate Information Bulletin (CIB), get the latest official updates on the CISSP certification, register and schedule your exam, pay your annual dues, and log your Continuing Professional Education (CPE) credits — it's also where you can find out about local (ISC)² chapters, network with other CISSPs, participate in security blogs, and download valuable security resources. Make it a habit to check the Chapters, Social Responsibility, Events, Industry Resources, and Blog tabs frequently!

INFOSYSSEC

www.infosyssec.com

INFOSYSSEC is the mother of all security websites and one of the largest security portals we've ever seen.

National Institute of Standards and Technology

www.nist.gov/itl

The U.S. National Institute of Standards and Technology (NIST) Information Technology Laboratory (ITL) provides access to NIST special publications, guides, standards, toolkits, projects, and a wealth of other helpful information and security resources. This site contains some of the best security standards and practices we have seen, and all of it is available for free.

PCI Security Standards Council

www.pcisecuritystandards.org

The Payment Card Industry (PCI) Security Standards Council website isn't a security website per se, but it is full of very useful and helpful security information related to the most far-reaching and comprehensive industry security standard today — the PCI Data Security Standard (DSS). PCI DSS is applicable to any organization that processes, transmits, or stores payment card data — whether it handles one transaction or one million transactions — so it is very likely that your organization or your clients are subject to or affected by PCI DSS in some way.

Check out the PCI Standards and Documents, Training, and News and Events tabs on the PCI website for useful resources such as incident response templates, self-assessment questionnaires, WiFi security guidelines, encryption and tokenization information, and secure virtualization tips. These resources are specific to PCI DSS, but since most data protection standards and regulations are based on security best practices, this isn't a bad place to go for good security information.

If you aren't familiar with PCI DSS, go to Chapter 12 (all about Legal, Regulations, Investigations, and Compliance) — go directly to Chapter 12. Do not pass Go, do not collect 200 dollars, and *do not* schedule your CISSP exam until you've read and understand Chapter 12 and can spell PCI frontwards and backwards while doing handstands blindfolded on a high wire!

The SANS Institute

www.sans.org

The SANS (Systems Administration, Networking, and Security) Institute sponsors the Global Information Assurance Certification (GIAC) program, a series of security certifications that have a more technical, hands-on focus than the CISSP certification. GIAC is an excellent complement to CISSP certification, and SANS offers a 40-percent discount on its GSEC (GIAC Security Essentials Certification) certification for those who have CISSP certification.

This website also includes SANS conference schedules, an extremely helpful "Internet Storm Center" and security digest, the SANS online bookstore, various projects, resources, security links, sample security policies, white papers, GIAC student practicals, and security tools.

The site also features the SANS/FBI Top Twenty Vulnerabilities list. This list, co-sponsored by the FBI, helps organizations prioritize security efforts by listing and describing the top 20 Internet security vulnerabilities in three categories: General Vulnerabilities, Windows Vulnerabilities, and UNIX Vulnerabilities.

WindowSecurity Network Security Library

www.windowsecurity.com

Don't be fooled by the name of the website — the Network Security Library deals with more than just Windows security issues. It's an excellent source of free online books, articles, FAQs, and how-to's on many subjects, including Windows, UNIX, Netware, firewalls, intrusion detection and prevention systems, security policy, the Internet, the National Computer Security Center (NCSC), the Department of Defense (DoD) Rainbow Series, harmless hacking, and many more.

Chapter 18

Ten Essential Reference Books

*I*nformation security is a hot topic, and new books on this important subject are being published every day. Some of those books are better than
others. Many outstanding information security books have been written, and
many more are likely to be published, so this chapter doesn't give you all the
books you may ever want to read on the subject. However, the following list
contains ten (well, actually, twelve) books that we highly recommend:

- *Applied Cryptography: Protocols, Algorithms, and Source Code in C,* 2nd
  Edition, by Bruce Schneier (John Wiley & Sons, Inc.). In case our chapter
  on Cryptography just whet your appetite and you're chomping at the bit
  to find out more, this book (written by one of cryptography's living legends) is the deep dive you're looking for!

- *Building Internet Firewalls,* 2nd Edition, by Elizabeth D. Zwicky, Simon
  Cooper, D. Brent Chapman, and Deborah Russell (O'Reilly Media, Inc.).
  This book contains the principles of deploying firewalls to implement an
  effective security strategy — and how to build an actual firewall.

- *Cyber Forensics: A Field Manual for Collecting, Examining, and Preserving
  Evidence of Computer Crimes,* Second Edition, by Albert J. Marcella,
  Jr., and Doug Menendez (Auerbach Publications). If you're tired of just
  watching *CSI,* this book will help you to properly conduct investigations!

- *Incident Response: Investigating Computer Crime,* Second Edition, by
  Kevin Mandia and Chris Prosise (McGraw-Hill/Osborne Media Group).
  This book has thorough coverage of investigations and evidence
  gathering.

- *Information Security: Protecting the Global Enterprise,* by Donald L. Pipkin
  (Prentice Hall). This book includes step-by-step guidance regarding
  important security management practices.

- *Network Intrusion Detection: An Analyst's Handbook,* 3rd Edition, by
  Stephen Northcutt and Judy Novak (New Riders Publishing); and
  Intrusion Signatures and Analysis, by Stephen Northcutt, Mark Cooper,
  Matt Fearnow, and Karen Frederick (New Riders Publishing). Okay, we
  technically just recommended two books, but (ISC)² includes only the
  first one on its website's Suggested Study Materials list. The second

book is an excellent (and logical) companion to the first — not listing both is like having yin but no yang, or mo but no jo. Both books are from the SANS Institute and provide practical, in-depth information.

✔ *Security Engineering: A Guide to Building Dependable Distributed Systems,* Second Edition, by Ross Anderson (John Wiley & Sons, Inc.). Read this book for excellent, in-depth coverage of some very complex subjects.

✔ *Security Warrior,* by Cyrus Peikari and Anton Chuvakin (O'Reilly Media, Inc.). The nuts and bolts of cracking software, network attacks, and operating system exploits — oh, and how to defend yourself from the bad guys!

✔ *The CERT Guide to System and Network Security Practices,* by Julia H. Allen (Addison-Wesley). Read this book to discover how to secure your systems and networks, step by step.

✔ *The Tao of Network Security Monitoring: Beyond Intrusion Detection* and *Extrusion Detection: Security Monitoring for Internal Intrusions,* both by Richard Bejtlich (Addison-Wesley). These two companion books are definitely worth your time and belong together. Two great tastes that taste great together — like peanut butter and chocolate, or peanut butter and jelly, or peanut butter and pickles!

Part IV
Appendixes

The 5th Wave By Rich Tennant

"A centralized security management system sounds fine, but then what would we do with all the dogs?"

In this part . . .

Whether you call 'em *appendixes* or *appendices,* they're chock-full of exam-passing and post-certification goodness that you don't want removed! In this book, the appendi-thingies include a complete 250-question practice exam and a glossary.

Appendix A

Practice CISSP Exam

. . . .

*1*f you've never taken a certification exam, you may be wondering what the exam will be like. The CISSP certification exam is fairly straightforward: Each question is multiple-choice and includes four possible answers. Only one answer is the *best* answer.

This chapter contains 250 questions — the same as in the real CISSP exam. You may consider this a practice run for the CISSP exam. You should time yourself and make sure you can finish in six hours.

Practice Test Questions

1 The number-one priority of disaster planning should always be:

A ○ Preservation of capital

B ○ Personnel evacuation and safety

C ○ Resumption of core business functions

D ○ Investor relations

2 An access control system that grants access to information based on that information's classification and the clearance of the individual is known as:

A ○ Identity-based access control

B ○ Mandatory access control

C ○ Role-based access control

D ○ Clearance-based access control

3 A database that contains the data structures used by an application is known as:

A ○ A data encyclopedia

B ○ A data dictionary

C ○ Metadata

D ○ A schema

4 The process of breaking the key and/or plaintext from an enciphered message is known as:

A ○ Decryption

B ○ Steganography

C ○ Cryptanalysis

D ○ Extraction

5 The Internet Worm incident of 1988 was perpetrated by:

A ○ The 414 Gang

B ○ Robert Morris

C ○ Kevin Mitnick

D ○ Gene Spafford

6 Access controls and card key systems are examples of:

A ○ Detective controls

B ○ Preventive controls

C ○ Corrective controls

D ○ Trust controls

7 **Why should a datacenter's walls go all the way to the ceiling and not just stop as high as the suspended ceiling?**

A ○ The walls will be stronger.

B ○ The HVAC will run more efficiently.

C ○ An intruder could enter the datacenter by climbing over the low wall.

D ○ The high wall will block more noise.

8 **Memory that's used to store computer instructions and data is known as:**

A ○ UART

B ○ SIMM

C ○ Cache

D ○ ROM

9 **Of what value is separation of authority in an organization?**

A ○ It limits the capabilities of any single individual.

B ○ It provides multiple paths for fulfilling critical tasks.

C ○ It accommodates the requirement for parallel audit trails.

D ○ It ensures that only one person is authorized to perform each task.

10 **UDP is sometimes called the "unreliable data protocol" because:**

A ○ It works only on low-speed wireless LANs.

B ○ UDP packets rarely get through because they have a lower priority.

C ○ Few know how to program UDP.

D ○ UDP does not guarantee delivery.

11 **Which of the following is NOT a goal of a Business Impact Assessment (BIA)?**

A ○ To inventory mutual aid agreements

B ○ To identify and prioritize business critical functions

C ○ To determine how much downtime the business can tolerate

D ○ To identify resources required by critical processes

12 **An access control system that grants access to information based on the identity of the user is known as:**

A ○ Identity-based access control

B ○ Mandatory access control

C ○ Role-based access control

D ○ Clearance-based access control

13 The purpose of a Service-Level Agreement is:

A ○ To guarantee a minimum quality of service for an application or function

B ○ To guarantee the maximum quality of service for an application or function

C ○ To identify gaps in availability of an application

D ○ To correct issues identified in a security audit

14 The method of encryption in which both sender and recipient possess a common encryption key is known as:

A ○ Message digest

B ○ Hash function

C ○ Public key cryptography

D ○ Secret key cryptography

15 Forensics is the term that describes:

A ○ Due process

B ○ Tracking hackers who operate in other countries

C ○ Taking steps to preserve and record evidence

D ○ Scrubbing a system in order to return it to service

16 Audit trails and security cameras are examples of:

A ○ Detective controls

B ○ Preventive controls

C ○ Corrective controls

D ○ Trust controls

17 How does water aid in fire suppression?

A ○ It reduces the fire's oxygen supply.

B ○ It isolates the fire's fuel supply.

C ○ It lowers the temperature to a degree at which the fire can't sustain itself.

D ○ It extinguishes the fire through a chemical reaction.

18 Firmware is generally stored on:

A ○ ROM or EPROM

B ○ Tape

C ○ RAM

D ○ Any removable media

19 The term *open view* refers to what activity?

A ○ Reclassifying a document so that anyone can view it

B ○ Viewing the contents of one's private encryption key

C ○ Leaving classified information where unauthorized people can see it

D ○ Using a decryption key to view the contents of a message

20 TCP is a poor choice for streaming video because:

A ○ It is too bursty for large networks.

B ○ Acknowledgment and sequencing add significantly to its overhead.

C ○ Checksums in video packets are meaningless.

D ○ TCP address space is nearly exhausted.

21 The longest period of time that an organization can accept a critical outage is known as:

A ○ Maximum Acceptable Downtime

B ○ Greatest Tolerated Downtime

C ○ Maximum Tolerable Downtime

D ○ Recovery Time Objective

22 An access control system that gives the user some control over who has access to information is known as:

A ○ Identity-based access control

B ○ User-directed access control

C ○ Role-based access control

D ○ Clearance-based access control

23 CRCs, parity checks, and checksums are examples of:

A ○ Corrective application controls

B ○ Message digests

C ○ Preventive application controls

D ○ Detective application controls

24 Why would a user's public encryption key be widely distributed?

A ○ So that cryptographers can attempt to break it

B ○ Because it's encrypted

C ○ Because the user's private key can't be derived from his or her public key

D ○ So that the user can decrypt messages from any location

25 **An expert witness:**

A ○ Offers an opinion based on the facts of a case and on personal expertise

B ○ Is someone who was present at the scene of the crime

C ○ Has direct personal knowledge about the event in question

D ○ Can testify in criminal proceedings only

26 **Reboot instructions and file restore procedures are examples of:**

A ○ Detective controls

B ○ Preventive controls

C ○ Corrective controls

D ○ Trust controls

27 **Drain pipes that channel liquids away from a building are called:**

A ○ Positive drains

B ○ Tight lines

C ○ Storm drains

D ○ Negative drains

28 **What's the purpose of memory protection?**

A ○ It protects memory from malicious code.

B ○ It prevents a program from being able to access memory used by another program.

C ○ Memory protection is another term used to describe virtual memory backing store.

D ○ It assures that hardware refresh happens frequently enough to maintain memory integrity.

29 **Which individual is responsible for classifying information?**

A ○ Owner

B ○ Custodian

C ○ Creator

D ○ User

30 **How many layers does the TCP/IP protocol model have?**

A ○ 4

B ○ 5

C ○ 6

D ○ 7

31 **The primary difference between a hot site and a warm site is:**

A ○ The hot site is closer to the organization's datacenters than the warm site.

B ○ The warm site's systems don't have the organization's software or data installed.

C ○ The warm site doesn't have computer systems in it.

D ○ The warm site is powered down, but the hot site is powered up and ready to go.

32 **Encryption, tokens, access control lists, and smart cards are known as:**

A ○ Discretionary access controls

B ○ Physical controls

C ○ Technical controls

D ○ Administrative controls

33 **Data mining:**

A ○ Can be performed by privileged users only

B ○ Is generally performed after hours because it's resource-intensive

C ○ Refers to searches for correlations in a data warehouse

D ○ Is the term used to describe the activities of a hacker who has broken into a database

34 **Reading down the columns of a message that has been written across is known as:**

A ○ A columnar transposition cipher

B ○ Calculating the hash

C ○ Calculating the checksum

D ○ Calculating the modulo

35 **A witness:**

A ○ Offers an opinion based on the facts of a case and on personal expertise

B ○ Is someone who was present at the scene of the crime

C ○ Has direct personal knowledge about the event in question

D ○ Can testify in criminal proceedings only

36 **Covert channel analysis is used to:**

A ○ Detect and understand unauthorized communication

B ○ Encipher unauthorized communications

C ○ Decipher unauthorized communications

D ○ Recover unauthorized communications

37 Of what value is pre-employment screening?

A ○ Undesirable medical or genetic conditions could diminish productivity.

B ○ Only certain personality types can work effectively in some organizations.

C ○ Employees need to have knowledge of security.

D ○ Background checks could uncover undesirable qualities.

38 The mapping of existing physical memory into a larger, imaginary memory space is known as:

A ○ Virtual memory

B ○ Swapping

C ○ Thrashing

D ○ Spooling

39 Which individual is responsible for protecting information?

A ○ Owner

B ○ Custodian

C ○ Creator

D ○ User

40 ARP is:

A ○ Access Routing Protocol

B ○ Address Resolution Protocol

C ○ Access Resolution Protocol

D ○ Address Recovery Protocol

41 Which of the following is NOT a concern for a hot site?

A ○ Programs and data at the hot site must be protected.

B ○ A widespread disaster will strain the hot site's resources.

C ○ A hot site is expensive because of the controls and patches required.

D ○ Computer equipment must be shipped quickly to the hot site for it to be effective.

42 Supervision, audits, procedures, and assessments are known as:

A ○ Discretionary access controls

B ○ Safeguards

C ○ Physical controls

D ○ Administrative controls

43 **Object-oriented, relational, and network are examples of:**

A ○ Types of database tables
B ○ Types of database records
C ○ Types of database queries
D ○ Types of databases

44 **An asymmetric cryptosystem is also known as a:**

A ○ Message digest
B ○ Hash function
C ○ Public key cryptosystem
D ○ Secret key cryptosystem

45 **Entrapment is defined as:**

A ○ Leading someone to commit a crime that they wouldn't otherwise have committed
B ○ Monitoring with the intent of recording a crime
C ○ Paying someone to commit a crime
D ○ Being caught with criminal evidence in one's possession

46 **Least privilege means:**

A ○ Analysis that determines which privileges are required to complete a task.
B ○ People who have high privileges delegate some of those privileges to others.
C ○ The people who have the fewest access rights do all the work.
D ○ Users should have the minimum privileges required to perform required tasks.

47 **Which of the following is NOT a part of a building's automated access audit log?**

A ○ Time of the attempted entry
B ○ The reason for the attempted entry
C ○ Location of attempted entry
D ○ Entry success or failure

48 **Systems that have published specifications and standards are known as:**

A ○ Open source
B ○ Copyleft
C ○ Freeware
D ○ Open systems

49 **Which of the following is NOT a criterion for classifying information?**

A ○ Marking

B ○ Useful life

C ○ Value

D ○ Age

50 **What is the purpose of ARP?**

A ○ When given an IP address, ARP returns a MAC address.

B ○ When given a MAC address, ARP returns an IP address.

C ○ It calculates the shortest path between two nodes on a network.

D ○ It acquires the next IP address on a circular route.

51 **The Disaster Recovery Plan (DRP) needs to be continuously maintained because:**

A ○ The organization's software versions are constantly changing.

B ○ The organization's business processes are constantly changing.

C ○ The available software patches are constantly changing.

D ○ The organization's data is constantly changing.

52 **Security guards, locked doors, and surveillance cameras are known as:**

A ○ Site-access controls

B ○ Safeguards

C ○ Physical access controls

D ○ Administrative controls

53 **Neural networking gets its name from:**

A ○ The make and model of equipment in a network

B ○ Patterns thought to exist in the brain

C ○ Its inventor, Sigor Neura

D ○ Observed patterns in neural telepathy

54 **The process of hiding a message inside a larger dataset is known as:**

A ○ Decryption

B ○ Steganography

C ○ Cryptanalysis

D ○ Extraction

55 Enticement is defined as:

    A ○ Being caught with criminal evidence in one's possession

    B ○ Leading someone to commit a crime that they wouldn't otherwise have committed

    C ○ Monitoring with the intent of recording a crime

    D ○ Keeping the criminal at the scene of the crime long enough to gather evidence

56 The practice of separation of duties:

    A ○ Is used to provide variety by rotating personnel among various tasks

    B ○ Helps to prevent any single individual from compromising an information system

    C ○ Is used to ensure that the most experienced persons get the best tasks

    D ○ Is used in large 24x7 operations shops

57 Tailgating is a term describing what activity?

    A ○ Logging in to a server from two or more locations

    B ○ Causing a PBX to permit unauthorized long distance calls

    C ○ Following an employee through an uncontrolled access

    D ○ Following an employee through a controlled access

58 Which of the following is NOT a security issue with distributed architectures?

    A ○ Lack of security awareness by some personnel.

    B ○ Difficulty in controlling the distribution and use of software.

    C ○ Protection of centrally stored information.

    D ○ Backups might not be performed on some systems, risking loss of data.

59 What's the purpose of a senior management statement of security policy?

    A ○ It defines who's responsible for carrying out a security policy.

    B ○ It states that senior management need not follow a security policy.

    C ○ It emphasizes the importance of security throughout an organization.

    D ○ It states that senior management must also follow a security policy.

60 What is the purpose of RARP?

    A ○ When given an IP address, RARP returns a MAC address.

    B ○ When given a MAC address, RARP returns an IP address.

    C ○ It traces the source address of a spoofed packet.

    D ○ It determines the least cost route through a multipath network.

61 **How is the organization's DRP best kept up-to-date?**

A ○ With regular audits to ensure that changes in business processes are known

B ○ By maintaining lists of current software versions, patches, and configurations

C ○ By maintaining personnel contact lists

D ○ By regularly testing the DRP

62 **Role-based access control and task-based access control are examples of:**

A ○ Mandatory access controls

B ○ Administrative controls

C ○ Discretionary access controls

D ○ Non-discretionary access controls

63 **The verification activity associated with coding is called:**

A ○ Unit testing

B ○ Design review

C ○ System testing

D ○ Architecture review

64 **Steganography isn't easily noticed because:**

A ○ Monitor and picture quality are so good these days.

B ○ Most PCs' speakers are turned off or disabled.

C ○ The human eye often can't sense the noise that steganography introduces.

D ○ Checksums can't detect most steganographed images.

65 **The purpose of a honeypot is to:**

A ○ Log an intruder's actions.

B ○ Act as a decoy to keep the intruder interested while his or her origin and identity are traced.

C ○ Deflect Denial of Service attacks away from production servers.

D ○ Provide direct evidence of a break-in.

66 **Which of the following tasks would NOT be performed by a security administrator?**

A ○ Changing file permissions

B ○ Configuring user privileges

C ○ Installing system software

D ○ Reviewing audit data

67 **What does *fail open* mean in the context of controlled building entrances?**

A ○ Controlled entrances permit no one to pass.

B ○ Controlled entrances permit people to pass without identification.

C ○ A power outage won't affect control of the entrance.

D ○ A pass key is required to enter the building.

68 **TCB is an acronym for:**

A ○ Trusted Computing Baseline

B ○ Trusted Computing Base

C ○ Tertiary Computing Base

D ○ Trusted Cache Base

69 **What is the purpose of an "advisory policy"?**

A ○ This is an optional policy that can be followed.

B ○ This is an informal offering of advice regarding security practices.

C ○ This is a temporary policy good only for a certain period of time.

D ○ This is a policy that must be followed but is not mandated by regulation.

70 **132.116.72.5 is a:**

A ○ MAC address

B ○ IPv4 address

C ○ Subnet mask

D ○ IPv6 address

71 **An organization that's developing its DRP has established a 20 minute Recovery Time Objective (RTO). Which solution will best support this objective?**

A ○ Cluster

B ○ Cold site

C ○ Hot site

D ○ Virtualization

72 **Audits, background checks, video cameras, and listening devices are known as:**

A ○ Discretionary controls

B ○ Physical controls

C ○ Preventive controls

D ○ Detective controls

73 **What's the primary input of a high-level product design?**

A ○ Feasibility study

B ○ Integration rules

C ○ Unit testing

D ○ Requirements

74 **What historic event was the backdrop for breakthroughs in strategic cryptography?**

A ○ The Gulf War

B ○ World War I

C ○ World War II

D ○ The Six-Day War

75 **Which of the following is NOT a precaution that needs to be taken before monitoring e-mail?**

A ○ Establishing strict procedures that define under what circumstances e-mail may be searched

B ○ Posting a visible notice that states e-mail is company information subject to search

C ○ Issuing monitoring tools to all e-mail administrators

D ○ Making sure that all employees know that e-mail is being monitored

76 **What's the potential security benefit of rotation of duties?**

A ○ It reduces the risk that personnel will perform unauthorized activities.

B ○ It ensures that all personnel are familiar with all security tasks.

C ○ It's used to detect covert activities.

D ○ It ensures security because personnel aren't very familiar with their duties.

77 **What does *fail closed* mean in the context of controlled building entrances?**

A ○ Controlled entrances permit no one to pass.

B ○ Controlled entrances permit people to pass without identification.

C ○ The access control computer is down.

D ○ Everyone is permitted to enter the building.

78 **The sum total of all protection mechanisms in a system is known as a:**

A ○ Trusted Computing Base

B ○ Protection domain

C ○ Trusted path

D ○ SPM (Summation Protection Mechanism)

79 **What is the definition of a "threat"?**

A ○ Any event that produces an undesirable outcome.
B ○ A weakness present in a control or countermeasure.
C ○ An act of aggression that causes harm.
D ○ An individual likely to violate security policy.

80 **04:c6:d1:45:87:E8 is a:**

A ○ MAC address
B ○ IPv4 address
C ○ Subnet mask
D ○ IPv6 address

81 **Which of the following is NOT a natural disaster?**

A ○ Tsunami
B ○ Pandemic
C ○ Flood
D ○ Communications outage

82 **Smart cards, fences, guard dogs, and card key access are known as:**

A ○ Mandatory controls
B ○ Physical controls
C ○ Preventive controls
D ○ Detective controls

83 **The main improvement of the Waterfall software life cycle model over earlier process models is:**

A ○ System and software requirements are combined into one step.
B ○ Developers can back up one step in the process for rework.
C ○ Coding and testing is combined into one step.
D ○ The need for rework was eliminated.

84 **Non-repudiation refers to:**

A ○ The technology that shoots down the "I didn't send that message" excuse
B ○ Re-verification of all Certificate Authority (CA) certificate servers
C ○ The annual competency review of system authentication mechanisms
D ○ The annual competency review of network authentication mechanisms

85 Intellectual property laws apply to:

A ○ Trade secrets, trademarks, copyrights, and patents

B ○ Trademarks, copyrights, and patents

C ○ Trademarks only

D ○ Patents only

86 The process of reviewing and approving changes in production systems is known as:

A ○ Availability management

B ○ Configuration management

C ○ Change management

D ○ Resource control

87 A water sprinkler system that's characterized as always having water in the pipes is known as:

A ○ Dry-pipe

B ○ Wet-pipe

C ○ Preaction

D ○ Discharge

88 The mechanism that overlaps hardware instructions to increase performance is known as:

A ○ RISC

B ○ Pipeline

C ○ Pipe dream

D ○ Multitasking

89 A weakness in a security control is called a:

A ○ Risk

B ○ Vulnerability

C ○ Threat

D ○ Hole

90 The "ping" command sends:

A ○ IGRP Echo Reply packets

B ○ IGRP Echo Request packets

C ○ ICMP Echo Request packets

D ○ UDP Echo Request packets

91 The term *remote journaling* refers to:

A ○ A mechanism that transmits transactions to an alternative processing site

B ○ A procedure for maintaining multiple copies of change control records

C ○ A procedure for maintaining multiple copies of configuration management records

D ○ A mechanism that ensures the survivability of written records

92 Is identification weaker than authentication?

A ○ Yes: Identity is based only on the assertion of identity without providing proof.

B ○ Yes: Identification uses ASCII data, whereas authentication uses binary data.

C ○ No: Identification and authentication provide the same level of identity.

D ○ No: They are used in different contexts and have nothing to do with each other.

93 A project team is at the beginning stages of a new software development project. The team wants to ensure that security features are present in the completed software application. In what stage should security be introduced?

A ○ Requirements development

B ○ Test plan development

C ○ Application coding

D ○ Implementation plan development

94 The amount of effort required to break a given ciphertext is known as:

A ○ The Work function

B ○ The Effort function

C ○ Cryptanalysis

D ○ Extraction

95 In order to be admissible, electronic evidence must:

A ○ Be legally permissible

B ○ Not be copied

C ○ Have been in the custody of the investigator at all times

D ○ Not contain viruses

96 The process of maintaining and documenting software versions and settings is known as:

A ○ Availability management

B ○ Configuration management

C ○ Change management

D ○ Resource control

97 A water sprinkler system that charges the pipes when it receives a heat or smoke alarm, and then discharges the water when a higher ambient temperature is reached, is known as:

A ○ Dry-pipe

B ○ Wet-pipe

C ○ Preaction

D ○ Discharge

98 FORTRAN, BASIC, and C are known as:

A ○ Structured languages

B ○ Nested languages

C ○ Second-generation languages

D ○ Third-generation languages

99 A security control intended to reduce risk is called a:

A ○ Safeguard

B ○ Threat

C ○ Countermeasure

D ○ Partition

100 SMTP is used to:

A ○ Manage multiple telnet sessions.

B ○ Tunnel private sessions through the Internet.

C ○ Simulate modems.

D ○ Transport e-mail.

101 Backing up data by sending it through a communications line to a remote location is known as:

A ○ Transaction journaling

B ○ Off-site storage

C ○ Electronic vaulting

D ○ Electronic journaling

102 Two-factor authentication is so called because:

A ○ It requires two of the three authentication types.

B ○ Tokens use two-factor encryption to hide their secret algorithms.

C ○ Authentication difficulty is increased by a factor of two.

D ○ It uses a factor of two prime numbers algorithm for added strength.

103 Which of the following is NOT a value of change control in the software development life cycle?

  A ○ Changes are documented and subject to approval.
  B ○ Scope creep is controlled.
  C ○ It gives the customer veto power over proposed changes.
  D ○ The cost of changes is considered.

104 What's one disadvantage of an organization signing its own certificates?

  A ○ The certificate-signing function is labor intensive.
  B ○ Anyone outside the organization will receive warning messages.
  C ○ The user-identification process is labor intensive.
  D ○ It's much more expensive than having certificates signed by a Certification Authority (CA).

105 Which agency has jurisdiction over computer crimes in the United States?

  A ○ The Department of Justice
  B ○ The Electronic Crimes Task Force
  C ○ Federal, state, or local jurisdiction
  D ○ The FBI and the Secret Service

106 Configuration Management is used to:

  A ○ Document the approval process for configuration changes.
  B ○ Control the approval process for configuration changes.
  C ○ Ensure that changes made to an information system don't compromise its security.
  D ○ Preserve a complete history of the changes to software or data in a system.

107 Why would a dry-pipe sprinkler be preferred over a wet-pipe sprinkler?

  A ○ Dry-pipe systems put out a fire more quickly.
  B ○ Dry-pipe systems consume less water.
  C ○ Dry-pipe systems have a smaller likelihood of rust damage.
  D ○ Dry-pipe systems have a potentially useful time delay before water is discharged.

108 The purpose of an operating system is to:

  A ○ Manage hardware resources.
  B ○ Compile program code.
  C ○ Decompile program code.
  D ○ Present graphic display to users.

109 **The purpose of risk analysis is:**

A ○ To qualify the classification of a potential threat.

B ○ To quantify the likelihood of a potential threat.

C ○ To quantify the net present value of an asset.

D ○ To quantify the impact of a potential threat.

110 **Which of the following is a disadvantage of SSL?**

A ○ It requires a certificate on every client system.

B ○ It is CPU intensive.

C ○ All clients must be retrofitted with HTTP v3 browsers.

D ○ An eavesdropper can record and later play back an SSL session.

111 **Which of the following is NOT a method used to create an online redundant data set?**

A ○ Remote journaling

B ○ Off-site storage

C ○ Electronic vaulting

D ○ Database mirroring

112 **The phrase *something you are* refers to:**

A ○ A user's security clearance

B ○ A user's role

C ○ Type 2 authentication

D ○ Type 3 authentication

113 **How does the Waterfall software development life cycle help to assure that applications will be secure?**

A ○ Security requirements can be included early on and verified later in testing.

B ○ The testing phase includes penetration testing.

C ○ The Risk Analysis phase will uncover flaws in the feasibility model.

D ○ A list of valid users must be approved prior to production.

114 **The ability for a government agency to wiretap a data connection was implemented in the:**

A ○ Skipjack chip

B ○ Magic lantern

C ○ Cutty chip

D ○ Clipper chip

115 Under what circumstance may evidence be seized without a warrant?

A ○ If it's in the public domain
B ○ If it's believed that its destruction is imminent
C ○ In international incidents
D ○ If it's on a computer

116 The traces of original data remaining after media erasure are known as:

A ○ Data remanence
B ○ Data traces
C ○ Leakage
D ○ Data particles

117 Why should a datacenter's walls go all the way to the ceiling and not just stop as high as the suspended ceiling?

A ○ The walls will serve as an effective fire break.
B ○ The HVAC will run more efficiently.
C ○ The walls will be stronger.
D ○ The high wall will block more noise.

118 Protection rings are used for:

A ○ Implementing memory protection
B ○ Creating nested protection domains
C ○ Modeling layers of protection around an information object
D ○ Shielding systems from EMF

119 Annualized Rate of Occurrence refers to:

A ○ The exact frequency of a threat.
B ○ The estimated frequency of a threat.
C ○ The estimated monetary value of a threat.
D ○ The exact monetary value of a threat.

120 An access control list is NOT used by:

A ○ A firewall or screening router to determine which packets should pass through.
B ○ A router to determine which administrative nodes may access it.
C ○ A bastion host to determine which network services should be permitted.
D ○ A client system to record and save passwords.

121 A DRP that has a high RPO and a low RTO will result in:

A ○ A system that takes more time to recover but has recent data

B ○ A system that recovers quickly but has old data

C ○ A system that recovers quickly and has recent data

D ○ A system that has never been tested

122 Two-factor authentication is stronger than single-factor authentication because:

A ○ It uses a factor of two prime numbers algorithm for added strength.

B ○ It relies on two factors, such as a password and a smart card.

C ○ Authentication difficulty is increased by a factor of two.

D ○ The user must be physically present to authenticate.

123 The main purpose of configuration management is to:

A ○ Require cost justification for any change in a software product.

B ○ Require approval for any desired change in a software product.

C ○ Maintain a detailed record of changes for the lifetime of a software product.

D ○ Provide the customer with a process for requesting configuration changes.

124 The cipher device used by Germany in World War II is known as:

A ○ M-922

B ○ M-902

C ○ Enigma

D ○ Turing

125 Motive, means, and opportunity:

A ○ Are required prior to the commission of a crime

B ○ Are the required three pieces of evidence in any criminal trial

C ○ Are the three factors that help determine whether someone may have committed a crime

D ○ Are the usual ingredients in a sting operation

126 Software controls are used to:

A ○ Perform input checking to ensure that no buffer overflows occur.

B ○ Keep running programs from viewing or changing other programs' memory.

C ○ Perform configuration management-like functions on software.

D ○ Ensure the confidentiality and integrity of software.

127 **Which of the following are NOT fire detectors?**

A ○ Dial-up alarms

B ○ Heat-sensing alarms

C ○ Flame-sensing alarms

D ○ Smoke-sensing alarms

128 **The TCSEC document is known as the Orange Book because**

A ○ It's orange in color.

B ○ It covers the major classes of computing system security, D through A.

C ○ Its coverage of security was likened to the defoliant Agent Orange.

D ○ No adequate model of computing system security was available at the time.

129 **Single Loss Expectancy refers to:**

A ○ The expectation of the occurrence of a single loss.

B ○ The monetary loss realized from an individual threat.

C ○ The likelihood that a single loss will occur.

D ○ The annualized monetary loss from a single threat.

130 **What is the purpose of the DHCP protocol?**

A ○ It's used to diagnose network problems.

B ○ It assigns IP addresses to servers.

C ○ It assigns IP addresses to stations that join the network.

D ○ It's used to dynamically build network routes.

131 **The purpose of a BIA is:**

A ○ To determine the criticality of business processes

B ○ To determine the impact of disasters on critical processes

C ○ To determine the impact of software defects on critical business processes

D ○ To determine which software defects should be fixed first

132 **An organization has recently implemented a palm-scan biometric system to control access to sensitive zones in a building. Some employees have objected to the biometric system for sanitary reasons. The organization should:**

A ○ Switch to a fingerprint-scanning biometric system.

B ○ Educate users about the inherent cleanliness of the system.

C ○ Allow users who object to the system to be able to bypass it.

D ○ Require employees to use a hand sanitizer prior to using the biometric system.

133 A security specialist has discovered that an application her company produces has a JavaScript injection vulnerability. What advice should the security specialist give to the application's developers?

A ○ Implement input filtering to block JavaScript and other script languages.
B ○ Upgrade to the latest release of Java.
C ○ Re-compile the application with safe input filtering turned on.
D ○ Re-compile the application by using UTF-8 character set support.

134 Cryptography can be used for all the following situations EXCEPT:

A ○ Performance
B ○ Confidentiality
C ○ Integrity
D ○ Authentication

135 The burden of proof in U.S. civil law is:

A ○ The preponderance of the evidence
B ○ Beyond a reasonable doubt
C ○ Beyond all doubt
D ○ Based on the opinion of the presiding judge

136 An organization may choose to perform periodic background checks on its employees for all the following reasons EXCEPT:

A ○ To determine whether the employee has earned any additional educational degrees
B ○ To determine whether a detrimental change in an employee's financial situation might entice him or her to steal from the employer
C ○ To determine whether a criminal offense has occurred since the person was hired that would impact the risk of continued employment
D ○ To uncover any criminal offenses that weren't discovered in the initial background check

137 Which class of hand-held fire extinguisher should be used in a datacenter?

A ○ Class B
B ○ Class C
C ○ Class A
D ○ Class D

138 All the following CPUs are CISC design EXCEPT:

A ○ PDP-11
B ○ Intel x86
C ○ SPARC
D ○ Motorola 68000

139 A system architect has designed a system that is protected with redundant parallel firewalls. This follows which security design principle?

A ○ Avoidance of a single point of failure

B ○ Defense in depth

C ○ Fail open

D ○ Fail closed

140 The type of cable that is best suited for high RF and EMF environments is:

A ○ Fiber-optic

B ○ Shielded twisted-pair

C ○ Coaxial

D ○ Thinnet

141 A Disaster Recovery Planning team has been told by management that the equipment required to meet RTO and RPO targets is too costly. What's the best course of action to take?

A ○ Classify the system as being out of scope.

B ○ Reduce the RTO and RPO targets.

C ○ Look for less expensive methods for achieving targets and report to management if no alternatives can be found.

D ○ Ask for more budget for recovery systems.

142 A security manager is planning a new video surveillance system. The manager wants the video surveillance system to be both a detective control and a deterrent control. What aspect of the system's design will achieve this objective?

A ○ Include a video-recording capability in the system.

B ○ Make video cameras conspicuously visible and post warning notices.

C ○ Hide video cameras and don't post warning notices.

D ○ Make video monitors conspicuously visible.

143 Privacy advocacy organizations are concerned about the practice of aggregation, which involves:

A ○ Selling highly sensitive data to the highest bidder

B ○ Distributing highly sensitive data to third parties

C ○ Combining low-sensitivity data elements that results in highly sensitive data

D ○ Disclosing highly sensitive data to government agencies

144 A cipher uses a table to replace plaintext characters with ciphertext characters. This type of cipher is known as:

A ○ Stream
B ○ Block
C ○ Substitution
D ○ Transposition

145 Under U.S. law, the amount of a fine and the length of imprisonment are based on:

A ○ The opinion of the judge
B ○ The opinion of the jury
C ○ The evidence introduced in a trial
D ○ Federal sentencing guidelines

146 An organization has identified a high-risk activity that's performed by a single individual. The organization will change the activity so that two or more individuals are required to perform the task. This new setup is known as:

A ○ Single point of failure
B ○ Shared custody
C ○ Split custody
D ○ Separation of duties

147 An organization wants to erect fencing around its property to keep out determined intruders. What are the minimum specifications that the organization should consider?

A ○ Eight feet in height and three strands of barbed wire at the top
B ○ Twelve feet in height and three strands of barbed wire at the top
C ○ Eight feet in height
D ○ Twelve feet in height

148 Which type of technology is a computer designer most likely to use for main memory?

A ○ EAROM
B ○ Dynamic RAM
C ○ Flash
D ○ Hard drive

149 A document that lists the equipment brands, programming languages, and communications protocols to be used in an organization is a:

A ○ Policy
B ○ Guideline
C ○ Requirement
D ○ Standard

150 Which of the following is true about Digital Subscriber Line:

A ○ Digital Subscriber Line is synonymous with DOCSIS (Digital Over Cable Services Interface Specification).
B ○ Digital Subscriber Line is a simplex protocol.
C ○ Digital Subscriber Line has been superseded by ISDN.
D ○ Digital Subscriber Line has superseded ISDN.

151 A DRP has an RTO of 24 hours and an RPO of 56 hours. This indicates that:

A ○ The system will be operational within 24 hours and the maximum data loss is 56 hours.
B ○ The system will be operational within at least 24 hours and the maximum data loss is 56 hours.
C ○ The system will be operational within 56 hours and the maximum data loss is 24 hours.
D ○ The system will be operational within 24 hours and the maximum data loss will be 32 hours.

152 The ability to associate users with their actions is known as:

A ○ Non-repudiation
B ○ Accountability
C ○ Audit trails
D ○ Responsibility

153 A database administrator has tuned a transaction processing database for optimum performance. Business users now want to use the same database for business intelligence and decision support. What action should the database administrator take?

A ○ Implement a separate data warehouse that's tuned for decision support.
B ○ Tune the transaction processing database to optimize performance of decision support queries.
C ○ Implement a database server cluster and tune the passive server for decision support.
D ○ Establish separate user IDs for transaction use and decision-support use, and tune each for their respective purposes.

154 **The Advanced Encryption Standard algorithm is based on:**

A ○ The Rijndael block cipher

B ○ The Rijndael stream cipher

C ○ The Skipjack cipher

D ○ The triple-DES cipher

155 **An organization has developed a new technique for compiling computer code and wants to protect that technique by using applicable intellectual property law. Which type of protection should the organization use?**

A ○ Patent

B ○ Trademark

C ○ Service mark

D ○ Copyright

156 **An organization is reducing the size of its workforce and has targeted the lead database administrator for termination of employment. How should the organization handle this termination?**

A ○ Terminate the employee's user accounts within 24 hours of notification.

B ○ Terminate the employee's user accounts immediately after notification.

C ○ Terminate the employee's user accounts within 48 hours of notification.

D ○ Retain the employee's user accounts until a replacement can be trained.

157 **What's one disadvantage of the use of key cards as a building access control?**

A ○ Key card readers are expensive.

B ○ The False Accept Rate (FAR) may exceed the False Reject Rate (FRR).

C ○ Any party who finds a lost key card can use it to enter a building.

D ○ A key card's PIN code is easily decrypted.

158 **All the following are components of an operating system EXCEPT:**

A ○ Compiler

B ○ Kernel

C ○ Device driver

D ○ Tools

159 **A document that describes the steps to be followed to complete a task is known as a:**

A ○ Process

B ○ Procedure

C ○ Guideline

D ○ Standard

160 Which routing protocol transmits its passwords in plaintext?

A ○ RIPv2

B ○ RIPv1

C ○ BGP

D ○ EIGRP

161 Damage assessment of a datacenter after an earthquake should be performed by:

A ○ The chief security officer

B ○ The datacenter manager

C ○ An unlicensed structural engineer

D ○ A licensed structural engineer

162 The primary reason users are encouraged to use passphrases, rather than passwords, is:

A ○ They'll choose longer passwords that are inherently stronger than shorter ones.

B ○ Their passwords will include spaces, which make passwords more complex.

C ○ Newer systems don't support passwords.

D ○ Passphrases can be coupled with biometric systems.

163 An application that was previously written to support a single user has been changed to support multiple concurrent users. The application encounters errors when two users attempt to access the same record. What feature should be added to the application to prevent these errors?

A ○ Load balancing

B ○ Replication

C ○ Record locking

D ○ Clustering

164 Two users, A and B, have exchanged public keys. How can user A send a secret message to user B?

A ○ User A encrypts a message with user B's public key; user B decrypts the message with user B's private key

B ○ User A encrypts the message with user A's private key; user B decrypts the message with user B's private key

C ○ User A encrypts the message with user A's private key; user B decrypts the message with user A's public key

D ○ User A encrypts the message with user B's public key; user B decrypts the message with user A's public key

165 An intruder has been apprehended for breaking into an organization's computer systems to steal national security secrets. Under what U.S. law will the intruder likely be charged?

A ○ Cybercrime Act of 2001

B ○ Federal Information Security Management Act of 2002

C ○ U.S. Computer Fraud and Abuse Act of 1986

D ○ U.S. Computer Security Act of 1987

166 The process of including text such as Company Confidential: For Internal Use Only on a document is known as:

A ○ Branding

B ○ Classification

C ○ Watermarking

D ○ Marking

167 An organization wants to install a motion detector in a portion of a building that has variable ambient noise. Which type of motion detector should be considered?

A ○ Wave pattern or capacitance

B ○ Wave pattern

C ○ Capacitance

D ○ Photo-electronic

168 An organization uses a Windows-based server to act as a file server. The owners of individual files and directories are able to grant read and write permissions to other users in the organization. This capability most closely resembles which security model?

A ○ Discretionary access control (DAC)

B ○ Mandatory access control (MAC)

C ○ Access matrix

D ○ Take-Grant

169 The relationship between threat, vulnerability, and risk is defined as:

A ○ Risk = vulnerability × threat

B ○ Threat = vulnerability × risk

C ○ Vulnerability = threat × risk

D ○ Risk = vulnerability + threat

170 Which of the following WiFi protocols has not been compromised:

A ○ WEP

B ○ WPA

C ○ WPA2

D ○ TKIP

171 The purpose of software escrow is:

A ○ Secure storage of software source code in the event of a disaster or the failure of the company that produced it

B ○ Third-party confirmation of the integrity of a software application

C ○ Secure storage of software object code in the event of a disaster or the failure of the company that produced it

D ○ Third-party delivery of a software application

172 A system has been designed to include strong authentication and transaction logging so that subjects can't deny having performed actions. This inability for a subject to deny having performed an action is known as:

A ○ Irresponsibility

B ○ Culpable deniability

C ○ Non-repudiation

D ○ Dissociation

173 An organization is considering the purchase of a business application. What should the organization develop before making a product decision?

A ○ Application code

B ○ Specifications

C ○ Design

D ○ Requirements

174 Two users want to establish a private communications link. The two users have never communicated before. How should a symmetric encryption key be communicated to both parties?

A ○ The encryption key should be kept by one party only.

B ○ The encryption key should be transmitted as part of initial communications.

C ○ The encryption key should be transmitted by using an in-band communications channel.

D ○ The encryption key should be transmitted by using an out-of-band communications channel.

175 An organization has developed a new method for building a mechanical device. The organization doesn't want to reveal the method to any third party. Which type of protection should be used?

A ○ Copyright

B ○ Patent

C ○ Trade secret

D ○ Trademark

176 An intruder has broken into an organization's computer systems to steal industrial designs. This action is known as:

A ○ Robbery

B ○ Cracking

C ○ Hacking

D ○ Espionage

177 For fire suppression in a commercial datacenter, all the following types of fire-suppression systems may be considered EXCEPT:

A ○ FM-200

B ○ Inert gas

C ○ Preaction

D ○ Deluge

178 TCSEC has been superseded by which standard?

A ○ Common Criteria

B ○ ITSEC

C ○ ISO 27002

D ○ DITSCAP

179 When is it prudent to perform a quantitative risk analysis?

A ○ When the probability of occurrence is low.

B ○ When the value of assets is high.

C ○ When the value of assets is low.

D ○ When the probability of occurrence is high.

180 Two users wish to establish a private communications link. The two users have never communicated before. What algorithm should be used to establish a symmetric encryption key?

A ○ Merkle

B ○ Diffie-Hellman

C ○ Babbage

D ○ RSA

181 The purpose of Layer 1 in the OSI model is to:

A ○ Transmit and receive bits.

B ○ Sequence packets and calculate checksums.

C ○ Perform application-to-application communications.

D ○ Transmit and receive frames.

182 The main reason for incorporating a CAPTCHA is:

A ○ To slow down brute-force attacks.

B ○ To prevent non-human interaction.

C ○ To improve application performance.

D ○ To reduce false-positives.

183 A set of SQL statements that are stored in the database is known as a:

A ○ Callout

B ○ Subroutine

C ○ Prepared statement

D ○ Stored procedure

184 Two users have exchanged public keys. User A has encrypted a message with User B's public key. What must User B do to read the message?

A ○ Decrypt the message with User A's private key.

B ○ Decrypt the message with User A's public key.

C ○ Decrypt the message with User B's public key.

D ○ Decrypt the message with User B's private key.

185 The USA PATRIOT Act:

A ○ Makes it illegal to encrypt international e-mail messages.

B ○ Makes it illegal to export strong encryption technology.

C ○ Gives law enforcement greater power of surveillance, search, and seizure.

D ○ Means judges no longer need to approve search warrants.

186 An organization has added bank account numbers to the data it backs up to tape. The organization should:

A ○ Back up only the hashes of bank account numbers and not the numbers themselves.

B ○ Split bank account numbers so they reside on two different backup tapes.

C ○ Stop sending backup tapes off-site.

D ○ Encrypt backup tapes that are sent off-site.

187 The purpose of a motion sensing request-to-exit sensor on an exterior doorway is:

A ○ Count the number of persons exiting the door.

B ○ Count the number of persons entering the door.

C ○ Unlock an exterior door and permit a person to exit.

D ○ Detect when a person is approaching an exterior exit from the inside.

188 The risks associated with outsourcing computing to the Cloud are all of the following EXCEPT:

A ○ Data ownership.

B ○ Data jurisdiction.

C ○ Control effectiveness.

D ○ Availability.

189 A system architect has designed a system that is protected with two layers of firewalls, where each firewall is a different make. This follows which security design principle?

A ○ Avoidance of a single point of failure

B ○ Defense in depth

C ○ Fail open

D ○ Fail closed

190 The range of all possible encryption keys is known as:

A ○ Keyrange.

B ○ Keyspace.

C ○ Elliptic curve.

D ○ Cryptospace.

191 2001:0F56:45E3:BA98 is a:

A ○ MAC address

B ○ IPv4 address

C ○ Subnet mask

D ○ IPv6 address

192 An authentication system does not limit the number of invalid login attempts. This system is:

A ○ Designed for machine interaction only.

B ○ Integrated to a single sign-on (SSO) service.

C ○ Vulnerable to brute force attacks.

D ○ Not used to store sensitive data.

193 An attacker has discovered a way to change his permissions from an ordinary end user to an administrator. This type of attack is known as:

A ○ Back door.

B ○ Denial of Service.

C ○ Privilege injection.

D ○ Escalation of privilege.

194 **A user has lost the password to his private key. The user should:**

A ○ Create a new password for his private key

B ○ Decrypt his private key

C ○ Retrieve the password from his public key

D ○ Generate a new keypair

195 **The burden of proof in U.S. criminal law is:**

A ○ The preponderance of the evidence

B ○ Beyond a reasonable doubt

C ○ Beyond all doubt

D ○ Based on the opinion of the presiding judge

196 **The best approach for patch management is:**

A ○ Install only those patches that scanning tools specify are missing.

B ○ Install patches only after problems are experienced.

C ○ Install all available patches.

D ○ Perform risk analysis and install patches that are relevant.

197 **In addition to video surveillance, how can a public reception area be best protected?**

A ○ Duress alarm

B ○ Pepper spray

C ○ Hand signals

D ○ Emergency telephone numbers

198 **The main weakness of a homogeneous environment is:**

A ○ A variety of systems is more difficult to manage effectively.

B ○ Inconsistent management among systems in the environment.

C ○ A vulnerability in one system is likely to be found in all systems in the environment.

D ○ Port scans will take longer to complete.

199 **A security manager has designed a building entrance that will lock doors in the event of a power failure. This follows which security design principle?**

A ○ Avoidance of a single point of failure

B ○ Defense in depth

C ○ Fail open

D ○ Fail closed

200 An effective cryptosystem is all of the following EXCEPT:

A ○ Efficient.

B ○ Easy to crack.

C ○ Easy to use.

D ○ Strong, even if its algorithm is known.

201 255.255.0.0 is a:

A ○ MAC address

B ○ IPv4 address

C ○ Subnet mask

D ○ IPv6 address

202 The main reason for preventing password re-use is:

A ○ To increase password entropy.

B ○ To prevent a user from reverting to their old, familiar password.

C ○ To encourage users to use different passwords on different systems.

D ○ To prevent users from using the same passwords on different systems.

203 A software developer has introduced a feature in an application that permits him to access the application without the need to log in. This feature is known as a:

A ○ Bypass

B ○ Front door

C ○ Side door

D ○ Back door

204 A cryptosystem uses two-digit numerals to represent each character of a message. This is a:

A ○ Concealment cipher

B ○ Vernam cipher

C ○ Substitution cipher

D ○ Transposition cipher

205 California state law SB-1386:

A ○ Requires organizations to publish their privacy policies.

B ○ Requires organizations to encrypt bank account numbers.

C ○ Requires organizations to disclose security breaches to affected citizens.

D ○ Requires organizations to encrypt private data.

206 The purpose of penetration testing is:

A ○ Simulate an attack by insiders.

B ○ Confirm the presence of application vulnerabilities.

C ○ Confirm the effectiveness of patch management.

D ○ Simulate a real attack and identify vulnerabilities.

207 An advantage of video surveillance motion sensing recording over continuous recording is:

A ○ Date and time stamping on video frames.

B ○ Improved durability of storage media.

C ○ Lower cost of storage media.

D ○ Relevant content can be retained for a longer period of time.

208 The four basic requirements in the Orange Book are:

A ○ Security policy, assurance, accountability, and documentation.

B ○ Security policy, availability, accountability, and documentation.

C ○ Security policy, assurance, confidentiality, and documentation.

D ○ Security policy, assurance, accountability, and integrity.

209 A document that is unclassified:

A ○ Is a threat to national security.

B ○ Is not sensitive.

C ○ Is secret and must be protected.

D ○ Is not a threat to national security.

210 In a symmetric cryptosystem, two users who wish to exchange encrypted messages exchange cryptovariables. The next thing the users should do is:

A ○ Re-issue encryption keys.

B ○ Begin to exchange encrypted messages.

C ○ Change encryption algorithms.

D ○ Change to an asymmetric cryptosystem.

211 In the resource \\usdb01\symm\dev\src\ usdb01 is a:

A ○ Server.

B ○ Directory.

C ○ File.

D ○ Network.

212 **An attacker has obtained a file containing hashed passwords. The fastest way to crack the hashed passwords is:**

A ○ Unsalt the hashes

B ○ Brute-force attack

C ○ Rainbow tables

D ○ Cryptanalysis

213 **The best method for defending against cross-site request forgery (CSRF) attacks is:**

A ○ Encrypt traffic with SSL/TLS.

B ○ Block JavaScript execution.

C ○ Filter input fields to reject injection strings.

D ○ Include a transaction confirmation step with every critical application function.

214 **A cryptosystem uses a key that is the same length of the message. The key is used only for this message. This is a:**

A ○ Transformation cipher.

B ○ Transposition cipher.

C ○ Substitution cipher.

D ○ Vernam cipher.

215 **The purpose of the Sarbanes-Oxley Act of 2002 is to:**

A ○ Restore investors' confidence in U.S. companies.

B ○ Ensure privacy of all U.S. citizens.

C ○ Increase penalties for security breaches.

D ○ Reduce securities fraud.

216 **A disadvantage of a HIDS is all of the following EXCEPT:**

A ○ A server-based HIDS system cannot be a choke point like a NIDS/NIPS can.

B ○ A separate HIDS instance must be installed and maintained on every server.

C ○ HIDS can only perform signature-based detection, not anomaly-based detection.

D ○ It will not detect port scans on unused IP addresses.

217 The primary advantage for remote monitoring of datacenter access controls is:

A ○ Local monitoring cannot identify all intrusions.

B ○ Remote monitoring is more effective than local monitoring.

C ○ Reduction of costs.

D ○ It compensates for the possibility that personnel in the datacenter are unavailable or compromised.

218 TCSEC evaluation criteria are:

A ○ Certification, inspection, and accreditation.

B ○ Confidentiality, integrity, and availability.

C ○ Measurement, guidance, and acquisition.

D ○ System architecture, system integrity, and covert channel analysis.

219 A document that lists approved protocols is known as a:

A ○ Process

B ○ Procedure

C ○ Guideline

D ○ Standard

220 An encryption algorithm that rearranges bits, characters, or blocks of data is known as a:

A ○ Substitution cipher.

B ○ Transposition cipher.

C ○ Vernam cipher.

D ○ Concealment cipher.

221 Systems on an internal network have RFC 1918 network addresses. To permit these systems to communicate with systems on the Internet, what should be implemented on the firewall?

A ○ NAT

B ○ NAC

C ○ NAP

D ○ NAS

222 The purpose of a user account access review is:

A ○ All of these.

B ○ To ensure that employee terminations were properly processed.

C ○ To ensure that all role assignments were properly approved.

D ○ To ensure that assigned roles are still needed.

223 The most effective countermeasure for session hijacking is:

A ○ Two-factor authentication.

B ○ Strong passwords.

C ○ Full disk encryption.

D ○ Full session HTTPS encryption.

224 A cryptologist has determined that a cryptosystem has a weak PRNG. This can lead to:

A ○ Compromise of the cryptosystem

B ○ Increased performance of the cryptosystem

C ○ Decreased performance of the cryptosystem

D ○ Collisions

225 Recordkeeping that is related to the acquisition and management of forensic evidence is known as:

A ○ Best evidence.

B ○ Burden of proof.

C ○ Chain of custody.

D ○ Certification.

226 The purpose of audit trails includes all of the following EXCEPT:

A ○ Event reconstruction.

B ○ Investigation support.

C ○ Enforcement of accountability.

D ○ Data recovery.

227 In a datacenter that provides dual power feeds to each equipment rack, components with dual power supplies are connected to each power feed. Why should power circuits not be loaded over 40% capacity?

A ○ To permit systems to be power-cycled without overloading circuits.

B ○ To permit systems to be rebooted without overloading circuits.

C ○ To permit power supplies to be swapped out.

D ○ If one power feed fails, power draw on alternate circuits will double.

228 A web application that uses sequential session identifiers:

A ○ Has high resilience.

B ○ Has low resilience.

C ○ Is vulnerable to session hijacking.

D ○ Is not vulnerable to session hijacking.

229 **All of the following statements about policies are true EXCEPT:**

A ○ They specify what should be done.

B ○ They specify how something should be done.

C ○ They should be reviewed annually.

D ○ They are formal statements of rules.

230 **An encryption algorithm that replaces bits, characters, or blocks in plaintext with alternate bits, characters, or blocks is known as a:**

A ○ Substitution cipher.

B ○ Transposition cipher.

C ○ Vernam cipher.

D ○ Concealment cipher.

231 **Two-factor authentication is preferred for VPN because:**

A ○ It is more resistant to a dictionary attack.

B ○ It is more resistant to a replay attack.

C ○ Encryption protects authentication credentials.

D ○ Encryption protects encapsulated traffic.

232 **An audit of user access has revealed that user accounts are not being locked when employees leave the organization. The best way to mitigate this finding is:**

A ○ Reset all account passwords.

B ○ Lock all user accounts and require users to re-apply for access.

C ○ Improve the termination process and perform monthly access reviews.

D ○ Discipline the culpable personnel.

233 **A blogging site allows users to embed JavaScript in the body of blog entries. This will allow what type of attack?**

A ○ Cross-frame scripting

B ○ Cross-site request forgery

C ○ Non-persistent cross-site scripting

D ○ Persistent cross-site scripting

234 **A system designer needs to choose a stream cipher to encrypt data. The designer should choose:**

A ○ 3DES

B ○ AES

C ○ RC1

D ○ RC4

235 Evidence that is obtained through illegal means:

A ○ May be used in a legal proceeding.

B ○ May be used as indirect evidence.

C ○ Cannot be used in a legal proceeding.

D ○ Must be returned to its owner.

236 A particular type of security incident occurs frequently in an organization. What should be performed to reduce the frequency of these incidents?

A ○ Audit log correlation

B ○ Root cause analysis

C ○ Incident forensics

D ○ Six Sigma analysis

237 What procedure should be followed by personnel in case of fire in a datacenter?

A ○ All personnel should remain to fight the fire.

B ○ One person should remain behind and fight the fire.

C ○ Collect backup media and evacuate.

D ○ Immediate evacuation.

238 The following statements about the Common Criteria are true EXCEPT:

A ○ It is the European version of ITSEC.

B ○ It has been adopted as international standard ISO 15408.

C ○ It contains eight levels of evaluation assurance.

D ○ It supersedes TCSEC and ITSEC.

239 An organization has employees in many countries, where laws vary on the type of background checks that can be performed. The best approach for background checks is:

A ○ Perform background checks only in those countries that permit reasonable checks.

B ○ Perform the best background check in each country as permitted by law.

C ○ Perform the same background check in all countries by performing only what is allowed in all of them.

D ○ Do not perform background checks.

240 A disadvantage of a symmetric cryptosystem is:

A ○ It is far less efficient than an asymmetric cryptosystem.

B ○ Users who do not know each other will have difficulty securely exchanging keys.

C ○ It is difficult to publish a public key.

D ○ It is easy to publish a public key.

241 **Two organizations exchange data via FTP. The best choice to make this more secure is:**

A ○ Change the FTP protocol to SFTP or FTPS.

B ○ Encrypt transferred files with PGP.

C ○ Change password more frequently.

D ○ Change to longer, complex passwords.

242 **An attacker is capturing a user's keystrokes during authentication. The attacker may be preparing to launch a:**

A ○ Brute-force attack.

B ○ Cryptanalysis attack.

C ○ Replay attack.

D ○ Denial of service attack.

243 **Users in a company have received e-mail messages claiming to be from the company's IT department with instructions on installing a security patch. The URL points to a page that resembles the company's IT Helpdesk home page. This may be a:**

A ○ Whaling attack.

B ○ Pharming attack.

C ○ Phishing attack.

D ○ Spear phishing attack.

244 **A laptop containing several private encryption keys has been stolen. The owner of the encryption keys should:**

A ○ Generate new key pairs

B ○ Change the keys' passwords

C ○ Change encryption algorithms

D ○ No action is necessary

245 **A company outsources its credit card processing to a third-party organization. The company should:**

A ○ Require the third-party organization to be PCI-compliant.

B ○ Require the third-party organization to be GLBA-compliant.

C ○ Sign a contract with the third-party organization.

D ○ Perform penetration tests on the third party's systems.

246 **Administration of a centralized audit log server should be performed by:**

A ○ Database administrators.

B ○ IT auditors.

C ○ The same administrators who manage servers being logged.

D ○ Separate administrators from those who administer servers being logged.

247 The ideal level of relative humidity for datacenter computing equipment is:

A ○ Between 0% and 20%.

B ○ Between 20% and 40%.

C ○ 0%.

D ○ Between 40% and 60%.

248 A security manager wishes to establish a set of access control rules that specify which organization job titles are permitted to have which roles in a system. The model that the security manager should use as a model is:

A ○ Access Matrix.

B ○ Information Flow.

C ○ Non-Interference.

D ○ Biba.

249 A decision on how to resolve an identified risk is known as:

A ○ Risk control.

B ○ Risk treatment.

C ○ Risk management.

D ○ Risk mitigation.

250 The advantage of Cipher Block Chaining (CBC) is:

A ○ Each block of ciphertext has a less random result.

B ○ Each block of ciphertext has a more random result.

C ○ Each block of ciphertext is encrypted separately.

D ○ Each block of ciphertext is decrypted separately.

Answers

1 **B.** See Chapter 11. People and their safety always come first!

2 **B.** See Chapter 4. Mandatory access control is based on the user's clearance level, the classification of the information, and the user's need-to-know.

3 **B.** See Chapter 7. A data dictionary contains information about an application's data structures, including table names, field names, indexes, and so on.

4 **C.** See Chapter 8. Cryptanalysis is the process of getting the key and/or the original message the hard way.

5 **B.** See Chapter 7. Robert Tappan Morris wrote and released what's now known as the Internet Worm in 1988. Researcher Gene Spafford wrote several papers on the topic.

6 **B.** See Chapter 10. Preventive controls are designed to prevent a security incident.

7 **C.** See Chapter 13. The primary concern here is to keep intruders out, which is why computer room walls should extend from the true floor to the true ceiling.

8 **C.** See Chapter 9. Cache memory holds instructions and data that are likely to be frequently accessed. Cache memory is faster than RAM, so it can contribute to faster performance.

9 **A.** See Chapter 6. Separation of authority makes it difficult for an individual to steal an organization's assets because it requires others to cooperate with the would-be criminal.

10 **D.** See Chapter 5. UDP has no guarantee of delivery, nor sequencing or acknowledgement.

11 **A.** See Chapter 11. Mutual aid agreements aren't a significant concern of a Business Impact Assessment (BIA). They're instead a part of contingency planning.

12 **A.** See Chapter 4. Identity-based access control is used to grant access to information based on the identity of the person requesting access.

13 **A.** See Chapter 7. A Service-Level Agreement (SLA) defines minimum performance metrics of an application or service.

14 **D.** See Chapter 8. Secret key cryptography is used when all parties possess a common key.

15 **C.** See Chapter 12. Forensics is the activity of discovering, preserving, and recording evidence.

16 **A.** See Chapter 10. Detective controls are designed to record security events.

17 **C.** See Chapter 13. Water cools the fuel to the point where the fire can't continue. Also, to some extent, water is a physical barrier between the fuel and oxygen.

18 **A.** See Chapter 9. Firmware is software that's seldom changed. Firmware is generally used to control low-level functions in computer hardware and embedded systems.

19 **C.** See Chapter 6. *Open view* is the act of leaving a classified document out in the open so that it can be viewed by anyone.

20 **B.** See Chapter 5. TCP adds unnecessary overhead. Streaming video can afford to lose a packet now and then.

21 **C.** See Chapter 11. Maximum Tolerable Downtime (MTD) is the length of time that an organization can tolerate critical processes being inoperative.

22 **B.** See Chapter 4. User-directed access control, a form of discretionary access control, permits the user to grant access to information based on certain limitations.

23 **D.** See Chapter 4. Cyclical Redundancy Checks (CRCs), parity checks, and checksums are examples of detective application controls because they're designed to help discover security breaches (as well as network malfunctions and other undesired events) in a network.

24 **C.** See Chapter 8. In public key cryptography, the value of the public key doesn't in any way betray the value of the secret key.

25 **A.** See Chapter 12. An expert witness offers his or her opinion based on the facts of the case and on personal expertise.

26 **C.** See Chapter 10. Corrective controls are used to resume business operations after a security incident.

27 **A.** See Chapter 13. Positive drains are those that carry liquids away from a building.

28 **B.** See Chapter 9. Memory protection is a machine-level security feature that prevents one program from being able to read or alter memory assigned to another program.

29 **A.** See Chapter 6. The information owner is ultimately responsible for the information asset and for its initial classification.

30 **A.** See Chapter 5. There are four layers in the TCP/IP model: Network Access, Internet, Transport, and Application.

31 **B.** See Chapter 11. Warm sites are mostly like hot sites, except that the organization's software and data aren't on the warm site's systems.

32 **C.** See Chapter 4. Encryption, tokens, access control lists, and smart cards are examples of technical, or logical, controls.

33 **C.** See Chapter 7. Data mining is the term used to describe searches for correlations, patterns, and trends in a data warehouse.

34 **A.** See Chapter 8. In this cipher, the cryptographer writes across but reads down.

35 **C.** See Chapter 12. A witness testifies the facts as he or she understands them.

36 **A.** See Chapter 10. Covert channel analysis is used to detect, understand, and help security personnel to prevent the creation and operation of covert channels.

37 **D.** See Chapter 6. It's infinitely better to find undesirable qualities, such as a criminal history, prior to making an employment decision.

38 **A.** See Chapter 9. The virtual memory model is used to create a memory space that's larger than the available physical memory.

39 **B.** See Chapter 6. The custodian protects the information on behalf of its owner.

40 **B.** See Chapter 5. ARP is the Address Resolution Protocol.

41 **D.** See Chapter 11. The hot site already has computer equipment.

42 **D.** See Chapter 4. Administrative access controls consist of all the policies and procedures that are used to mitigate risk.

43 **D.** See Chapter 7. Object-oriented, relational, and network are types of databases.

44 **C.** See Chapter 8. Asymmetric cryptosystems are also known as public key cryptosystems.

45 **A.** See Chapter 12. Entrapment refers to the activities that lure an individual into committing a crime that he or she wouldn't have otherwise committed.

46 **D.** See Chapter 10. Least privilege is the principle that states users should have access only to the data and functions required for their stated duties.

47 **B.** See Chapter 13. Building access systems don't know why people are coming and going.

48 **D.** See Chapter 9. Open systems are those in which specifications are published and freely available, permitting any vendor to develop components that can be used with it.

49 **A.** See Chapter 6. Useful life, value, and age are some of the criteria used to classify information.

50 **A.** See Chapter 5. ARP is used to translate an IP address into a MAC address.

51 **B.** See Chapter 11. The Disaster Recovery Plan (DRP) must contain an up-to-date record of all critical business processes.

52 **C.** See Chapter 4. Physical access controls include security guards, locked doors, and surveillance cameras, as well as other controls such as backups, protection of cabling, and card-key access.

53 **B.** See Chapter 7. Neural networks are systems that can detect patterns after a period of training.

54 **B.** See Chapter 8. Steganography is the science of inserting messages into larger datasets so that the existence of the message is unknown.

55 **D.** See Chapter 12. Enticement is used to keep a criminal at the scene of the crime. In the context of electronic crime, a honeypot is a great way to keep an intruder sniffing around while his or her origin is traced.

56 **B.** See Chapter 10. Separation of duties is used to ensure that no single individual has too much privilege, which could lead to a security incident or fraud.

57 **D.** See Chapter 13. Tailgating is a common method used by someone who wants to enter a controlled area but has no authorization to do so.

58 **C.** See Chapter 9. In a distributed architecture, information isn't centrally stored, but rather stored in a multitude of locations. The other answers *are* security issues in distributed architectures.

59 **C.** See Chapter 6. A senior management statement of security policy underscores the importance of and support for security.

60 **B.** See Chapter 5. RARP is used to translate a MAC address into an IP address.

61 **A.** See Chapter 11. Audits will uncover changes that are needed in the DRP.

62 **D.** See Chapter 4. Role-based access control and task-based access control are known as non-discretionary controls, which match information to roles or tasks, not individual users.

63 **A.** See Chapter 7. Unit testing is the testing of small modules of code, which is used to verify that the coding was done correctly.

64 **C.** See Chapter 8. Steganography can be difficult to detect visually in an image.

65 **B.** See Chapter 12. A honeypot is designed to keep an intruder sniffing around long enough for investigators to determine his or her origin and identity.

66 **C.** See Chapter 10. Installing system software is a system administrator function; the rest are security administrator functions.

67 **B.** See Chapter 13. *Fail open* refers to any controlling mechanism that remains in the unlocked position when it fails. In the case of controlled building entrances, anyone can enter the building.

68 **B.** See Chapter 9. TCB stands for Trusted Computing Base.

69 **D.** See Chapter 6. An advisory policy is required by the organization but is not mandated by a local or national government.

70 **B.** See Chapter 5. This is an IPv4 address.

71 **C.** See Chapter 11. A short Recovery Time Objective (RTO) usually requires a hot site because you have very little time available for setting up replacement systems.

72 **D.** See Chapter 4. Detective controls are those controls that are designed to detect security events, but can't prevent them in the way that preventive controls can.

73 **D.** See Chapter 7. Requirements are the single largest input used in the high-level product design phase.

74 **C.** See Chapter 8. World War II saw a significant advancement in the science of cryptography. World War II became a war of cryptanalysis wherein each participant was sometimes able to break the code of the others, resulting in strategic advantages.

75 **C.** See Chapter 12. Issuing monitoring tools to all e-mail administrators isn't a precaution at all — it's not even a step that would be considered. The other items do need to occur before any monitoring is performed.

76 **A.** See Chapter 10. Rotation of duties is used to keep mixing up the teams in order to prevent situations in which individuals are tempted to perform unauthorized acts.

77 **A.** See Chapter 13. *Fail closed* refers to any controlling mechanism that remains in the locked position when it fails. In the case of controlled building entrances, no one can enter the building by normal means.

78 **A.** See Chapter 9. A Trusted Computing Base is the complete picture of protection used in a computer system.

79 **A.** See Chapter 6. A threat is a possible undesirable event that may cause harm or damage.

80 **A.** See Chapter 5. This is a MAC address.

81 **D.** See Chapter 11. A communications outage is considered a man-made disaster (although it can be caused by a naturally occurring event).

82 **C.** See Chapter 4. Preventive controls are controls that are used to prevent security events.

83 **B.** See Chapter 7. Going back one step for rework (of requirements, design, coding, testing — whatever the step is that needs to be reworked) was the main improvement of the Waterfall model. This is important because sometimes any of the steps may fail to consider something that the next step uncovers.

84 **A.** See Chapter 8. Non-repudiation helps to prove that a specific individual did create or sign a document, or did transmit data to or receive data from another individual.

85 **A.** See Chapter 12. Intellectual property laws apply to trade secrets, trademarks, copyrights, and patents.

86 **C.** See Chapter 10. Change management is the complete management function that controls changes made to a production environment.

87 **B.** See Chapter 13. Wet-pipe is the sprinkler system type in which water is always in the pipe.

88 **B.** See Chapter 9. Pipelining is the mechanism used to overlap the steps in machine instructions in order to complete them faster.

89 **B.** See Chapter 6. A vulnerability is a weakness that can permit an undesirable event.

90 **C.** See Chapter 5. Ping uses ICMP Echo Requests.

91 **A.** See Chapter 11. Remote journaling keeps data at an alternative site up-to-date at all times.

92 **A.** See Chapter 4. Identification is only the assertion of identity, whereas authentication is the proof of identity.

93 **A.** See Chapter 7. Security should be included in the earliest possible phases of a software development project. The requirements phase is the earliest among the choices offered.

94 **A.** See Chapter 8. Work function is the term used to describe the amount of time and/or money required to break a ciphertext.

95 **A.** See Chapter 12. Evidence gathered in violation of any laws can't be admitted in court.

96 **B.** See Chapter 10. Configuration management is the support function that's used to store version information about its systems.

97 **C.** See Chapter 13. Preaction, a combination of dry-pipe and wet-pipe, is increasingly popular in datacenters because it reduces the likelihood that a water discharge will actually occur — and a discharge will be limited to a small area in the datacenter.

98 **D.** See Chapter 9. FORTRAN, BASIC, and C are third-generation languages.

99 **A.** See Chapter 6. Safeguards exist to reduce risk in some way.

100 **D.** See Chapter 5. SMTP, or Simple Mail Transport Protocol, is used to send and receive e-mail messages.

101 **C.** See Chapter 11. *Electronic vaulting* is the term that describes backing up data over a communications line to another location.

102 **A.** See Chapter 4. Two-factor authentication requires any two of Type 1 (something you know), Type 2 (something you have), and Type 3 (something you are) authentication methods.

103 **C.** See Chapter 7. Veto power is unlikely, but the other choices listed are value-added features of change control.

104 **B.** See Chapter 8. The lack of a top-level (root) signature on a certificate results in warning messages stating that the certificate lacks a top-level signature.

105 **C.** See Chapter 12. Federal, state, and local laws cover computer crime. Depending on the crime, one or more levels of government may have jurisdiction.

106 **D.** See Chapter 10. Configuration management is used to preserve all prior settings or versions of software or hardware, as well as to provide a check out/check in capability to avoid collisions.

107 **D.** See Chapter 13. Dry-pipe systems take a few moments (at least) before water discharge begins.

108 **A.** See Chapter 9. An operating system (OS) manages computer hardware and presents a consistent interface to application programs and tools.

109 **D.** See Chapter 6. The purpose of risk analysis is to quantify the impact of a potential threat; in other words, to put a monetary value on the loss of information or functionality.

110 **B.** See Chapter 5. Because it encrypts and decrypts packets over the network, SSL consumes a lot of CPU time.

111 **B.** See Chapter 11. Off-site storage is merely an alternate location for storing back-up media.

112 **D.** See Chapter 4. *Something you are* refers to authentication that measures a biometric, which means something physical, such as a fingerprint, retina scan, or voiceprint.

113 **A.** See Chapter 7. The greatest value in the development life cycle is getting security requirements in at the beginning so that security will be "baked in."

114 **D.** See Chapter 8. The Clipper Chip implemented a capability to provide encryption for users and also provided a legal wiretap capability.

115 **B.** See Chapter 12. Evidence may be seized only if law enforcement believes that it's about to be destroyed (which the law calls *exigent circumstances*).

116 **A.** See Chapter 9. Erasure is seldom 100-percent effective. Despite complex and time-consuming methods, the slightest traces of data on media that have been erased may always remain.

117 **A.** See Chapter 13. Walls that go all the way up to the ceiling do a better job of keeping fires from spreading into or out of the datacenter.

118 **B.** See Chapter 9. Protection rings are layers of protection domains, with the most protected domain in the center.

119 **B.** See Chapter 6. Annualized Rate of Occurrence (ARO) is a risk management term that describes the likelihood of the occurrence of a threat.

120 **D.** See Chapter 5. Access control lists are used on firewalls, routers, and bastion hosts, but not on client systems (at least not for recording passwords!).

121 **B.** See Chapter 11. A high Recovery Point Objective (RPO) means that data on a recovered system will be older. A low Recovery Time Objective (RTO) means that the system will be recovered quickly.

122 **B.** See Chapter 4. Two-factor authentication requires any two of Type 1 (something you know), Type 2 (something you have), and Type 3 (something you are) authentication methods.

123 **C.** See Chapter 7. Configuration management produces a highly detailed record, including details of each and every copy of a software product that was created.

124 **C.** See Chapter 8. The famous device used by Germany to encrypt and decrypt secret messages was the Enigma.

125 **C.** See Chapter 12. Motive, means, and opportunity are the standard criteria when considering a possible suspect in a crime.

126 **D.** See Chapter 10. Software controls are used to protect software from unauthorized disclosure or tampering.

127 **A.** See Chapter 13. Dial-up alarms don't detect fire; they respond to a fire detector and call the fire department by using a telephone line to play a prerecorded message.

128 **A.** See Chapter 9. The Orange Book was one of several books in the Rainbow Series, each describing various levels and contexts of computer security, and each with its own unique color.

129 **B.** See Chapter 6. Single Loss Expectancy (SLE) is the monetary value associated with an individual threat.

130 **C.** See Chapter 5. The DHCP (dynamic host configuration protocol) is used to assign IP addresses to stations that join a network.

131 **B.** See Chapter 11. A Business Impact Assessment (BIA) is used to determine the impact that different types of disasters have on critical business processes.

132 **D.** See Chapter 4. It's reasonable for some employees to voice concerns regarding the cleanliness of a hand scanner that many employees will be using. Making hand-sanitizing agents available and requiring all users to use those hand sanitizers is a reasonable precaution to help prevent the spread of illnesses.

133 **A.** See Chapter 7. An application that has a script injection vulnerability needs to be modified so that data accepted in input fields is sanitized by removing script tags and other scripting commands.

134 **A.** See Chapter 8. Cryptography can be used for confidentiality (by encrypting a message), integrity (through the use of digital signatures), and authentication (through the use of digital signatures to prove the origin of a message). Cryptography isn't used for performance.

135 **A.** See Chapter 12. The burden of proof in U.S. civil law is based on the preponderance of the evidence.

136 **A.** See Chapter 10. Periodic background checks can be used to discover any new events in an employee's criminal or financial background, as well as uncover any criminal records that weren't found in the initial background check.

137 **B.** See Chapter 13. A Class C fire extinguisher should be used in a datacenter; this type is most effective against electronics and electrical fires.

138 **C.** See Chapter 9. PDP-11, Intel x86, and Motorola 68000 are CISC design CPUs. SPARC is a RISC design CPU.

139 **A.** See Chapter 6. An architecture with parallel components generally is following the avoidance of a single point of failure.

140 **A.** See Chapter 5. Because it transmits light instead of electrical signals, fiber-optic cabling is virtually immune to RF and EMF environments.

141 **C.** See Chapter 11. When management has determined that a proposed disaster recovery architecture is too expensive, the project team needs to find less costly alternatives. If none can be found, the project team needs to inform management, who may approve of longer RPO and RTO targets that should be less costly.

142 **B.** See Chapter 4. A video surveillance system can be an effective deterrent control if its cameras are visible. Warning notices provide even greater deterrent ability.

143 **C.** See Chapter 7. Aggregation is the process of combining data, which can result in the creation of highly sensitive information.

144 **C.** See Chapter 8. A substitution cipher uses a lookup table for substituting one character for another.

145 **D.** See Chapter 12. Federal sentencing guidelines provide the range of possible monetary fines and length of imprisonment.

146 **D.** See Chapter 10. Separation of duties is the concept that supports a process design in which two or more individuals are required to perform a critical task. The classic example is the three activities carried out by three separate individuals in an accounting system: creating a payee, making a payment request, and making a payment.

147 **A.** See Chapter 13. To keep out determined intruders, an organization should consider fencing that's at least eight feet in height and includes three strands of barbed wire.

148 **B.** See Chapter 9. Most computers' main memory uses dynamic RAM (DRAM) or static RAM (SRAM).

149 **D.** See Chapter 6. A standards document defines the equipment brands, programming languages, communications protocols, and other components to be used in an organization.

150 **D.** See Chapter 5. Digital Subscriber Line has superseded ISDN in most areas. The other statements are false.

151 **A.** See Chapter 11. An RTO of 24 hours means a recovery system will be operational within 24 hours of a disaster. An RPO of 56 hours means the maximum data loss will be 56 hours.

152 **B.** See Chapter 4. When users are associated with their actions (which is usually achieved through audit logs), they're made to be accountable.

153 **A.** See Chapter 7. It's rarely possible to tune a database management system to provide adequate performance for both transaction processing and decision support. A separate data warehouse should be implemented, and that database tuned for that purpose. The original database should be tuned for optimum transaction processing performance.

154 **A.** See Chapter 8. AES (Advanced Encryption Standard) is based on the Rijndael block cipher.

155 **A.** See Chapter 12. A patent is the type of legal protection used for the design of a mechanism.

156 **B.** See Chapter 10. A position such as database administrator, network administrator, or system administrator usually has high privileges. The safest course of action when terminating employment for a person in such a position is to immediately terminate all access immediately after (or just prior to) notification.

157 **C.** See Chapter 13. Unless coupled with a PIN pad or biometric reader, any person can use a key card to enter a building.

158 **A.** See Chapter 9. Operating systems consist of a kernel, device drivers, and tools.

159 **B.** See Chapter 6. A procedure describes the steps used to complete a task.

160 **A.** See Chapter 5. The RIP (Routing Information Protocol) version 2 transmits passwords in plaintext. RIPv1 did not use passwords at all.

161 **D.** See Chapter 11. Only a licensed structural engineer is qualified to examine the structure of a building after an earthquake and determine whether that building can be safely used. The other parties aren't qualified to make this assessment.

162 **A.** See Chapter 4. The term *passphrase* simply means a longer password. The longer a password, the more difficult it can be to crack.

163 **C.** See Chapter 7. *Record locking* is a mechanism used to arbitrate access to resources in multiuser applications.

164 **A.** See Chapter 8. In public key cryptography, a sender encrypts a message with the recipient's public key; the recipient decrypts the message with the recipient's private key.

165 **C.** See Chapter 12. An intruder who steals national security secrets in the U.S. is likely to be charged with a violation of the Computer Fraud and Abuse Act of 1986.

166 **D.** See Chapter 10. Classifying, or marking, is the term used to describe the action of including text such as Company Confidential on a document.

167 **A.** See Chapter 13. A wave pattern or capacitance motion detector would be a candidate for an area that experiences ambient noise.

168 **A.** See Chapter 9. The capability for end users to grant permissions to others corresponds to the discretionary access control (DAC) model.

169 **A.** See Chapter 6. The basic relationship between threat, vulnerability, and risk is that the risk is equal to the threat times the vulnerability.

170 **C.** See Chapter 5. WPA2 with AES has not been compromised.

171 **A.** See Chapter 11. The purpose of a software escrow agreement (also known as a source code escrow agreement) is the secure off-site storage of software source code in the event of a disaster or the complete failure of the organization.

172 **C.** See Chapter 4. Non-repudiation is a property of a system to be able to prevent a subject from denying that he or she performed an action. This is accomplished through strong authentication and audit (or transaction) logging.

173 **D.** See Chapter 7. An organization should develop requirements that define the desired characteristics of an application that it will consider purchasing.

174 **D.** See Chapter 8. For two parties that have not communicated before, a symmetric encryption key must be sent from one party to another through an out-of-band channel. For example, an encryption key for network communications should be sent via fax or courier.

175 **C.** See Chapter 12. An organization that doesn't want to disclose a method can't file a copyright, trademark, or patent because these filings would disclose the method. Instead, the organization must carefully guard the method and consider it a trade secret.

176 **D.** See Chapter 10. Espionage is the process of spying on an organization in order to discover its military or industrial secrets.

177 **D.** See Chapter 13. Fire suppression in a commercial datacenter may include an inert gas system, FM-200 (which is one commercial brand of an inert gas system), or preaction (if local fire codes require some type of a water sprinkler system). A deluge system would never be considered.

178 A. See Chapter 9. The Trusted Computer System Evaluation Criteria (TCSEC) has been superseded by the Common Criteria.

179 B. See Chapter 6. A quantitative risk analysis is more difficult and time-consuming to perform, and is usually done only on high-value assets.

180 B. See Chapter 8. The Diffie-Hellman (DH) key exchange algorithm permits the safe establishment of a symmetric encryption key over a communications channel.

181 A. See Chapter 5. Layer 1 of the OSI model is concerned only with sending and receiving bits.

182 B. See Chapter 4. The primary reason for using CAPTCHA (Completely Automated Public Turing test to tell Computers and Humans Apart) is to ensure that a human is interacting with an application.

183 D. See Chapter 7. A *stored procedure* is a set of one or more SQL statements that are stored in the database management system, usually in the data dictionary.

184 D. See Chapter 8. In *public key cryptography*, a sender encrypts a message with the recipient's public key. The recipient decrypts the message with his own private key.

185 C. See Chapter 12. The USA PATRIOT Act gives law enforcement organizations greater search and seizure powers, primarily to combat terrorism.

186 D. See Chapter 10. An organization that backs up sensitive data such as bank account numbers should consider encrypting its backup media.

187 D. See Chapter 13. The purpose of a request-to-exit (REX) sensor is to detect when a person is approaching a doorway — usually an exterior exit door from the inside. If an exterior door is opened from the outside without the use of a key card and without a person inside the door, then the door is assumed to have been opened with a key or forced open by an intruder.

188 A. See Chapter 9. Data jurisdiction, control effectiveness, and availability are risks associated with cloud computing. Data ownership is not usually an issue.

189 B. See Chapter 6. A network that uses two different makes of firewalls follows the principle of defense in depth. A weakness in one firewall is not likely to be present in the other.

190 B. See Chapter 8. The complete range of possible keys in a cryptosystem is known as the keyspace.

191 D. See Chapter 5. 2001:0F56:45E3:BA98 is an IPv6 address.

192 C. See Chapter 4. A system that does not limit the number of invalid login attempts is vulnerable to mechanized password guessing attacks. The attacker can attempt to log in thousands of times until the correct password is discovered.

193 **D.** See Chapter 7. An attack that results in increased permissions is known as *escalation of privilege*.

194 **D.** See Chapter 8. If a user has lost the password to his private key, the key can no longer be used; the user must generate a new keypair.

195 **B.** See Chapter 12. The burden of proof in U.S. criminal law is "beyond a reasonable doubt."

196 **D.** See Chapter 10. The best approach for patch management is to perform risk analysis on each patch, and install those that are relevant. Applying all available patches consumes more resources and may reduce system integrity.

197 **A.** See Chapter 13. A duress alarm can be used to signal other personnel that there is an emergency in a specific area of a building.

198 **C.** See Chapter 9. The main weakness of a homogeneous environment is that all of the systems are the same. If one system has a vulnerability or weakness, many or all of the other systems in the environment are likely to have the same vulnerability or weakness.

199 **D.** See Chapter 6. A system that blocks all access in the event of a power failure (or other type of failure) follows the principle of *fail closed*.

200 **B.** See Chapter 8. An effective cryptosystem is easy to use, strong even if its algorithm is known, and makes efficient use of resources. A cryptosystem that is easily broken is not effective.

201 **C.** See Chapter 5. 255.255.0.0 is an IPv4 subnet mask.

202 **B.** See Chapter 4. Preventing password re-use discourages users from trying to revert to familiar passwords, which can slightly increase the risk of system compromise.

203 **D.** See Chapter 7. A *back door* is a feature that permits covert access to a system, usually through bypassing access controls.

204 **C.** See Chapter 8. A cryptosystem where message characters are converted to two-digit numerals is a *substitution cipher*, because ciphertext characters are substituted for message characters.

205 **C.** See Chapter 12. The California Security Breach Information Act, SB-1386, requires organizations to disclose security breaches of specific personal data to all affected citizens, unless that data was encrypted. The law does not require that any data be encrypted.

206 **D.** See Chapter 10. The purpose of penetration testing is to simulate an attack by malicious outsiders or insiders who may be attempting to compromise a target system.

207 **D.** See Chapter 13. In a motion-sensing surveillance system, only content with actual motion is recorded. This enables content to be retained for a greater period of time (because recording of no-activity is eliminated).

208 **A.** See Chapter 9. The four basic requirements described in the Orange Book are security policy, assurance, accountability, and documentation.

209 **B.** See Chapter 6. A document that is unclassified does not contain sensitive information.

210 **B.** See Chapter 8. When two users have exchanged *cryptovariables* (also known as *encryption keys*), they may begin exchanging encrypted messages.

211 **A.** See Chapter 5. In Uniform Naming Convention (UNC) for \\usdb01\symm\dev\src\, usdb01 is the name of a server.

212 **C.** See Chapter 4. An attacker who obtains a list of hashed passwords may be able to use a rainbow table to simply find the matching hashes and learn their corresponding passwords.

213 **D.** See Chapter 7. The best defense against cross-site request forgery (CSRF) attacks is to include subsequent steps such as transaction confirmation.

214 **D.** See Chapter 8. A *Vernam cipher*, or *one-time pad*, is a cryptosystem where the encryption key is the same length of the message, and is used only one time – for that message alone.

215 **A.** See Chapter 12. The purpose of the Sarbanes-Oxley Act of 2002 is to renew public trust in U.S. public companies by strengthening company controls related to financial reporting.

216 **C.** See Chapter 10. Because it has to be installed on every host, an organization may have many HIDS systems to maintain. And, because HIDS runs on individual hosts, a HIDS system cannot act as a network choke point in the way a network-based IDS can. A HIDS system can only detect traffic sent directly to any host it's running on.

217 **D.** See Chapter 13. One of the main reasons for employing remote monitoring of physical access controls in a datacenter is the ability to observe physical access controls even if local staff are unavailable or compromised.

218 **C.** See Chapter 9. TCSEC (Orange Book) system evaluation criteria are measurement, guidance, and acquisition.

219 **D.** See Chapter 6. A document that lists approved protocols, technologies, or suppliers is known as a *standard*.

220 **B.** See Chapter 8. An encryption algorithm that rearranges bits, characters, or blocks of data is known as a *transposition cipher*, because it transposes data.

221 **A.** See Chapter 5. In order to facilitate communication to the Internet on systems with RFC 1918 (private) addresses, implement NAT (network address translation) on a firewall.

222 **A.** See Chapter 4. The purpose of a user account access review can serve many purposes, including making sure that employee terminations resulted in timely access terminations, that all user roles were properly approved, and that users still require their access roles.

223 **D.** See Chapter 7. Session hijacking occurs when an attacker obtains session cookies from a victim user. Full session encryption with HTTPS is an effective countermeasure, since attackers will not be able to obtain session cookies.

224 **A.** See Chapter 8. A weak pseudo-random number generator (PRNG) may result in a weak cryptosystem that can be broken through cryptanalysis.

225 **C.** See Chapter 12. The Chain of Custody is the recordkeeping that describes the handling of forensic evidence in support of an investigation.

226 **D.** See Chapter 10. Audit trails support event reconstruction, investigation support, problem identification, and enforcement of accountability. Audit trails are not used for recovery purposes.

227 **D.** See Chapter 13. When dual power supply components are connected to different circuits, those circuits should not be loaded to a load greater than 40% of capacity. If one power circuit fails, the other circuit can expect its load to increase to 80%.

228 **C.** See Chapter 9. A web application that uses sequential session identifiers is vulnerable to a *state attack*, where an attacker can easily guess other session identifiers and attempt to steal other users' sessions.

229 **B.** See Chapter 6. Policies are formal statements of business rules; they specify *what* should be done, but not *how* they should be done. Policies should be reviewed periodically.

230 **A.** See Chapter 8. An encryption algorithm that replaces bits, characters, or blocks of data is known as a *substitution cipher*.

231 **A.** See Chapter 5. Two-factor authentication is preferred for VPN because it is more resistant to a dictionary attack.

232 **C.** See Chapter 4. When it has been discovered that many user accounts were not locked for users who left the organization, the termination process should be improved by whatever means necessary. Monthly access reviews will help to ensure that process changes are effective.

233 **D.** See Chapter 7. Any site that permits users to embed JavaScript is susceptible to cross-site scripting (XSS) attacks.

234 **D.** See Chapter 8. A system designer in need of a stream cipher should choose RC4. The other ciphers are block ciphers.

235 **C.** See Chapter 12. Any evidence obtained through illegal means cannot be used in any legal proceeding.

236 **B.** See Chapter 10. If a specific type of incident occurs over and over, root cause analysis should be performed so that the factors responsible for incident recurrence can be corrected.

237 **D.** See Chapter 13. In case of a fire in a datacenter, personnel should evacuate immediately. Personnel safety is the highest priority in a datacenter.

238 **A.** See Chapter 9. The Common Criteria has been adopted as international standard ISO 15408, it contains eight levels of evaluation assurance, and it supersedes TCSEC and ITSEC.

239 **B.** See Chapter 6. An organization should perform the best background check available and permitted by law in each country.

240 **B.** See Chapter 8. In a *symmetric cryptosystem*, both users must possess the same encryption key. If these users do not know each other, it may be difficult to securely exchange a key.

241 **A.** See Chapter 5. The best choice for making an FTP connection more secure is to change to FTPS or SFTP. Encrypting the payload does not protect authentication credentials.

242 **C.** See Chapter 4. An attacker who is able to record the keystrokes of a user logging in to a system is preparing to launch a *replay attack*.

243 **D.** See Chapter 7. An e-mail-based attack that points users to a website that resembles a company's own website is a *spear phishing attack*, because it is targeting users in a specific organization.

244 **A.** See Chapter 8. If a laptop containing private encryption keys has been stolen, the attacker may be able to guess the passwords for private keys and compromise the cryptosystem. The owner of the encryption keys should generate new key pairs.

245 **A.** See Chapter 12. Any company that outsources credit card processing to another organization should require the organization to be PCI-compliant.

246 **D.** See Chapter 10. Personnel who administer centralized audit log servers should be separate personnel from those who administer systems being logged. Otherwise administrators would be able to manipulate the contents of audit log servers and cover up their activities.

247 **D.** See Chapter 13. The ideal level for relative humidity in a datacenter is between 40% and 60%. If humidity falls below 40%, there is risk of static discharge that can damage computing equipment. If the humidity rises above 60%, condensation can damage computing equipment.

248 **A.** See Chapter 9. The access model described here is the Access Matrix, which specifies which persons (or job titles) are permitted to access which system roles.

249 **B.** See Chapter 6. A decision on how to resolve an identified risk is known as *risk treatment*.

250 **B.** See Chapter 8. In Cipher Block Chaining (CBC), each plaintext block is XORed with the ciphertext of the preceding block, making it more random.

Appendix B

Glossary

· ·

3DES (Triple DES): An enhancement to the original DES algorithm that uses multiple keys to encrypt plaintext. *See also **Data Encryption Standard (DES)**.*

AAA: Shorthand for the system controls *authentication, authorization,* and *accountability.*

abstraction: A process that involves viewing an application from its highest-level functions, which makes lower-level functions abstract.

access control: The capability to permit or deny the use of an *object* (a passive entity, such as a system or file) by a *subject* (an active entity, such as a person or process).

access control list (ACL): Lists the specific rights and permissions assigned to a subject for a given object.

Access Matrix Model: Provides object access rights (read/write/execute or R/W/X) to subjects in a DAC system. An access matrix consists of ACLs and capability lists. *See also **access control list (ACL)** and **discretionary access control (DAC)**.*

accreditation: An official, written approval for the operation of a specific system in a specific environment, as documented in a certification report.

active-active: A clustered configuration in which all of the nodes in a system or network are load balanced, synchronized, and active. If one node fails, the other node(s) continue providing services seamlessly.

active-passive: A clustered configuration in which only one node in a system or network is active. If the primary node fails, a passive node becomes active and continues providing services, usually after a short delay.

Address Resolution Protocol (ARP): The network protocol used to query and discover the MAC address of a device on a LAN.

address space: A programming instruction that specifies where memory is located in a computer system.

administrative controls: The policies and procedures that an organization implements as part of its overall information security strategy.

administrative (or regulatory) laws: Legal requirements passed by government institutions that define standards of performance and conduct for major industries (such as banking, energy, and healthcare), organizations, and officials.

Advanced Encryption Standard (AES): A block cipher based on the Rijndael cipher, which is expected to eventually replace DES. *See also **Data Encryption Standard (DES)**.*

adware: Legitimate, albeit annoying, software that's commonly installed with a freeware or shareware program. It provides a source of revenue for the software developer and runs only when you're using the associated program or until you purchase the program (in the case of shareware).

agent: A software component that performs a particular service.

aggregation: A database security issue that describes the act of obtaining information classified at a high sensitivity level by combining other items of low-sensitivity information.

Annualized Loss Expectancy (ALE): A standard, quantifiable measure of the impact that a realized threat will have on an organization's assets. ALE is determined by the formula Single Loss Expectancy (SLE) × Annualized Rate of Occurrence (ARO) = ALE.

- ✔ **Single Loss Expectancy (SLE):** Asset Value × Exposure Factor (EF). A measure of the loss incurred from a single realized threat or event, expressed in dollars.

- ✔ **Exposure Factor (EF):** A measure, expressed as a percentage, of the negative effect or impact that a realized threat or event would have on a specific asset.

- ✔ **Annualized Rate of Occurrence (ARO):** The estimated annual frequency of occurrence for a specific threat or event.

antivirus software: Software that's designed to detect and prevent computer viruses and other malware from entering and harming a system.

applet: A component in a distributed environment (various components are located on separate systems) that's downloaded into and executed by another program, such as a web browser.

application firewall: A firewall that inspects OSI Layer 7 content in order to block malicious content from reaching or leaving an application server.

application scan: A test used to identify weaknesses in a software application.

application software: Computer software that a person uses to accomplish a specific task.

application-level firewall: *See application firewall.*

archive: In a PKI, an archive is responsible for long-term storage of archived information from the CA. *See also Certification Authority (CA) and Public Key Infrastructure (PKI).*

asset: A resource, process, product, system, and so on that has some value to an organization and must therefore be protected. Assets can be hard goods, such as computers and equipment, but can also be information and intellectual property.

asset valuation: The process of assigning a financial value to an organization's information assets.

asymmetric key system (or asymmetric algorithm; public key): A cryptographic system that uses two separate keys — one key to encrypt information and a different key to decrypt information. These keys are known as *public* and *private key pairs.*

Asynchronous Transfer Mode (ATM): A very high-speed, low-latency, packet-switched communications protocol.

audit: The independent verification of any activity or process.

audit trail: The auxiliary records that document transactions and other events.

authentication: The process of verifying a subject's claimed identity in an access control system.

Authentication Header (AH): In IPSec, a protocol that provides integrity, authentication, and non-repudiation. *See also Internet Protocol Security (IPSec).*

authorization (or establishment): The process of defining the rights and permissions granted to a subject (what you can do).

automatic controls: Controls that are automatically performed by information systems.

availability: The process of ensuring that systems and data are accessible to authorized users when they need it.

background check: The process of verifying a person's professional, financial, and legal backgrounds, usually in connection with employment.

baseline: A process that identifies a consistent basis for an organization's security architecture, taking into account system-specific parameters, such as different operating systems.

Bell-LaPadula model: A formal confidentiality model that defines two basic properties:

- ✔ **simple security property (ss property):** A subject can't read information from an object that has a higher sensitivity label than the subject (no read up, or NRU).
- ✔ **star property (* property):** A subject can't write information to an object that has a lower sensitivity label than the subject (no write down, or NWD).

best evidence: Original, unaltered evidence, which is preferred by the court over secondary evidence. *See also* **best evidence rule.**

best evidence rule: Defined in the Federal Rules of Evidence; states that "to prove the content of a writing, recording, or photograph, the original writing, recording, or photograph is (ordinarily) required."

Biba model: A formal integrity model that defines two basic properties:

- ✔ **simple integrity property:** A subject can't read information from an object that has a lower integrity level than the subject (no read down, or NRD).
- ✔ **star integrity property (*-integrity property):** A subject can't write information to an object that has a higher integrity level than the subject (no write up, or NWU).

biometrics: Any of various means used, as part of an authentication mechanism, to verify the identity of a person. Types of biometrics used include fingerprints, palm prints, signatures, retinal scans, voice scans, and keystroke patterns.

Birthday Attack: A type of attack that attempts to exploit the probability of two messages using the same hash function and producing the same message digest. *See also* **hash function.**

black-box testing: A security test wherein the tester has no prior knowledge of the system being tested.

blackout: Total loss of electric power.

block cipher: An encryption algorithm that divides plaintext into fixed-size blocks of characters or bits, and then uses the same key on each fixed-size block to produce corresponding ciphertext.

bridge: A network device that forwards packets to other devices on a network.

brownout: Prolonged drop in voltage from an electric power source, such as a public utility.

brute-force attack: A type of attack in which the attacker attempts every possible combination of letters, numbers, and characters to crack a password, passphrase, or PIN.

buffer (or stack) overflow attack: A type of attack in which the attacker enters an out-of-range parameter or intentionally exceeds the buffer capacity of a system or application to effect a Denial of Service (DoS) or exploit a vulnerability.

bus (computer architecture): The logical interconnection between basic components in a computer system, including Central Processing Unit (CPU), memory, and peripherals.

bus (network topology): A network topology in which all devices are connected to a single cable.

Business Impact Assessment (BIA): A risk analysis that, as part of a Business Continuity Plan, describes the impact to business operations that the loss of various IT systems would impose.

caller ID: The protocol used to transmit the calling party's telephone number to the called party's telephone equipment during the establishment of a telephone call.

CAN: Campus area network.

Central Processing Unit (CPU): The electronic circuitry that performs a computer's arithmetic, logic, and computing functions.

certification: A formal methodology that uses established evaluation criteria to conduct comprehensive testing and documentation of information system security safeguards, both technical and nontechnical, in a given environment.

Certification Authority (CA): In a PKI, the CA issues certificates, maintains and publishes status information and Certificate Revocation Lists (CRLs), and maintains archives. *See also **Public Key Infrastructure (PKI)**.*

chain of custody (or chain of evidence): Provides accountability and protection for evidence throughout that evidence's entire life cycle.

Challenge Handshake Authentication Protocol (CHAP): A remote access control protocol that uses a three-way handshake to authenticate both a peer and a server. *See also **three-way handshake**.*

Change Management: The formal business process that ensures all changes made to a system are properly requested, reviewed, approved, and implemented.

chosen plaintext attack: An attack technique in which the cryptanalyst selects the plaintext to be encrypted and then analyzes the resulting ciphertext.

C-I-A: Confidentiality, integrity, and availability.

cipher: A cryptographic transformation.

Cipher Block Chaining (CBC): One of four operating modes for DES. Operates on 64-bit blocks of plaintext to produce 64-bit blocks of ciphertext. Each block is XORed with the ciphertext of the preceding block, creating a dependency (or chain), thereby producing a more random ciphertext result. CBC is the most common mode of DES operation. *See also **Cipher Feedback (CFB), Data Encryption Standard (DES), Electronic Code Book (ECB), Exclusive Or (XOR),** and **Output Feedback (OFB).***

Cipher Feedback (CFB): One of four operating modes for DES. CFB is a stream cipher most often used to encrypt individual characters. In this mode, previously generated ciphertext is used as feedback for key generation in the next keystream, and the resulting ciphertext is chained together. *See also **Cipher Block Chaining (CBC), Data Encryption Standard (DES), Electronic Code Book (ECB),** and **Output Feedback (OFB).***

ciphertext: A plaintext message that has been transformed (encrypted) into a scrambled message that's unintelligible.

circumstantial evidence: Relevant facts that can't be directly or conclusively connected to other events, but about which a reasonable inference can be made.

civil (or tort) law: Legal codes that address wrongful acts committed against an individual or business, either willfully or negligently, resulting in damage, loss, injury, or death. Unlike criminal law, U.S. civil law cases are determined based on a preponderance of evidence, and punishments are limited to fines.

Clark-Wilson model: A formal integrity model that addresses all three goals of integrity (preventing unauthorized users from making any changes, preventing authorized users from making incorrect changes, and maintaining internal and external consistency) and identifies special requirements for inputting data.

classification: The process of assigning to a document a security label that defines how the document should be handled.

closed system: A system that uses proprietary hardware and/or software that may not be compatible with other systems or components. *See also* ***open system.***

cluster: A system or network configuration containing multiple redundant nodes for resiliency. *See also* ***active-active*** *and* ***active passive.***

clustering (or key clustering): When identical ciphertext messages are generated from a plaintext message by using the same encryption algorithm but different encryption keys.

code of ethics: A formal statement that defines ethical behavior in a given organization or profession.

cold site: An alternative computer facility that has electricity and HVAC, but no computer equipment located onsite. *See also* ***hot site, HVAC,*** *and* ***warm site.***

Common Criteria: An international effort to standardize and improve existing European and North American information systems security evaluation criteria.

compensating controls: Controls that are implemented as an alternative to other preventive, detective, corrective, deterrent, or recovery controls.

compensatory damages: Actual damages to the victim including attorney/legal fees, lost profits, investigative costs, and so on.

Complex-Instruction-Set-Computing (CISC): A microprocessor instruction set architecture in which each instruction can execute several low-level operations. *See also* ***Reduced-Instruction-Set-Computing (RISC).***

Computer Emergency Response Team (CERT): *See* ***Computer Incident Response Team (CIRT).***

Computer Incident Response Team (CIRT) or Computer Emergency Response Team (CERT): A team that comprises individuals who are properly trained in incident response and investigation.

concealment cipher: A technique of hiding a message in plain sight. The key is knowing where the message lies.

concentrator: *See* ***hub.***

conclusive evidence: Incontrovertible and irrefutable . . . you know, the *smoking gun.*

confidentiality: Prevents the unauthorized use or disclosure of information, ensuring that information is accessible only to those authorized to have access to the information.

confidentiality agreement. *See **non-disclosure agreement (NDA).***

Configuration Management: The process of recording all changes to information systems.

Continuity of Operations Planning (COOP): A blending of Disaster Recovery Planning (DRP) and Business Continuity Planning (BCP) into a single coordinated activity.

copyright: A form of legal protection granted to the author(s) of "original works of authorship," both published and unpublished.

corrective controls: Controls that remedy violations and incidents or improve existing preventive and detective controls.

corroborative evidence: Evidence that supports or substantiates other evidence presented in a legal case.

countermeasure: A device, control, or action required to reduce the impact or probability of a security incident.

covert channel: An unintended communications path; it may be a covert storage channel or a covert timing channel.

criminal law: Defines those crimes committed against society, even when the actual victim is a business or individual(s). Criminal laws are enacted to protect the general public. Unlike civil law, U.S. criminal cases are decided when a party is guilty beyond a reasonable doubt and punishments may include fines, incarceration, and even execution.

Criticality Assessment: The part of a BIA that ranks the criticality of business processes and IT systems. *See also **Business Impact Assessment (BIA).***

cross-frame scripting (XFS): *See **frame injection.***

Crossover Error Rate (CER): In biometric access control systems, the point at which the FRR equals the FAR, stated as a percentage. *See also **False Accept Rate (FAR; or Type II Error)** and **False Reject Rate (FRR; or Type I Error).***

cross-site request forgery (CSRF): An attack where an attacker is attempting to trick a victim into clicking a link that will perform an action the victim would not otherwise approve.

cross-site scripting (XSS): An attack where an attacker is attempting to inject client-side script into web pages viewed by other intended victims.

cryptanalysis: The science of deciphering ciphertext without using the cryptographic key.

cryptography: The science of encrypting and decrypting information, such as a private message, to protect its confidentiality, integrity, and/or authenticity.

cryptology: The science that encompasses both cryptography and cryptanalysis.

cryptosystem: The hardware or software implementation that transforms plaintext into ciphertext (encrypts) and back into plaintext (decrypts).

cryptovariable (or key): A secret value applied to a cryptographic algorithm. The strength and effectiveness of the cryptosystem is largely dependent on the secrecy and strength of the cryptovariable.

culpable negligence: A legal term that may describe an organization's failure to follow a standard of due care in the protection of its assets and thereby expose the organization to a legal claim. *See also **due care.***

custodian: An individual who has day-to-day responsibility for protecting information assets.

data dictionary: A database of databases.

Data Encryption Standard (DES): A commonly used symmetric key algorithm that uses a 56-bit key and operates on 64-bit blocks. *See also **Advanced Encryption Standard (AES).***

data warehouse: A special-purpose database used for decision support or research purposes.

database management system (DBMS): Restricts access by different subjects to various objects in a database.

DCE: Data Communications Equipment. *See also **DTE.***

decryption: The process of transforming ciphertext into plaintext.

defense in depth: The principle of protecting assets by using layers of dissimilar mechanisms.

Defense Information Technology Security Certification and Accreditation Process (DITSCAP): A program that formalizes the certification and accreditation process for U.S. Department of Defense information systems.

demonstrative evidence: Evidence that is used to aid the court's understanding of a legal case.

Denial of Service (DoS): An attack on a system or network with the intention of making the system or network unavailable for use.

detective controls: Controls that identify violations and incidents.

deterrent controls: Controls that discourage violations.

Diameter: The next-generation RADIUS protocol. *See also **Remote Authentication Dial-In User Service (RADIUS).***

dictionary attack: A focused type of brute-force attack in which a predefined word list is used. *See also **brute-force attack.***

Diffie-Hellman: A key-agreement algorithm based on discrete logarithms.

digital certificate: A certificate that binds an identity with a public encryption key.

Digital Signature Standard (DSS): Published by NIST in Federal Information Processing Standard (FIPS) 186-1, DSS specifies two acceptable algorithms in its standard: The RSA Digital Signature Algorithm and the Digital Signature Algorithm (DSA). *See also **NIST** and **Rivest, Shamir, Adleman (RSA).***

Digital Subscriber Line (xDSL): A high-bandwidth communications protocol that operates over analog telecommunications voice lines.

direct evidence: Oral testimony or a written statement based on information gathered through the witness's five senses that proves or disproves a specific fact or issue.

discretionary access control (DAC): An access policy determined by the owner of a file or other resource. *See also **mandatory access control (MAC) system.***

disk mirroring (RAID Level 1): When a duplicate copy of all data is written to another disk or set of disks.

disk striping (RAID Level 0): When data is written across multiple disks but doesn't provide redundancy or fault tolerance.

disk striping with parity (RAID Level 5): When data is written across multiple disks, along with parity data that provides fault tolerance if one disk fails.

distributed application: A software application whose components reside in several systems or locations.

Distributed Denial of Service (DDoS): An attack where the attacker initiates simultaneous denial of service attacks from many systems.

documentary evidence: Evidence that is used in legal proceedings, including originals and copies of business records, computer-generated and computer-stored records, manuals, policies, standards, procedures, and log files.

domain: A collection of users, computers, and resources that have a common security policy and single administration.

DTE: Data Terminal Equipment. *See also **DCE**.*

due care: The steps that an organization takes to implement security best practices.

due diligence: The prudent management and execution of due care.

dumpster diving: The process of examining garbage with the intention of finding valuable goods or information.

dynamic password: A password that changes at some regular interval or event.

Electromagnetic Interference (EMI): Electrical noise generated by the different charges between the three electrical wires (hot, neutral, and ground) and can be *common-mode noise* (caused by hot and ground) or *traverse-mode noise* (caused by hot and neutral).

Electronic Code Book (ECB): One of four operating modes for DES. ECB operates on 64-bit blocks of plaintext independently and produces 64-bit blocks of ciphertext, and it's the native mode for DES operation. *See also **Cipher Block Chaining (CBC), Cipher Feedback (CFB), Data Encryption Standard (DES)**, and **Output Feedback (OFB)**.*

Encapsulating Security Payload (ESP): In IPSec, a protocol that provides confidentiality (encryption) and limited authentication. *See also **Internet Protocol Security (IPSec)**.*

encryption: The process of transforming plaintext into ciphertext.

end-to-end encryption: A process by which packets are encrypted once at the original encryption source and then decrypted only at the final decryption destination.

enticement: Luring someone toward certain evidence after that individual has already committed a crime.

entrapment: Encouraging someone to commit a crime that the individual may have had no intention of committing.

escalation of privilege: An attack where the attacker is using some means to bypass security controls in order to attain a higher privilege level on the target system.

Escrowed Encryption Standard (EES): Divides a secret key into two parts, and places those two parts into escrow with two separate, trusted organizations. Published by NIST in FIPS PUB 185 (1994). *See also **NIST.***

espionage: The practice of spying or using spies to obtain proprietary or confidential information.

Ethernet: A common bus-topology network transport protocol.

ethics: Professional principles and duties that guide decisions and behavior. *See also **code of ethics.***

European Information Technology Security Evaluation Criteria (ITSEC): Formal evaluation criteria that address confidentiality, integrity, and availability for an entire system.

evidence life cycle: The various phases of evidence, from its initial discovery to its final disposition. The evidence life cycle has the following five stages: collection and identification; analysis; storage, preservation, and transportation; presentation in court; and return to victim (owner).

Exclusive Or (XOR): A binary operation applied to two input bits. If the two bits are equal, the result is zero. If the two bits are not equal, the result is one.

exigent circumstances: If probable cause exists and the destruction of evidence is imminent, property or people may be searched and/or evidence may be seized by law enforcement personnel without a search warrant.

expert systems: A type of artificial intelligence system based on an inference engine (a program that attempts to derive answers) and knowledge base.

Extensible Authentication Protocol (EAP): A remote access control protocol that implements various authentication mechanisms, including MD5, S/Key, generic token cards, and digital certificates. Often used in wireless networks.

extranet: An intranet that has been extended to include external parties, such as customers, partners, and suppliers. *See also **intranet.***

fail closed: A control failure that results in all accesses being blocked.

fail open: A control failure that results in all accesses being permitted.

failover: A failure mode in which the system automatically transfers processing to a hot backup component, such as a clustered server, if a hardware or software failure is detected.

fail-safe: A failure mode in which program execution is terminated, and the system is protected from compromise, if a hardware or software failure is detected.

fail-soft (or resilient): A failure mode in which certain, noncritical processing is terminated, and the computer or network continues to function in a degraded mode, if a hardware or software failure is detected.

False Accept Rate (FAR; or Type II Error): In biometric access control systems, the percentage of unauthorized users who are incorrectly granted access. *See also **Crossover Error Rate (CER)** and **False Reject Rate (FRR; or Type I Error)**.*

False Reject Rate (FRR; or Type I Error): In biometric access control systems, the percentage of authorized users who are incorrectly denied access. *See also **Crossover Error Rate (CER)** and **False Accept Rate (FAR; or Type II Error)**.*

fault: Momentary loss of electric power.

fault-tolerant: A system that continues to operate after the failure of a computer or network component.

Fiber Distributed Data Interface (FDDI): A star topology, token-passing, network transport protocol.

FIPS: Federal Information Processing Standard. Standards and guidelines published by the U.S. National Institute of Standards and Technology (NIST) for federal computer systems. *See also **NIST**.*

firewall: A device or program that controls traffic flow between networks.

firmware: A program or code that's stored in ROM memory.

forensics (or computer forensics): The science of conducting a computer crime investigation in order to determine what's happened and who's responsible for what's happened. One major component of computer forensics involves collecting legally admissible evidence for use in a computer crime case.

frame injection: An attack where the attacker is attempting to load arbitrary code into a browser in order to steal data from other frames in the browser session.

Frame Relay (FR): A packet-switched network protocol used to transport WAN communications.

fraud: Any deceptive or misrepresented activity that results in illicit personal gain.

fuzzy logic: An artificial intelligence method that's used to address uncertain situations to determine whether a given condition is true or false.

gateway: A system, connected to a network, which performs any real-time translation or interface function; for example, a system that converts Exchange e-mail to Lotus Notes e-mail.

goals: Specific milestones that an organization hopes to accomplish.

gray-box testing: A security test wherein the tester has some prior knowledge of the system being tested.

guidelines: Similar to standards, but considered recommendations, rather than compulsory requirements.

hardware: The physical components in a computer system.

hardware segmentation: The practice of isolating functions by placing them on separate hardware platforms.

hash function: A mathematical function that creates a unique representation of a larger set of data (such as a digest). Hash functions are often used in cryptographic algorithms and to produce checksums and message digests. *See also **message digest.***

Health Insurance Portability and Accountability Act (HIPAA): A federal Act that addresses security and privacy requirements for medical systems and information.

hearsay evidence: Evidence that isn't based on the witness's personal, first-hand knowledge, but was instead obtained through other sources.

hearsay rule: Under the Federal Rules of Evidence, hearsay evidence is normally not admissible in court.

heterogeneous environment: A systems environment that consists of a variety of types of systems. *See also **homogeneous environment.***

hidden code: An attack in which secret (and usually malicious) computer code is embedded within another program.

High-Speed Serial Interface (HSSI): A point-to-point WAN connection protocol.

homogeneous environment: A systems environment that consists largely of one type of system. *See also **heterogeneous environment.***

honeypot: A decoy system deployed by a security administrator to discover the attack methods of potential hackers.

hot site: A fully configured alternative computer facility that has electrical power, HVAC, and functioning file/print servers and workstations. *See also **cold site, HVAC, and warm site.***

hub: A network device used to connect several LAN devices together. Also known as a *concentrator.*

HVAC: Heating, ventilation, and air conditioning.

identification: The means by which a user claims a specific, unproven identity to a system. *See also* **authentication.**

identity management: The processes and procedures that support the life cycle of people's identities in an organization.

IETF: Internet Engineering Task Force.

inference: The ability of users to figure out information about data at a sensitivity level for which they're not authorized.

inference channel: A link that allows inference to occur.

inference engine: An artificial intelligence system that derives answers from a knowledge base.

information custodian (or custodian): The individual who has the day-to-day responsibility of protecting information assets.

information flow model: A lattice-based model in which each object is assigned a security class and value, and their direction of flow is controlled by a security policy.

information owner (or owner): The individual who decides who's allowed access to a file and what privileges are granted.

inrush: Initial electric power surge experienced when electrical equipment is turned on.

Integrated Services Digital Network (ISDN): A low-bandwidth communications protocol that operates over analog telecommunications voice lines.

integrity: Safeguards the accuracy and completeness of information and processing methods, and ensures that

- ✔ Modifications to data aren't made by unauthorized users or processes.
- ✔ Unauthorized modifications to data aren't made by authorized users or processes.
- ✔ Data is internally and externally consistent, meaning a given input produces an expected output.

intellectual property: Includes patents, trademarks, copyrights, and trade secrets.

Internet: The worldwide, publicly accessible network that connects the networks of organizations.

Internet Control Message Protocol (ICMP): An Internet Protocol used to transmit diagnostic messages.

Internet Protocol (IP): The Open Systems Interconnection (OSI) Layer 3 protocol that's the basis of the modern Internet.

Internet Protocol Security (IPSec): An IETF open-standard Virtual Private Network (VPN) protocol for secure communications over public IP-based networks.

Internetwork Packet Exchange (IPX): A network packet-oriented protocol that's the basis for Novell Netware networks. IPX is analogous to IP.

intranet: An organization's private network that's used to securely share information among the organization's employees.

intrusion detection system (IDS): A hardware or software application that detects and reports on suspected network or host intrusions.

intrusion prevention system (IPS): A hardware or software application that both detects and blocks suspected network or host intrusions.

job rotation: The practice of moving employees from one position to another, for cross-training and security reasons.

Kerberos: A ticket-based authentication protocol, in which "tickets" are used to identify users, developed at the Massachusetts Institute of Technology (MIT).

key logging: The practice of recording keystrokes, usually for illicit purposes, such as acquiring user IDs, passwords, and other confidential information.

known-plaintext attack: An attack technique in which the cryptanalyst has a given plaintext message and the resulting ciphertext.

KryptoKnight: A ticket-based single sign-on (SSO) authentication system, in which "tickets" are used to identify users, developed by IBM.

LAN: Local area network.

lattice-based access controls: A method for implementing mandatory access controls in which a mathematical structure defines greatest lower-bound and least upper-bound values for a pair of elements: for example, subject and object.

Layer 2 Forwarding Protocol (L2F): A Virtual Private Network (VPN) protocol similar to Point-to-Point Tunneling Protocol (PPTP).

Layer 2 Tunneling Protocol (L2TP): A Virtual Private Network (VPN) protocol similar to Point-to-Point Tunneling Protocol (PPTP) and Layer 2 Forwarding Protocol (L2F).

least privilege: A principle requiring that a subject is granted only the minimum privileges necessary to perform an assigned task.

Lightweight Directory Access Protocol (LDAP): An Internet Protocol (IP) and data storage model that supports authentication and directory functions.

link encryption: Packet encryption and decryption at every node along the network path; requires each node to have separate key pairs for its upstream and downstream neighbors.

logic bomb: A program, or portion thereof, designed to perform some malicious function when a predetermined circumstance occurs.

maintenance hook: A back door that allows a software developer or vendor to bypass access control mechanisms in order to perform maintenance. These back doors are often well known and pose a significant security threat if not properly secured.

malware: Malicious software that typically damages, takes control of, or collects information from a computer. This classification of software broadly includes viruses, worms, Trojan horses, logic bombs, spyware, and (to a lesser extent) adware.

MAN: Metropolitan area network.

mandatory access control (MAC) system: A type of access control system in which the access policy is determined by the system, rather than by the owner. *See also **discretionary access control (DAC)**.*

Man-in-the-Middle Attack: A type of attack in which an attacker intercepts messages between two parties and forwards a modified version of the original message.

mantrap: A physical access control method consisting of a double set of locked doors or turnstiles.

manual controls: Controls that must be performed manually by people.

Maximum Tolerable Downtime (MTD): An extension of a Criticality Assessment that specifies the maximum period of time that a given business process can be inoperative before experiencing unacceptable consequences. *See also **Criticality Assessment**.*

Maximum Tolerable Period of Disruption (MTPD). *See **Maximum Tolerable Downtime (MTD)**.*

media controls: Controls that are used to manage information classification and physical media.

Meet-in-the-Middle Attack: A type of attack in which an attacker encrypts known plaintext with each possible key on one end, decrypts the corresponding ciphertext with each possible key, and then compares the results *in the middle.*

memory addressing: The method used by the Central Processing Unit (CPU) to access the contents of memory.

memory space: The amount of memory available in a computer system.

message digest: A condensed representation of a message that is produced by using a one-way hash function. *See also **hash function.***

metadata: "Data about data" that may present a security risk by revealing private information about a document or its history.

MIME Object Security Services (MOSS): Provides confidentiality, integrity, identification and authentication, and non-repudiation by using MD2 or MD5, RSA asymmetric keys, and DES. *See also **Data Encryption Standard (DES), Multipurpose Internet Mail Extensions (MIME), and Rivest, Shamir, Adleman (RSA).***

mission statement: A statement that defines an organization's reason for existence.

mobile app: An application that runs on a mobile device and has the capability to interact with the user, communicate over the Internet, and store data locally.

mobile device: A general term encompassing all smaller devices such as smartphones and tablet computers, which run operating systems such as iOS and Android.

monitoring: Activities that verify processes, procedures, and systems.

monoalphabetic substitution: A cryptographic system that uses a single alphabet to encrypt and decrypt an entire message.

multi-level system: A single computer system that handles multiple classification levels between subjects and objects.

multiprocessing: A system that executes multiple programs on multiple processors simultaneously.

multiprogramming: A system that alternates execution of multiple programs on a single processor.

Multi-Protocol Label Switching (MPLS): An extremely fast method of forwarding packets through a network by using labels inserted between Layer 2 and Layer 3 headers in the packet.

Multipurpose Internet Mail Extensions (MIME): An IETF standard that defines the format for messages that are exchanged between e-mail systems over the Internet. *See also* ***IETF.***

multitasking: A system that alternates execution of multiple subprograms or tasks on a single processor.

National Information Assurance Certification and Accreditation Process (NIACAP): Formalizes the certification and accreditation process for U.S. government national security information systems.

NCSC: National Computer Security Center. A U.S. government organization, within the U.S. National Security Agency (NSA), that is responsible for evaluating computing equipment and applications that are used to process classified data.

need-to-know: A status, granted to an individual, that defines the essential information needed to perform his or her assigned job function.

Network Address Translation (NAT): The process of converting internal, privately used addresses in a network to external, public addresses.

network interface card (NIC): An adaptor that permits a computer or other system to be connected to a network.

neural network: A type of artificial intelligence system that approximates the function of the human nervous system.

NIST: U.S. National Institute of Standards and Technology. A federal agency, within the U.S. Department of Commerce, that is responsible for promoting innovation and competitiveness through standards, measurement science, and technology.

non-compete agreement: A legal agreement in which an employee agrees not to accept employment in a competing organization.

non-disclosure agreement (NDA): A legal agreement in which one or more parties agrees to refrain from disseminating confidential information related to other parties.

non-interference model: Ensures that the actions of different objects and subjects aren't seen by, and don't interfere with, other objects and subjects on the same system.

non-repudiation: The inability for a user to deny an action; his or her identity is positively associated with that action.

object: A passive entity, such as a system or file.

object reuse: The process of protecting the confidentiality of objects that are reassigned after initial use. *See also **Trusted Computer System Evaluation Criteria (TCSEC)**.*

objectives: Specific milestones that an organization wants to perform in order to meet its goals. *See also **goals**.*

one-time pad: A cryptographic keystream that can be used only once.

one-time password: A password that's valid for only one log-on session.

one-way function: A problem that's easy to compute in one direction but not in the reverse direction.

open message format: A message encrypted in an asymmetric key system by using the sender's private key. The sender's public key, which is available to anyone, is used to decrypt the message. This format guarantees the message's authenticity. *See also **secure and signed message format** and **secure message format**.*

open system: A vendor-independent system that complies with an accepted standard, which promotes interoperability between systems and components made by different vendors. *See also **closed system**.*

Open Systems Interconnection (OSI) model: The seven-layer reference model for networks. The layers are *Physical, Data Link, Network, Transport, Session, Presentation,* and *Application.*

operating system (OS): Software that controls computer hardware and resources and facilitates the operation of application software. *See also **application software**.*

Orange Book: *See **Trusted Computer System Evaluation Criteria (TCSEC)**.*

Output Feedback (OFB): One of four operating modes for DES. OFB is a stream cipher often used to encrypt satellite communications. In this mode, previous plaintext is used as feedback for key generation in the next keystream; however, the resulting ciphertext isn't chained together (unlike with CFB). *See also **Cipher Block Chaining (CBC), Cipher Feedback (CFB),** and **Data Encryption Standard (DES)**.*

owner: An individual in an organization who's responsible for management of an asset, including classification, handling, and access policy.

Packet (or password) sniffing: A type of attack in which an attacker uses a sniffer to capture network packets and analyze their contents.

packet-filtering firewall: A type of firewall that examines the source and destination addresses of an incoming packet, and then either permits or denies the packet based on an ACL. *See also **access control list (ACL).***

PAN: Personal area network.

password: A string of characters (a word or phrase) that a subject provides to an authentication mechanism in order to authenticate to a system.

Password Authentication Protocol (PAP): A remote access control protocol that uses a two-way handshake to authenticate a peer to a server when a link is initially established.

patent: As defined by the U.S. Patent and Trademark Office (PTO), a patent is "the grant of a property right to the inventor."

penetration testing: A test that attempts to penetrate a system and identify potential software vulnerabilities. Also known as *pen testing.*

personal identification number (PIN): A numeric-only password, usually used when only a numeric keypad (versus an alphanumeric keyboard) is available. *See also **password.***

pharming: A phishing attack that's targeted towards a specific organization. *See also **phishing.***

phishing: A social-engineering cyber-attack technique widely used in identity-theft crimes. An e-mail, purportedly from a known legitimate business (typically financial institutions, online auctions, retail stores, and so on), requests the recipient to verify personal information online at a forged or hijacked website. *See also **pharming** and **spear phishing.***

physical controls: Controls that ensure the safety and security of the physical environment.

plaintext: A message in its original readable format or a ciphertext message that's been properly decrypted (unscrambled) to produce the original readable plaintext message.

Point-to-Point Protocol (PPP): A protocol used in remote access service (RAS) servers to encapsulate Internet Protocol (IP) packets and establish dial-in connections over serial and Integrated Services Digital Network (ISDN) links.

Point-to-Point Tunneling Protocol (PPTP): A Virtual Private Network (VPN) protocol designed for individual client-server connections.

policy: A formal high-level statement of an organization's objectives, responsibilities, ethics and beliefs, and general requirements and controls.

polyinstantiation: Allows different versions of the same data to exist at different sensitivity levels.

port scan: A test used to determine which Transmission Control Protocol/Internet Protocol (TCP/IP) service ports on a system are running.

prepared statement: A canned database command that can be called by an application.

Pretty Good Privacy (PGP): A freely available, open-source e-mail application that provides confidentiality and authentication by using the International Data Encryption Algorithm (IDEA) cipher for encryption and the RSA asymmetric system for digital signatures and secure key distribution. *See also* ***Rivest, Shamir, Adleman (RSA).***

preventive controls: Controls that prevent unwanted events.

privacy: The security and protection of personal information.

Privacy Enhanced Mail (PEM): A protocol that provides confidentiality and authentication by using 3DES for encryption, MD2 or MD5 message digests, X.509 digital certificates, and the RSA asymmetric system for digital signatures and secure key distribution. *See also* ***3DES (Triple DES)*** *and* ***Rivest, Shamir, Adleman (RSA).***

privilege escalation: *See* ***escalation of privilege.***

procedures: Detailed instructions about how to implement specific policies and meet the criteria defined in standards.

process isolation: An operating system feature whereby different user processes are unable to view or modify information related to other processes.

process table: The collection of processes that are active in an operating system.

promiscuous mode: A setting on a network adapter that passes all network traffic to the associated device for processing, not just traffic that is specifically addressed to that device. *See also* ***sniffing.***

Protected Extensible Authentication Protocol (PEAP): An open standard used to transmit authentication information in a protected manner.

protection domain: Prevents other programs or processes from accessing and modifying the contents of an address space that has already been assigned to an active program or process.

protection rings: A security architecture concept that implements multiple domains that have increasing levels of trust near the center.

proximate causation: An action taken or not taken as part of a sequence of events that result in negative consequences.

proxy server: A system that transfers data packets from one network to another.

prudent man rule: Under the Federal Sentencing Guidelines, senior corporate officers are required to perform their duties in good faith, in the best interests of the enterprise, and with the care and diligence that ordinary, prudent people in a similar position would exercise in similar circumstances.

pseudo flaw: A form of social engineering in which the attacker attempts to trick people into performing certain actions to remedy a supposed security situation.

public key cryptography: A cryptographic method that permits parties to communicate with each other without exchanging a secret key in advance.

Public Key Infrastructure (PKI): A system that enables secure e-commerce through the integration of digital signatures, digital certificates, and other services necessary to ensure confidentiality, integrity, authentication, non-repudiation, and access control.

punitive damages: Determined by a jury and intended to punish the offender.

Radio Frequency Interference (RFI): Electrical noise caused by electrical components, such as fluorescent lighting and electric cables.

real (or physical) evidence: Tangible objects from the actual crime, such as the tools or weapons used and any stolen or damaged property.

recovery controls: Controls that restore systems and information.

Recovery Point Objective (RPO): The maximum period of time in which data may be lost if a disaster occurs.

Recovery Time Objective (RTO): The period of time in which a business process must be recovered (during a disaster) in order to ensure the survival of the organization.

Reduced-Instruction-Set-Computing (RISC): A microprocessor instruction set architecture that utilizes a smaller and simpler instruction set than CISC, which makes RISC more efficient than CISC. *See also Complex-Instruction-Set-Computing (CISC).*

redundancy: Multiple systems, nodes, or network paths that provide the same functionality for resiliency and availability in the event of failure.

reference monitor: An abstract machine (a theoretical model for a computer system or software program) that mediates all access to an object by a subject.

Registration Authority (RA): In a PKI, the RA is responsible for verifying certificate contents for the CA. *See also **Certification Authority (CA)** and **Public Key Infrastructure (PKI)**.*

remote access service (RAS): A remote access protocol typically used over dial-up facilities.

Remote Authentication Dial-In User Service (RADIUS): An open-source, User Datagram Protocol (UDP)–based client-server protocol used to authenticate remote users.

remote backup: A backup operation where the target backup media is located in a remote location.

replication: The process of copying data transactions from one system to another.

repository: In a PKI infrastructure, a repository is a system that accepts certificates and Certificate Revocation Lists (CRLs) from a CA and distributes them to authorized parties. *See also **Certification Authority (CA)** and **Public Key Infrastructure (PKI)**.*

Reverse Address Resolution Protocol (RARP): A protocol used by diskless workstations to query and discover their own IP addresses.

Rijndael: The encryption algorithm used by the AES. *See also **Advanced Encryption Standard (AES)**.*

ring: A network topology in which all devices are connected to a closed loop.

risk acceptance: Accepting the loss associated with a potential risk.

risk analysis: A method used to identify and assess threats and vulnerabilities in a business, process, system, or activity.

risk assignment (or transference): Transferring the potential loss associated with a risk to a third party, such as an insurance company.

risk mitigation: Reducing risk to a level that's acceptable to an organization.

risk reduction: Mitigating risk by implementing the necessary security controls, policies, and procedures to protect an asset.

Rivest, Shamir, Adleman (RSA): A key transport algorithm based on the difficulty of factoring a number that's the product of two large prime numbers.

role-based access control (RBAC): A method for implementing discretionary access controls in which access decisions are based on group membership, according to organizational or functional roles.

rotation of duties (or job rotation): Regularly transferring key personnel into different positions or departments within an organization.

router: A network device that forwards packets among dissimilar networks.

rule-based access control: A method for applying mandatory access control by matching an object's sensitivity label and a subject's sensitivity label to determine whether access should be granted or denied.

safeguard: A control or countermeasure implemented to reduce the risk or damage associated with a specific threat.

sag: A short drop in voltage.

scan: A technique used to identify vulnerabilities in a system, usually by transmitting data to it and observing its response.

scareware: A type of social engineering attack wherein a Trojan horse program or a browser popup is intended to trick the user into thinking that there is a security problem in their computer. The intended victim is asked or tricked to click a button or link to fix a security problem; in reality the consenting user is enabling malware to run on the computer.

screening router: A firewall architecture that consists of a router that controls packet flow through the use of ACLs. *See also **access control list (ACL)** and **firewall.***

script injection: An attack in which the attacker injects script code, in hopes that the code will be executed on a target system.

secondary evidence: A duplicate or copy of evidence, such as a tape backup, screen capture, or photograph.

secure and signed message format: A message encrypted in an asymmetric key system by using the recipient's public key and the sender's private key. This encryption method protects the message's confidentiality and guarantees the message's authenticity. *See also **open message format** and **secure message format.***

Secure Electronic Transaction (SET): Developed by MasterCard and Visa to provide secure e-commerce transactions by implementing authentication mechanisms while protecting the confidentiality and integrity of cardholder data.

Secure European System and Applications in a Multi-vendor Environment (SESAME): A ticket-based authentication protocol similar to Kerberos, with additional security enhancements. *See also* **Kerberos.**

Secure HyperText Transfer Protocol (S-HTTP): An Internet protocol that provides a method for secure communications with a webserver.

secure message format: A message encrypted in an asymmetric key system by using the recipient's public key. Only the recipient's private key can decrypt the message. This encryption method protects the message's confidentiality. *See also* **open message format** *and* **secure and signed message format.**

Secure Multipurpose Internet Mail Extensions (S/MIME): Provides confidentiality and authentication for e-mail by using the RSA asymmetric key system, digital signatures, and X.509 digital certificates. *See also* **Rivest, Shamir, Adleman (RSA).**

Secure Shell (SSH): A secure character-oriented protocol that's a secure alternative to *Telnet* and *rsh*. *See also* **Telnet.**

Secure Sockets Layer/Transport Layer Security (SSL/TLS): A transport layer protocol that provides session-based encryption and authentication for secure communication between clients and servers on the Internet.

security awareness: The process of providing basic security information to users in an organization to help them make prudent decisions regarding the protection of the organization's assets.

security kernel: The combination of hardware, firmware, and software elements in a TCB that implements the reference monitor concept. *See also* **Trusted Computing Base (TCB).**

security modes of operation: Designations for U.S. military and government computer systems based on the need to protect secrets stored within them. The modes are *Dedicated, System High, Multi-Level,* and *Limited Access.*

security perimeter: The boundary that separates the TCB from the rest of the system. *See also* **Trusted Computing Base (TCB).**

segregation of duties. *See* **separation of duties and responsibilities.**

Sensitive but Unclassified (SBU): A U.S. government data classification level for information that's not classified but requires protection, such as private or personal information.

sensitivity label: In a MAC-based system, a subject's sensitivity label specifies that subject's level of trust, whereas an object's sensitivity label specifies the level of trust required for access to that object. *See also **mandatory access control (MAC) system.***

separation of duties and responsibilities: A concept that ensures no single individual has complete authority and control of a critical system or process.

Serial Line Internet Protocol (SLIP): An early Point-to-Point Protocol (PPP) used to transport Internet Protocol (IP) over dial-up modems. PPP is more commonly used for this purpose.

Service-Level Agreement (SLA): Formal minimum performance standards for systems, applications, networks, or services.

session hijacking: Similar to a Man-in-the-Middle Attack, except that the attacker impersonates the intended recipient instead of modifying messages in transit. *See also **Man-in-the-Middle Attack.***

shoulder surfing: A social engineering technique that involves looking over someone's shoulder to obtain information such as passwords or account numbers.

Simple Key Management for Internet Protocols (SKIP): A protocol used to share encryption keys.

single sign-on (SSO): A system that allows a user to present a single set of log-on credentials, typically to an authentication server, which then transparently logs the user on to all other enterprise systems and applications for which that user is authorized.

smartphone: *See mobile device.*

Smurf: A Denial of Service attack in which the attacker sends forged Internet Control Message Protocol (ICMP) echo request packets into a network with the intention of having large numbers of nodes on the network sending ICMP echo replies to the target system. *See also **Denial of Service (DoS).***

sniffing: The practice of intercepting communications for usually covert purposes.

social engineering: A low-tech attack method that employs techniques such as dumpster diving and shoulder surfing.

software: Computer instructions that enable the computer to accomplish tasks. *See also **application software** and **operating system (OS).***

software development life cycle (SDLC): The business-level process used to develop and maintain software.

SONET: *See* **Synchronous Optical Networking (SONET).**

spam (or Unsolicited Commercial E-mail [UCE]): Junk e-mail, which currently constitutes about 85 percent of all worldwide e-mail.

spear phishing: A phishing attack that's highly targeted; for example, at a particular organization or part of an organization. *See also* **phishing.**

spike: A momentary rush of electric power.

SPIM: Spam over instant messaging.

SPIT: Spam over Internet telephony.

spoofing: A technique used to forge TCP/IP packet information or e-mail header information. In network attacks, IP spoofing is used to gain access to systems by impersonating the IP address of a trusted host. In e-mail spoofing, the sender address is forged to trick an e-mail user into opening or responding to an e-mail (which usually contains a virus or spam).

spyware: A form of malware that's installed on a user's computer, usually without his or her knowledge, often for the purpose of collecting information about a user's Internet usage or for taking control of his or her computer. Spyware increasingly includes keystroke loggers and Trojan horses.

SQL injection: A type of attack where the attacker injects SQL commands into a computer input field, in hopes that the SQL command will be passed to the database management system.

standards: Specific, mandatory requirements that further define and support high-level policies.

star: A network topology in which all devices are directly connected to a central hub or concentrator.

state attack: An attack where the attacker is attempting to steal other users' session identifiers, in order to access a system using the stolen session identifier.

state machine model: An abstract model in which a secure state is defined and maintained during transitions between secure states.

stateful inspection firewall: A type of firewall that captures and analyzes data packets at all levels of the Open Systems Interconnection (OSI) model to determine the state and context of the data packet and whether it's to be permitted access to the network.

static password: A password that's the same for each log-on.

statutory damages: Mandatory damages determined by law and assessed for violating the law.

steganography: The art of hiding the very existence of a message; for example, in a picture.

stored procedure: A subroutine that is accessible by software programs, and which is stored in a relational database management system.

stream cipher: An encryption algorithm that operates on a continuous stream of data, typically bit-by-bit.

strong authentication: A means of authentication that requires two or more independent means of identification. *See also* ***two-factor authentication.***

Structured Query Language (SQL): A computer language used to manipulate data in a database management system.

subject: An active entity, such as an individual or a process.

substitution cipher: Ciphers that replace bits, characters, or character blocks in plaintext with alternate bits, characters, or character blocks to produce ciphertext.

Supervisor mode: A level of elevated privilege, usually intended for only system administration use. *See also* ***User mode.***

surge: A prolonged rush of electric power.

switch: An intelligent hub that transmits data to only individual devices on a network, rather than all devices (in the way that hubs do). *See also* ***hub.***

Switched Multimegabit Data Service (SMDS): A high-speed, packet-switched, connectionless-oriented, datagram-based technology available over public switched networks.

symmetric key system (or symmetric algorithm, secret key, single key, private key): A cryptographic system that uses a single key to both encrypt and decrypt information.

SYN flood: An attack in which the attacker sends large volumes of Transmission Control Protocol (TCP) SYN (synchronize) packets to a target system. A SYN flood is a type of Denial of Service attack. *See also* ***Denial of Service (DoS).***

Synchronous Optical Networking (SONET): A telecommunications carrier-class protocol used to communicate digital information over optical fiber.

system access control: A control that prevents a subject from accessing a system unless the subject can present valid credentials.

system high mode: A state in which a system operates at the highest level of information classification.

Take-Grant model: A security model that specifies the rights that a subject can transfer to or from another subject or object.

Teardrop attack: A type of stack overflow attack that exploits vulnerabilities in the Internet Protocol (IP).

technical (or logical) controls: Hardware and software technology used to implement access control.

Telnet: A network protocol used to establish a command line interface on another system over a network. *See also **Secure Shell (SSH)**.*

Terminal Access Controller Access Control System (TACACS): A User Datagram Protocol (UDP)–based access control protocol that provides authentication, authorization, and accounting.

threat: Any natural or man-made circumstance or event that can have an adverse or undesirable impact, whether minor or major, on an organizational asset.

threat modeling: A systematic process used to identify likely threats, vulnerabilities, and countermeasures for a specific application and its uses during the design phase of the application (or software) development life cycle.

three-way handshake: The method used to establish and tear down network connections in the Transmission Control Protocol (TCP).

token: A hardware device used in two-factor authentication.

Token-Ring: A star-topology network transport protocol.

trade secret: Proprietary or business-related information that a company or individual uses and has exclusive rights to.

trademark: As defined by the U.S. Patent and Trademark Office (PTO), a trademark is "any word, name, symbol, or device, or any combination, used, or intended to be used, in commerce to identify and distinguish the goods of one manufacturer or seller from goods manufactured or sold by others."

traffic analysis: A method of attack in which an attacker observes network traffic patterns in order to make deductions about network utilization, architecture, behavior, or other discernable characteristics.

transient: A momentary electrical line noise disturbance.

Transmission Control Protocol (TCP): A connection-oriented network protocol that provides reliable delivery of packets over a network.

transposition cipher: Ciphers that rearrange bits, characters, or character blocks in plaintext to produce ciphertext.

trap door: A feature within a program that performs an undocumented function (usually a security bypass, such as an elevation of privilege).

Trojan horse: A program that purports to perform a given function, but which actually performs some other (usually malicious) function.

trusted computer system: A system that employs all necessary hardware and software assurance measures and meets the specified requirements for reliability and security.

Trusted Computer System Evaluation Criteria (TCSEC): Commonly known as the *Orange Book.* Formal systems evaluation criteria developed for the U.S. Department of Defense by the National Computer Security Center (NCSC) as part of the Rainbow Series.

Trusted Computing Base (TCB): The total combination of protection mechanisms within a computer system — including hardware, firmware, and software — that are responsible for enforcing a security policy.

Trusted Network Interpretation (TNI): Commonly known as the *Red Book* (of the Rainbow Series). Addresses confidentiality and integrity in trusted computer/communications network systems. *See also **Trusted Computer System Evaluation Criteria (TCSEC).***

trusted path: A direct communications path between the user and the Trusted Computing Base (TCB) that doesn't require interaction with untrusted applications or operating system layers.

trusted recovery: Safeguards to prevent the disclosure of information during the recovery of a system after a failure.

two-factor authentication: An authentication method that requires two ways of establishing identity.

uninterruptible power supply (UPS): A device that provides continuous electrical power, usually by storing excess capacity in one or more batteries.

USA PATRIOT Act (Uniting [and] Strengthening America [by] Providing Appropriate Tools Required [to] Intercept [and] Obstruct Terrorism Act of 2001): A U.S. law that expands the authority of law enforcement agencies for the purpose of combating terrorism.

user: A person who has access to information and/or information systems.

User Datagram Protocol (UDP): A network protocol that doesn't guarantee packet delivery or the order of packet delivery over a network.

user entitlement: The data access privileges that are granted to an individual user.

User mode: A level of privilege, usually intended for ordinary users. *See also Supervisor mode.*

vernam cipher: *See one-time pad.*

view: A logical operation that can be used to restrict access to specific information in a database, hide attributes, and restrict queries available to a user. Views are a type of constrained user interface that restricts access to specific functions by not allowing a user to request it.

violation analysis: The process of examining audit logs and other sources in order to discover inappropriate activities.

virtual memory: A type of secondary memory addressing that uses both installed physical memory and available hard drive space to present a larger apparent memory space than actually exists to the Central Processing Unit (CPU).

Virtual Private Network (VPN): A private network used to communicate privately over public networks. VPNs utilize encryption and encapsulation to protect and simplify connectivity.

Virtual Tape Library (VTL): A disk-based storage system that is used like magnetic tape storage for use in backup operations.

virus: A set of computer instructions whose purpose is to embed itself within another computer program in order to replicate itself.

Voice over Internet Protocol (VoIP): Telephony protocols that are designed to transport voice communications over TCP/IP networks.

vulnerability: The absence or weakness of a safeguard in an asset, which makes a threat potentially more harmful or costly, more likely to occur, or likely to occur more frequently.

WAN: Wide area network.

war dialing: A brute-force attack that uses a program to automatically dial a large block of phone numbers (such as an area code), searching for vulnerable modems or fax machines.

war driving: A brute-force attack that involves driving around, looking for vulnerable wireless networks.

warm site: An alternative computer facility that's readily available and equipped with electrical power, HVAC, and computers, but not fully configured. *See also **cold site, hot site**, and **HVAC**.*

white-box testing: A security test in which the tester has complete knowledge of the system being tested.

WiFi (wireless fidelity): Wireless network technology that utilizes 802.11 protocols.

Wired Equivalent Privacy (WEP): A means of encrypting communications; specifically, 802.11/WiFi networks.

Wireless Transport Layer Security (WTLS): A protocol that provides security services for the Wireless Application Protocol (WAP) commonly used for Internet connectivity by mobile devices.

WLAN: Wireless local area network. *See also **WiFi**.*

work factor: The difficulty (in terms of time, effort, and resources) of breaking a cryptosystem.

worm: Malware that usually has the capability to replicate itself from computer to computer without the need for human intervention.

X.25: The first wide-area, packet-switching network.

Index

• F •

Notes

Notes

Notes

Apple & Mac

iPad 2 For Dummies,
3rd Edition
978-1-118-17679-5

iPhone 4S For Dummies,
5th Edition
978-1-118-03671-6

iPod touch For Dummies,
3rd Edition
978-1-118-12960-9

Mac OS X Lion
For Dummies
978-1-118-02205-4

Blogging & Social Media

CityVille For Dummies
978-1-118-08337-6

Facebook For Dummies,
4th Edition
978-1-118-09562-1

Mom Blogging
For Dummies
978-1-118-03843-7

Twitter For Dummies,
2nd Edition
978-0-470-76879-2

WordPress For Dummies,
4th Edition
978-1-118-07342-1

Business

Cash Flow For Dummies
978-1-118-01850-7

Investing For Dummies,
6th Edition
978-0-470-90545-6

Job Searching with Social Media For Dummies
978-0-470-93072-4

QuickBooks 2012
For Dummies
978-1-118-09120-3

Resumes For Dummies,
6th Edition
978-0-470-87361-8

Starting an Etsy Business
For Dummies
978-0-470-93067-0

Cooking & Entertaining

Cooking Basics
For Dummies, 4th Edition
978-0-470-91388-8

Wine For Dummies,
4th Edition
978-0-470-04579-4

Diet & Nutrition

Kettlebells For Dummies
978-0-470-59929-7

Nutrition For Dummies,
5th Edition
978-0-470-93231-5

Restaurant Calorie Counter
For Dummies,
2nd Edition
978-0-470-64405-8

Digital Photography

Digital SLR Cameras &
Photography For Dummies,
4th Edition
978-1-118-14489-3

Digital SLR Settings
& Shortcuts
For Dummies
978-0-470-91763-3

Photoshop Elements 10
For Dummies
978-1-118-10742-3

Gardening

Gardening Basics
For Dummies
978-0-470-03749-2

Vegetable Gardening
For Dummies,
2nd Edition
978-0-470-49870-5

Green/Sustainable

Raising Chickens
For Dummies
978-0-470-46544-8

Green Cleaning
For Dummies
978-0-470-39106-8

Health

Diabetes For Dummies,
3rd Edition
978-0-470-27086-8

Food Allergies
For Dummies
978-0-470-09584-3

Living Gluten-Free
For Dummies,
2nd Edition
978-0-470-58589-4

Hobbies

Beekeeping
For Dummies,
2nd Edition
978-0-470-43065-1

Chess For Dummies,
3rd Edition
978-1-118-01695-4

Drawing For Dummies,
2nd Edition
978-0-470-61842-4

eBay For Dummies,
7th Edition
978-1-118-09806-6

Knitting For Dummies,
2nd Edition
978-0-470-28747-7

Language &
Foreign Language

English Grammar
For Dummies,
2nd Edition
978-0-470-54664-2

French For Dummies,
2nd Edition
978-1-118-00464-7

German For Dummies,
2nd Edition
978-0-470-90101-4

Spanish Essentials
For Dummies
978-0-470-63751-7

Spanish For Dummies,
2nd Edition
978-0-470-87855-2